Concepts of Leisure in Western Thought

A Critical and Historical Analysis

Byron Dare
Associate Professor of Political Science
Fort Lewis College, Durango, Colorado

George Welton
Professor of Recreation and Leisure Studies
California State University, Northridge

William Coe
Professor of Philosophy
Fort Lewis College, Durango, Colorado

Kendall/Hunt Publishing Company
Dubuque, Iowa

Credits

We are grateful to the copyright holders for permission to reprint material from the following sources:

Excerpts from "Flash of Fire" and "Darrell and Judy" by Hoyt Axton. Copyright © Lady Jane Music. All rights reserved, reprinted by permission.

Excerpt from *To the Finland Station* by Edmund Wilson. Copyright © 1972 by Edmund Wilson. Copyright 1940, renewed 1968 by Edmund Wilson. Reprinted by permission, Farrar, Straus and Giroux, Inc.

Excerpts from *Before the Industrial Revolution,* Second Edition, by Carlo M. Cipolla. Copyright © 1976, 1980. Reprinted by permission, W. W. Norton and Company.

Excerpts from *Les Philosophes,* edited by Norman L. Torrey. Copyright © 1960. Reprinted by permission, The Putnam Publishing Group.

Excerpts from *The Iliad of Homer,* translated by Richard Lattimore. Copyright © 1951, 1961. Reprinted by permission, University of Chicago Press.

Excerpts from *The Worldly Philosophers,* Revised Edition, by Robert L. Heilbroner. Copyright © 1953, 1961, 1972 by Robert L. Heilbroner. Reprinted by permission, Simon & Schuster, Inc.

Excerpt from "Five to One," written and composed by The Doors. Copyright © 1967 Doors Music Company. All rights reserved. Reprinted by permission.

Cover key: Western civilization space-time diagram

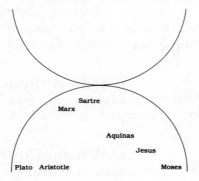

Cover design by Victoria Romero Coe

Copyright © 1987 by Kendall/Hunt Publishing Company

Library of Congress Catalog Card Number: 87–50617

ISBN 0–8403–4417–1

Printed in the United States of America
10 9 8 7 6 5 4 3 2 1

Contents

Foreword

Leisure: The Essence of Culture

Leisure has had a prophetic existence since the dawn of Western Civilization. The Greek ideal of leisure served to promote its "essence" as the wellspring of culture. Leisure's "essence" was derived from an interpretation of the word *skole;* a state of being free *from* the necessity of being occupied or freedom from the necessity of work. In today's high technology, post-industrial, information-based society, leisure has come to mean free *after* the obligation or necessity of work and existence requirements have been met. Culture is the "basis" of attitudes towards leisure in contemporary Western society. Leisure has emerged as free time, time to be pursued by individuals for purposes of personal satisfaction.

Professors Dare, Welton and Coe have undertaken a massive project to decipher over two thousand years of changes in social conditions and interpret the resulting changes in attitudes toward leisure. This highly important intellectual activity is successfully achieved through their skillful interpretation of the writings and teachings of selected scholars and philosophers.

For all students of leisure this text will serve as a valuable asset to aid the understanding interpretation of how ideas influenced by our political, social, economic, and intellectual environments have acted, in turn, to influence further political, social, economic and intellectual change. The classical Greek ideal of leisure as the contemplative life, the pursuit of the highest human aspects of truth and wisdom, was destroyed by developments in Western thought in succeeding centuries by those seeking to establish labor, in an expanding market economy, as our unique human capacity. This occurrence resulted in the promotion of work, and therefore humans as primarily economic beings, as the foundation of culture. Intellectual wisdom was replaced with material wealth, reason with desire, leisure with work.

In contemporary society the humanism which has emerged from existentialist thought serves to focus attention on the individual who can transcend the material situation to pursue "authentic" contemplation. According to existentialists, to be free, to engage in truly personally liberating experiences, one must be able to engage in creative self-expression. In the classical Greek ideal the contemplative life put one in touch with the essence of man, the universe, God and the good life. These essences according to Professors Dare, Welton and Coe existed independent of one's contemplation of them. In the existentialist vision, the authenticity of the contemplation itself rather than any essences which are its objects, make contemplation essential to the good life.

The emerging thesis for Western society, now in the midst of a synergistic amalgamation with Eastern social, political, economic and intellectual thought may well serve to spur a new cultural ideal—leisure as an integral, interactive spiritual and rational form of personal freedom. Leisure may become both the reason for our being and the basis for our liberating transcendence, linking human beings to all previous and future cultures.

James F. Murphy, Ph.D.
Professor and Chairperson
Department of Recreation and Leisure Studies
San Francisco State University

Preface

Sometimes life is full of laughs—
Sometimes it ain't funny.

Hoyt Axton

We are tempted to begin this book by detailing its genesis in countless conversations while commuting, backpacking, building decks, and drinking beer. And while such an approach might prove to be highly entertaining, it could easily deter us from the subject at hand—a sociological and historical analysis of changing attitudes toward leisure in western civilization. Our focus is on coherent sets of ideas (philosophies) as they relate to leisure time and the human potential, and we hope that a wide variety of students (in the broadest possible definition of the word) will benefit from this book. For students of western civilization, we offer a supplement to standard texts that stresses changing views toward leisure time in our intellectual heritage. For students of philosophy, we try to clarify the pivotal issues and introduce you to some of the major figures in western thought. Ideally, a focus on a specific concept (leisure time) will provide an introduction that will stimulate your interest in, and discovery of, the more intricate dimensions of western philosophy. For students of leisure studies and recreation, we have attempted to write a book that clarifies and enhances the significance of your discipline.

To some, the work involved in the study of leisure may sound contradictory. But even a cursory glance at leisure and recreation in the United States today suggests that, in fact, many people spend a great deal of time attempting to understand these phenomena. The 19th Edition of the *College Bluebook* lists 11 institutions of higher education offering degrees (including 5 at the graduate level) in Leisure Studies. Under the heading of Recreation, nearly 400 institutions and programs are listed, with 72 granting graduate degrees (including 11 at the Ph.D. level). Programs range from recreation administration and management to high risk outdoor activities, and from leisure studies to therapeutic recreation. Descriptions of these offerings suggest that the discipline has reached a consensus on the significance of leisure time, and has moved toward more specific studies of recreational activities that occur during such free, or discretionary, time.

The availability of more amounts of discretionary time in the United States and other industrial societies is well documented. In their encyclopedic study of recreation behavior and resources entitled *One Third of Our Time?*, Michael and Holly Chubb note that the decreasing industrial workweek in the twentieth century has produced a 331% increase in free time since the late 1800s, and that most people in the United States spend nearly 4½ hours per day engaging in "identifiable recreation activities." These trends are generally interpreted in a highly optimistic fashion, with an increase in discretionary time viewed as providing the opportunity for greater human fulfillment. In *The Third Wave* and *Megatrends,* Alvin Toffler and John Naisbitt argue that the increasing amount of free time is leading us into a realm of hitherto unknown accomplishment. Abraham Maslow's suggestion that human self-actualization cannot be accomplished until more basic biological needs are satisfied is often interpreted as suggesting that, somehow, satisfaction of lower needs (food, clothing, shelter, safety, et cetera) will automatically lead to human fulfillment. Hence, as free time and hope intermingle in our society, we have noticed the temptation to interpret the increase in discretionary time (which suggests that more basic needs have been satisfied) as both necessary and sufficient to automatically produce a brighter future for self-actualization and an unprecedented pursuit of the human potential.

While this optimism is appealing, it should strike a note of caution among even the most casual observers of the evening news, where we are constantly reminded that addiction to various drugs is a reality in nearly all segments of our society. In addition, alcoholism and suicide are well-recognized plagues that provide a stark counterpoint to the promise of greater human fulfillment that tends to be linked (explicitly or implicitly) to the increase of leisure time. Significantly, these manifestations of self-destruction (as opposed to self-fulfillment) appear to be on the rise among middle-class youth in the United States—those who we would expect to be the primary beneficiaries of the increase in discretionary time.

The obvious tension between expectations for leisure time and indications that it does not automatically lead to human happiness and fulfillment had much to do with our decision to write this book. In the process, a haunting question was reiterated more forcefully with each chapter— a question that you should internalize before proceeding: did industrialization necessitate the destruction of a positive and creative view toward leisure time? The irony becomes even more pronounced if we view the historical process that provided us with this blossoming of discretionary time (industrialization and post-industrial development) as bringing with it the destruction of our ability to view such time positively and creatively. And our dilemma is compounded when we recognize that our positive expectations of leisure time are primarily derived from the classical philosophical tradition associated with the ancient Greeks—a tradition that has been systematically attacked and emasculated since the sixteenth century. Are we left, then, with enormous amounts of free time that we don't know how to use?

A Note on Organization

We are aware of the possibility that, in trying to pursue so many goals, we may have made it difficult to accomplish any of them. Our colleagues who have been reviewing drafts of the current book have noted that the historical and philosophical detail occasionally tended to draw them away from our primary focus. Wherever possible, we have responded to their suggestions—but we view the remaining historical and philosophical details as essential in order to recognize the subtleties and significance of the process that has created what might be summarized as the current dilemma of leisure. In order to minimize any problems that might remain in the relationship of detail to concept, the following summary is offered at the outset.

The book is divided into an Introduction and five parts. The first chapter in each part is devoted to outlining the historical factors that shaped the context of specific philosophers. Some readers may not view these chapters (Chapters 1, 5, 8, 11, and 14) as crucial to the analysis, but we do. Remember that we are not specifically dealing with leisure time in these discussions of historical change; instead, we are attempting to describe the environments in which changing concepts of leisure were developed.

The second chapter in each part (Chapters 2, 6, 9 and 12) is designed to supplement the description of the social, economic and political context with a discussion of the intellectual environment in which the major perspectives on leisure were developed. Again, these chapters are not designed to specifically discuss leisure; instead, we try to stress the scope and depth of debate over key issues that influenced more focused views toward leisure time. In Chapters 3, 4, 7, 10, 13 and 15, we attempt to clarify the ways in which the pivotal thinkers (Plato, Aristotle, Thomas

Aquinas, Adam Smith, Karl Marx and Jean-Paul Sartre) integrated their socio-historical and intellectual environment into coherent views that clearly had an impact on concepts of leisure.

Each part is prefaced by an introduction and followed by a brief summary and conclusion. If, at times, you find yourself wondering "what does this have to do with leisure?", you should refer to them. We might also suggest that you begin by reading the Introductions and Conclusions to all five parts. They are designed to keep you focused on concepts of leisure and, hopefully, will provide quick references at any point in the text.

Acknowledgments

Once there was a flock of geese. They were kept in a wire cage, by a farmer. One day, one of the geese looked up and saw that there was no top to the cage. Excitedly, he told the other geese: "Look, look: There is no top. We may leave here. We may become free."

Few listened, and none would turn his head to the sky. So, one day, he simply spread his wings and flew away—alone.

Søren Kierkegaard

For Chris, Clellan, Justin, Matthew, Nathan and Sarah—may you find someone to fly with. Or better yet, stay out of the cage to begin with—and for their grandparents. And for Terry and Sal, Harry and Betty, Jeannie and Robert, John and Cindy, Darryl and Elyse, and Norm and Sue.

Several friends and colleagues were kind enough to read parts of the manuscript and contribute suggestions and encouragement. We accepted all of the encouragement and most of the suggestions from Red Bird, Rita Blaylock, John Bullaro, John Crowder, Reece Kelly, Norman Linton, Kathy Poer and Isabelle Walker. William C. Langworthy provided support from the Fort Lewis College Research and Creative Endeavor funds.

Rita Blaylock, Kathy Poer and Holly Daniel made it all possible with their editing and typing skills, while Janalee Dare (who knew that there was no top to the cage without ever looking) contributed years of love and encouragement.

Byron Dare
Durango, Colorado
April, 1987

Introduction

The strongest innovating attitudes find in leisure an expression which challenges the primacy given to a utilitarian transformation of nature and rehabilitates disinterested contemplation. . . . Leisure is a rebellion against repressive culture.

Joffre Dumazedier

Trading your hours for a handful of dimes. . . .

The Doors

The story's not pretty but you better believe it's true.

Hoyt Axton

Besides, there are some things that can't be the truth even if they did happen.

Ken Kesey

To teach to live without certainty, and yet without being paralyzed by hesitation, is perhaps the chief thing that philosophy, in our age, can still do for those who study it.

Bertrand Russell

Definition of Terms
Philosophy and Leisure Defined

Before any inquiry can be undertaken the terms of that inquiry need to be defined. If not, the reader can be misled into confusing one author's intention for that of another. But the importance of defining terms is not just limited to scholarly inquiry; even in our daily discourse, it is not uncommon to be confused about the meaning of words. How many times have you debated an issue only to reach a stalemate because the terms used by the debaters had different definitions? In this chapter, then, we seek to establish a common ground with you, the reader, by defining the terms crucial to this inquiry. The terms defined are "philosophy" and "leisure." We have approached each term in the form of a question—"What is philosophy"?, and "What is leisure"? In answering these questions, we hope to establish a common point of departure and plant the seed of a greater understanding of a magnificent idea: Leisure.

What Is Philosophy?

It has been suggested that the world is composed of two types of thinkers: the ordinary and the philosophical. The difference between these two types is probably best depicted by the ancient Greek philosopher, Plato, in a story about an even more ancient philosopher, Thales.[1] It seems that while studying the stars on an evening stroll, Thales stumbled into a well. A maiden witnessing the act reproached Thales for being so entranced with the heavens that he was unaware of what lay at his feet—as if Thales was wasting time. The maiden can be seen as representing the ordinary thinker, one concerned solely with immediate answers to daily problems for which philosophy seems to have little relevance. We encourage you to consider this view before proceeding because we assert that the way we all perceive and react to daily problems actually reflects assumptions derived from some philosophical perspective. In the case of the philosopher, such assumptions and perspectives are subject to explicit analysis, best described as an inner search for truth. In the case of the ordinary thinker, chances are that these perspectives have been implicitly accepted, without critical analysis of their origins and ramifications; nevertheless, they determine the way in which we view the world—including daily problems. For instance, do you view war as a problem—or is it a solution to problems such as overpopulation, unemployment, or new military technology that has not yet been tested in combat? Is abortion a problem—or is it a solution to the problem of unwanted pregnancy? And does your view of an "unwanted pregnancy" depend on economic factors (insufficient money to support the child), or morality (cases of incest, rape, or both)? Would destroying your charge card create a problem—or would it be a solution to your problem of debt? Is debt a problem—or a solution to the problem of not being able to afford what you want? Your answers to these questions are likely to be influenced by answers (either yours or someone else's) to the broader questions of philosophy. As T. Z. Lavine notes, such questions include:

> What is real? What can we know? What does it mean to be moral, to live a good life? What is the difference between right and wrong? What is a good government and what are its functions with respect to citizens? Does human history have any meaning, pattern, purpose?[2]

We suggest, then, that philosophy is concerned with daily living because our answers to these fundamental questions determine the way we view ourselves, other human beings, our world (past, present and future), and even our leisure time. While these links between ordinary thinking and philosophy appear clear to us, we must also stress the difference that separates them. Epictetus, an ancient Roman philosopher, said that true peace of mind, freedom and tranquility only come about from the philosopher's inner search. From a purely practical point of view, we suggest that the implicit acceptance of someone else's answers to the major questions of life (without seriously considering the origins and ramifications of these answers) is, at best, absurd. At its worst, this failure to analyze our actions and assumptions is subhuman.

To the extent that philosophy is an inner search, we can say that it is a search for understanding. Born with the ancient Greek word *Philosophia,* it is an attempt to better understand the world and our place in it. For this reason, philosophy is unrestricted in scope; it cuts across all human endeavors, disciplines, and institutions. Philosophy is at the center of individual and social actions: there are philosophical problems in science, art, law, and politics, as well as leisure. We can say that the problems of philosophy are the problems of human life. So, as we investigate the philosophical problem of leisure we simultaneously investigate philosophy.

Philosophical Problems and Processes

The mode of inquiry and the spirit of the question separate a philosophical treatment of daily problems from an "ordinary" approach. For example, in their quest to learn about leisure, social scientists are generally content to describe and classify it, while philosophers use a mode of inquiry that seeks to understand the meaning of leisure. The other part of the philosophical approach to a problem, the spirit of questioning, comes from a desire to know more than is evident—to go beyond immediate appearance to underlying complexities.

Epictetus suggested that explanations began to take on a philosophical mode and spirit with urbanization. The close living conditions of the cities brought out an awareness of differences in ideas as people from various backgrounds met and shared points of view. As these differences were ironed out, civilization formed and lives were shaped according to certain criteria. The examination of the criteria is philosophy:

> Here you see the beginning of philosophy, in the discovery of the conflict of men's minds with one another, and the attempt to seek for the reason of this conflict, and the condemnation of mere opinion, as a thing not to be trusted; and a search to determine whether your opinion is true, and an attempt to discover a standard, just as we discover the balance to deal with weights and the rule to deal with things straight and crooked. This is the beginning of philosophy.[3]

Thus, a society has standards for measuring the physical world and standards for measuring such qualities as right and wrong, good and bad, et cetera. The way these standards are examined is called a "process of philosophy."

Concepts which can be used to analyze this process of philosophy are thesis, antithesis, and synthesis. The thesis represents an initial system of beliefs. The antithesis, as the word suggests, contrasts the thesis and presents an alternative system of beliefs. The synthesis may be a combination of the two beliefs, as the term suggests, or it may be a rejection of one belief which appears to be more false than the other. Once a synthesis is agreed upon it becomes a thesis which is subject to a new antithesis, and the process continues. It is essential that this be recognized as an ongoing process because it is by continually questioning and re-examining beliefs that humans attempt to find the closest approximation of truth. Socrates said during his trial:

> I cannot 'mind my own business,' you will not believe that I am serious. If on the other hand I tell you that to let no day pass without discussing goodness and all the other subjects about which you hear me talking and examining both myself and others is really the very best thing that a man can do, and that life without this sort of examination is not worth living, you will be even less inclined to believe me.[4]

History and our daily lives are full of examples of the philosophical process. In day to day living, this process occurs when we are confronted with a situation that challenges or tests our beliefs. Of course, not all such situations (in fact, only a small percentage in a lifetime) are of the type which will alter basic beliefs. Only the major confrontations test our philosophical ideals, and what constitutes a major confrontation is often an individual interpretation. Let us look at an elementary example: a college student is required to register for the military draft, but he believes war is immoral and to register would be to acknowledge that he would fight in a war, contradicting his belief. The young man must either register or not. The seriousness with which this person considers 1) the effects of not registering—possible imprisonment and 2) the effects of registering—going against his conscience, will determine whether this situation has serious philosophical implications or not. In this way, every situation presents the possibility of using the process of philosophy. In a majority of cases, however, people tend to see themselves through situations without analyzing, and possibly, restructuring the foundations from which they view life.

Speculative and Practical Philosophy

The process of philosophy is a mode of inquiry that searches for a solution through critical analysis of concepts and meanings. While its resolution is rarely (if ever) conclusive, it can be either practical or speculative, representing two types of concerns. David Hume, an 18th century Scottish philosopher, clarified the differences:

The one considers man chiefly as born for action; and as influenced in his measures by taste and sentiment; pursuing one object, and avoiding another, according to the value which these objects seem to possess, and according to the light in which they present themselves. . . . They make us *feel* the difference between vice and virtue. . . . The other species of philosophers considers man in the light of a reasonable rather than an active being, and endeavors to form his understanding more than cultivate his manners. They regard human nature as a subject of speculation; and with narrow scrutiny examine it, in order to find those principles, which regulate our understanding, excite our sentiments; and make us approve or blame any particular object, action, or behavior.[5]

The latter part of Hume's description refers to speculative philosophy. Aristotle defined speculative philosophy as "scientific knowledge, combined with intuitive reason, or the things that are highest by nature."[6] It is, thus, a search for wisdom that penetrates to the source, or "first principles" of nature. Practical philosophy, considered in the first part of Hume's description, is the search for pragmatic understanding. Calling it practical wisdom, Aristotle said:

It is thought to be the mark of a man of practical wisdom to be able to deliberate well about what is good and expedient for himself, not in some particular respect, e.g. about what sorts of thing conduce to health or to strength, but about what sorts of thing conduce to the good life in general.[7]

While there are two types of philosophy, speculative and practical, they are not mutually exclusive. In fact, the ancient Greeks felt the link was so strong that solutions to the problems of conduct could be sought in the speculative as well as the practical realm. Plato, near the end of the *Timaeus,* said that "by learning the harmonies and revolutions of the universe, . . . and having assimilated them [each man] may attain to that best life which the gods have set before mankind, both for the present and the future."[8]

Although the ancient Greek philosophers believed that an understanding of reality helps one understand how to live, be cautious; for there is no guarantee that a step by step solution to practical problems will be found. Philosophy, whether speculative or practical, can promote your ability to see beyond the immediate and mundane toward deeper and more profound answers to problems. But these answers may not always be as precise and assuring as you would like them to be.

This section began with a story about Thales' mishap, so it is fitting that it conclude with another story about Thales. This one was told by Aristotle, and reminds us that philosophers are philosophers by choice, not by default:

He [Thales] was reproached for his poverty, which was supposed to show that philosophy was of no use. According to the story, he knew by his skill in the stars while it was yet winter that there would be a great harvest of olives in the coming year; so, having a little money, he gave deposits for the use of all the olive-presses in Chinos and Miletus, which he hired at a low price because no one bid against him. When the harvest-time came, and many were wanted all at once and of a sudden, he let them out at any rate which he pleased, and made a quantity of money. Thus he showed the world that philosophers can easily be rich if they like, but that their ambition is of another sort.[9]

While philosophers are so by choice, we must keep in mind (as Epictetus mentioned earler) that philosophers are first and always philosophers. Philosophy, to be philosophy, cannot be directed toward anything other than itself. It is not pursued in order to gain material wealth, but rather pursued for its ability to satisfy the intellect and conscience, and enhance understanding of the self and the world. Its value does not rest in utilitarian application to practical problems, but in shedding the light of reason on a problem: in this case, the problem of leisure.

What Is Leisure?

The term leisure has its origins in the languages of ancient Greece and Rome. While both civilizations made a contribution, the ancient Greek views are by far the most significant.

Leisure as Reflected in the Ancient Greek and Latin Languages

Leisure in the ancient Greek was called *skole*. It originally referred to quiet or peace and to rest and to think without distraction. Later it became known as time to spare or, more accurately, time to oneself; that is, time dedicated to personal enhancement with no utilitarian implication; it was the goal, or end, of life.

It is crucial to recognize that *skole* did not mean free or unobligated time, as time remaining after work; instead, it meant a state of being free from the necessity of work. Perhaps this subtlety can be more fully grasped when compared to the opposite of *skole, askolia*. Literally, the absence of leisure, *askolia* is unleisure or being occupied. *Askolia* is having an occupation or occupying time with necessary activities. But life in ancient Greece was not simply a division between leisure and work. There was also *paidia* (amusements) and *anapasis* (recreation). While these activities were not classified as work, they were not labeled as leisure either. Amusement and recreation were not looked upon as ends-in-themselves. An amusement is simply a diversion having no consequence, as when something is found to be "amusing." Recreation is, as the word suggests, a "recreation" of self. It was considered a renewal for work; something that "refreshes."

While *skole* is freedom from the necessity of work, it does not imply a lack of activity. On the contrary, within this freedom activity must take place. The sociologist de Grazia defines leisure from the ancient Greek perspective as a state of being in which activity is performed for its own sake or as its own end.[10] But not any activity can be considered an end-in-itself. Only the activity called *diagoge,* cultivation of the mind, so qualifies. It is, says De Grazia, being:

> occupied in something desirable for its own sake—hearing of noble music and noble poetry, intercourse with friends chosen for their own worth and above all the exercise, alone or in company, of the speculative faculty.[11]

In our culture, this is commonly thought of as contemplation. The word contemplation is derived from the Latin translation of the Greek *theorein,* to behold. *Theoria* in Greek is the "theoretical life." In Latin it becomes the "contemplative life." Contemplation is the search for and dwelling in truth. In the ancient Greek sense of the word it is a search for the understanding of theoretical "first principles." Hence, its link to speculative philosophy is obvious.

The ancient Roman notion of leisure is rooted in the Latin word *otium*. The opposite of *otium* is *negotium,* a person's occupation. While the Greek definition of leisure and occupation are unrelated, the Latin definitions are related. *Otium* and *negotium* are complementing terms. *Otium* is thought of as a well earned rest from *negotium,* such as a vacation or retirement. The Latin definition of leisure is not in the spirit of the ancient Greek, because one cannot have *otium* without first experiencing *negotium*. *Otium* comes after a life of *negotium*. It is a contemplative existence but it is viewed as a reward for a life of *negotium*. In one respect it is similar to the classical Greek idea of *skole* and *theoria*. But in another respect, given its dependence on occupation, it is not. The philosopher Seneca tells us of Cicero (a Roman statesman, orator, and writer), who sought *otium* not for itself—but because he was tired of *negotium*. When Cicero finally realized the blessing of *otium* and was ready to pursue it for its own sake, it was too late. Seneca concludes that Cicero never really lived, as no one really can live until leisure is valued for its own sake.[12]

While Roman philosophers and intellectuals may have realized what they were missing, they could not fuse the Greek ideal with the political and economic aspects of their lives. Unlike the Greek city-state, the demands of the Roman empire required a stoic sense of duty, which precluded the contemplative life. The situation created what can be called the Roman "problem of leisure," which gives us insight into our present dilemma. We also have political and economic demands that distract us from living a life of leisure in the Greek sense. This dilemma gives rise to two definitions of leisure, one for the classical Greek world and one for the Romans and the modern world.

Definitions of Leisure

Classical leisure. The ancient Greek idea of contemplation is commonly referred to as classical leisure. David Gray, a contemporary scholar of leisure, calls classical leisure "an activity which involves pursuit of truth and self-understanding. . . . It is an act of aesthetic, psychological, religious and philosophical contemplation."[13] To contemplate, says Josef Pieper, "means to open one's eyes receptively to whatever offers itself to one's vision, and the things seen enter into us, so to speak, without calling for any effort or strain on our part to possess them."[14] These short definitions fail to give a complete understanding; hence, to help us more clearly envision classical leisure, the very act of thinking needs to be analyzed in more detail.

Pieper suggests that by the Middle Ages two ways of understanding were clearly recognized, *ratio* and *intellectus. Ratio* is "logical thought, of searching and of examination, of abstraction, of definition and drawing conclusions." *Intellectus* is a simple vision of truth: contemplation.[15] We can elucidate the difference through the example of a rose bush: employing *ratio* powers in the study of a rose leads to an experiential understanding, based on the logic of experimentation. We analyze, observe, calculate, and record. An *intellectus,* or meditative, understanding of a rose goes beyond description and demonstrated fact to the "roseness" of the rose. We contemplate the essence of a rose, its beauty, entirety and meaning.

Pieper notes that in our world of "total work," there is not much room for *intellectus.* Society holds in esteem the effort of work and sees the effortless activity of contemplation as worthless, often confusing it with idleness. By discounting *intellectus,* we must hold to the assumption that all knowledge is a result of *ratio* thought and, says Pieper, "the effort which knowledge requires is a criterion of its truth."[16] Learning truth becomes hard work, resulting in a society that turns its thinkers into "intellectual workers":

> Like the wage-earner, the manual worker and the proletarian, the educated man, the scholar, too, is a worker, in fact an "intellectual worker," and he, too, is harnessed to the social system and takes his place in the division of labour . . . he is a functionary in the world of "total work;" he may be called a specialist, but he is a functionary.[17]

So important is *ratio* understanding and so forgotten is *intellectus* understanding that many of our educational institutions virtually neglect the liberal or "free" arts in favor of the utilitarian aspects of knowledge. This focus has created a professional class of workers who are not educated, but trained functionaries.[18] It should be clear that classical leisure in modern society is, basically, non-existent. Our goal is to trace its decline in the history of western philosophy. First, however, we must discuss the attitudes that have replaced it.

Modern Leisure. There has been a historical journey, writes Pieper, in which the notion of work has grown to envelop every sphere of life.[19] The result is a work–non-work dichotomy with no hint of classical leisure. Hannah Arendt describes it as a labor–play dichotomy:

Whatever we do, we are supposed to do for the sake of making a living; such is the verdict of society . . . to level down all serious activities to the status of making a living is manifest in present-day labour theories, which almost unanimously define labour as the opposite of play. As a result, all serious activities, irrespective of their fruits, are called labour, and every activity which is not necessary either for the life of the individual or for the life process of society is subsumed under playfulness.[20]

From this modern perspective, work captures all seriousness while leisure time is left empty.

In an effort to salvage a place for leisure in modern society, the sociologist Stanley Parker abandons the classical notion and tries to forge a new idea of leisure. In a modern society, both work and leisure must be defined within the dimensions of time and activity. Thus, a complete definition of leisure must include its relationship to work. To grasp the work–leisure dichotomy, Parker suggests that there are five ways of spending time; two are devoted to work and three are devoted to non-work.[21] They are:

1. *Work, working time, sold time, subsistence time.* This is time devoted to earning a living.
2. *Work-related time, work obligations.* This includes time traveling to and from work, preparing for work, work related meetings and education, et cetera.
3. *Existence time, meeting physiological needs.* This is time engaged in meeting the physiological needs, such as eating and sleeping, et cetera.
4. *Non-work obligations, semi-leisure.* These include obligations to home and commitments to others.
5. *Leisure, free time, spare time, uncommitted time, discretionary time, choosing time.* This can be thought of, say Charles Brightbill and Tony Mobley, as "time left over after work and other activities necessary for self-maintenance or basic requirements of existence."[22]

Parker's work–leisure continuum places the time dimension of leisure into perspective by defining leisure time as that time which is not bound by obligation; it does not qualify leisure by its other dimension: activity. For this we turn to Joffre Dumazedier, another sociologist, for help. He says that leisure activities are so called if they display four characteristics: liberating, disinterested, hedonistic, and personal.

1. *Liberating.* Leisure is freedom "from a certain number and from certain kinds of obligation." These obligations are institutional and are listed as occupational, family, socio-political, and socio-spiritual.[23]
2. *Disinterested.* Leisure cannot be at the service of any material or social end. It has no utilitarian or ideological goal.[24]
3. *Hedonistic.* Leisure is characterized by the search for a "state of satisfaction." This makes it intrinsically hedonistic.[25]
4. *Personal.* Leisure is not concerned with obligations imposed by society. It is engaged in for the self; it serves one or more of three functions:
   a. "It offers man the possibility of freeing himself from . . . physical and nervous strains."
   b. "It provides an opportunity to free oneself from the daily boredom generated by repetitive and frequent tasks."
   c. "It gives everyone a chance to escape the routine and the stereotypes imposed by the operation of basic institutions, it enables man to go beyond the confines of the self and it frees his creative powers, whether to conform with the dominant values of civilization or to challenge them."[26]

xix

Brightbill suggests that leisure activity has various potential, ranging from a rejuvenator for work to "the foundation of culture beyond the utilitarian world."[27] Similarly, Norman Miller and Duane Robinson, in *The Leisure Age,* define leisure as "that portion of available free time devoted to the pursuit of leisure values."[28] Leisure values are defined as "the complex of self-fulfilling and self-enriching values achieved by the individual as he uses leisure time in self-chosen activities."[29] Finally, we return to Dumazedier, who states that the function of modern leisure is to free one from "tiredness by resting, from boredom by entertainment, from functional specialization by developing the aptitudes of his body or his mind."[30] Modern leisure, then, is generally defined as nearly any activity that is performed during "free time." Hence, modern leisure tends to be defined within the dimensions of time and activity; upon reflection, it is evident that classical leisure is also defined within these dimensions.

Leisure Time and Activity

Classical and modern leisure can be distinguished in terms of the activity dimension. The activity of Classical leisure is the cultivation of self, the pursuit of truth and the exercise of wisdom. It originates in the intellect in the form of contemplative thought. Modern leisure is not nearly as specific. From the modern perspective, any activity engaged in during free time is designated as leisure—as long as it is free from obligation, self-satisfying, self-serving and socially acceptable.

The two definitions of leisure, modern and classical, can also be viewed from the dimension of time. Classical leisure has its time—freedom from the necessity of work, and modern leisure has its time—unobligated time. The difference between the two is their relationship or lack of relationship to work. On the one hand, leisure time in the classical sense is not dependent upon work. Classical leisure is a way of life, or state of mind, and cannot be turned on and off to meet the demands of work. On the other hand, the modern perspective of leisure time comes after work time. In fact, leisure is thought of as dependent upon work because it can only be derived from work. Brightbill, from the modern perspective, goes so far as to distinguish between the unobligated time resulting from work and unobligated time resulting from a lack of work. The former is called true leisure and the latter enforced leisure:

> there are two modes of leisure—true leisure and enforced leisure. *True* leisure is not imposed upon us. Enforced leisure is the leisure we do not seek—it is the time the victim of the confining illness has on his hands, it is the "time off" which grandpa gets when the company says he has reached the retirement age.[31]

Because of the importance of work in the modern world, there is little appreciation of classical leisure. Certainly there is an inverse relationship between work and classical leisure—a relationship that is clarified by the importance a culture places upon one over the other.

Leisure and Culture

A definition of modern and classical leisure is not complete until their differing positions with regard to culture is appreciated. Pieper describes classical leisure as the basis of culture—it is the "centre-point about which everything revolves."[32] There is but one leisure, and the exercise of it determines but one true culture. But the modern view of leisure relates to culture differently, reversing Pieper's position by suggesting that culture is the basis of leisure. Because there are many cultures, there are many forms of leisure. According to Dumazedier, leisure is a product of "economic and social evolution."[33] And that product, in the modern world, is a person's "social right to dispose of time for his own satisfaction."[34]

While initially it may seem that we are free in our leisure time, a more critical look can raise questions about this assumption. Herbert Marcuse has argued that leisure time thrives in advanced industrial society but that it is "unfree to the extent to which it is administered by business and politics."[35] Marcuse's observation raises a crucial issue: the possibility that society, or culture, influences our ideas. In this case, our idea of what it is to be at leisure, our idea of what it is to be free, and our idea of what a human being is, may well be influenced by our culture. This point suggests the necessity of a brief discussion of the relationship between culture and ideas.

Leisure and the Sociology of Knowledge

An underlying approach to this study can be broadly characterized as the sociology of knowledge, the study of the relationship between society and ideas. While it is not necessary to deliver a treatise of this approach to how ideas are formed, a few words are appropriate concerning its assumptions and goals.

From our perspective, the roots of the sociology of knowledge lie in the proposition that human beings are, to some degree, influenced by their social environments. This position is held, in varying degrees, by others as well. For example, most histories of philosophy have accepted this proposition to a limited degree, as evidenced by their tendency to begin discussion of a particular system of thought by noting dimensions of the historical context in which the ideas were developed.[36] Some scholars are more explicit in the degree to which they stress the impact of social conditions on ideas. An example can be found in the introduction to George Sabine's *A History of Political Theory:*

> This history of political theory is written in the light of the hypothesis that theories of politics are themselves a part of politics. In other words, they do not refer to an external reality but are produced as a normal part of the social milieu in which politics itself has its being.[37]

Finally, there is a group of scholars whose activity centers on identifying social factors that influenced specific types of ideas.[38] As a result of this narrow focus, they are able to conduct in-depth analyses of the relationship between social conditions and thought. While such an approach is denied us due to the scope of this study, we view the impact of social conditions on ideas as a critical consideration. Hence, while we admire the goals of the sociology of knowledge, we are currently limited by space and scope (attitudes toward leisure over a period exceeding 2000 years) in our ability to pursue them to our satisfaction. A brief summary of these goals should clarify the source of our limitations.

While the origins of the sociology of knowledge have been traced to Vico, Montesquieu, G. W. F. Hegel, and Karl Marx, the modern delineation of the concept, as well as the phrase itself, was developed by Max Scheler in 1924, and introduced to the United States in 1936 by Karl Mannheim's *Ideology and Utopia.* Mannheim's thesis states that "there are modes of thought which cannot be adequately understood as long as their social origins are obscured."[39] Those attempting to contribute to the field of study are challenged to "analyze . . . all the factors in the actually existing social situation which may influence thought."[40] And if this challenge does not clarify the complexity of the task, a final quote should:

> The problem is to show how, in the whole history of thought, certain intellectual standpoints are connected with certain forms of experience, and to trace the intimate interaction between the two in the course of social and intellectual change.[41]

Being mere mortals, who are interested in the phenomenon of leisure, we have found it necessary to substitute "changing concepts of leisure" for Mannheim's "whole history of thought." This substitution narrows the topic to manageable proportions, though it is still sufficiently broad to inhibit the degree of sophistication we would prefer in the analysis of "certain forms of experience." Ultimately, it is up to each reader to determine our success in relating changes in social conditions to changes in attitutes toward leisure.

Philosophy and Leisure in Context

We have attempted to define our essential terms: philosophy and leisure. This was important because our goals in this study are to a) clarify the historical process that gradually replaced the classical concept of leisure with the modern view, and b) show how this change is reflected in the process of philosophy in western civilization. To bring you this story we will journey through a time span of over 2000 years. We will focus on the writings and teachings of selected, key people—those who we feel had the most to say on the subject of leisure. Our attempt is to place each philosopher in his historical and intellectual context in the belief that ideas are products of the political, social, economic, and intellectual environment. In addition, it will be obvious that these ideas acted, in turn, to influence further political, economic, intellectual and social change—as they challenged or reinforced the historical realities that originally stimulated them.

If we combine the concepts and definitions noted above, we can recognize that changing views toward leisure time are crucial dimensions of the process of philosophy in western civilization. In the succeeding chapters, we will clarify and add detail to the following conceptual diagram.

1. *THESIS* (Parts I and II)
   Classical Leisure: humans as contemplative beings. Hence, leisure and human essence linked. Leisure viewed positively, but only a small percentage of humans are in a position to benefit from it.

2. *ANTITHESIS* (Part III)
   Modern Leisure: humans as active, economic beings. Hence, leisure viewed negatively. This negative view is democratized, i.e. denial of leisure's significance is applicable to all humans.

3. *ATTEMPTED SYNTHESIS* (Part IV)
   Work and leisure integrated, as humans are viewed as contemplative economic beings. Democratization of classical leisure and, hence, human essence.

References

1. Plato, *Theaetetus,* 174 a–c, *The Collected Dialogues of Plato,* ed. Edith Hamilton and Huntington Cairns (New York: Pantheon Books, 1961) p. 879.
2. T. Z. Lavine, *From Socrates to Sartre: The Philosophical Quest* (New York: Bantam Books, 1984) p. 5.
3. Epictetus, *The Discourse of Epictetus, Book II,* Chap. 11, trans. P. E. Matheson, in *The Stoic and Epicurean Philosophers,* ed. Whitney J. Oates (New York: The Modern Library, 1940) p. 301.
4. Plato, *Apology,* 38a, Hamilton and Cairns, p. 23.
5. David Hume, *An Enquiry Concerning Human Understanding and Concerning the Principles of Morals,* ed. L. A. Selby-Biggs (Oxford: Clarendon Press, 1967) p. 526.

6. Aristotle, *Nicomachean Ethics,* 1141b2, *The Basic Works of Aristotle,* ed. Richard McKeon (New York: Random House, 1941) p. 1028.
7. Aris. 1140a26–28, Ibid., p. 1026.
8. Plato, *Timaeus,* 90d–e, Hamilton and Cairns, p. 1209.
9. Aristotle, *Politics,* 1259a10–12, McKeon, p. 1142.
10. Sebastian de Grazia, *Of Time, Work and Leisure* (New York: Twentieth Century Fund, 1962) p. 21.
11. Ibid., p. 19.
12. Ibid., p. 22.
13. David Gray, "This Alien Thing Called Leisure," in *Reflections on the Park and Recreation Movement,* ed. David Gray and Donald Pelegrino (Dubuque, Iowa: Wm. C. Brown Company Publishers, 1973) p. 8.
14. Josef Pieper, *Leisure: the Basis of Culture* (New York: Pantheon Books, 1952) p. 9.
15. Ibid., p. 11.
16. Ibid., p. 19.
17. Ibid.
18. Ibid., p. 20.
19. Ibid., p. 6.
20. Hannah Arendt, *The Human Condition* (Chicago: Chicago University Press, 1958) p. 127.
21. Stanley Parker, *The Future of Work and Leisure* (New York: Praeger Publishers, 1971) pp. 25–27.
22. Charles K. Brightbill and Tony A. Mobley, *Educating for Leisure Centered Living,* 2nd ed. (New York: John Wiley and Sons, 1966) p. 8.
23. Joffre Dumazedier, *Sociology of Leisure,* trans. M. A. McKenzie (New York: Elsevier, 1974) p. 73.
24. Ibid., pp. 74–75.
25. Ibid., pp. 75–76.
26. Ibid., p. 76.
27. Charles K. Brightbill, *The Challenge of Leisure* (Englewood Cliffs, NJ: Prentice-Hall, 1960) p. 6.
28. Norman Miller and Duane Robinson, *The Leisure Age* (Belmont, Ca.: Wadsworth, 1967) p. 6.
29. Ibid., p. 6.
30. J. Dumazedier, p. 71.
31. C. Brightbill, pp. 4–5.
32. J. Pieper, p. 5.
33. J. Dumazedier, p. 71.
34. Ibid., p. 72.
35. Herbert Marcuse, *One Dimensional Man* (Boston: Beacon Press, 1964) p. 49.
36. See, for example, T. Z. Lavine's excellent summary of western thought, *From Socrates to Sartre: The Philosophic Quest.*
37. George H. Sabine, *A History of Political Theory* 3rd ed. (New York: Holt, Rinehart and Winston, 1961) p. v.
38. See, for example, Leopold Haimson's *The Russian Marxists and the Origins of Bolshevism* (Cambridge, Mass: Harvard University Press, 1955) and C. B. McPherson, *The Political Theory of Possessive Individualism* (New York: Oxford University Press, 1979).
39. Karl Mannheim, *Ideology and Utopia,* trans. L. Wirth and E. Shils (New York: Harcourt, Brace and World, 1936) p. 2.
40. Ibid., p. 78.
41. Ibid., p. 80.

Part I
Leisure as Essence: The Athenian Ideal

You don't know if you can have any real impact on the future, but you act as if you can.

Robert Heilbroner

The rise of Hellenic, or Greek, Civilization serves as our historical point of departure for the analysis of concepts of leisure in western thought. For it was during this period, basically from 900 to 400 B.C., that many seeds of what is generally referred to as western civilization were planted. Even Bertrand Russell, whose reputation as a twentieth-century philosopher is not based on his sense of mystery in the historical process, displays the slightest hint of awe in the first paragraph of his *A History of Western Philosophy:*

> In all history, nothing is so surprising or so difficult to account for as the sudden rise of civilization in Greece. . . . What occurred was so astonishing that, until very recent times, men were content to gape and talk mystically about the Greek Genius.[1]

And while Russell would undoubtedly argue that his analysis of the course of western philosophy has removed much of the awe and mystery, many of us are still inclined to be overpowered when studying this phenomenon.

The following four chapters (Part I) attempt to sort out and clarify the critical philosophical arguments underlying the classical view of leisure, as well as the historical and intellectual antecedents that contributed to them. The social thought of Plato and Aristotle serves as the cornerstone of classical leisure, and forms the thesis for our analysis of the changing attitudes toward leisure time in western thought. Part II traces the thesis of classical leisure through the Middle Ages, where it stayed essentially intact as an ideal until confronted with its antithesis (modern leisure: Part III), which fully blossomed during the period from the sixteenth to the eighteenth century. Parts IV and V discuss the attempts to synthesize the classical and modern views of leisure, from the early nineteenth century to the present time.

Chapter One outlines what we consider to be the most important social, political, and economic realities that influenced Plato and Aristotle. Chapter Two summarizes dimensions of the intellectual legacy bequeathed to them, from Homer through Socrates. Chapter Three focuses on Plato's thought, divided into sections on a) Theory of Knowledge, b) Individual, Society and the State, and c) Leisure. Chapter Four uses the same categories to analyze Aristotle's perspectives.

If, at times, the subject seems difficult and too complex to follow, do not hesitate to put the book down and stare at the sky—or whatever you get pleasure from staring at—and take comfort in the following story. Its characters include three famous thinkers of the twentieth century—the

1

economist John Maynard Keynes, the mathematician Max Planck, and the philosopher Bertrand Russell:

> Keynes was having dinner with Professor Max Planck, the mathematical genius who was responsible for the development of quantum mechanics, one of the more bewildering achievements of the human mind. Planck turned to Keynes and told him that he had once considered going into economics himself. But he had decided against it—it was too hard. Keynes repeated the story with relish to a friend back at Cambridge. "Why, that's odd," said the friend. "Bertrand Russell was telling me just the other day that he'd also thought about going into economics. But he decided it was too easy."[2]

References

1. Bertrand Russell, *A History of Western Philosophy* (New York: Simon and Schuster, 1945) p. 3.
2. Robert L. Heilbroner, *The Worldly Philosophers,* Rev. Ed. (New York: Simon and Schuster, 1961) p. 227.

Chapter 1
The Greek City-State:
Origins, Conflicts, and Decline

They were beaten at all points and altogether; all that they suffered was great; they were destroyed, as the saying is, with a total destruction

Thucydides

The goal of this chapter is to summarize the important dimensions of the Greek City-State, which provided the social context for the ideas of Plato and Aristotle. Significantly, both of these pivotal thinkers lived during the period when the city-state was crumbling. And, as we will note, this relationship between the development of significant new philosophies and the decline of political and social stability is a recurring phenomenon throughout history. In the early nineteenth century, G. W. F. Hegel accounted for this tendency by suggesting that historical epochs can be fully understood only as they are coming to an end; hence, philosophy cannot alter the course of events, but only summarize them. Hegel, the epitome of the philosopher of history, viewed philosophies as intellectual expressions of historical epochs, and we encourage you to think about his proposition from your own perspective.[1]

The origins of ancient Greece can be traced to the period around 1600 B.C. when Indo-European peoples migrated southward from northern and central Europe, overcoming the Mycenaeans. A second series of invasions (led by the Dorians) began in 1100 B.C. and eventually undermined the Mycenaean civilization. As was typical of most warrior societies, political power depended upon the prowess and personality of the warrior-leader to such a degree that political structures, as we know them today, did not exist. Recall that in the war against Troy (c. 1180 B.C.—note that all of the dates in this chapter refer to B.C.) Achilles decided to pull his forces out of battle due to a dispute with Agamemnon, the king. We will look deeper into the story below, but at this point we wish to point out the fact that while his troops were sorely missed, there is little to suggest that Achilles did not have the right to make such a decision, which ran counter to Agamemnon's wishes.

The major economic focus was agriculture and herding, with manufacturing mostly limited to the creation of implements of war. Unlike ancient Crete, which had a flourishing trade, commerce was virtually nonexistent; barter was the means of exchange. Slavery existed (primarily for the personal convenience of the warriors), but the majority of laborers worked the land and manned the armies through an essentially feudal relationship with their leaders.

The *Iliad* and the *Odyssey* provide us with a glimpse into the view of the world of the ancient Greeks. As in most primitive societies, the forces of nature served as the primary focus of religion; hence, we find these mysterious and uncontrollable forces transformed into deities, to be courted and placated for the benefit of humans. The sun, rain, wind, and sea were much more threatening prior to the development of technological means to dampen their effects and, without such control, it is not surprising that other methods were developed to regulate these forces.

3

In contrast to modern western ideas of the deity, the Greek gods were a rowdy bunch, as likely to cause problems as they were to solve them. Zeus, the father of the gods, often appears as a harrassed husband and father who enjoys parties and his sleep. And to the degree that morality and ethics can be derived from the epic poems, the gods are seen as enforcers of fate and the principle of moderation. The tendency to perceive divine forces in human images, then, was taken to an extreme in ancient Greece. An illustration of many of these points is found in Book One of the *Iliad*.

The scene is Troy, besieged by the Greek troops who have traveled across the sea to rescue a beautiful woman who was captured (that's their version—actually she ran away from her Spartan husband and loves her "captor") by a Trojan prince. In the course of the siege, the daughter of Apollo's priest is captured for Agamemnon, and he refuses her father's offer to ransom her, invoking the wrath of Apollo. With Apollo actively supporting the Trojans, many Greeks are killed, and Agamemnon finally agrees to give up his captive—but only if Achilles will replace her with one of his. Achilles responds by pulling his troops out of the battle and sulks in his tent, feeling that he has been dishonored. Thetis, Achilles' mother, is a sea goddess and he appeals to her to convince Zeus that, in order to restore his honor, the gods should help the Trojans further so Agamemnon will recognize that Achilles' presence is critical for victory. The plot works, the Trojans gain the upper hand, and Agamemnon apologizes—but Achilles is still too offended to fight. As the Trojans prepare to burn the Greek ships, Achilles' best friend is killed trying to stop them. Finally, in a rage, Achilles agrees to fight and the Trojans are defeated, but he is killed.

Possibly the most obvious point to be drawn from this Hellenic soap opera is the view of women. Like Eve in the *Old Testament,* women are viewed as the source of the men's problems. Each of the critical events in the story can be traced back to a woman and, clearly, the view presented is not a positive one. The idea of "woman as troublemaker," then, is deeply imbedded in the western tradition—a suggestion that might help to illuminate the depth of opposition towards the women's movement in our own society. Another way of viewing the story is to focus on the childishness of the great warriors. And, from this perspective, we can begin to recognize another dominant theme that has influenced western thought: the conflict between desire and passion, on the one hand, and reason, on the other. As outside observers, we can see the tension, and it appears that if the characters thought about what they were doing for a moment, they would recognize that their lust and pride are the sources of their problems—problems that might be transcended with reason. The two themes are combined with the recognition that women tend to be viewed as objects of desire and passion; hence, anyone stressing the evil of women reveals an underlying view which assumes the weakness of men.

As noted, not even the gods are safe from such concerns, and the above points can be seen coming through the discussion between Thetis and Zeus when she is making her appeal for Achilles. Note the obviously human dimensions of their interaction (remembering that Zeus is the father, and king, of the gods), as well as Thetis' style; finally, note the reaction of Hera, Zeus' wife, to the plot. The "gods who live forever" are assembling for a feast, and Thetis arrives early to catch Zeus alone:

> She came and sat beside him with her left hand embracing his knees, but took him underneath the chin with her right hand and spoke in supplication to the lord Zeus . . . : 'Father Zeus, if ever before in word or action I did you favour among the immortals, now grant what I ask for. Now give honour to my son short-lived beyond all other mortals. Since even now the lord of men Agamemnon dishonours him, who has taken away his prize and keeps it. Zeus of the counsels, lord of Olympos, now do him honour. So long put strength into the Trojans, until the Achaians give my son his rights, and his honour is increased among them.'

4

She spoke thus. But Zeus . . . made no answer but sat in silence a long time. And Thetis, as she had taken his knees, clung fast to them and urged once more her question. . . .

Deeply disturbed Zeus . . . answered her: 'This is a disastrous matter when you set me in conflict with Hera, and she troubles me with recriminations'

Finally, Zeus agrees, but, as he feared, his wife had seen him and Thetis together:

Hera was not ignorant, having seen how he had been plotting counsels with Thetis . . . and at once she spoke revilingly to Zeus. . . . 'Treacherous one, what god has been plotting counsels with you? Always it is dear to your heart in my absence to think of secret things and decide upon them. Never have you patience to speak forth to me the thing that you purpose. . . .'

Then in return Zeus . . . made answer: 'Dear lady, I never escape you, you are always full of suspicion. . . . If what you say is true, then that is the way I wish it. But go then, sit down in silence, and do as I tell you, for fear all the gods, as many as are on Olympos, can do nothing if I come close and lay my unconquerable hands upon you.'[2]

Clearly, Zeus is caught between the two women, and the pressure threatens to push him beyond moderation, as evidenced by his threat to strike his wife. The lesser gods fear a "brawl," as the family begins to take sides with their father or mother. Finally, when all are reminded of Zeus' strength and temper, the nectar is passed, the music starts, and the party continues. Book One of the *Iliad* ends by noting that when the festival was over, Zeus and Hera were sufficiently reconciled to share the same bed—very human, indeed.

Both Achilles and Zeus stepped beyond the line of moderation, but the mortal man did not know when to stop. In the end, we have the impression that while there are many similarities between the two male figures, it is Zeus' relative degree of moderation (he ultimately controls his temper when Achilles does not) that separates the two. This practical object lesson seems to be ready-made for a warrior society.

The City-State

Sometime between 900 and 750, the Greeks embarked on a political experiment that would guarantee their place in western history. In some cases (such as Athens), the city-state can be identified as the original context for the development of modern political ideas such as individual freedom and popular participation. In others (notably Sparta), the siege mentality that accompanied constant military threat contributed to different configurations of social norms, which can best be viewed as more highly structured extensions of the warrior society. The city-states, then, represent a political transition from the ancient to the modern world, and we are continually struck by the similarities between their problems and ours. While numerous city-states grew and flourished around the Mediterranean before and after the rise of Athens and Sparta, these two "superpowers" provided the major historical contrasts that influenced the life and thought of Plato.

As Plato noted in *The Laws,* many differences in social and political systems can be attributed to geographical factors—notably, the relative ease of access to the sea. The proximity of Athens to port facilities stimulated the growth of commerce, introducing foreign ideas and peoples into the clan-based milieu of the city-state. The focus on commerce undermined the self-sufficiency of the isolated agricultural community, enhancing desires for more material possessions and causing wars when merchants extended their areas of operation into hostile lands. These wars drained the treasury and opened the doors for demagogues to appeal to the frightened and confused people. The once-united society became factionalized, adding civil tensions to the burdens of foreign war, and massive discrepancies in the distribution of wealth served to further polarize the community. Sparta's geographical location hindered the growth of commerce, maintaining the self-sufficient virtues of agricultural life and the importance of community. This brief outline suggests the continued importance of the ancient concept of moderation. Plato viewed desire (greed) and passion (excessive pride) as destructive forces in both individuals and societies. Ironically, then, while our society tends to glorify Athens, Plato (for reasons that will become clear) was highly critical of it. In some ways, Plato was lauding Sparta—and, at the very least, he suggested that the ideal state will be based on moderation. With this point in mind, we will sketch some of the differences between these two major city-states.

Sparta

The origins of Sparta, the major city of Laconia, date back to the Dorian invasion (1100), and the continuity of the warrior-society norms is striking. While history is full of examples of conquerors gradually substituting new institutions and world views for their warrior norms, the Spartans maintained and strengthened their conquerors' attitudes, creating a city-state best described as a garrison. The extension of Spartan power throughout Laconia from the eighth to the sixth centuries created a society in which the vast majority of people were conquered subjects. These "Helots" were treated as either sharecroppers or slaves and, along with a small group of state-sanctioned merchants (the Perioeci), their function was to provide the "Spariates" (the Dorian elite) with means of support. With their necessities provided by the Helots, and forbidden to engage in commerce, the Spariates were free to devote all of their time and energy to affairs of state and military training.

The Spartan conquest of the Peloponnese, and the repression of a major Helot rebellion, were barely completed when the wars with Persia (499 to 479) temporarily united Sparta, Athens and other Greek city-states against a common enemy. By 431 B.C., Sparta and Athens were at war against each other. The siege mentality of Sparta, which can be traced to the Spariates' fears of Helot rebellion, was clearly reinforced by these wars.

This siege mentality was transformed into strict social and political regulations, with the Spariates exercising total control over the inhabitants of Laconia. And such control necessitated that life would be just as regimented for the Spariates as it was for the Helots. Hence, the Spariates devoted their lives, from the age of seven years, to military training and state service. Their families were secondary to the interests of the city-state, they owned few private possessions, they spent most of their time in military barracks, and even the children were considered property of the state. Political and social status was the reward for the Spariates, not material wealth or personal freedom. And with the number of potentially hostile Helots estimated at around 200,000 and the citizens "never more than 8,000 strong," the degree of militancy and the sacrifice of individualism seems harsh, but understandable.[3]

The institutions of government reflected and supported the social norms, with a system based on kingship, an assembly, a council, and a powerful five member group called the Ephorate. On most occasions, the monarchy appears as primarily symbolic. The Council, which was made up of the kings (Sparta had a dual monarchy) and 28 nobles (each had to be over 60 years of age), carried out the administration of government affairs and prepared legislation for the Assembly to consider. Above all of this stood the five Ephors, who could veto any piece of legislation; in addition, they exercised strict control over the distribution of wealth, judicial matters, and the content of education.

Sparta's legacy included concepts of discipline, simplicity, loyalty, and self sacrifice, along with its legendary military and athletic skills. Its early period of expansion was, essentially, over by the sixth century, but the militaristic norms remained intact to protect what had already been created. Hence, by the fifth century, when Athens and Sparta went to war, it was the expansion of Athens, not Sparta, that sparked the conflict.

Athens: Rise to Prominence

The origins of Athens, the major city of Attica, are also traceable back to tribal organizations. Significantly, however, these organizations were not subjected to the continual pressures that we noted as factors influencing the Spartan state. Hence, while remnants of aristocratic society existed, they were not as closely associated with a warrior caste. Whereas the Spartan ideal rested on single-minded devotion to the state, the Athenian prided himself on his multi-dimensional character. Pericles' (who ruled Athens during the "Golden Age" from 461 to 429) famous funeral oration summarizes this view in its comparison between the Athenians and the Spartans:

> Our constitution does not copy the laws of neighboring states; we are rather a pattern for others to follow. . . .
> Further, we provide plenty of means for the mind to refresh itself from business. We celebrate games and sacrifices all the year round, and the elegance of our private establishments forms a daily source of pleasure. . . .
> If we turn to our military policy, there also we differ from our antagonists. We throw open our city to the world, and never by alien acts exclude foreigners from any opportunity of learning or observing . . . ; while in education, where our rivals from their very cradles by a painful discipline seek after manliness, we live exactly as we please, and yet are just as ready to encounter any legitimate danger.[4]

Significantly, the address was given in 431. In the course of the next 27 years, the Athenians tendency to do exactly as they pleased led to their destruction by the highly disciplined Spartans. But before we discuss the fall, we should note the important aspects of the rise of Athens.

The cohesion derived from the ancient tribal organizations succeeded in holding the Athenians together until the eighth century, when the growing emphasis on olive oil production contributed to social tension. Many independent small farmers were unable to compete, losing their land and, in many cases, their freedom. As the movement of the aristocracy into commercial activity concentrated land ownership into fewer and fewer hands, the growth of a plantation economy stimulated the growth of slavery, making it even harder for the small landowner to compete. The aristocrats, secure in their power, abolished the monarchy, and transformed their Council into the governing body. Unlike the aristocrats in the days of Homer, who appear as paternal leaders who inspire the people, the upper class became bent on exploitation, enhancing their wealth and power by destroying other Athenians. Intellectually, this introduced a new twist to the ancient view of the gods, which we will note in the writings of Hesiod in Chapter Two. Socially, it brought Attica to the brink of chaos.

By 594, social unrest (which included popular movements demanding the cancellation of all debts and massive land reform) became so intense that Solon was given absolute power by his fellow aristocrats to reform Athens. Solon's reforms included limitations on the size of landholdings and the abolition of debtors' slavery. Critically, he also embarked Athens on a course of commercial development by turning the focus of economic activity away from subsistence agriculture toward the export of olive oil. In conjunction, citizenship was opened to foreign merchants and artisans, and legislation was passed mandating that each boy learn a trade. These reforms would have a crucial impact on Athens during the following two centuries, as its economy became increasingly oriented toward manufacturing and commerce. Politically, Solon altered the traditional form of suffrage, substituting property ownership for blood lines as a requirement to hold office in executive and administrative positions. In addition, the Popular Courts were established and the common peoples' influence in the Assembly was enhanced.[5]

In retrospect, Solon's reforms contributed to major changes in the society, but the conflict was too intense to be overcome immediately and social unrest continued. Appealing to the peasants, Pisistratus seized power in 546, exiled many aristocrats and redistributed their land; he also instigated extensive irrigation projects, and extended and popularized the ancient rituals. Pisistratus died in 527 and was followed by his son, Hippias (whose brother was murdered in the course of Athenian court intrigue). Meanwhile, the exiled aristocrats had convinced the Spartan leaders to intervene against the "tyrants" in order to stop the spread of the peasant-oriented reforms. Sparta restored the aristocrats to power in 510, and shortly thereafter a new set of reforms was introduced which ushered Athens into the "Golden Age."

Cleisthenes' reforms altered the voting system by establishing electoral districts that cut across clan and economic identities—two longstanding sources of conflict in Athens. In addition, the electoral districts became a new focus of the citizens' identity, serving to stimulate loyalty to the city-state, as opposed to other groupings. The power of the Aristocratic Council was also limited, being replaced with greater influence in the Assembly and its Administrative Council. Each of the new electoral districts chose candidates for the Assembly (all men who were citizens and over 30 years of age were eligible) and the final 500 Council members were chosen by lot from this group. The Assembly was given control over financial affairs and the power to declare war; in its meetings, the adult male citizens of Athens discussed and debated the issues of the day.

The right to discuss was expanded into the right to initiate legislation in the Assembly under Pericles. And as the powers of the Assembly to order the affairs of state and formulate specific laws were expanded (these powers were maintained in the Council of 500 under Cleisthenes), the power of the Council declined. Payment for service in the government was also introduced, enabling even the poorest citizens to participate in civic affairs. With the assembled male citizens making the laws, the Board of Generals (consisting of 10 generals chosen by the Assembly for one year terms) became an increasingly significant force in administering the government; all other administrative officials were chosen by lot. Finally, Pericles (who was chosen President of the Board of Generals for 30 consecutive terms) extended the tradition of popular juries. Six thousand male citizens, chosen by lot, made up the pool of potential jurists. Juries were chosen from this pool to preside over trials, and the verdict was based on the vote of a majority.

While the changes in governmental structures and social status from Solon through Pericles were often introduced as last-ditch attempts to placate potentially-revolutionary masses of people, their results were impressive. Unlike Sparta, whose agrarian practices remained essentially unchanged during this period of time, Athens developed a highly-efficient commercial society. In addition, the extension of participatory democracy and vigorous growth of the arts established the reputation that is still highly esteemed today, nearly 25 centuries later. But there is also a dark side to the story of this growth of democracy, commerce, and the attitude that everyone should live "exactly as we please." The focus on commerce turned the Athenians away from the simple, self-sufficient agrarian life that their ancestors had known. The need to supply the commercial city-state with food stimulated the growth of a vast empire and a large navy to protect its precious products. Hence, while the wealth grew, so did the cost of defending the opportunity to pursue it.

And while it is unfair to suggest that commercial expansion made war with neighboring states inevitable, such expansion was a critical factor.

We have suggested that Cleisthenes' reforms of the electoral laws were, in part, an attempt to unify Athens, and we have noted that, under Pericles, Athens was highly unified. Hence, the reforms appear to have worked; but from our perspective, the Persian Wars were an even more critical factor serving to unite Athens.

With the growth of power under Cyrus in the sixth century, the Persians extended their control westward to Aegean Sea, conquering numerous Greek cities and islands in and near Asia Minor. By 499, an anti-Persian revolt spread in the conquered areas, and an offensive against Persia was organized. While Sparta refused to participate, Athens committed naval forces—but they arrived after the revolt had been suppressed. This attempt to support Miletus (the center of the revolt where, in 494, the Persians annihilated the population) triggered the Persian Wars. Persian troops attacked Athens in 490, but were defeated at the battle of Marathon. They retreated, but returned 10 years later with a massive fleet and army, prepared to conquer all of Greece. With Athens and the other city-states united under Spartan leadership, the Persians were unable to achieve their objective. But the war continued until 479, and peace was not formally established until 448.

The common threat and the hardships shared by all Greeks during the war served to unite them, if only temporarily. Sparta and its allies began to withdraw from the fighting after the Persian fleet was destroyed at Salamis in 480, and continued to do so after the decisive Greek victories during the following year at Plataea and Mycale nullified the threat to the mainland. The Spartan leaders, always fearful of a Helot revolt, wanted their troops back home as soon as the foreign threat subsided. For Athenians, the wars boosted the spirit of unity and equality to its highest point. Most citizens had contributed something to the war effort, the victories at Marathon and Salamis were clearly Athenian victories, and the Persian threat had been so great that, at one point, the entire population of Athens was forced to evacuate the city. Robinson's summary paints the picture of a united society ready to tackle any problem:

> After Salamis, clearly, things could never be quite the same again; first the mass evacuation, in itself a great leveller, a breaker-up of traditions as well as homes, and then the victory in which every man equally had played a part. . . . The twofold experience was bound to breed a sense of social and political equality. The tide of Athenian democracy now set in at full flood; and more and more through the coming years the People's will determined the city's policy.[6]

But the democratic process does not necessarily guarantee that the laws it produces are conducive to social harmony and stability. And it is crucial to stress that at the same time that governmental procedures were becoming more democratized, the substance of the laws was, in fact, laying the basis for the self-destruction of Athens.

Athens: Decline

With the Persian threat to the mainland severely weakened in 479, the Athenian leaders made some decisions that contributed to the decline of Athens. The first was to extend the fight outward from the mainland in order to liberate the area surrounding the Aegean Sea from Persian influence. With the massive fleet that had been assembled since the victory at Marathon, Athens became the obvious leader in this effort. To coordinate the task and guard against any future encroachments into the Greek world, the Delian League was created, with Athens supplying the leaders and the ships. The other member states paid yearly assessments to the common treasury, located on the island of Delos. All of this sounds logical enough, but by 467 (only 10 years after its creation) some of the allies attempted to secede from the League, accusing Athens of manipulating policy for its own benefit. In short, the former protector had become the new exploiter of the Greek cities in the Aegean and Asia Minor:

> Since Athens donated ships instead of money, it soon exercised, through its sea power, an effective control over its allies; and rapidly the confederacy of equals was transformed into an Athenian Empire.[7]

Hence, by the time Pericles came to power in 461, Athens was attempting to maintain a far-flung, and increasingly unloyal, empire. The importance of the earlier decisions to turn Athens into a center of trade should now be clear—for Athens had become dependent on the importing of food and, hence, could not allow the Empire to crumble. Pericles exacerbated the tension when, in 454, he moved the treasury from Delos to Athens, proposing that its funds be used to rebuild and beautify the central city of the Athenian Empire.

As the Empire grew, tension increased between Athens and Corinth, another maritime power. The competition between Athens and Corinth to extend their alliances and subvert those created by the other (and, clearly, Athens was on the offense, with Corinth acting defensively) sparked the Peloponnesian War, which destroyed Athens. Briefly, the scenario from 433 to 431 unfolded as follows: in response to the extension of Athenian power in the western sea lanes, Corinth attacked an Athenian ally. Corinth then encouraged another Athenian ally to revolt; Athens then responded with troops, and declared an Empire-wide boycott on goods from the city of Megara, which had half-heartedly supported Corinth. In 431, Corinth called a meeting of the Peloponnesian League (a loose alliance of the city-states in the area) "and after much argument her delegates pushed the reluctant Spartans into a decision for war."[8] Hence, Sparta (which had also been reluctant to encourage the war against Persia) reluctantly declared war on Athens in response to the growth of Athenian power. Sparta's stated goal was to free Greece from Athenian domination.

Secure in its naval power, Athens avoided a confrontation with Sparta's superior army. As a result, Sparta was able to invade Attica, forcing its inhabitants to seek protection in the walled fortress of Athens. The walls, which extended from the city to the sea, kept the Spartans out, but the overcrowding contributed to an outbreak of plague in 429. Thucydides' description of a corpse-ridden Athens is chilling: he notes that nearly one quarter of the population (including Pericles) died, and the high degree of unity forged during the Persian Wars was destroyed. In addition, he suggests that the plague produced a nearly complete collapse of morals and social order:

> So they resolved to spend quickly and enjoy themselves, regarding their lives and riches alike as things of a day. Perseverance in what men called honour was popular with none, it was so uncertain whether they would be spared to attain the object; but it was settled that present enjoyment, and all that contributed to it, was both honourable and useful. Fear of gods or law of man there was none to restrain them. As for the first, they judged it to be just the same whether they worshipped them or not, as they saw all alike perishing; and for the last, no one expected to live to be brought to trial for his offences.[9]

The longstanding tensions between the landowning aristocrats and the commercial interests of Athens (loosely organized into the political parties known as Oligarchs and Democrats) grew into open hostility after the plague. Robinson notes that the aristocrats and peasants were most affected by the war because their land was being destroyed; hence, they pushed for peace. But the merchants, whose fortunes were relatively safe behind the walls of Athens, insisted on extending the war: The mercantile class . . . were evidently making a good thing out of the war. The chance of crushing Corinth was not to be missed.[10] With unity destroyed, the vaunted democratic institutions of Athens became tools for struggle between economic factions, with each side contributing its share of short range, selfish, and absurd acts.

Domestic conditions under Pericles may deserve the title "Golden Age," but the international relations present a far different picture. And, not unlike the realities of England in the late nineteenth century, reform at home was coupled with repressive arrogance abroad. Clearly, the benefactor in the wars against Persia became the exploiter, continually raising the yearly assessments for the maintenance of the Empire (which, again, Athenians did not pay), forcing unwilling cities to join the League, and suppressing any rebellions. In addition, Athens reserved the power to try all cases arising from imperial disputes in the Athenian courts. Pericles did, however, recognize that the continuation of these policies was possible only as long as Sparta was not offended, and there is evidence to suggest that he tried to bribe the Spartan leaders to stay out of the war.[11] Following Pericles' death, the commercial interests gained power and, whether out of greed, pride, or ignorance, they decided to press the war against Sparta. Cleon, a wealthy merchant who masqueraded as a commoner, used his oratory skills to convince the Assembly to support this course of action. He sweetened this proposal by including in it an increase in the League's assessment, so that no Athenian taxes would be used to pursue the war. If Pericles seduced the Empire, Cleon raped it—forcing members to pay for a war that began when they wanted out of the League.

By 425, Sparta offered to negotiate a peace, but the confident Athenians, driven by military success and stimulated by Cleon's rousing speeches, refused. The tide of battle turned, Cleon was killed, and moderate Oligarchs came to power in 421. Sparta offered peace again, and the Treaty of Nicias was signed by the Oligarchs.

With the peace, the aristocrats and peasants returned to their land and, it seems, Athens had the opportunity to learn from its mistakes. But the commercial interests had their eyes on extending the Empire even further, into Sicily and Italy. Their leaders immediately began to encourage revolts among Sparta's allies and, in 416, the island of Melos (which had steadfastly refused to join the League) was reduced to rubble as Athenian troops killed the men and sold the women and children into slavery. In the wake of the slaughter, Athenian colonists occupied the island.

The commercial interests found their leader in Alcibiades, a flamboyant playboy and military genius with sufficient reputation and oratory skills to convince the Assembly that imperial wars were good for Athens. With the raw materials (including grain) of Sicily and Italy as their goal, the Athenians moved into areas historically claimed by Syracuse, and a new war began. Confident, but overextended, the Athenian fleet and army were destroyed near Syracuse. Seeing Athens weakened, the cities of the League began full scale revolts, refused to pay their assessments, and called Sparta in for the kill. Sparta declared war on Athens in 413, accusing Athens of breaking the Treaty of Nicias. Through the imposition of rigid taxes (this time levied on its own citizens), Athens was able to rebuild its navy. From 413 until 405, Sparta and Athens fought numerous battles, which completely drained the Athenian economy (recall that the primary stimulus for all of this was the expansion of the economy), to the point that valuable metals were extracted from the statues on the Acropolis to help finance the war. Finally, the rebuilt Athenian fleet was destroyed and the food shortage in Athens had become critical. In 404 a bankrupt, starving and totally demoralized Athens—with only one-third of its citizenry still alive—surrendered.

The picture is bleak, but it is even more discouraging when the domestic dimensions of Athens' "suicide" are noted. While it is obvious that the ancient value of moderation was flagrantly violated internationally, Athens' mere lip-service to temperance became even more pronounced at home. While Thucydides' description of the plague presents a hedonistic response to desperation, the Athenian society collapsed when this hedonism was combined with hope for victory. By the time Athens surrendered, a domestic legacy of court intrigue, treason, mass murder, and recriminations so plagued the society that it is a wonder that any semblance of cohesion was restored.

The Democrats clearly kept the wars going for their own economic gain, while the Oligarchs often conspired for peace with the enemy. The Oligarchs, however, had no patents on treason—anti-aristocratic elements were ready to open the gates of Athens to the Persians in 490, while the aristocrats led the defense at Marathon. Even Alcibiades, who helped stimulate the anti-Syracuse fervor, ended up conspiring with the Spartans and the Persians. The pressure of war intensified the economic and social tensions, leaving the famous democratic institutions open to absurdity: in 406, the Athenian navy won a decisive battle against the Spartan fleet, but many Athenian warriors were drowned. The Assembly liked the victory, but lamented the loss of life—so after a debate, its members voted to have their victorious admirals executed. Shortly thereafter (but not soon enough to save the admirals), the Assembly voted to execute those who proposed the execution. Reeling from the defeat, the Spartans offered peace but, as Aristotle notes:

> although some of the Athenians supported this proposal, the majority refused to listen to them. In this they were led astray by Cleophon, who appeared in the Assembly drunk and wearing his breastplate.[12]

Each shift of power during the second phase of the war brought with it recriminations against the previous leaders. The Oligarchs revolted and seized the government in 411, assassinating Democrats and disbanding the Assembly. A second coup was led by Theramenes four months later, establishing a balance between democracy and oligarchy that later served as a historical example for Aristotle's "polity," or best possible state.[13] But the navy, historically aligned with the commercial interests, got word of the first coup and threatened to lay siege to its own port if the democracy was not restored. By 410 the Democrats were back in power and they sent for Alcibiades to return. With the surrender to Sparta in 404, the Oligarchs again assumed power. With Sparta's support, they abolished the Assembly and created the Council of Thirty, which confiscated merchant's property and exiled or executed its opponents. Critias, the leader, forbade Socrates (his former teacher) to engage in public activity and teaching. In 403, an army of Democrat exiles overthrew Critias and re-created the Assembly.

Virtually all historians stress the degree of moderation exercised by the new government in dealing with its opponents. And while it seems fair to suggest that after Critias' tyrannical rule anything would seem moderate, it is significant that decades of internal violence subsided under the new leadership of Thrasybulus. Most of the Oligarchic leadership that survived the coup were exiled, not executed, and a general amnesty was declared. But the intensity of the previous conflicts combined with the moderation exercised by the new government created an environment ripe for the discovery of a scapegoat to purge Athens of its problems. Fortunately for Athens, a 70-year old man was available to perform this function; unfortunately for Athens, that man was Socrates, whose students (especially Plato) were sufficiently prolific and enraged that they would not let the world forget this final act of absurdity. Hence, along with all of its accomplishments, Athenian society is still remembered as the one that caused the execution of Socrates—thereby creating the most famous martyr of western philosophy.

From our modern perspective, it is difficult to imagine that a lone philosopher who "wore his poverty as a badge of his honesty" could be viewed as a threat to the Athenian state, but others saw it differently. Socrates' direct role in the politics of Athens presents inconclusive evidence: true to his Oligarchic sympathies, he strongly opposed the execution of the admirals in 406 (he was the presiding officer in the Assembly the day the issue was raised, and the decision was passed over his attempt to table the motion), but he was also critical of Critias and the Rule of the Thirty. In short, Socrates refused to become totally aligned with either faction; (recall that Critias had forbidden him to teach). It is also true that Socrates had, at one time or another, taught several of the most controversial figures of the time—including Critias, Alcibiades, Charmides (a general under Critias), and the son of Anytus (an Athenian leader in 403, and the author of Socrates' indictment). In the end, it seems to us that Socrates' major crime was encouraging those he contacted to examine their lives ("life without this sort of examination is not worth living") in the context of an overwhelmingly hypocritical society.[14] Such questioning has always been threatening to such a society, and the politicians (not the philosophers) are those with the power to enforce their definition of what is patriotic and what is subversive. In Athens, the quest for the truth was considered subversive, and Socrates was convicted of impiety and corruption of the Athenian youth.

Socrates' execution was witnessed by his closest friends and students, including Plato. And many of the themes emerging from Plato's philosophy can be traced to this jolting experience. Plato's family was aligned with the Oligarchs; they had initially supported Pericles, but turned against the Democrats during the Peloponnesian War. He was even related to Critias (his uncle) and Charmides (his cousin). And, certainly, his inherent distrust of democracy was strengthened by the Democrats' charges against his mentor. The hypocrisy of the system (and its relationship to democracy in general) comes through in Plato's works, and the ideal system he developed in *The Republic* beckons us to respect the discipline and simplicity of Sparta, although not the entire system. Finally, Plato's lineage suggests that if it had not been for the timing of his birth, he probably would have played a significant role in Athenian politics—but he was deprived of the opportunity by the excesses of his relatives and the public reaction to them. Athens had declined, the ancient values of moderation and reason had been replaced by greed and pride. Plato was 28 years old when Socrates was executed—the Golden Age was past, and Athens would never recover.

If Sparta initially held an inkling of hope for the re-establishment of the ancient Greek ideals for Plato, such hopes were dashed by the end of the fourth century. After destroying the Athenian Empire in order to free Greece, Sparta replaced Athens with its own empire, including renewed yearly assessments, Spartan governors, and Spartan troops.[15] The increase in wealth at home was concentrated in the hands of a small group, undermining the discipline and simplicity, and adding new dimensions of economic inequality to the society. Greed, it seems, had spread throughout the Greek world as a motivating force for wars between the city-states. Athens briefly regained imperial influence from 378 to 354, but the power of the warring city-states was eclipsed by the rise of Macedonia.

The decline of the city-states and the rise of Macedonia serve as the immediate historical context for Aristotle, who was born in the Macedonian city of Stagira in 384 and died in the Greek city of Chalcis in 323. His father was a physician at the Macedonian court, and Aristotle grew up with Philip—the future king, and father of Alexander the Great. Philip became King of Macedonia in 359, while Aristotle was in the midst of his 20 year course of study with Plato at the Academy. Posing as a defender of Greece, Philip succeeded in seducing or conquering the Greek world by the time he was murdered in 338. Aristotle left the Academy after Plato's death in 347, dismayed because the new director had chosen to focus on the mathematical dimensions of Plato's thought to the detriment of his philosophical inquiries. When Alexander came to power in

13

Macedonia following his father's death, Aristotle enjoyed a privileged position. He had tutored the young Alexander, and their relationship continued until the conqueror degenerated into an egomaniac and declared himself a god. In 334, Aristotle established the Lyceum, his school in Athens.

Alexander died in 323, stimulating a strong anti-Macedonian movement throughout Greece, and Aristotle was forced to flee from Athens to Chalcis, where he died within the year. Once again, the Athenians were looking for a scapegoat to blame for their troubles, and Aristotle (who had advised Philip and defended Alexander until the latter lost touch with reality) was as good a choice as any. Like Socrates, Aristotle was accused of impiety, but his self-imposed exile deprived Athens of its chance to "sin a second time against philosophy."[16]

Like Plato, Aristotle lived through the decline of the city-state. Unlike Plato, Aristotle lived during a period when a degree of social order was being established. Granted, it was Macedonian order, but both Philip and Alexander admired and supported Greek culture, and Aristotle's life presents a picture far different than Plato's total alienation from his society. It is also interesting to note that Aristotle's father taught him anatomy and natural science before he went to Athens to study with Plato. And whereas Socrates' rigorous system of logical deduction (as opposed to empirical observation) served as the basis of Plato's method, Aristotle stressed the importance of scientific inquiry.

Suggesting that Plato and Aristotle did not develop their systems of thought in a social and intellectual vacuum, we have attempted to summarize critical historical events influencing their social contexts. In the following chapter, we turn to an examination of the rich intellectual legacy they inherited from ancient Greece.

References

1. We will discuss Hegel's ideas in more depth in Chapter Twelve.
2. Homer, *Iliad of Homer,* trans. Richard Lattimore (Chicago: Phoenix Books, 1961) pp. 72–74.
3. C. E. Robinson, *Hellas* (Boston: Beacon Press, 1955) p. 37. Originally published in 1948, Pantheon Books.
4. Thucydides *History,* II, 37–39, in M. I. Finley, ed. *The Portable Greek Historians* (New York: Viking, 1960) pp. 267–268.
5. For detail on these, and the following reforms, see Robinson, Chapter IV and Will Durant, *The Life of Greece* (New York: Simon and Schuster, 1939), Chapter V. *The Story of Civilization,* Part II. Aristotle also summarizes them in *The Athenian Constitution.*
6. C. E. Robinson, p. 68.
7. W. Durant, p. 245.
8. C. E. Robinson, p. 107.
9. Thucydides, *History, II,* 53, in M. Finley, p. 277.
10. C. E. Robinson, p. 110.
11. The following summary is drawn primarily from W. Durant, Chapter XVIII, aptly entitled "The Suicide of Greece."
12. Aristotle, *The Athenian Constitution,* 34, quoted in W. Durant, p. 450.
13. W. Durant, p. 449, also Ernest Barker, *Greek Political Theory* (New York: University Paperbacks, 1960) p. 380. Originally published in 1918, Methuen and Company.
14. Plato, *Apology,* 38, in E. Hamilton and H. Cairns, p. 23.
15. For details, see W. Durant, Chapter XIX.
16. Ibid., p. 553.

Chapter 2
Origins of Western Philosophy:
The Disciplines That Try to Explain and the First Western Philosophers

The story of leisure is part of the story of human understanding—in which religion, science, and philosophy have each staked their territory. The first part of this chapter gives recognition to all three approaches. The second part focuses on the early Greek natural philosophers, who established important themes that served as the intellectual background for Plato and Aristotle. When added to the historical considerations previously discussed, this chapter should further clarify the legacy bequeathed to them from ancient Greece.

Science, Religion, and Philosophy

Philosophy attempts to give sense to our world and our actions in it. To say it another way, philosophy is an effort to explain the universe. From this perspective, it shares a common purpose with religion and science, which also claim a role in universal knowledge. The Medieval philosopher Thomas Aquinas acknowledged their role: it was necessary for man's salvation that there should be a knowledge revealed by God, in addition to the philosophical sciences built on human reason.[1] In the time of Aquinas, science had not yet emerged from philosophy as an independent discipline. It is often difficult to talk philosophically without also speaking religiously or scientifically, making a clear separation difficult—for at times each may possess attributes of the others. The boundaries of philosophy are sometimes so vague that Bertrand Russell likened philosophy to a "No Man's Land" between religion and science.[2]

Because they share attributes, science, philosophy and religion serve as each other's midwives and, throughout history, each has been stimulated by the perceived inadequacies of the other. For example, Sigmund Freud reflected a total confidence in the power of science, suggesting that philosophy and religion present no problems that cannot be solved by science. According to Freud, "It is not permissible to declare that science is one field of human mental activity and that religion and philosophy are others, at least its equal in value, and that science has no business to interfere with the other two." Freud thought that it was valid for scientific research to regard "every sphere of human activity as belonging to it" and to criticize the unscientific formulations of philosophy.[3] Freud's statements represent our period of history—a period when science is given the most credit for contributing to human understanding. The following section investigates another period—that of the early Greek natural philosophers. From this source, western philosophy was born from religion, and the stage was set for the classical elaboration of leisure.

Early Greek Natural Philosophers

The western struggle to come to grips with the world began with Homer and Hesiod. They provide the intellectual origins of the early Greek philosophers examined here: Thales, Anaximander, Anaximenes, Heraclitus, Pythagoras, Democritus, the Sophists, and Socrates. By looking at these early Greeks, a gradual growth in intellectual sophistication can be seen—as well as a struggle to differentiate between religion on the one hand, and philosophy and science on the other.

We recognize that our brief overview of these thinkers can be confusing, because there are so many different points of view presented in a few pages. Hence, to help you understand the material, we suggest that you remember that these people were searching for answers to the basic questions of life. The fact that they developed divergent perspectives may be confusing, but it is also testimony to human creativity. Note, especially, how concepts that were raised by one thinker acted as a point of departure for others, and allow yourself to become fascinated by the ways in which some perspectives filtered through the process from one philosopher to another. Most of the basic questions of western philosophy, religion and science were raised prior to Plato's birth—and humans have been trying to answer them for over 2,000 years.

Homer and Hesiod

In 900 B.C. the universe, as seen through Greek eyes, was ruled by gods that held nature together by regulating the sea, earth and sky. To imagine a world governed by these gods is to imagine a haphazard world, where there are few natural laws to order nature in a consistent way. Thus, there are few consistent social guidelines and little sense of justice. Homer's *Iliad* (c. 804 B.C.) provides some direction out of this world of unpredictability by defining the gods and the universe as subject to destiny, or fate—an initial concept leading toward the idea of natural order and regularity. To subscribe to this destiny is the path to happiness for both gods and humans. But within the parameters of destiny, there is leeway for various types of activity, and the virtues that contribute to the likelihood of happiness and honor (for both individuals and societies) are reason and moderation—that inner discipline which makes us responsible for our actions. Both virtues are cornerstones for the classical concept of leisure.

Hesiod (c. 750 B.C.), writing in a period when the toil of the serf and small farmer provided wealth for the aristocracy, accepted the notion of destiny, but redefined the gods. Hesiod did this by turning fate into moral law, envisioning a natural order to correct the unjust exploitation of the poor. The gods, proposed Hesiod, do not touch human life for their own pleasure, but for the good of humankind. So Zeus is no longer controlled by the whims of those who have his ear; instead, he is the enforcer of justice. Hesiod elevated the position of humans by holding "man to be different in kind, not merely in degree of complexity, from the rest of nature." This being the case, "man has a destiny different from that of the rest of nature."[4] People are the creation of gods and, as such, they share a mutual destiny with the gods. Again, the way they meet their destiny is through reason and moderation.

Homer and Hesiod have sown the seeds of western philosophy. Their concept of fate, or destiny suggests that the causes of events are regulated by natural laws and not the erratic will of capricious gods. And Hesiod's extension of fate into moral law provided a point of departure for the Greek natural philosophers.

Thales, Anaximander and Anaximenes

As long as the causes of events were attributed to the will of the gods, science and philosophy were impossible. It required a time and place where ideas could be exchanged, customs and beliefs observed, and superstitions cancelled for reason to dominate. The time was the sixth century B.C.; the place was the Ionian city of Miletus, the richest city in the Greek world. Thales, Anaximander and Anaximenes were citizens of Miletus and collectively represented the Milesian School. They were the first Greeks to suggest a natural process underlying world order, stimulating the growth of philosophy and science. These three philosophers postulated a single cause for all things, as they reformulated the writings of Homer and Hesiod.

Thales, the first of the Milesians, asked the question "What is the source of all things?" His answer was water, the ancient symbol of life. It could have seemed to Thales that in evaporation water becomes air, and in rain the process reverses. In the formation of a delta, water becomes earth and in a spring, earth becomes water.[5] So for Thales water was the basic "substance" of all things. This concept provided the foundation of the natural philosophers' quest by proposing that a) there is a unifying principle of the universe resulting from natural causes, not divine action, and b) that the cause of the universe can be determined. For these contributions, Thales is considered the father of western philosophy.

Anaximander was a generation younger than Thales. He reasoned that it is impossible for Thales' basic "substance," water, to take on all forms of existence. If substance is a particular thing, how can it come to be its opposite, asks Anaximander. Opposites stand to each other in a relation of opposition, such as hot and cold, or wet and dry; therefore, if one of them was made universal substance, the other could not continue to exist.[6] It was evident to Anaximander that "only something which was no one thing in particular could turn itself with equal facility into anything and everything."[7] The substance that Anaximander spoke of was only defined as boundless, or infinite.

Anaximenes was a pupil of Anaximander and rejected Anaximander's "boundless" because it conveyed no meaning. Boundless is nothing in particular, so it cannot explain specific qualities. It is like saying there is color, but no particular color.[8] To solve this problem, Anaximenes synthesized aspects of Thales' and Anaximander's arguments:

> Anaximenes differs from Anaximander in that his primary substance is not merely something infinite without any more exact definition, but in common with that of Thales a substance with definite qualities; but he agrees with Anaximander in that he chooses for this purpose a substance which seems to possess the real qualities of the latter's primary matter, that is boundlessness and perpetual movement.[9]

The substance Anaximenes selected was Air; it can spread itself out into the boundlessness of space and yet be in continual motion and change. Without the benefits of scientific techniques to test his position, Anaximenes had to move directly from hypothesis to assertion. Thus, he stated that when air "is dilated into a rarer form it becomes fire, while on the other hand air that is condensed forms winds . . . if this process goes further, it gives water, still further earth, and the greatest condensation of all is found in stones."[10]

Anaximenes' synthesis refined Thales' approach to understanding the universe. As air condenses, it changes from wind to water to earth to stone; each change is a change in the quality of substance (air) but is measured quantitatively through the thing it becomes. Anaximenes is saying that whatever the substance of the universe is, it can be observed. This is the foundation of the quantifiable and precise description of nature, which stimulated a quest for understanding guided by the view that the universe is a unified entity and provided a cornerstone for the development of natural science. There is another philosophical quest that began in early Greek philosophy: the attempt to explain the structure of particular things, and Pythagoras serves to illustrate this view.

Pythagoras and the Pythagoreans

During the sixth century B.C., Croton, on the east coast of southern Italy, was along the trade route between Greece and Italy. It was here, about 520 B.C., that Pythagoras (a native of Samos, an island off the Ionian coast just north of Miletus) settled, gathered his disciples, and developed his philosophy. Because his teachings were kept secret, within the cult of Pythagoreans, it is difficult to distinguish between the philosophy of Pythagoras and that of his followers, such as Democedes, Alcmaeon, Heppasus and Philolaus.

Unlike the Milesians, who focused their attention on the study of nature, the Pythagoreans searched for truth in the abstractions of mathematics. Their fundamental proposition was that the nature of things is derived from "number." Aristotle's description is still, perhaps, the most succinct:

> The so-called Pythagoreans, who were the first to take up mathematics, not only advanced this study, but also having been brought up in it they thought its principles were the principles of all things. Since of these principles numbers are by nature the first, and in numbers they seemed to see many resemblances to things that exist and come into being—more than in fire and earth and water (such and such a modification of numbers being justice, another being soul and reason, another being opportunity—and similarly almost all other things being numerically expressible); since, again, they saw that the modifications and the ratios of the musical scales were expressible in numbers; since, then, all other things seem in their whole nature to be modelled on numbers, and numbers seemed to be the first things in the whole of nature, they supposed the elements of numbers to be the elements of all things, and the whole heaven to be a musical scale and a number.[11]

Numbers explain everything; for example, in musical studies the Pythagoreans noted "that the pitch of tones depends on the length of the strings on musical instruments and that musical harmony is determined by definite mathematical propositions."[12] Applying mathematics to the universe, they expressed harmony as an arithmetic mean.

Projecting their ideas about numbers onto Anaximander's idea of the "boundless," the Pythagoreans developed the theory of the limited and the unlimited. The world consists of limited forms and unlimited basic substance. Form is provided by a series of mathematical constructs. Hence numbers, while distinguished from unlimited substance, are closely connected to it—for they limit the unlimited and give it shape. In this view, the Pythagoreans preserve Anaximander's "boundless" as the unlimited and show how particular objects take form. While the Pythagoreans tried to make sense out of the many particular things in the universe through their notion of the limiting factor of numbers, Heraclitus followed on their heels by reopening the arguments of Thales and Anaximenes, which focused on an identifiable universal substance.

Heraclitus

A hundred years separate Heraclitus from Thales. Born in the famous Ionian city of Ephesus, he began contributing to the debate around 500 B.C. Heraclitus noted that Thales and Anaximenes had reduced the world to a single principle, water or air, that remained itself as it changed into other things. Finding these propositions inadequate (as did Anaximander), because they do not solve the problem regarding how one universal substance can be the many different things of nature, he proposed another solution. But, unlike Anaximander's theory, it was an answer that accepted the notion of a single, identifiable universal substance. As the water of Thales and the air of Anaximenes were deemed insufficient when faced with the problem of change, Heraclitus proposed fire because it is in a state of constant motion. Thus, says Heraclitus, all things in nature must also be undergoing constant change; truly, one cannot step into the same river twice. "Upon those that step into the same rivers different and different waters flow. . . . It scatters and . . . gathers . . . it comes together and flows away . . . approaches and departs."[13] While it is obvious that a river is in constant motion, what about more stable objects, such as the chair you sit in or the book you read? Aristotle gives us Heraclitus' answer: And some say not that some existing things are moving, and not others, but (I say) that all things are in motion all the time, but that this escapes our perception.[14] Things only give an illusion of stability, but in reality they are in constant motion. With this idea, Heraclitus presented two worlds, the world as things appear to be (stable) and the world as things must really be (continually changing).

Heraclitus' account of nature as appearance and reality provides the starting point for his account of human nature. Substance (through its many changes) comprises natural law, and the human reflection of natural law is justice. Previous thinkers, such as Hesiod, had suggested that it was the gods, through fate, that gave guidance to social order and justice. Heraclitus modified this concept by subscribing to substance as the source of all change. True natural laws (as changing substance) are hidden from human perception, making human natural laws (true justice) also hidden from humans. The problem is to uncover these concealed human laws. They are, he said, housed in each person and we need only draw them out. Unfortunately, people tend to base their ideas of right and wrong upon a narrow perspective by judging events only in relation to how they personally affect them. But in reality natural human laws are objective and, thus, truly just.[15] Heraclitus' pursuit of reality led him to rely on reason rather than the senses, an approach that was further refined by Parmenides.

Parmenides

Thales introduced the notion of change and Heraclitus proposed that all things are in a state of constant change. Parmenides (of Elea on the west coast of southern Italy) argued, around 475 B.C., that change is impossible. So, whereas Heraclitus concluded that things only give an illusion of stability, Parmenides argued that change is the illusion. But Parmenides' major contribution was not his conclusion concerning the impossibility of change; instead, it is found in his method of pure logical argumentation without the aid of sense perception to explain reality.

Parmenides began with the idea of existence. If something exists, we say it is a being. And the opposite of existence is non-existence, which is to say that the opposite of being is not being. We can think about what exists, but we cannot think of non-existence or not being; in other words, one cannot think of what is not, only what is. What is not has no substance, it is impossible and will always remain so because it is impossible for nothing to change into something. And for something to change into something else it must become what it is not. The old disappears, becomes nothing, and the new appears—changing into something from nothing—a logical impossibility. "What is," says Parmenides, "is uncreated and imperishable, for it is entire, immovable, and without end."[16] This logical argument is based on the belief that truth can only be reached through the use of reason. Only reason can reach universal truth because logical statements are true in every case. Sense perceptions can only lead to falsehoods because they only verify particular cases. But if, as Parmenides says, change is impossible, how is it that our senses observe change? Democritus attempts to formulate an answer.

Democritus

Democritus of Abdera, in northern Greece, wrote about 420 B.C. He represents a school of philosophy called Atomism, characterized by a focus on an infinite universe made up of an infinite number of minute "things" called atoms. Each atom is viewed as an individual Parmenidian being. Atoms comprise substance, while space is nothingness—the unbound. These atoms group together, with each grouping emitting different properties, to make up the particular things we experience in the world. Only atoms and the void of space are real while the things we experience (such as plants, water and other humans) are an illusion comprised of various atomic arrangements. In this way, individual judgments can vary, because they are based upon the illusion of individual experience.

While subjectivity comes from the senses, not all experience is subjective. In the process of determining reality, our senses act on things while things act on our senses, and out of this interaction a criterion of truth can be derived. Given this, Democritus suggested that there are two ways of knowing, one obscure and one genuine. Obscure understanding is a product of sensations (sight, hearing, smell, taste and touch); and tells us what appears evident. Genuine understanding is a product of reason:

> Since only atoms and space have absolute unchanging existence, only knowledge of them can be real; but since the atoms are removed from perception, it follows that only the intellectual concept of atoms and space is genuine knowledge; all else, all that is communicated by the senses, is an appearance.[17]

Truth does exist, but it is not evident. It is discovered by reason, the genuine way of knowing.

All the previously-noted philosophers (Thales through Parmenides) suggested that universal order and its understanding rests upon some form of a conscious and intelligent force. The Atomists attacked this tradition by proposing that sensations, as well as ideas, are only arrangements of atoms which themselves are incapable of sensitivity or thought. If atoms are the essence of all things and are incapable in themselves of consciousness or intelligence, then there can be no conscious force that guides the universe. Human sensation and thought, then, are only the result of atomic movement. Sensation is caused by atoms stimulating the senses which, in turn, stimulate the mind, and thought occurs as atoms pass through the body and directly stimulate the mind. Thus, thought is a direct and true form of knowledge. And while there is no conscious force as discussed above, neither is there free will. All atoms, including those of the mind, are set in motion by antecedent atomic motion, so you may think you decide to do something but, in reality, your decision is determined by such motion.

With the motion of atoms serving as the basis of all reality, Democritus developed a system of ethics based on enhancing our knowledge of this motion. The basis of ethics, and the goal of life, is seen as happiness. And happiness results from the exercise of reason or genuine knowledge as opposed to its obscure counterpart derived from the senses. The pursuit of happiness, then, is a personal, inward process, far removed from the desires of the external world of our sense perception. And, warns Democritus, the major factor in achieving it is the exercise of moderation. "To overstep due measure makes the most pleasant things unpleasant, while moderation multiplies pleasures and magnifies pleasure."[18] Through a life of moderation and the employment of reason, happiness is found in the contemplation of truth and beauty.

From the point of view of this study, Democritus and the Atomists were the culmination of early Greek natural philosophy—and the reader with a background in later Greek thought will already have recognized the presence of several Greek ideals, such as reason, moderation, and contemplation, which served as a basis for classical leisure. But the Atomists' view of the universe as a purposeless combination of purposeless atoms did not logically support their ethical prescriptions for the good life. Hence, there was no way to deduce their ethics from their science, and they left Greek thought in this critical void.

The Sophists

With the extension of popular participation in the Athenian Assembly and courts during the rule of Pericles, a group of philosophers and teachers collectively called the Sophists (literally, teachers of wisdom) emerged as an influence in Athens. Their reputation as merchants of rhetoric and advocates of crass self-interest is derived primarily from Plato, who spared no effort to discredit them. But Plato's concern goes beyond the fact that they charged students for their teaching; there is also an obvious clash of values present in the conflict between the Sophist and the Socratic/Platonic view of the world. These two approaches to philosophy can be viewed as extensions of the problem noted in Democritus' conclusions: the early Sophists tended to view humans only from his scientific perspective; hence, they denied the universality of his ethics. Socrates and Plato stressed the ethics, denying the atomists' scientific view of the world. Aristotle attempted to synthesize the ethical and scientific dimensions of this legacy. Protagoras, Gorgias, Hippias, Antiphon, and Callicles will be noted as illustrations of the Sophists' arguments.

The Sophists' views were derived from a strictly empirical epistemology. This approach fits nicely with the Greek tradition of natural science and can be seen as laying the basis for modern empiricism, introduced by John Locke and extended by David Hume. It is interesting to note that from our perspective, Plato tends to sound foreign, while much of what the Sophists said strikes familiar chords.[19] Their stress on education as a means to enhance efficiency in "practical" pursuits, their moral relativism, their skepticism, and even their suggestion that "might makes right," are probably more widespread in our society than most of us would like to admit. Be that as it may, their views ran counter to the ethical concerns of traditional Greek philosophy:

> Broadly speaking, they were prepared, like modern lawyers, to show how to argue for or against any opinion, and were not concerned to advocate conclusions of their own. Those to whom philosophy was a way of life, closely bound up with religion, were naturally shocked; to them, the Sophists appeared frivolous and immoral.[20]

Protagoras' insistence on sense perceptions as a means to truth appears as a direct attack on Parmenides. And because different people perceive reality differently, Protagoras concluded that there is no such thing as absolute reality; from this assertion, he determined that an absolute standard to measure truth, ethics, and morality is impossible. Perception of truth and right, then, is a purely subjective experience, and no one can expect others to perceive these in similar ways. Different experiences stimulate different realities, on a personal and a social level; therefore, there is no reason to expect individuals or societies to agree on answers to important questions, and there is nothing restraining them from altering values they hold one day, replacing them with entirely new standards the next. Obviously, such a view threatened every tradition in society, so Protagoras was banished from Athens in 411 B.C. for impiety, after publishing a book that casually stated his skepticism concerning the existence of the gods (all available copies of the book were publicly burned, by order of the Assembly). His most famous statement, though, is found in Plato's dialogue *Theaetetus*, where Socrates quotes Protagoras, stressing his untrammeled individualism:

> Then my perception is true for me, for its object at any moment is my reality, and I am, as Protagoras says, a judge of what is for me, that it is, and of what is not, that it is not.[21]

The passage is often recapitulated as "man is the measure of all things."

Gorgias arrived in Athens in 427; his skill at practicing and teaching rhetoric attracted numerous students, and his attack on Parmenides makes Protagoras' sound tame. His main argument can be summarized as follows:

> (1) Nothing exists beyond the senses; (2) if anything existed beyond the senses it would be unknowable, for all knowledge comes through the senses; (3) if anything suprasensual were knowable, the knowledge of it would be incommunicable, since all communication is through the senses.[22]

Obviously, such assertions challenged the Greek ideas of divine order and ethical imperatives.

Hippias extended the critique of the ethical and divinely guided state by suggesting that universal, higher laws exist above and beyond the boundaries of any particular city-state. All Greek citizens, then, are governed by the same laws of nature, and states have no right to violate these laws. Thus, Hippias challenged the classical Greek view that the city-state is the medium for the fulfillment of the individual. And, as Barker argues, he formed the basis for the concept of a universal humanity guided by a law higher than any individual state is capable of producing. Loyalty, then, is owed to human beings, suggesting the transcendence of the city-state:

> Gentlemen, he said, I count you all my kinsmen and family and fellow citizens—by nature, not by convention. By nature like is kin to like, but custom, the tyrant of mankind, does much violence to nature.[23]

Antiphon was more explicit in his development of this argument, suggesting that the ancient distinctions between Greek and non-Greeks should be transcended because all human beings are alike. In addition, he went so far as to suggest that laws of the state that promote conflict within the universal human community are contrary to nature, and should not be obeyed.[24]

Focusing on the conflict between nature and political conventions, Callicles extended the argument to the point that the laws of the state are totally opposed to nature and actually serve to weaken the best and wisest men by enforcing standards of mediocrity. Challenging the conventional wisdom, Callicles laid the basis for the suggestion that "might makes right," which was stated by Thrasymachus in Plato's *Republic*. Thrasymachus' character combines the various dimensions of Sophistry as follows: if sense perceptions do not reveal universal truths, then none exist. If there are no universal truths, then there are no moral guidelines for behavior. All morality, then, is mere convention. Given this situation, those in power will inevitably exercise their control over others for their own benefit. Thus, the ability to enforce laws is all that counts: I affirm that the just is nothing else than the advantage of the stronger.[25]

The Sophists were clearly a threat to the religious and social traditions of ancient Greece. So much so, in fact, that it would seem that anyone who attacked their arguments (notably Socrates and Plato) should have been held up as heroic, conservative defenders of the traditional ideals. And from this perspective, the fact that Socrates was executed points (again) to the hypocrisy that had grown in Athens. Given their empirical focus, it seems fair to suggest that Protagoras, Gorgias, Callicles, and Thrasymachus were merely reflecting the reality of Athens during its decline. Protagoras observed the rampant hedonism stimulated by the plague, and Gorgias taught throughout Athens when this individualism supported the factional strife in the Assembly. Democracy, of course, is based on the assumption that the majority can determine truth and justice; by necessity, then, absolute standards are eliminated, with truth and justice becoming something that the majority can agree on—in short, a head count. Hippias can be seen as responding to this new reality in which the state was no longer a tool for justice but the arm of factional interests. Whereas Hippias and Antiphon offer an alternative to the chaos and self-destruction by suggesting a new unit of reference (universal humanity), Callicles and Thrasymachus rely on their analysis of the crumbling society, presenting themselves as realists. Might had become right in Athens, as illustrated by the selfishness of the factions (particularly the Democrats) and the absurdity of the bloody recriminations instituted when the power shifted (especially by the Oligarchs).

Pericles' boast that the Athenians lived "exactly as we please" epitomizes the society in which Sophistry germinated. If a majority of the Assembly determined that conquest and war was right, then it was right. If a majority decided to annihilate the inhabitants of a city who would not subordinate themselves to the Empire, then genocide was just. Cleon admitted the truth when he warned the Assembly about the realities of the Empire in 428:

> entirely forgetting that your empire is a tyranny and your subjects disaffected conspirators, whose obedience is insured not by your suicidal concessions but by the superiority given you by your own strength and not their loyalty.[26]

His solution, of course, was to increase the repression of freedom. He went on to argue in favor of the execution of all adult males in the rebellious city of Mytilene. That the Athenian Assembly eventually accepted such a view is illustrated in the declaration prepared prior to the complete destruction of the city of Melos in 416:

> Of the gods we believe and of men we know, that by a necessary law of their nature they rule wherever they can. And it is not as if we were the first to make this law, or act upon it; we found it existing before, and shall leave it to exist forever after us; all we do is make use of it, knowing that you and everybody else, having the same power as we have, would do the same as we do.[27]

Having thus justified the slaughter of fellow-Greeks, the Athenians sold the women and children into slavery.

We conclude that Socrates' and Plato's attacks on the Sophists were also indictments of the entire society during the decline of Athens. We understand the need of the Democrats to reunite the fragmented society when they returned to power in 403. But we also suggest that their chances of doing so might have been enhanced if they had listened to Socrates instead of executing him. For it was Socrates who summoned Athens back to its traditional ideals, challenging its citizens to admit their hypocrisy. Instead of responding, they acted as if the Golden Age was still a reality and voted to execute their strongest link to it.

Socrates

The final person to be considered in this Chapter is Socrates, born in 469 B.C. in Athens. Given his influence on later western thought, some readers might question our relatively brief treatment here—but we have chosen to view him, essentially, as a major influence on the thought of Plato. Following a typical education, Socrates worked as a sculptor, like his father; he also served in the army and, as previously noted, was a member of the Athenian Assembly. In addition, he educated himself in philosophy. His studies of the natural philosophers, whose ideas we have reviewed, convinced him that their works lacked purpose because their explanations of the world were limited to physical phenomena. To subscribe to these philosophers was to explain all human actions simply in terms of physical movements—or, in the case of Democritus, the movement of atoms. This notion that the understanding of natural order was an understanding of humans was rejected by

Socrates. Instead, he focused on the human predicament: the knowledge of truth, justice, goodness.[28] As he turned his back on natural philosophy, he also took issue with the Sophists. To counteract the Sophists and establish his own position, Socrates looked to Parmenides. Where Parmenides argued that the physical world is unchanging, Socrates argued that "truth and justice are unchanging and the same for all."[29] Socrates sought to establish a standard for justice above the situational morality advocated by the Sophists. He pursued the good life and happiness, paving the way for the classical notions of leisure, as described in the writings of Plato and Aristotle.

While Socrates' end was goodness and truth, he did not teach a doctrine. Instead, he advocated a method of discovery:

> The essence of the Socratic Method is to convince the interlocuter that whereas he thought he knew something, in fact he does not. The conviction of ignorance is a necessary first step to the acquisition of knowledge, for no one is going to seek knowledge on any subject if he is under the delusion that he already possesses it.[30]

Only when we have recognized our ignorance are we ready to learn. This is the aim of the Socratic Method, but it does not end there. It is "a process of continual questioning which reveals the implications of the questioned belief."[31] In turn, this process leads to a continual revising of beliefs in the pursuit of objective truth. Through the Socratic Method each person discovers truth, goodness, and justice for him or her self. Yet these ideas are unchanging and the same for all. Thus, Socrates argued that differences of opinion as to what is good, true, or just are a result of ignorance; "virtue must be equated with knowledge."[32] Knowledge of Good will result in good actions.

Socrates' career as a philosopher attracted much public attention. As previously noted, it was the wrong kind. He refused to defend himself at his trial, opting to instruct the jury on its incompetence; in closing, he stressed the hypocrisy behind the charges of his impiety, stating:

> I have a more sincere belief, gentlemen, than any of my accusers, and I leave it to you and to God to judge me as it shall be best for me and for yourselves.[33]

While awaiting execution, his friends arranged for an escape. But despite emotional appeals, Socrates refused to flee—telling his companions that such an act would be illegal. Finally, 30 days after his conviction, with a few friends at hand, Socrates drank hemlock and died. Socrates directed western philosophy toward a serious questioning of the significance of human life—a spirit of questioning that continues today. Not answering false charges, refusing to flee (as Protagoras had done), and his dignity in death reflected his commitment and left an undeniable impact on Plato and future generations.

References

1. Thomas Aquinas, *Summa Theologica,* Part I, Q.I., A.I., trans. Fathers of the English Dominican Province (San Francisco: Benziger Bros., Inc., 1947).
2. B. Russell, p. xiii.
3. Sigmund Freud, *New Introductory Lectures on Psycho-Analysis,* trans. James Strachey (New York: W. W. Norton, 1965) p. 160.
4. W. T. Jones, *A History of Western Philosophy* (New York: Harcourt, Brace and World, 1952) p. 31.
5. Ibid., p. 32.
6. Reginald E. Allen, *Greek Philosophy: Thales to Aristotle* (New York: The Free Press, 1966) p. 2.

7. B. A. G. Fuller, *History of Greek Philosophy: Thales to Democritus* (New York: Greenwood Press, 1968) p. 87. Originally published in 1923, Henry Holt.
8. W. T. Jones, p. 36.
9. Eduard Zeller, *Outline of the History of Greek Philosophy* (New York: World Publishing Co., 1955) p. 45.
10. W. T. Jones, p. 37.
11. Aristotle, *Metaphysics,* I.5.985B24–32, R. McKeon, p. 698.
12. E. Zeller, p. 51.
13. R. Allen, p. 43.
14. Aristotle, 253b9 in R. Allen, p. 42.
15. R. Allen, p. 41.
16. Ibid., p. 45.
17. Kathleen Freeman, *The Pre-Socratic Philosophers* (Oxford: Basil Blackwell, 1953) p. 309.
18. Ibid., p. 316.
19. We are not alone in this observation. See T. Z. Lavine, p. 25.
20. B. Russell, p. 78.
21. Plato, *Theaetatus,* 160, Hamilton and Cairns, p. 866.
22. W. Durant, p. 360.
23. Plato, *Protagoras,* 337, Hamilton and Cairns, p. 331. Barker's discussion of the Sophists is from *Greek Political Theory,* pp. 66–94.
24. E. Barker, pp. 77–79.
25. Plato, *Republic,* 338, Hamilton and Cairns, p. 588.
26. Thucydides, *History,* III, 37, Finley, p. 281.
27. Thucydides, *History,* V. 15, quoted in W. Durant, p. 444.
28. G. F. Parker, *A Short Account of Greek Philosophy from Thales to Epicurus* (New York: Barnes and Noble, Inc., 1967) p. 86.
29. Francis H. Parker, *The Story of Western Philosophy* (Bloomington, Ind.: Indiana University Press, 1967) p. 37.
30. W. K. C. Guthrie, *The Greek Philosophers from Thales to Aristotle,* (New York: Harper & Row Publishers, 1960) p. 74.
31. F. H. Parker, p. 38.
32. G. F. Parker, p. 87.
33. Plato, *Apology,* 35d, Hamilton and Cairns, p. 21.

Chapter 3
Plato: Idealism and the Philosopher-King

Thales is recognized as the first Greek philosopher and represents the beginning of the first philosophical school of thought, which later included Anaximander and Anaximenes. All of these philosophers lived in the Greek City of Miletus during the same historical epoch, and they all derived their thoughts from a common foundation—the necessity of universal substance. While these Milesian philosophers represent the first "school" of Greek philosophy, the Athenian philosophers (we have grouped the Sophists, Socrates, Plato and Aristotle into this category) comprise the most renowned school of Greek philosophy.

Faced with the decline of Athens, Socrates and the Sophists directed philosophy away from its preoccupation with natural order and focused it on the human predicament. If all is in constant change, as Heraclitus said, then there can be no universal notions of truth and good. As we have noted, this position was adopted by the Sophists. Socrates, recognizing this path as leading to an ethical dead end, argued that universal, unchanging truth and good must exist; without them there can be no notion of ethics and justice. While this conclusion seemed self-evident to Socrates, he did not develop a consistent philosophy from it. Plato pursued this task, following Democritus' lead in distinguishing between appearance and reality. Like Democritus, his goal was the good life of reason, moderation, and contemplation. Unlike Democritus, he pushed beyond the void between these ethical imperatives and atomism, developing a tightly reasoned argument in support of his ethics.

Theory of Knowledge

Students of Plato's works are immediately struck by his distinctive style—it is a manner that presents ideas in the form of a conversation, usually between Socrates and other individuals. During the discussion, characters question their beliefs and seek answers through dialogue. This mode of learning is called the Socratic Method and, for Plato, it is not just a convenient writing style; instead, it is based upon and consistent with his theory of knowledge. Simply, this theory says reality exists as ideas, and the physical world is only an imperfect copy; knowledge of ideas is housed in the soul, where it lies dormant for reason to discern. Thus, the teacher's role is not to lecture or impart knowledge, but to skillfully ask questions that guide the student into recalling the knowledge already possessed.

In his theory, Plato establishes two realms of existence: ideas and the physical world. If these two realms could be put side by side, we would see that they are very different. The physical world is composed of all material things, including human beings and their materialized abstractions (such as a society's legal system), while ideas are pure abstractions that can only be objectified in thought. In addition, the physical world is in constant change as day turns to night, flowers bloom then wilt, and people are born, grow old and die; on the other hand, ideas cannot change— they always were and always will be truth. By securing these two realms, Plato steps around the

Sophists' arguments and proposes that truth is not in the world of the particular, relative and material.

Because ideas are perfection, they constitute reality—and our knowledge of ideas provides a standard to explain and evaluate the physical world. For example, if while cleaning out your garage you come across a chair with only three legs, you will immediately notice its imperfection. Your assessment can only be made because you have an idea of what a chair is. Your idea has shaped your observation into an explanation; thus, it is the idea that is real and the physical world (as represented by the chair) that is an imperfect copy of reality. Here Plato strikes a chord with the Pythagoreans, who professed that the physical world merely imitates perfect, abstract "numbers." But rather than "numbers" constituting reality, Plato uses the concept of abstract ideas. For Plato, the idea of a human being allows us to evaluate a particular person, just as the idea of a chair allows us to evaluate the particular three-legged chair.

While we possess knowledge, it is not obvious; it only becomes explicit through the process of education. During this process we attain various stages of awareness, ultimately acquiring truth and good. The two major steps toward the comprehension of truth are classified as knowledge and opinion. Knowledge must be of unchanging ideas and reality, while opinion must be of the changing physical world, which gives the appearance of reality. Opinion (the lowest step of comprehension) gives only an image of what seems to be reality; at best, it helps to develop beliefs about truth and perfection. Knowledge begins when we understand that certainty is not found in the shadowy, transient things of the physical world, but in the lasting permanency of abstractions. Plato suggested that the best training for stepping past opinion is the study of mathematics, the science of abstract symbols and forms. With sufficient education and discipline, ideals are revealed to us through reason; and finally, says Plato, we behold the origin of absolute perfection—Good.[1]

Ascending the steps of knowledge to the Good is likened to the struggle of a prisoner in a cave who breaks from the chains of ignorance and, through effort and determination, makes his way out to the freedom of knowledge. Just such an allegory is related by Socrates to Glaucon in the Seventh Book of the *Republic,* where we find a group of prisoners who have been chained in a cave, so that they can only see the back wall. Behind is a fire and between the prisoners and the fire, guards continually pass so that shadows of images are cast on the uneven surface of the back wall. This is all that the prisoners have seen and so they surmise that this appearance of reality is reality itself. There comes a time when one of the prisoners releases his chains, for they were never locked, and turns around. The glare of the fire causes him discomfort, but soon he sees the guards marching by, the fire burning, and the state of his fellow prisoners. As he sees these physical things he has a belief about his situation, although it is only a fragment of true reality. While investigating the cavern, he discovers a tunnel that leads up; curious, he enters it. The climb is difficult because the passage is steep and as he nears the opening the light of the sun becomes intense, causing him to proceed no more quickly than his eyes can adjust. At the entrance he looks out at the world before him, which is true reality, and passes from opinion to knowledge. Finally, with great effort he tries to gaze at the sun, the source of all life. While he cannot see it directly, its light illuminates his entire soul—revealing truth. After a time of dwelling on his newly-found knowledge and reflecting on his comrades below, he feels compelled to share his discovery. The way back is difficult, and his eyes cannot see in the dark. At last he stumbles into the cavern and tells his friends of the wonderful treasures that await, but they do not listen and refuse to believe.[2]

The "Allegory of the Cave" summarizes how people view truth. The great majority will always remain at the lowest step of awareness, comfortable in the conviction that their changing, distorted images are reality. Only a few will turn toward the fire and of those, only a small fraction

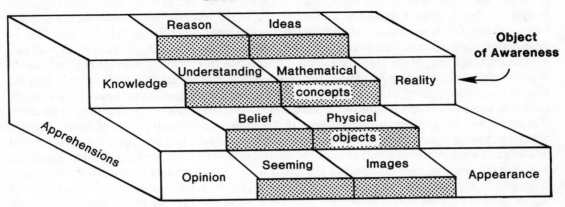

Steps of Knowledge

Good

Reason — Ideas

Knowledge — Understanding — Mathematical concepts — Reality

Object of Awareness

Apprehensions

Belief — Physical objects

Opinion — Seeming — Images — Appearance

will find their way to the outside. Those who reach truth must share their discovery—but those in the cave will not want to be told, finding solace in their ignorance and more than willing to apply the fate of Socrates to those who reveal the illusion of their existence.

Individual, Society and the State

Recall that Protagoras and Thrasymachus insisted that morality and good are relative to each individual and to each society, and they concluded that there is no standard by which to determine the good of individual behavior or actions of states. Plato counters that there are absolute ethical ideas, they are knowable, and they are standards by which we can measure the goodness of our lives and our state. From this position, he outlines the relationship between the just individual and just state.

Individual and Society

Everyone has a soul, which is spiritual—meaning that while it does not take up space as a bodily part, it does occupy us. The soul represents our essence and vitality as the house of knowledge and individual disposition toward knowledge. The human disposition is comprised of three elements: reason, passion, and desire—making the soul tripartite. The way these elements work together determines the level of knowledge a person acquires, the good to which that knowledge is applied, and the happiness attained in this life. To this end the tripartite soul is a place of continual struggle, where each element attempts to exert itself over the others to become the dominant trait of our personality.

The soul, then, has three essential functions (reason, passion, desire) that in the best souls combine to produce happiness. The lowest element, desire, is first concerned with basic physical needs such as eating and sleeping. If unchecked, desire will go beyond necessities to a preoccupation with material wealth and luxury, a diversion that can never satisfy the human soul; such obsession seeks the Good in the objects of possession, which are nothing more than transitory images of what is good. Unrestrained desire results in the restlessness of inconsistency and unreliability but, for those naturally dominated by the appetites, this appears to be the good life. To help reason temper desire, the soul is equipped with passion—which is the part of us that recognizes excessive immediate pleasure as only a distraction from reality, and that has ambition to bring about true and lasting happiness; but this enthusiasm is rooted in intuition, for it does not possess the rational power to know true good. Therefore, passion must courageously trust the direction of reason and suppress the extravagance of desire. The result is a middle level of goodness that rises above the shadowy opinion of good that is evident in the materialism of desire, but falls below the absolute good of reason. If passion becomes our overriding principle, it neglects reason and wages a kind of constant war toward the control of other people, seeking to fill an insatiable drive for the accumulation of influence and recognition. While passion is concerned with acquisition of the abstract luxuries of fame and power rather than material luxury, it can achieve a higher state of happiness than desire. But because passion is a drive for possessions (even though they are intangible), true happiness is beyond reach. Unbridled passion brings an endless series of victories, each increasing power and fame and each leaving the soul unsatisfied, and for those naturally dominated by passion this appears to be the good life. The highest element of the soul, reason, is the only part of us that has insight into knowledge. Thus, of all the elements, reason is the only one which knows reality and understands true goodness; hence it should command the other two, as it is not corruptible and knows best. When functioning well, reason attains the virtue of wisdom and, to the extent that it dominates desire with the aid of passion, it leads the soul to the good life.

The relationship of the three elements was described by Plato in a myth about a charioteer. Imagine a chariot pulled by two horses, one called Passion and the other Desire, and driven by a charioteer called Reason. Only the charioteer is capable of directing the chariot to its goal because only he knows the final destination and how the two horses relate to each other. The horse called Passion, while unable to comprehend the final goal or its pathway, trusts the commands of the charioteer and, in responding to him, keeps the other horse on the proper path. The horse called Desire wishes only to stop at every bush to eat and every trail to explore; it is only concerned with the satisfaction of immediate appetites. This horse is kept moving on the correct path only by the force of Passion, which responds to the commands of Reason. Only by this mutual effort will the chariot reach its final destination.[3] And only in this mutual effort will each participant function to its highest degree. Likewise, as we move through life toward our ultimate goal, reason must command us wisely, passion must obey through courage, and desire must be tempered if we are to live the Good life.

Plato's ideal is a disciplined life where passion is governed by reason and, in turn, subordinates desire. It is only in this proper relationship that wisdom prevails and creates the just, good individual.[4] But we are all born with divergent capacities within the soul, so we cannot all be expected to reach harmony. Most have desire as their dominant principle, others have passion, and a small fraction have reason. Because inherent proportions cannot be added or deleted from the soul, the function of the state is to make the most of each individual by allowing all members of the society to utilize their dominant principles in the most effective way. If successful, says Plato, the three types of people, "the philosopher or lover of wisdom, [the] lover of victory, [and the] lover of gain" will emerge in their rightful positions and all will be happy according to their natural ratio.[5]

Society and State

The character of the ideal state is the same as the character of the ideal individual, so as there are three elements to individual character (reason, passion and desire), there are corresponding classes in society: rulers, auxiliaries and industrialists.[6] The lowest class of society, industrialists, should be concerned only with material gain and accumulation of wealth. This overriding occupation with profit and loss would make it ideal for supplying material needs of the state; its members have only an unreliable image of reality, so they should not be expected to have vision. But the highest class (the rulers) know truth through reason, so it should be expected to have vision. For rulers to govern, they need wisdom—the result of knowledge and inner harmony. Their concerns should be the welfare of the entire state and they should care little for personal gain and honor. Between these two classes are the auxiliaries, who should understand how the industrialists must function to be successful, and yet believe in the decisions of the rulers. They should simultaneously be able to glance at reality above and appearance of reality below. As the link between the other classes, they should display the virtues of courage and strength, for which suitable fame and honor should come their way.

Organizationally, all individuals in the state should do what they do best, according to their dominant trait. Not all people should be rulers, nor all auxiliaries, nor all industrialists; if a state is to function harmoniously, it is necessary that each individual perform in the class where that person functions best. This leads to a good, just, and harmonious society—one that separates individuals into their proper class, yet allows each class to function as it functions best (rule, defend, or serve). Each class must respect the position and responsibilities of the other, recognizing that it is the rulers' duty to command wisely, the auxiliaries' duty to obey courageously, and the industrialists' duty to obey temperately. As Socrates says to Glaucon in the *Republic:*

> the same kinds equal in number are to be found in the state and in the soul of each one of us. . . . Then does not . . . [it] follow, that as and whereby the state was wise, so and thereby is the individual wise? . . . and as the individual is brave, thereby and so is the state brave, and that both should have all the other constituents of virtue in the same way?[7]

Levels of Society and Soul

Classes of Society	Level	Virtues	Elements of Soul
Rulers	Highest	Wisdom	Reason
Auxiliaries	Middle	Courage	Passion
Industrialists	Lowest	Temperance	Desire

To keep this utopia of individual and state in harmony, there needs to be a highly regimented and propagandized education for those deemed rulers and auxiliaries, to insure the virtues of wisdom, courage and moderation; justice rests on their goodness and incorruptability. On the other hand, the industrial class needs little regulation or education—except in practical affairs of commerce and craft. Education begins in nursery school, where children are told carefully censored fables and fairy tales espousing the noble virtues of temperance, courage, wisdom and justice. As teaching progresses, the students (both male and female) are introduced to gymnastics and music for strength and harmony of the body and soul; exposure is balanced and fundamental, blending wisdom and courage. Training in the arts is regulated by avoiding extravagance so that the pupil can appreciate good and beauty. From here, education advances to a more abstract curriculum, including mathematics, astronomy and the other sciences. At the age of thirty, students take a series of examinations; those passing advance on to what amounts to a five-year training course in the dialectic (logical argumentation). At the end of this study students are required to complete a fifteen-year probationary period during which time they are given experience in everyday military and political affairs. At the age of fifty, those who have demonstrated their thirst for truth and justice become philosopher-kings. This educational system, to Plato, can be used to sort out the wise and courageous from the materialistic and, later, the wise from the courageous.

Hence, while Plato's rigidity is initially offensive to some, it is easy to see that each person's basic drive would determine how long he or she remained in the process. The natural industrialist would want out of the educational system as soon as possible, in order to pursue a private career. The natural auxiliary would find a rewarding public career somewhere during the process, leaving only a small group of natural rulers by the time it was possible to rule. But Plato also recognized that absolute power might lead to lower-level temptations, so he instituted a further system of safeguards to guarantee that the rulers would not become corrupt. With the stringent educational system as the first safeguard, Plato added the requirement that philosopher-kings and auxiliaries would not be allowed to own any private property. Plato had witnessed the results of factional greed in Athens—so to guard against the possibility of corruption emerging, he eliminated the possibility of any personal gain for the two highest classes. Furthermore, he stipulated that they would not be allowed to raise their own children. Recognizing that a parent's love for a child might distort the existing balance of drives, the pleasures of family were also denied to those in a position of power. In short, Plato offers a form of socialism, or communalism, as a safeguard against the abuse of power and corruption among those who have a say over the state's policy. These regulations would not apply to the industrialists, whose social function is to pursue wealth, and who have the luxury of enjoying their families. To rule a state, or to be in a position to enforce its laws, requires the sacrifice of personal pleasures and desires. Of course, according to Plato, those truly belonging in the higher classes would not consider this a sacrifice because their souls drive them toward different types of self-fulfillment.

Implications for Leisure

Plato's idealism should be obvious in its application to individuals, society and the state. Reality is the ideal, while people and their social arrangements are imperfect physical manifestations. And people (as living, breathing individuals), along with their collective expressions (as diverse, dynamic societies and states) only change to reach perfection. If this change is governed by a rationally-dominated self-restraint, the ideals will materialize. But the realization of perfection, for both individual and the state, is dependent upon a mutual, complementary effort. For the state to govern rationally, its citizens must act rationally—and citizens can live rationally only if the state is rational. This unity of citizen and state is where the good life is achieved.

Plato identifies three conditions necessary for the good life: economic security, statesmanship and commitment.

Economic Security

Only after the material necessities of life have been acquired do individuals begin to have rational control of their lives. Desire secures our material needs, but reason limits materialism to a moderate level, freeing the individual to pursue higher functions. Plato realized that while temperance is rationally enforced, it needs the support of the state: individuals cannot be expected to live moderately in a society dominated by greed. His solution is the Greek city-state, governed by an Aristocracy where wise rulers temper greed by leading the state toward economic self-sufficiency. The effect is to limit the material desires of the populace by limiting their material expectations, thus enhancing reason's control over desire.

Statesmanship

The good life requires that people have individual and political control of their lives. Once the material necessities of life have been guaranteed, individuals are in a position to take rational control of their personal and political future if the political structures will allow it. Just such a social arrangement is found in Plato's utopia, as the rationally-ruled Greek city-state. Here, statesmanship can be employed on a personal and social level, as reason directs passion to limit desire. The true philosopher-king is the wise ruler of self, household and state, who meets responsibilities for the sake of Good and not for material gain or personal fame.

Commitment

The ability to contribute to society at your highest level of competence (ruler, auxiliary, industrialist) is necessary for the good life. Finding each person's proper niche in society, which requires assistance from the state, allows all individuals to perform best what they do best. The result is the harmonious function of society and individual, as each is committed to the other for mutual enhancement.

Just as there are hierarchies of knowledge, social classes and natural drives, there is a hierarchy of happiness. Considering people unequal (that is, acknowledging that the citizens of any society possess various amounts of reason), Plato knew that only a few have the capacity to rule, while the many can only function optimally in the lower classes as auxiliaries and industrialists. This led Plato to conclude that if the state is able to channel all individuals into their proper social class, as determined by prevailing virtue (that is, those predominantly controlled by desire into the industrial class, those controlled by passion into the auxiliary class, and those controlled by reason into the ruling class), then each individual can make the best contribution to society and self. Such an arrangement produces harmony because all would be able to realize their ideal by having reason, passion and desire work as harmoniously as possible:

> There being then three kinds of pleasure, the pleasure of that part of the soul whereby we learn is the sweetest, and the life of the man in whom that part dominates is the most pleasurable. . . . At any rate the man of intelligence speaks with authority when he commends his own life. And to what life and to what pleasure, I said, does the judge assign the second place? Obviously to that of the warrior and honor-loving type, for it is nearer to the first than is the life of the money-maker. And so the last place belongs to the lover of gain.[8]

A complete understanding of Plato's notion of happiness requires an appreciation of its two-dimensional nature; in short, it is simultaneously absolute and relative. Those in the lower levels cannot envision the greater happiness that exists at the higher levels, yet those on the higher levels can "see down" to the less pleasurable lives below. Thus, only rulers enjoy the absolute, true ideal of happiness while they "see down" at the relative, inferior happiness of auxiliaries and industrialists. But those below cannot comprehend a greater happiness than they enjoy; the happiness they possess appears to be absolute. So as there is the absolute idea of happiness by which to measure the quality of each individual's life, there is also, for each individual, a personal ideal to be attained. While an individual's particular ideal may be less than the absolute ideal, he or she need only exercise the virtues as harmoniously as possible to reach relative happiness (although, from this individual's perspective, it would be absolute happiness because it would be defined according to the dominant part of the soul).

Plato leaves us with fascinating perspectives on leisure, happiness and the human potential. Different types of humans are best suited to occupy different levels and categories, which limit their possibilities for absolute fulfillment. And yet, within these categories, different levels of fulfillment and happiness are possible—if, and only if, the society is properly organized. Clearly, the contemplative life is proposed as the highest form of humanity, and the degree to which a society is ruled by those who are driven by reason will determine the degree to which it is a good society. Within the three categories there are degrees of happiness, but individuals cannot achieve even these relative degrees of happiness unless the society is ruled by the contemplative philosophers. Hence, contemplative leisure is not only a prerequisite for absolute human fulfillment among the philosopher-kings, it is also necessary to achieve the relative possibilities of the good life throughout the entire society.

Major Philosophical Points

Plato's solution to the problem of change was to synthesize the ancient philosophers, Heraclitus and Parmenides. The result was his famous Doctrine of Ideas, designed to denigrate the Sophists' arguments. From the Doctrine of Ideas, Plato developed notions of the ideal society and individual, both governed by reason and guided by good. If the conditions of utopia can be created, happiness will be available to all.

- The Doctrine of Ideas resolves the dichotomy between the physical and ideal.
- The Soul has knowledge of ideas.
- Reality is the ideal, not the physical world.
- Knowledge is a virtue.
- Good citizens make good states and good states make good citizens.
- People make their best contributions when they are functioning at their proper level in society.
- Social class is determined by virtue, not by material wealth or inheritance.
- Knowledge and virtue intertwine with society to create happiness.
- With leadership from the proper state, all individual interests will find their proper place, promoting their own good, and the good of the society.

References

1. Plato's classification appears in the *Republic,* 533e–534a, Hamilton and Cairns, p. 765. The following diagram is our conceptualization.
2. Plato, *Republic,* 514a–521a, Ibid., pp. 747–753.
3. Plato, *Phaedrus,* 253d–255, Ibid., pp. 499–500.
4. Plato, *Republic,* 443d–444a, Ibid., p. 686.
5. Plato, 581c, Ibid., p. 808.
6. Plato, 435e–436a, Ibid., p. 677.
7. Plato, 441c–d, Ibid., p. 683.
8. Plato, 582e–583a, Ibid., pp. 809–810.

Chapter 4
Aristotle: Cause and Contemplation

If the Athenian school is the most renowned of the classical schools of thought, Aristotle was arguably the most influential of the Athenian philosophers: nearly every aspect of human endeavor (from biology to astronomy, and from human anatomy to political theory) is touched upon in his works, and virtually no stone or idea is left unturned in his quest for the truth about both the physical and the metaphysical.

Our attraction to Aristotle is enhanced by his contribution to the concept of leisure. But to understand his conclusions, we must first examine his theory of knowledge and how it relates to the individual, society, and the state. During the course of this inquiry you will recognize the familiar themes of reason, moderation, and virtue. While all of these topics have been previously noted, Aristotle presented them in a more comprehensive manner than his predecessors. He blends theory and practice, universal truth and nature, and individual and the state in such a fashion that we recognize his thought as the synthesis of prior Greek philosophy. Essentially, every Greek philosopher and every divergent view is accounted for in this synthesis.

Theory of Knowledge

Parmenides hinted at it, Pythagoras declared it, and Plato reaffirmed it: the objects of this world take their shape from abstract ideas. Their arguments suggested that the essence of a thing had to be maintained in an unchanging, abstract realm while the physical object changed. Aristotle took a different view—he proposed that essence, while abstract, must exist in the physical object itself. Knowledge is not innate, but derived from the physical: reason seeks mental images of the physical, not replications of ideas.

Aristotle's position means that we are not endowed with an all-knowing soul (making learning recollection), but that our soul is initially devoid of knowledge, and we begin through our senses (taste, touch, smell, sight, hearing) to collect information. Eventually, with the aid of reason, our soul develops the knowledge that Plato thought was inherent. It is a building-block process, beginning with vague sense perceptions where the object of thought is not recognized. Repeated sense perceptions accumulate into memories, where the object of thought is remembered when encountered, being called to mind in conversation or upon reflection. Memories constitute experience, from which we gain the knowledge that allows us to define the object's composition, structure, quality, and purpose:

> So out of sense-perception comes to be what we call memory, and out of frequently repeated memories of the same thing develops experience; for a number of memories constitute a single experience. From experience again—i.e. from the universal now stabilized in its entirety within the soul, the one beside the many which is a single identity within them all—originate the skill of the craftsman and the knowledge of the man of science.[1]

Knowledge is of two types: practical and speculative. "Skill," or practical knowledge, is applied for a particular purpose—as when the craftsman uses his skill to make a product. "Science," as speculative knowledge, seeks pure understanding, as when the astronomer studies the universe. Whatever the type of knowledge, it is retained in the soul as universal principles, not as ideas.

As you reflect upon the way you learn, Aristotle's propositions should sound familiar. We are considered ignorant from birth and sent to school where we are educated, based on a design to convert memories to experience to knowledge. The source of our knowledge is outside of us in the form of books, field trips, lectures, and so on. We investigate all these sources through our senses by reading, writing and listening, then we assimilate them through discussion and reflection; finally, we are considered knowledgeable because we have been educated. While all this is taken for granted today, it was not during the time of Aristotle. To justify this view of the the learning process, he had to demonstrate that truth (as unchanging) can be found in the physical world, which is in constant change.

Science was Artistotle's strength, and he spent much of his life observing and classifying everything from the stars to systems of government. All knowledge, whether speculative or practical, of physical bodies or human values, was gained by applying scientific methods (in ancient Greece, these were limited to observation, recording, and logical deduction). By applying these methods to the study of facts (as opposed to the Socratic method, which only considers the plausible), Aristotle believed that truth could be discovered. With his reliance upon observation and logic, Aristotle accepted the ancient view of substance as the substratum of the changing harmonious universe. This position holds that underlying the physical world there is a substance that is nondescriptive—it takes no shape but is present in everything that does. There is, then, a definable form that objects take, which is imposed on an undefinable substance. To explain this phenomenon, Aristotle presents four causes in nature: Material, Formal, Efficient and Final. The Material Cause is the substance that makes possible the existence of things. We can consider it as simply the potential to be a particular thing. The Formal Cause is the form or structure given to material, such as the size, shape, texture of a particular thing, the sculptor's plan for a statue, or the individual soul of a person. The Efficient Cause imposes form on substance by actualizing potential in a determinate way. The Final Cause is the purpose actualized by imposing form on substance. Thus, to have knowledge of something is to understand its composition (Material Cause), the structure of the composition (Formal Cause), the forces which make the thing actual (Efficient Cause) and the goal toward which the forces are directed (Final Cause).

While the four causes overcome what Aristotle perceived to be the weakness of Plato's ideas by establishing a commonality between change and non-change, and perfection and imperfection, they do not explain how change perpetuates itself. Aristotle accepted the premise that nature is in constant change; it is everlasting, without beginning and without end. But because nothing can actualize itself, there must be a First Cause (unmoved mover) that transcends nature, causing "a motion that is eternal and does cause it during an infinite time."[2] By virtue of its absolute firstness, it must itself be unchangeable, making it purely actual (identical property of the Final Cause) and, as such, not a natural thing.

Aristotle brought knowledge to "earth," so to speak, and made the world of philosophy a real place—a place of error and answer, falsity and truth, change and continuity, substance and form, struggle and hope. By bringing knowledge to "earth" he also brought humanity to "earth," firmly planting us within nature. Such a naturalistic approach has its consequences with regard to the essence of the individual, society and state, as they take on physical and pragmatic characteristics, rather than metaphysical and ideal attributes.

Individual, Society and State

Aristotle's keen interest in science permeated all of his writings. We have seen how it caused him to differ from Plato concerning the source of truth; now we will investigate how it further steered him away from Plato in terms of the human predicament and the role of society and state. Placing human beings within the bounds of natural processes, Aristotle held that humans can only be explained in natural terms, like other earthly things. Thus, as there are causes by which we understand nature (material, formal, efficient and final), the same causes lead to an understanding of human nature. Our essence is not something beyond any natural process; instead, we are interpreted in the same way we interpret nature. By applying the principles of nature to human beings, the good life and the means of attaining it can be identified. From Aristotle's perspective, the natural destiny of people is to seek the good life, and the responsibility of the state is to foster this quest.

Individual

Belief in the soul was deeply rooted in ancient Greek thought, and while Aristotle accepted this tradition, he added dimensions to the soul's function. Reason is the hallmark of humanity to Aristotle, setting us apart from all other living things. Virtue is the employment of reason as an intellectual exercise, the habit of acting morally. A comprehension of these three concepts provides the foundation for Aristotle's views concerning the way we relate to each other and the entire universe.

Tripartite Soul. Anything that is alive has a soul because the soul is considered the first actuality or life-giving force, of a living thing: What has soul in it differs from what has not in that the former displays life.[3] But the soul does more than impart life to a physical body; it determines essence—what a living body is to be. For Aristotle, there are three categories of living things: vegetative (plants), sensitive (animals), and rational (humans); each category has a soul with unique properties. Plants have only a vegetative quality—which is the ability to grow, reach maturity, and decay; this quality is basic to all living things as it represents the first actuality, or basic evidence, of life. Animals also enjoy the sensitive dimension, which provides a capacity to distinguish between pleasure and pain: It is the possession of sensation that leads us for the first time to speak of living things as animals.[4] Desire to pursue pleasure and avoid pain characterizes this animal level. With humans, Aristotle adds a third quality to the vegetative and sensitive—the unique human capacity to reason.

Types of Reason. For Aristotle, the highest faculty of the human soul is reason, and he identifies two types: passive and active. Passive reason is the capacity to record simple intelligible forms, such as appearances and memories. Along with the vegetative and sensitive parts of the soul, it is within the capacity of animals: The animals other than man live by appearances and memories, and have but little of connected experience.[5] Active reason changes passive reason into knowledge by converting potentially knowable universals, which lie in memories and experience, into actual knowledge of them. The capacity to generalize and originate—the unique function of humans—distinguishes our souls from those of other living things. To be truly human is to exercise our uniqueness, active reason. The function of the human soul is to fully actualize the human being through active reason. Hence, we can say that a human life is good to the degree to which reason is employed in both the active and contemplative spheres of life. To Aristotle, the measure of such goodness, or excellence, is virtue.

Virtue is being good in thought and deed. Thus, Aristotle distinguishes two kinds of virtue: intellectual and moral. Intellectual virtue is the pursuit and realization of universal knowledge, and is the seat of wisdom. As the highest virtue, it is the pure, uncorrupted contemplation that converts the potential to know (passive reason) into knowledge as an end in itself, with no utilitarian goal. For this it is considered the "most finished of the forms of knowledge."[6] Moral virtue is the habit of proper action, consistently choosing the mean between the vices of excess and defect. Aristotle uses the example of a soldier. The virtue of a soldier is courage, which is a "mean" somewhere between its excess (rashness) and deficiency (cowardliness): For the man who flies from and fears everything and does not stand his ground against anything becomes a coward, and the man who fears nothing at all but goes to meet every danger becomes rash.[7] But the habit of charging forward and retreating back at the proper moment is the virtue of courage—truly a "golden" mean.

Society and State

While the accumulation of theoretical knowledge through contemplation is the ultimate human end, we must first act and interact to secure the contemplative life. Thus, practical knowledge is a prerequisite to theoretical knowledge. This fact motivated Aristotle's discussion of virtue in the previous section, just as it underlies his discussion of politics in this section. For as moral virtue concerns itself with individual action, the state deals with collective, social interactions. And both find their justification in the promotion of the good life.[8] Yet in his outline of society and state, Aristotle was not utopian in the Platonic sense. He did not subscribe to an absolute, rigid social structure which is good in all cases, but to general rules which can be adapted to social circumstances. He presented a fluid concept of state dependent upon the background (education level, economic status, family arrangements, environmental conditions, et cetera) of its citizens.

In one way Aristotle is an extension of Plato's utopian dream in that he agreed with his teacher that an aristocracy in the form of the Greek city–state is the best possible government. But he acknowledged that because optimum conditions can never exist in nature, a pragmatic approach must be taken to politics, which reflects the intellectual and moral level of a state's citizenry. For example, in ancient Greece, when living conditions were difficult (economics unpredictable, affluence unknown and education non-existent), a monarchy (rule by one) was the best possible state because there were few who could be trusted to direct society toward its true goal.[9] As circumstances improve, the number of rulers can be expanded because there are more citizens with greater intellectual and moral capacity to guide society toward its proper end. But the extension of political control is a delicate process and must be conditioned by wisdom. The solution to the problem of the scope of political participation is, again, found in the notion of the "golden" mean. The good state involves as many good citizens as possible and does so by seeking a balance between the vices of defect (rule by a few wealthy individuals) and excess (rule by the masses of poor people).[10] This mean is a "polity," and serves as Aristotle's answer to the inherent problems of Plato's aristocracy, as well as the forces that had destroyed Athens. It is where political power is held by a middle class, a mean between extravagance and poverty.

Aristotle, like Plato, held that the purpose of the state is to promote the good life and that oligarchy and democracy tend to divert the state from this natural goal. In an oligarchy, the state becomes a tool for the material desires of a small propertied class; in a democracy, chaos prevails as all scramble for power and possession. But a polity, for Aristotle, is a practical compromise. It can offset the excesses of the two extremes by directing energies toward self-sufficiency rather than the external dependency on colonialism. The polity reflects the evolutionary development of society and state: beginning with rule by one, the state naturally expands influence, wealth, education, and virtue, as conditions permit, toward an ultimate aristocracy (where all citizens can take part in the contemplative life). Only in a life characterized by individual and social moderation can contemplation be actualized.

An integral component of the polity is labor; without it, Aristotle's thoughts on the good society are only utopian dreams. There must be a labor force to harvest crops and manufacture goods, and there must be merchants to sell the products of labor. These people cannot have a life of contemplation. To justify this view, Aristotle recognized two social classes. One is a leisure class made up of those citizens who can participate in the contemplative life, while the other is a working class comprised of those people who lack the potential for the proper use of leisure. This working class should be a non-citizen class populated by slaves and free people (non-Greeks and freed slaves). Hence, while Aristotle's views of the good society stress the contemplative life and, through it, the actualization of the human potential, he reserved this process for a limited class (citizens) in the society.

Aristotle, then, was not a democrat—he entices us with a view of the good life, but reserves it for a limited social group. In absolute terms, this is Aristotle's view of society. But if changes in social circumstances (economics, education, morality, et cetera) influence political reality, then viewing Aristotle in relative terms (which his method suggests is the proper approach) presents an entirely different picture. In short, is slavery a necessary, universal condition—or is it a temporary condition necessitated by social circumstances in the third century B.C.? And it should be obvious that whether we choose to view Aristotle in absolute or in relative terms will have a critical impact on how we evaluate his social and political thought. From one perspective (absolute) the good life is reserved for the few; from another (relative), the process of history holds out the possibility of expanding contemplation (and leisure) throughout the society, given changes in economic, moral and social circumstances. We will return to this point in Part IV where we suggest that the ideas of Aristotle and Karl Marx become meshed through the relative approach to Aristotle's thought.

Implications for Leisure

The Greeks' intellectual search for the good life culminated in the philosophy of Aristotle, and his philosophy culminates with leisure. Throughout Part I, Leisure as Essence, we have noted the struggle to find order, justice, peace, and harmony. At times this struggle has shown signs of desperation, particularly with Socrates and Plato (understandable given the tumultuous realities of their day). Aristotle's vantage point caused him to share their concerns, but he was sufficiently removed from the chaos to develop what he considered to be a pragmatic, sensible, and objective approach to the good life. Aristotle unifies us, individually and collectively, with history—as a lifetime becomes the measure of individual goodness, and conformity to the natural process becomes the measure of social goodness. Both of these measures find their standard in individual leisure and its social equivalent—peace:

> Since the end of individuals and of states is the same, the end of the best man and the best constitution must also be the same; it is therefore evident that there ought to exist in both of them the virtues of leisure; for peace . . . is the end of war, and leisure of toil.[11]

The goal of the state is the good life. A necessary condition for the pursuit of the good life is peace, which can only be accomplished through self-sufficiency and moderation. The goal of the

39

individual is the proper use of leisure, which needs the prerequisites of self-sufficiency and moderation of desires. And while peace is difficult to acquire (as history undeniably shows), so is leisure. Because peace and leisure are not innate, they must be cultivated, placing a double burden upon the rulers of any state; securing peace and self-sufficiency does not guarantee the proper use of leisure:

> military states are safe only while they are at war, but fall when they have acquired their empire; like unused iron they lose their temper in time of peace. And for this the legislator is to blame, he never having taught them how to lead a life of peace.[12]

The only proper cause for war is peace and the reason for peace is individual fulfillment through creative leisure. Hence, if a good state goes to war to ensure peace, it follows that when peace is attained, the state exists for the sake of leisure. The citizenry needs sufficient intellectual and moral guidance to temper its material demands, and to use leisure for its proper end—the contemplative life. For Aristotle, as for Plato, excessive greed signifies an inferior society; and, if contemplation can be lived, then true happiness will ensue because contemplation is the one human activity that is self-sufficient, complete and uncorrupted:

> the activity of reason, which is contemplative, seems both to be superior in serious worth and to aim at no end beyond itself, and to have its pleasure proper to itself . . . and the self-sufficiency, leisureliness, unweariedness . . . and all the other attributes ascribed to the supremely happy man are evidently those connected with this activity, it follows that this will be the complete happiness of man, if it be allowed a complete term of life. . . .[13]

The importance of leisure and peace is not only justified by our natural, and often frantic, yearnings to be rid of weariness and disturbance. Aristotle went beyond this self-evident suggestion and provided external, logical evidence to support his position. In the Doctrine of Cause, as applied to human nature, he rests his case: the goodness of anything is found in actualizing its uniqueness; so we, as humans, are good when performing our unique function—active reason. For "If reason is divine . . . in comparison with man, the life according to it is divine in comparison with human life."[14] Active reason, as contemplation, is final cause because it is that part of us which is purely actual, with no potential to be other than what it is.[15] Through the contemplative life of leisure, human essence is achieved, stretching out toward Aristotle's First Cause—or deity.

Major Philosophical Points

In our investigation of Aristotle we found that he had the same goals as Plato: truth, virtue and good. We also found that he took a different approach in his method—rather than Ideals as the source of knowledge, he reasoned that Nature had to be the source in the form of Universal Principles. Because human beings are part of nature, an explanation of nature is necessary if we are to understand humans; everything in nature is determined by the four causes: Material, Formal, Efficient and Final. For the good life, the Material Cause is the potential to know, the Formal Cause is actual knowing, the Efficient Cause is reasoning, and the Final Cause is leisure time spent in the contemplation of universal principles. It is the role of the state to encourage leisure throughout the society by securing peace, which is best accomplished through a polity and the practice of moral virtue.

- The universe changes and yet remains the same.
- Truth is derived from experience.
- To know is to understand cause.
- For anything to be, the First Cause must be.
- To be fully human is to actualize what is uniquely human—active reason.
- The "golden" mean insures moral virtue.
- Wisdom is the highest virtue.
- The polity promotes self-sufficiency and moderation.
- Leisure is contemplation.

References

1. Aristotle, *Posterior Analytics,* 100a4–10, Richard McKeon, p. 185.
2. Aristotle, *Physics,* 267b24–26, Ibid., p. 394.
3. Aristotle, *On the Soul,* 413a21, Ibid., p. 557.
4. Aris. 413b2, Ibid. p. 557.
5. Aristotle, *Metaphysics,* 980b25–981a7, Ibid. p. 689.
6. Aristotle, *Nicomachean Ethics,* 1141a16, Ibid., p. 1027.
7. Aris. 1104a21–23, Ibid., p. 954.
8. Aristotle, *Politics,* 1252a1–6, Ibid., p. 1127.
9. Aris. 1261a, Ibid., pp. 1146–1147.
10. Aris. 1295a25–1295b, Ibid., p. 1220.
11. Aris. 1334a11–16, Ibid., p. 1299.
12. Aris. 1334a6–11, Ibid., p. 1299.
13. Aristotle, *Nicomachean Ethics,* 1177b19–25, Ibid., p. 1105.
14. Aris. 1177b29–31, Ibid., p. 1105.
15. Aristotle, *Metaphysics,* 1075a5–10, Ibid., p. 885.

Part I Conclusion

The rise and fall of Athens reveals an underlying tone of tragedy. We find ourselves wondering why the Athenians could not identify and halt the process that, in retrospect, appears to have been a headlong rush toward self-destruction motivated by greed and the lust for power. We are fascinated by the sharp contrast between the ancient moral values (as elucidated by Homer) of moderation, balance and reason—and the actual practices of the Athenian citizenry. It would be nice if we could say that the tension between ideals and reality was a unique Greek phenomenon. Unfortunately, though, we are just beginning our journey through western civilization and you will be very familiar with this tension by the time the book is finished. In a way, it might be easiest to just chalk up the self-destruction of Athens to fate, or destiny—and leave it at that. But accepting destiny as the root cause of things was not part of the Greek intellectual spirit. Hence, at the same time that the society was laying the basis for self-destruction, Greek intellectuals embarked on a journey to explain the world around them that provided the foundations of science and philosophy.

The Milesians' (Thales, Anaximander and Anaximenes) search for the basis of reality, i.e., the source of all things, in nature obviously stressed the scientific approach to understanding. To us, their perspectives sound as odd as their names—but their concerns provided a basis for debate and refinement that must be appreciated as the origin of western science. Denying that the key to reality was the stuff of which it is made, the Pythagoreans searched elsewhere for reality and meaning, concluding that the logical abstractions of mathematics open the door to truth. Continuity and change fascinated Heraclitus, and he noted that the tension between the two can be solved by recognizing differences between the Milesians' world of physical stuff, or matter, and the Pythagorean focus on rational forms. Parmenides relied on reason to interpret reality, and Democritus argued that only atoms are real and unchanging; the combinations they form are constantly changing illusions.

If this all sounds too abstract, then you will appreciate Socrates' critique of natural science when he argued that it does not provide practical guidelines for human ethics and social interaction. Responding to the crass empiricism and individualistic hedonism of the Sophists, Socrates stressed individual understanding and social responsibility. Everyone is born having known all there is to know, and learning becomes a process of recalling truth through the mind. To be philosophical is to devote your life to the pursuit of knowledge; the unexamined life is not worth living. The classical concept of leisure is firmly established: leisure is not the absence of required activity, but a special type of activity that is based on the pursuit of truth and the development of wisdom—key requirements if one is to be truly human. Classical leisure is an exercise in speculative philosophy intended to identify and pursue truth. Far from being unobligated, or discretionary, time—it is the most important time and activity in a truly human life.

Having observed the execution of his teacher (the charges were impiety and corrupting the youth—but we have suggested that Socrates' "crimes" had more to do with politics and his penchant for reminding the Athenians of their hypocrisy)—Plato was determined to extend Socrates' message into a consistent philosophy. Once again, the role of the active mind is paramount—as Plato argued that sense perceptions are illusions, and that truth and goodness are to be found through rational thought. To transcend this world of material illusions, Plato suggested that we tame our passions and desires through reason and extricate ourselves from the shadowy cave of ignorance. But we cannot hope to accomplish this truly human goal by ourselves: we need a good society and a good state to be good individuals. Hence, Plato outlined the ideal environment for human development in the *Republic,* where those who are dominated by reason shall rule over those who are not. The "lover of gain" should not be allowed anywhere near political power, for he is consumed (like the Athenians) by his individual material self-interest. He has a place in society but, clearly, this place must be subordinated to those able and willing to live a life devoted to rational understanding of eternal truth.

Plato considered democracy to be absurd, and a strict social hierarchy was needed to guarantee good government, while providing the material necessities of life. But it would be as foolish to expect that those dominated by reason should directly contribute to the production of wealth as it would be to expect that those dominated by desire could rule properly. The role of reason (for individuals as well as societies) is to control desire. Would you want a philosopher in charge of your economic future? Recall Plato's story about Thales and your answer will be a resounding "no!" But do you want a person (or persons) whose entire focus in life revolves around individual material self-interest in charge of your morals and political system? From Plato's perspective, few are equipped with sufficient amounts of reason to appreciate the higher aspirations—and allowing just anyone to govern would be like allowing a child to plan a nutritious diet. The child would, in all likelihood, choose ice cream and cookies for every meal—just as the majority of the Athenians opted for greed and pride.

The classical concept of leisure became institutionalized in Plato's *Republic,* and the well-being of the entire society became dependent on the quest for absolute truth among the philosopher–kings. This drive is so powerful that they are not interested in material wealth or fame because concern over such tangible rewards would interfere with valuable time and energy that is better utilized engaging in the higher, truly human, search for truth and goodness.

While Plato, like Socrates, admonished people to submerge themselves in the rational search for absolute truth, he recognized that few would do so. Hence, classical leisure—as a life devoted to truth and goodness—became reserved for the tiny group that could effectively subordinate their desires and passions to reason. Recall that Homer reserved this ability for the Gods. Plato's open acceptance of inequality may strike the twentieth-century reader as threatening but, at least, he viewed some humans as willing and able to accept the challenge of classical leisure: the unhindered pursuit of truth and justice.

Aristotle integrated Greek natural science with Plato's social concerns by arguing that nature encompasses both the *actual* material manifestations of a thing and the *potential* form that the thing will become. He pulled Plato's thought out of the realm of metaphysics and argued that fulfillment and perfection are part of our physical existence. Each thing in nature is potentially something more than it actually appears to be. And because nature is responsible for this potential, the tendency of everything in nature is to actualize, or become, what it is capable of becoming. The hierarchy of nature, then, is established by the degree to which a thing actively participates in the actualization of its own potential. Humans are at the top of the hierarchy because we have the unique capacity of "active reason"—the ability to contemplate and generalize about our lives and society, our history, our future and nature.

Active reason allows us to go far beyond the blind acceptance of customary practices and rote memorization of detail. It allows us to recognize relationships between apparently unrelated things. Hence, we have the obligation—to ourselves and to nature—to function on a level of active reason to participate in the fulfillment of our own destiny. For Aristotle, this uniquely human capacity requires that both time and activity rise above the "mere" satisfaction of material comfort; animals satisfy their need for material comfort. Hence, if we deny our uniqueness we are relegating ourselves to the status of animals. The essence of animals is to survive. The essence of humans is

43

to contemplate the world around us. Hence, classical leisure is our goal in life—a state of mind—in which we actualize our potential humanity by pursuing our essence as rational beings.

Like Plato, Aristotle's political concerns focused on ways to maximize the ability of people to live their lives in classical leisure, or contemplation. He drew upon the traditional Greek versus non-Greek distinctions, suggesting that slaves should do the work to provide the material necessities so that Greek citizens could live classical leisure. Compared to Plato, he appreciably expanded the number of people who should be expected to pursue knowledge as the end, or goal, of life—but their ability to do so would still be dependent on denying the slaves similar opportunities. In addition, he maintained the intimate connection between individual, society and state that had been stressed by his former teacher.

The Athenian ideal of classical leisure was based on the assumption that humans are something more than they appear to be. We are not just the self-centered beings that the history of Athens suggests we might be. There is more to us than desire and passion: whether approached metaphysically or scientifically, Plato and Aristotle offered the promise of being something more. In order to a) discover what this "something more" is and b) become whatever we are capable of becoming, we must view our lives in a very different manner than most of us do. We must view ourselves as very special beings, with an essence that transcends the satisfaction of animal needs and physical desires. In short, we must view our lives as the opportunity to know truth and practice goodness. Everything we do—our time and our energy—should take this uniqueness into account and our priorities must begin with the discovery and pursuit of our uniqueness. We should insist that our society and state actively participate to strengthen the environment that is conducive to *skole*—classical leisure—the goal of life.

The classical view toward leisure time is worlds away from our own concept. Modern leisure tends to signify a lack of required activity, or unobligated time. It is generally viewed as the opposite of work (obligated time) and usually refers to recreation, diversion, amusement, and escape from reality. As part of the Athenian ideal, contemplative leisure was viewed as intimately related to human essence. It was the highest form of activity, and the truly human being was obligated to pursue it for its own sake as the highest goal in life. To the degree that subsistence-related work was necessary, it was viewed as the opposite of contemplation. And because contemplation was bound up with the pursuit of human essence, such work was relegated to a position of insignificance. In our society, work is considered paramount and leisure loses its positive meaning.

In Part II, we analyze the historical and intellectual process that gradually altered the classical view away from its focus on humans and toward a focus on God, while maintaining the crucial role of contemplation as human essence. Part III identifies the factors that destroyed all remnants of classical leisure by denying contemplation as the essence of human beings. Without this essence, we are left with labor as our unique capacity, and leisure loses its transcendental power—easily degenerating into recreation, amusement, diversion and escape—because there is nothing left to contemplate; we are exactly what we appear to be, with no potential to be anything more. In short, the Athenian world view was turned upside down in the seventeenth and eighteenth centuries—destroying classical leisure and its foundation of hope for the human potential.

Part II
Essence Altered: Rome, Catholicism, and Thomas Aquinas

If a man is just and resolute, the whole world may break and fall upon him and find him, in the ruins, undismayed.

Horace

With the death of Aristotle in 322 B.C., we move into a period in which the philosophical basis of western society was open to challenges from numerous fronts. Our approach suggests that we view the Greek philosophical legacy as open to attacks and alterations stimulated by variations in social contexts. And, indeed, this appears to be the case with Plato and Aristotle—at least through the early years of the sixteenth century. Those of you who are attracted to their perspectives may find yourselves lamenting these alterations. Other readers will find themselves on more familiar ground with the adaptations—especially those of Rome and medieval Europe. Regardless of your position, we think that most readers will agree that the power of their ideas is obvious if for no other reason than the fact that every major philosopher who lived after the fourth century B.C. based his thought, to some degree, on either Plato or Aristotle. What is most surprising, then, is not the disparity in later interpretations—given the changing conditions, disparities should be expected. The most remarkable point is that their arguments established the parameters for western thought for at least 1,800 years!

During this period, drastic changes in social norms and political structures took place: Rome was built from a city state into a far-flung empire, an empire that eventually crumbled due to imperialism, overextension, domestic corruption, social unrest and the pressure of invasions. In its wake, the Roman Catholic Church emerged as a new form of authority, justifying its power with a mixture of classical Greek, ancient Hebrew, and Christian ideas. Toward the end of this 1,800 year period, new political realities, which led to the growth of the secular nation state as the dominant form of social organization, developed. And to the degree that Catholicism was associated with the pre-nation state feudal systems (political organizations that grew out of the ashes of Rome), it became a target for the new ideas and movements.

Chapter Five focuses on the more important social changes from the ancient world through feudal Europe. Chapter Six analyzes the meshing of Greek, Hebrew, and Christian thought—a process that was well established by the time of the fall of Rome. Chapter Seven stresses the influence of Greek thought on the Catholic Church's best known theologian, Thoman Aquinas. Aquinas' major accomplishment was the synthesis of Aristotle with the Augustinian (Catholic) perspectives, which were already heavily influenced by Platonism.

Chapter 5

The Roman Empire: Origins, Decline, and European Feudalism

> Our generals urge their soldiers to fight for the graves and shrines
> of their ancestors. The appeal is idle and false. You cannot point
> to a paternal altar. You have no ancestral tomb. You fight and die
> to give wealth and luxury to others. You are called the masters of
> the world, but there is not a foot of ground that you can call your
> own.
>
> Tiberius Gracchus

As we trace the extension and decline of the Roman Empire and summarize dimensions of European feudalism, we will be outlining the social and historical realities that influenced Roman and medieval Christian thought. The period under consideration extends from the origins of Rome in the eighth century B.C. to the thirteenth century A.D., when Thomas Aquinas developed his synthesis of Aristotelian and Catholic perspectives. With Aquinas' thought serving as the focus for Part Two, the teachings of Christianity (and their antecedents drawn from ancient Hebrew civilization) will also be discussed.

The lasting impact of Roman Civilization can be found in its extension of Greek culture into Europe. Whereas Alexander the Great carried Hellenic views eastward, the Roman Empire integrated much of Europe into a system that was influenced by Greek ideas. But in the process of extending Roman Imperialism, other cultures were meshed with the Greek traditions. Rome's tolerance of cultural diversity within the Empire is noted by virtually all historians of the period. And while this toleration can be seen as a factor contributing to the disintegration of the Empire following the decline of Rome's power (as various cultures reestablished the primacy of their ancient traditions), it can also be seen as a critical dimension of Rome's legacy to Europe. When all is said and done, it is obvious that early Christianity was highly influenced by Hebrew culture, and that Christianity provided the basis for European unity—or, at least, commonality—in the wake of Rome's decline. Hence, while Roman culture was initially Hellenic, it gradually accomodated a mixture, or synthesis, of Greek and Hebrew–Christian views. And when Roman political power declined, this synthesis (as it emerged in the Roman Catholic Church) provided the cultural basis of feudal society during the Middle Ages. This synthesis was undermined by the scientific, technological, economic, and political changes of the late Middle Ages, which culminated in the final blow: the Protestant Reformation of the sixteenth century.

Rome

The origins of Rome are similar to those of ancient Greece. The same tide of Indo-European migrations that destroyed the Mycenaeans in Greece spilled over into what is now Italy. Sometime during the eighth century B.C., the Etruscans invaded and settled the interior regions, while Greeks established city–states along the southern coastline (in Naples and Tarentum on the mainland and at Syracuse, in Sicily). With the exception of trade in the few good port areas controlled by the Greek settlers, agriculture provided the focus of economic activity. This agricultural base, combined with the relative lack of natural geographical boundaries (which made invasion comparatively easy), produced a social reality not unlike that of Sparta. And as in Sparta, the consciousness of the early inhabitants appears to have been conditioned by these factors toward an overriding concern for stability and a corresponding focus on military power. The rise of Rome took place during the years from the eighth to the sixth century B.C., as neighboring cities were conquered and brought under its control.

The early government was based on the ancient customs of the warrior society. It included a king, an Assembly of all male citizens of fighting age, and a council of elder clan leaders known as the Senate. The focal point of power rested in the aristocratic Senate, whose members chose the king from their group. The king initiated laws, the Assembly ratified them, and the Senate held the power to veto them if they conflicted with hereditary and customary aristocratic rights. At the end of the sixth century, the Senate overthrew the monarchy and established the Roman Republic.

From the beginning of the Republic through the middle of the third century B.C., the extension of Roman power throughout the mainland meant constant war. The aristocrats in the Senate were bent on conquest and their policies created severe social tensions. Like Sparta, Rome was able to conquer numerous indigenous peoples—and like Sparta, this led to constant fear of revolts and a corresponding garrison mentality. In addition, the aristocrats faced challenges from their less fortunate fellow citizens, many of whom lost their small farms when they were forced to spend decades fighting to extend the system. The aristocrats, then, were able to acquire new areas in Italy and, because the common soldiers could not maintain their farms, the aristocrats also acquired their land. Ultimately, many citizens were transformed into tenants on large agricultural estates.

These conditions (which sound remarkably similar to those in Athens in the sixth century B.C. prior to Solon's reforms) stimulated a revolt by the plebians (small farmers) against the wealthy patricians, who dominated the land and exercised control through the Senate. Through a series of rebellions and reforms that lasted nearly 200 years, the plebians were gradually integrated into the Senate and administrative positions in the state. While the conditions causing the unrest were similar to those in Athens prior to Solon, the results were quite different. It seems as if the plebians had little interest in altering the policies of the patrician-ruled state; instead, they merely wanted to participate in the benefits produced by these policies. Hence, once the plebians were assured of a greater role in the decision making process, their movement disintegrated, and a unified Rome that had reconciled plebian and patrician interests turned outward to conquer the world. The Spartan-like attitudes that had accompanied Rome's location and conquests clearly surfaced in this arrangement. The glory of the state acted as a focal point for all Romans, much as it did in the nineteenth century in Germany—where Bismarck also eased social tensions through nationalism and external aggression. In both cases, the adaptation of democratic dimensions to authoritarian cultures created a popular and highly motivated military machine:

> To the troops of other empires, serving for pay and enlisted by force from the native populations, she could oppose an army as well trained and as numerous, and manned by citizens and allies, who fought, not for money nor by compulsion, but by the voluntary decision of the whole body of Roman citizens.[1]

The power of Rome in the third century B.C. propelled it onto a collision course with another Mediterranean power, Carthage. Beginning as an ancient Phoenician outpost in the eighth century B.C., Carthage had extended its influence throughout northern Africa and western Sicily. The first Punic War (which began in 264 B.C. and lasted 23 years) resulted from the expansion of Rome and Carthage into Sicily. Carthage was defeated, but a second war began in 218 B.C., stimulated by the question of control over Spain. Finally, in 149 B.C., Rome invaded North Africa and destroyed Carthage, razing the city and killing or enslaving all of its inhabitants. In the course of the wars, Philip V of Macedonia, alarmed at the growth of Roman influence, established an alliance with Carthage to thwart Rome's power. But the united Roman legions could not be stopped, and Macedonia (along with Greece and Egypt) fell as the power of Rome was extended throughout the areas surrounding the Mediterranean Sea.

During the course of this expansion, domestic problems growing out of the extension of empire began to undermine the plebian-patrician alliance. And, just as the decline of Athens can be traced to internal turmoil and imperial policies, Rome's power abroad was accompanied by internal disintegration:

> every new conquest made Rome richer, more rotten, more merciless. She had won every war but the class war; and the destruction of Carthage removed the last check to civil division and strife. Now through a hundred bitter years of revolution Rome would pay the penalty of gaining the world.[2]

The continuous expansionary wars had numerous disruptive effects on Roman society. Imports of cheap grains from throughout the Empire drove the price of domestic farm products down to such a point that Roman citizens working small farms could not compete. Forced to leave their land to search for jobs in the cities, they found that slaves had been imported from the colonies to perform virtually all manual labor. Aristocratic landowners, relying on the inexhaustible supply of slave labor, acquired the vacated farms and merged them into massive landed estates. With their economic independence eroded, the plebians were reduced to unemployed masses that congregated in Rome. The increase of slave labor in virtually all sectors of the economy lowered "the wages of free workers to a point where it was almost as profitable to be idle as to toil."[3] These factors seriously undermined the electoral process by encouraging some wealthy aristocrats to court the unemployed masses with bribes; with their land and labor meaningless, the only thing left for the urban masses to sell was their vote. The wars also encouraged profiteering, and a merchant class (inclined to flaunt its wealth) emerged alongside the increasingly degraded plebians. Slave revolts added to domestic tensions and rebellions were common throughout the Empire.

In 133 B.C. Tiberius Gracchus introduced a series of reforms designed to respond to the needs of the dispossessed plebians. Plans were made to limit the size of the aristocratic estates and to redistribute the confiscated land to its previous owners. The allotments were to be divided into twenty acre parcels that could not be sold, guaranteeing that the process that created the problems would not be repeated. There is no doubt that Tiberius' methods bordered on demagogy, but the significance of the proposed reforms should also be clear. Recognizing that the reforms threatened their economic and political control of Rome, the outraged aristocrats beat Tiberius to death in the Forum. In 124 B.C. Tiberius' younger brother introduced another series of reforms also designed to ease social tensions. Caius pushed his brother's land policy, but was careful to lay the groundwork for more widespread support. In addition to his plebian following, Caius guaranteed strong merchant support by pushing for the establishment of new colonies to enhance trade. He appealed to the army by offering soldiers increased fringe benefits for military service, and garnered the support of the unemployed masses by introducing government subsidies to lower the price of wheat by one-half. But Caius' aristocratic opponents outmaneuvered him by introducing a law forbidding the collection of taxes on the newly-redistributed land. Due in part to plebian short-sightedness in response to this offer, Caius' coalition began to falter and, in 121 B.C., he was forced to flee Rome; he died in the process.

The years immediately following Caius' death were characterized by intense struggle between the Senate and followers of the Gracchi. In 100 B.C., Saturninus extended the wheat subsidy, lowering the price of wheat nearly 90 per cent. The Senate reacted by calling upon Marius, a successful general who had just turned back a Teutonic invasion, to march on Rome to dislodge and kill Saturninus.[4] The established pattern continued throughout the first century B.C., with Rome watering the seeds of its own destruction. Foreign wars were used to divert attention from domestic problems. Generals pillaged the known world, keeping most of the spoils for themselves while dividing enough booty among their troops to create a number of armies not necessarily loyal to the state (which had never paid them well); instead, the troops' loyalty gradually shifted to the various generals. Heavy taxes were placed on the conquered territories and when they could not be paid, Roman bankers loaned them money at interest rates ranging as high as 48 per cent.[5] The citizen army degenerated into mercenaries fighting for a share in the spoils, while political decisions were increasingly made by generals with the strongest armies. The merchants and aristocrats joined forces to increase their wealth at the expense of conquered peoples of the Empire, while the masses of urban poor congregated in Rome, placated by cheap food and spectacular public entertainment sponsored by the state and the wealthy generals.

The social tensions produced two competing factions, or parties, struggling to dominate the system: the *populares* (appealing to the masses for support) and the *optimates* (based on aristocratic privilege). Different generals identified with different factions, leading to a series of wars between the forces of Marius (*populares*) and Sulla (*optimates*), Caesar (*populares*) and Pompey (*optimates*),and Octavius and Antony (*populares*) versus Caesar's assassins (*optimates*). When the latter group was defeated, Octavius turned against Antony and emerged as the single most powerful leader of Rome. He was given the title of Augustus (which had religious overtones; literally, it means "consecrated") and he ruled as Emperor from 27 B.C. until his death in 14 A.D. While the Senate continued to exist, it became subordinated to Augustus and his successors, most of whom are best characterized as incompetent tyrants. The actual power in Rome became concentrated in the military and civilian bureaucracy, removing any semblance of control even further away from the common citizen. There were a few leaders that appear as exceptions to the norm (including Nerva, Trajan and Marcus Aurelius), but it seems that Rome's past had finally caught up with it. Cruelty and violence dominated the society; crime was widespread and murder and assassination became the primary means of determining changes in leadership. In addition, the discrepancies between the increasingly decadent wealthy and the increasingly degraded poor continued to grow following the death of Augustus.

Hebrew Civilization

While Plato was working to develop Socrates' ethics into a consistent philosophy to promote human happiness in the good society and Aristotle was attempting to discover a principle of order in the universe, a well established religious tradition was offering its solutions to these concerns across the Mediterranean Sea. From one perspective, the Old Testament offers an alternative set of solutions to the problems stimulating the philosophies of Plato and Aristotle. Aristotle's first cause, or unmoved mover, clearly sounds similar to the Hebrew concept of YHWH, which was extended into the Christian God. In these traditions, human beings are viewed as potentially something more than they actually are and the proper goal for human beings is to work toward their actualization, or perfection, as provided for by the supreme being. With the supreme being as the model of pure actualization (perfection), the proper pathway for human beings is well established. To be human is to have a preeminent place in the hierarchy of creation and, thus, to be distinct from other animals. In addition, humans are divided into different groups, depending on the degree of favor they enjoy as a result of the supreme being's blessing: the Hebrew concept of a "Chosen People" was clearly extended into Christian perspectives. While human beings (and, especially, the chosen ones) enjoy a special status in nature, they also have increased responsibilities. For just as in Aristotle's view (we are truly human only to the degree that we actualize our potential), so in both Judaism and Christianity we have the obligation to live our lives according to the commandments established by our creator.

In addition to these commonalities (which should not surprise anyone who agrees with our brief discussion of religion and philosophy in Chapter Two), there are also interesting parallels in social and ethical concerns. Much of the Old Testament can be seen as the delineation of day-to-day guidelines for the establishment of the good society—and if Plato's system strikes you as being rigid, note the strictness of the social regulations proposed in both the Old and New Testaments. These regulations become significantly more critical if the *Bible* is viewed as the revealed word of the supreme being. If Plato (a mere philosopher) is ignored, we can look forward to an unfulfilled life. But if the creator's stringent outlines for society are ignored, the consequences should be expected to be greater. The *Bible* repeatedly reminds us that punishments for disobedience are not to be taken lightly: people, cities, and civilizations meet with destruction when they disobey the established rules—and the entire human population (with the exception of one family) was destroyed in the great flood due to its iniquity. With the theory of knowledge being relatively straightforward (the commands of the supreme being as revealed to the people through the prophets), we will briefly note the dominant Hebrew views toward the individual, state and society.

The enduring Hebrew contribution to western civilization was, clearly, the Old Testament—which makes up the bulk of the Christian Bible and is also important to the Islamic world view. The first five books (the Pentateuch) describe the creation, establish the children of Israel as the chosen people, and introduce regulations for their behavior. Delivered from slavery under the Egyptians by the prophet Moses, the ancient Hebrews were provided a promised land. And remarkably, the laws established to regulate human behavior within the promised land appear to be devised to guard against greed and excessive pride—precisely the drives that, as we have noted, destroyed Athens and Rome.

The origins of the promised land are clear: it is a gift from above, and although the children of Israel were forced to fight (under the able leadership of Joshua) to gain control of it, the act of conquest is not to be misconstrued to mean that the land is privately owned:

> Speak unto the children of Israel, and say unto them, When ye come into the land which I give you, then shall the land keep a sabbath unto the Lord.[6]
> The land shall not be sold forever: for the land is mine; for ye are strangers and sojourners with me.[7]
> If thy brother be waxen poor, and hath sold away some of his possession, and if any of his kin come to redeem it, then shall he redeem that which his brother sold.[8]

And if they brother be waxen poor, and fallen in decay with thee; then thou shalt relieve him: yea, though he be a stranger, or a sojourner; that he may live with thee.[9]

With the land divided along tribal lines, and viewed as communally owned (as opposed to private ownership), we can identify obvious attempts to prevent an inequitable distribution of wealth. But if these communal norms break down, there are social regulations to guarantee that collective ownership will be restored. In Leviticus 25, verses six through 20, the Jubilee Year is described as a mechanism to guard against concentration of land and wealth: every fiftieth year all land is to revert back to its original form of tribal distribution, with the repeated goal of returning "every man unto his possession."[10] Hence, not only does Leviticus suggest that the chosen people ("strangers and sojourners") humble themselves and avoid excessive pride, but strict social regulations guarding against greed are also introduced. In addition, lending money with interest is strictly forbidden in Leviticus 25:37, "thou shalt not give him thy money upon usury, nor lend him thy victuals for increase."

In Deuteronomy, these regulations are slightly eased through the allowance that usury is acceptable when dealing with "strangers," but it is still forbidden among the children of Israel.[11] In addition, another means of guarding against an inequitable distribution of wealth is introduced: the Year of Release. Scheduled to take place every seven years, the release is another obvious mechanism to control greed:

> And this is the manner of release: Every creditor that lendeth ought unto his neighbor shall release it; he shall not exact it of his neighbor, or of his brother; because it is called the Lord's release.[12]

Again, foreigners are not protected by the release, but the children of Israel are.[13] And the practice is to continue until "there shall be no more poor among you."[14] Throughout the description of the release, stress is placed on the fact that the land was provided by the supreme being for the benefit of his chosen people, and that these laws are to be considered part of the arrangement. And there is even a warning against failing to help the poor just because the Year of Release is coming:

> Beware that there be not a thought in thy wicked heart, saying, The seventh year, the year of release is at hand; and thine eye be evil against thy poor brother, and thou givest him nought; and he cry unto the Lord against thee, and it be sin unto thee.[15]

Having discussed the role of greed and pride in the social chaos that engulfed Athens and Rome, the supreme being's prescriptions for social organization sound extremely pragmatic. The focus is clearly on the society, and individual drives that disrupt social cohesion are to be checked. In short, the Law stresses the importance of the community, develops a concept of social responsibility, and promises retribution against those who do not follow the guidelines. These guidelines can be seen as the origin of socialist ideas that have resurfaced throughout western history:

> When thou comest into thy neighbor's vineyard, then thou mayest eat thy fill at thine own pleasure; but thou shalt not put any in thy vessel.
> When thou comest into the standing corn of thy neighbor, then thou mayest pluck the ears with thine hand; but thou shalt not move a sickle unto thy neighbor's standing corn.[16]

By the eighth century B.C., the chosen people had fallen prey to the same temptations that were to plague the populations of the fledgling city–states of Athens and Rome. The simple life of the nomadic shepherds had given way to agriculture, and the growing focus on trade in the cities was gradually replacing the rural values. Economic inequality grew as class distinctions began to split the once-united society; small farmers lost their land (their "possession") and their independence to debtors' slavery, while private ownership supplanted the Law of communal property. These violations of tradition were accompanied by severe hardship at the hands of Egyptian and Assyrian invaders. Isaiah, an aristocrat who was well versed in the ancient Law, emerged on the scene to call the chosen people back to the ways of their ancestors. As the first in a succession of Hebrew prophets who extended from the eighth century B.C. to Jesus of Nazareth, Isaiah equates the suffering of the people to their repeated violations of the guidelines that were established to ensure their happiness. In the famous allegory of the vineyard, the communal property norms are defended, and the peoples' violations condemned:

> My well beloved hath a vineyard in a very fruitful hill: And he fenced it, and gathered out the stones thereof, and planted it with the choicest vine, and built a tower in the midst of it, and also made a winepress therein; and he looked that it should bring forth grapes, and it brought forth wild grapes.
> And now, O inhabitants of Jerusalem, and men of Judah, judge, I pray you, betwixt me and my vineyard.
> What could have been done more to my vineyard, that I have not done in it? wherefore, when I looked that it should bring forth grapes, brought it forth wild grapes?
> And now go to; I will tell you what I will do to my vineyard: I will take away the hedge thereof, and it shall be eaten up; and break down the wall thereof, and it shall be trodden down:
> And I will lay it waste: it shall not be pruned, nor digged; but there shall come up briars and thorns: I will also command the clouds that they rain no rain upon it.
> For the vineyard of the Lord of hosts is the house of Israel, and the men of Judah his pleasant plant: and he looked for judgment, but behold oppression; for righteousness, but behold a cry.
> Woe unto them that join house to house, that lay field to field, till there be no place, that they may be placed alone in the midst of the earth![17]

These ominous warnings of impending doom are clearly the results of the denial of the covenants, and the transgressions are listed in the following order:

> For the vile person will speak villany, and his heart will work iniquity, to practice hypocrisy, and to utter error against the Lord, to make empty the soul of the hungry, and he will cause the drink of the thirsty to fail.
> The instruments of the churl are evil: he deviseth wicked devices to destroy the poor with lying words, even when the needy speaketh right.[18]

The solution to these problems seems to be as clear as the origins: the people must return to their ancient (communal) ways:

> Ho, everyone that thirsteth, come ye to the waters, and he that hath no money; come ye, buy, and eat; yea, come, buy wine and milk without money and without price.[19]

Isaiah was followed by Amos, a prophet of more humble origins. But while their social background differed, their message was the same: return to the ancient Laws. If anything, Amos is even more outspoken concerning the hypocrisy of the wealthy, who achieved their wealth and power by violating the Laws:

> Forasmuch therefore as your treading is upon the poor, and ye take from him burdens of wheat: ye have built houses of hewn stone, but ye shall not dwell in them; ye have planted pleasant vineyards, but ye shall not drink wine of them.

> For I know your manifold transgressions and your mighty sins: they afflict the just, they take a bribe, and they turn aside the poor in the gate of their right.[20]

Amos was followed by Micah, who echoed the same message:

> Woe to them that devise iniquity, and work evil upon their beds!
> And they covet fields, and take them by violence; and houses, and take them away: so they oppress a man and his house, even a man and his heritage.[21]

Note that throughout these passages the concepts of "right," "possession," and "heritage" are repeatedly used to refer to the ancient Laws established after the chosen people were led into the promised land.

Other prophets brought the same warnings. Ezekiel admonished the people to return to the communal norms of tribal ownership and the reestablishment of the Laws (Ezekiel 47:13, 14, 21). And Malachi called the people to recognize their abominations and return to the ancient ways. In Malachi, we are told of a messenger to come to prepare the way for the Lord (3:1). The Lord's coming will reward the righteous and punish the wicked, and we are, again, given a list of the sins of the wicked:

> And I will come near to you to judgment; and I will be a swift witness aginst the sorcerers, and against the adulterers, and against the false swearers, and against those that oppress the hireling in his wages, the widow, the fatherless, and that turn aside the stranger from his right. . . .
> Even from the days of your fathers ye are gone away from mine ordinances, and have not kept them. Return unto me, and I will return unto you, saith the Lord of hosts.[22]

By the second century B.C., the chosen people had sunk to new depths of degradation. Completely subjugated by the Seleucid King Antiochus Epiphanes, they were forbidden to practice what little was left of their ancient religious rites. Strongly influenced by Hellenic culture, Antiochus placed statues of Greek gods in the temple at Jerusalem. Having been promised a messenger to prepare the way for the coming of a savior and the reestablishment of justice, it is not surprising that Judas Maccabee found widespread support for his armed revolt against the Syrians in 167 B.C. Beginning with a demand for increased religious toleration, the Maccabees began a full scale revolution against Syrian control—with striking similarities to modern anti-colonial revolutions. And like other revolutions, the Maccabee revolt went through a series of stages that included military dictatorship, court intrigue, and factional strife. By 67 B.C., the two dominant factions appealed to Rome (which had conquered Syria) to intervene on their respective sides. Pompey obliged them; leading Roman troops into Jerusalem, he crushed the Maccabees and established the Empire's control over the chosen people of the Old Testament.

Jesus of Nazareth

Jesus of Nazareth was born into an environment of political repression, social instability, and widespread corruption. The words of the prophets had not been heeded, the people had been conquered repeatedly, and the society had become fragmented into several competing groups. The Sadducees (aristocratic, wealthy, and contemptuous of the masses) were adopting Greek culture. The Pharisees paid lip service to ancient Hebrew culture but they were also wealthy and highly contemptuous of the poor. The Essenes, however, heeded the warnings of the prophets. Insisting on a strict interpretation of the Pentateuch, the Essenes deserted the towns and developed a monastic lifestyle based on communal living, strict austerity, study of the scriptures, and obedience to the spirit (which ran counter to current practices) of the Laws. Under these circumstances, it is significant that Jesus chose John (an Essene who had been jailed repeatedly and, ultimately, was executed) to baptize him.

The New Testament presents Jesus as the fulfillment of the Old Testament prophecies (Matthew 2:23) and John the Baptist as the messenger predicted by Isaiah as the "voice of one crying in the wilderness, Prepare ye the way of the Lord."[23] John is described as dressed in camel's hair and leather, his food was provided by nature ("locusts and wild honey") and he attacked the Pharisees and Sadducees as a "generation of vipers."[24] Finally, it was John who sought to shake the chosen people from their iniquity by the warning "Repent ye: for the kingdom of heaven is at hand."[25] Such a promise might well have conjured up visions of a Maccabee-type political revolt in the minds of the oppressed, as well as the oppressors. And given Jesus' unrestrained attacks on the hypocrisy and iniquity of his society (which, obviously, could also have been applied to the Roman Empire), there were few influential voices to defend him while he pursued his ministry among the poor.

The charges against Jesus were the same as those against Socrates: 1) Impiety; he was initially accused of threatening to destroy the temple. Then, having agreed to the accusation that he presented himself as the "Son of the Blessed," he was accused of blasphemy.[26] 2) Corrupting the people through his teaching:

> We found this fellow perverting the nation. . . . He stirreth up the people, teaching throughout all Jewry, beginning from Galilee to this place.[27]

We will return to an analysis of Jesus' thought in the following Chapter. At this point, we ask that you reflect on the obvious similarities between the "crimes" of Socrates and those of Jesus of Nazareth.

Christianity and Rome

As the Roman Empire proceeded toward its destruction, inhabitants of areas under its control became increasingly attracted to views that stressed withdrawal and denial of the importance of the physical realities surrounding them. Mystical interpretations of nature flourished in the "mystery cults" of Isis and Osiris, The Great Mother, and Mithra. These cults based their views on the redemption of followers through a god-savior; each included elaborate rites and sacraments, and each stressed the importance of an eternal afterlife to replace physical suffering and social chaos. As conditions became more intolerable from the second to the fourth centuries A.D. (including a ruthless government, plague, and foreign invasions), the popularity of these cults grew:

> This sense of helplessness and world-weariness infected every class of society. At the bottom was the vast slave population, living in abject poverty and superstition; hardly better was the condition of the masses of impoverished and ignorant citizens; finally there was the small wealthy class, conscience-stricken at the difference between their lot and that of other men, but powerless to effect a change.[28]

In this environment, the followers of Jesus gradually established a set of practices and institutions that ultimately resulted in organized Christianity.

Unlike the mystery cults (in which widespread toleration of varying religious beliefs was the norm), the followers of Jesus became involved in questions of interpretation and orthodoxy in the century following the execution of their Messiah. Like Socrates, Jesus left no written records of his ministry, and the parables and ethical teachings were interpreted and reinterpreted as the years passed. There were early conflicts over reason versus faith, conflicts over how Jesus was to be viewed (divine, mortal, or a combination of both), conflicts over the status of Mary, and conflicts over the proper Christian attitudes toward the authority of the state. With the Hebrew tradition providing for one God, such questions could not be easily dismissed. These differences in interpretation eventually shattered the movement: the Donatists (Christians in North Africa who refused to cooperate with Rome) were "declared outlaws" by the Roman Emperor Honorius in 412.[29] Other disputes led to the ostracism of the Arian, Nestorian and Jacobite Christians. And, finally, the Roman West and the Greek East separated in the eleventh century.

In the course of these disputes, the Roman State shifted from persecutor of Christians to arbitrator in the conflicts! In the process, the crumbling Empire became identified with the views developed by Paul in the first century A.D. Paul's position (which we will discuss in the following chapter) forbade conflicts between the followers and the state, arguing that secular authority must be obeyed. Hence, when Constantine issued the Edict of Toleration for Christians in 313, Roman Christianity had been stripped of its potentially revolutionary dimensions. In 380, Emperor Theodosius declared Christianity the official religion of the dying Empire—a mere 30 years before the Visigoths sacked Rome. Such worldly pressures are not conducive to high levels of toleration, and Theodosius outlawed the mystery cults, which still existed as popular alternatives to Christianity. Hence, the marriage of Church and state was based on the assumption that absolute truth could be known, practiced, and enforced on non-believers. Theodosius' decree suggests that the strong, not the weak, will inherit the earth through the sword:

> We authorize the followers of this doctrine to assume the title of Catholic Christians, and we brand all others with the infamous name of heretics. They must expect to suffer the severe penalties which our authority, guided by the heavenly wisdom, shall think proper to inflict upon them.[30]

Obviously, things had changed in 400 years!

This 400 year period produced a highly institutionalized organization from the scattered followers of a teacher who stressed simplicity, brotherly (and sisterly) love, and attacked hypocrisy. In the course of this change, the meaning and practice of the "church" was altered. The word "church" is translated from the Greek *ecclesia,* meaning an assembly of people. In Acts 5:11 and 14, the "church" is clearly referred to in these terms, and equated with the community of "believers." As we will stress in Chapter Six, the early followers of Jesus formed themselves into such communities. Attempting to free themselves from material desires and pride, they provided each other with support and camaraderie—they were the church. From its beginning, the church provided for both social and religious needs. Socially, Christian life in Rome was described by Saint John Chrysostom as follows:

> None considered as being his what belonged to him, all their riches were in common . . . a great charity was in all of them. This charity consisted in that there were no poor among them, so much did those who had possessions hasten to strip themselves of them. They did not divide their fortunes into two parts, giving one and keeping the other back; they gave what they had. So there was no inequality between them; they all lived in great abundance.[31]

The religious practices focused on two sacraments: baptism and the eucharist, which also reinforced the social nature of the movement:

> It created the new ethic, which meant that all believers in Christ were united into one body against the world; this ethic also taught that individual believers must die unto sin and live unto righteousness, repeating in their own history the dying and the ressurrection of Christ by rising again to a new life in the spirit—a life of endeavour after personal holiness for the love of God, and of brotherly love.[32]

With these practices serving as the basis for the early church, obvious problems can be identified. Who should conduct the sacraments? Who should oversee the distribution of the collective wealth to those in need? And, with the growing discrepancies in Christian interpretations and practices throughout the Roman Empire, who should determine which ones are right? It is not surprising, then, that a hierarchy of functionaries developed to solve these administrative problems. In the course of time, the church functionaries became the Church, as described by Saint Ignatius in the second century:

> It is necessary that you should do nothing without the bishop, but be ye also in subjection to the presbytery; likewise let all respect the deacons as Jesus Christ, even as the bishop is also a type of the father, and the presbyters as the council of God, and the college of Apostles.[33]

In an attempt to guarantee the dominance of Rome over the local Chruches, Emperor Valentinian III decreed that the bishops in the Empire must recognize the ultimate power of the Bishop of Rome, or Pope, in 455.

With the formal conversion of the Roman Empire to Christianity, those holding positions of authority in the Church gained social status and political power. After years of being forced to practice their religion under threat of persecution, the "Catholic Christians" extended their visibility in society, which included constructing ornate buildings in which to worship. By the fifth century, the wealth of the Church was no longer shared equally among those in need; instead, it was divided into four portions: the first for the bishop, the second for the minor clergy, the third for the upkeep of the Church, and it was only the fourth part which was distributed among the needy.[34]

This is not to suggest that the institutionalized Church completely violated the norms of the early church. The monastic orders of the Middle Ages were based on communal living (reminiscent of both the early church and dimensions of Plato's *Republic*) and official voices occasionally called the Church back to its original values. Notable in this tradition was Pope Gregory I (the Great) in the sixth century:

> It is by no means enough not to steal the property of others; you are in error if you keep to yourself the wealth which God has created for you. He who does not give to others what he possesses is a murderer, a killer; when he keeps for his own use what would provide for the poor, one can say that he is slaying all those who could have lived from his plenty; when we share with those who are suffering, we do not give what belongs to us, but what belongs to them. This is not an act of pity, but the payment of a debt.[35]

But Christianity was now a widespread, flourishing religion—attracting the wealthy and poor alike. Almsgiving replaced the earlier surrender of all material possessions to the community and the Church replaced the Empire as the focal point of cohesion.

European Feudalism

As the power of the Roman Empire declined, local political leaders and Church officials united to maintain order and a degree of stability in Europe. Numerous conflicts plagued this alliance, but it served as the cornerstone of political power and social status through the sixteenth century. The Merovingian Kings succeeded in uniting the Franks (in what is now France) from the fifth to the eighth century with the support of the local and Roman clergy. This unity was extended by Charlemagne during his reign from 768 to 814. The interests of secular and clerical leaders (Charlemagne and Pope Leo III) clearly meshed in the last year of the eighth century: Leo had been beaten by conspirators who desired to make their leader pope; Charlemagne was in the process of conquering all of western and central Europe. Pope Leo gained protection from further attacks and Charlemagne gained the title "Emperor of the Romans" in 800. Under his rule, the Carolingian Empire was extended from Antwerp and Danzig in the north to Corsica and Rome in the south. Conflicts over the true source of power surfaced repeatedly between the two leaders, establishing a legacy of tension between the Franks and Rome that continued for centuries. Following the death of Charlemagne, the Empire was divided—adding another dimension of tension between the western Franks (French) and eastern Franks (Germans). Attempts were made to reunite the Holy Roman Empire but it remained a ghost empire, as local leaders filled the power void by establishing feudal systems.

Conflicts between Charlemagne's heirs combined with increased military pressure from the Saracens and Norsemen to stimulate the growth of feudalism:

> feudalism can be described as a series of responses to a certain kind of challenge. A challenge which affected a good many societies was that of the decay or weakening of a highly organized political system—an empire or a relatively large kingdom. The spasms of disintegration of such a system can sometimes produce by way of response a series of moves toward reconstruction which lead in a feudal direction.[36]

Hence, with the decline of Roman and Carolingian power, smaller economic and political structures arose to fill the void of the ghost empire. Common characteristics of European feudal societies can be summarized as follows:

1. Small areas of administration, with political power viewed as a personal possession held by a military leader. Government functions based on personal relationships between lord and vassal, with each level enjoying rights and responsibilities.
2. Limited scope of economic activity, with focus on agriculture; barter the primary means of exchange.
3. Strict social hierarchy with the vast majority of society (commoners) working the land and a hierarchy of elites (nobility) exercising control. Local clerics (religious leaders) support the hierarchy and enjoy specified privileges.

The need to survive appears to be the basis of such arrangements: The professional fighting man becomes the backbone of the feudal class.[37]

Military hierarchies growing in threatened areas are common throughout history. But in the European context, the traditions inherited from the Germanic warrior bands (based on an interacting system of mutual rights and responsibilities between the various levels of authority) gave these feudal hierarchies their special character. The military elite enjoyed special privileges but its members also had established responsibilities toward their vassals. In turn, the vassals had obligations, as well as rights, in relationship to the nobility: Under the onslaught of foreign invasion, defense became a local priority and those with privileges were forced to carry out responsibilities.[38] This pattern was especially pronounced in northwestern Europe, where independent farmers voluntarily submitted themselves to vassalage to gain protection from marauding Norsemen.

As generations passed, the positions in the vassalage system became well-established and hereditary. Hence, a farmer became subordinated to a local noble (paying him with a percentage of his crops and recognizing him as the source of law) in return for protection. While this local noble (a baron with his own soldiers, or knights) was lord over "his" peasants, he was vassal to a member of the higher nobility (count) who was lord in that context but also a vassal to an even higher power, the duke. Corresponding rights and responsibilities were established between all of these levels of authority; for instance, a baron would be required to supply knights to his superiors for service in wars but if the fighting went badly, he and his vassals could take refuge in the count's castle. Under these circumstances, it is not surprising that the hereditary elite totally dominated the agrarian economy and local administration; nor is it surprising that widely differing practices developed in the thousands of feudal areas that made up what is now western Europe. These variations in local customs were critical in later centuries when the strongest nobles attempted to unite these diverse areas into larger, more cohesive nation states—a process that we will return to in Chapter Eight.

In view of the high degree of diversity among feudal systems, the role of the Church as a cohesive entity is more clearly appreciated. The clergy developed along lines similar to the feudal nobility, but the hierarchy was subject to an ultimate leader, the pope. Hence, while the feudal lords were engaged in defending and controlling their holdings, the Church was providing a degree of continuity and cohesiveness. Again, there were numerous conflicts over the ultimate source of authority throughout the Middle Ages but, overall, the nobility and the Church can be recognized as the components of the medieval elite. In the attempt to maintain and strengthen its influence within this elite, the Church developed a virtual monopoly over education and stressed that its authority came from God. Hence, it was critical that the Church maintain a degree of certainty and continuity in its teachings and practices in order to justify its superiority. This necessity led to conflicts among the leaders of the Church, especially when alternative ideas and practices threatened their monopoly over interpreting the spiritual and physical world. These challenges were particularly intense during the thirteenth century, when Thomas Aquinas was born.

In the early years of the thirteenth century, the Church was in turmoil. A number of groups were in the process of breaking away from Rome—accusing the Church and Pope of corruption, greed, and immorality. Especially popular in the south of France, the Cathari (or Albigenses) and the Waldenses argued that the Church had corrupted the teachings of Jesus and called for the reestablishment of simplicity and virtue. They altered the sacraments and gained support from members of the local nobility, who were interested in seizing the Church's property. The threat to Rome posed by these "heretics" prompted Pope Innocent III to establish the Inquisition—in effect, a reign of terror exercised by the Church throughout Europe. Numerous similarities between these anti-papal movements and the Protestant Reformation can be identified, and we will return to this point in Chapter Eight; at this point, consider the suggestion that the anti-papal movement had its origins during this period, but it took another 200 years to gain sufficient momentum to seriously undermine the authority of Rome.

In addition to Rome's problems in France, conflicts grew between Innocent III and the head of the "ghost empire," the German Emperor Otto IV. The Pope was highly active in political affairs—he involved himself in the politics of several countries and when he came into conflict with Otto IV, he demanded that the Emperor be deposed. Frederick II cooperated with the Pope and replaced Otto but he soon came into conflict with Innocent's successors (Popes Honorius III and Gregory IX) and was excommunicated. Following a brief reconciliation, he was excommunicated again and full-scale war broke out between Frederick and the Lombard League (the latter fought with the Pope's blessing).

As the worldly violence grew in response to the "heretics," the Church also became increasingly threatened by intellectual dialogue.

The Rise of Islam

While feudal systems were filling the power vacuum in Europe following the decline of Rome, the Saracenic Empire was filling the southern void from Persia to North Africa. Based on the appeal of the Islamic religion, Saracenic culture expanded following the death of the prophet Mohammed in 632 and was extended into Spain by the middle of the eighth century. While the *Koran* provided religious guidelines, there was also an active interest in studying the writings of the Greek Philosophers. In Spain, the most influential scholar of Greek works was Averroes, who lived from 1126–1198. Averroes' concerns were similar to those of the early Christian theologians who focused on the question of faith versus reason. But whereas Paul opted for faith, Averroes stressed reason—revealing his Aristotelian interests. In short, Averroes concluded that the truths of reason (philosophy) are distinct from the truths of faith (religion). Faith and reason, then, were viewed as totally separate ways of understanding the world. Obviously, this argument was threatening to the Catholic Church because its actions were based on the dominance of faith. If Averroes' argument was accepted, and philosophy led to conclusions that were antithetical to the Church's, then these conclusions were just as "right" as the Chruch's doctrine. As we will stress in the following Chapter, the ancient conflict between Plato and Aristotle surfaced in this issue. The Church had been steeped in Neoplatonism since the fourth century, when Saint Augustine synthesized Christianity and Plato. Aristotle, via Averroes, was now questioning the source of knowledge—stressing reason as opposed to religious faith, and opening the door to still another heresy.

Averroes' perspectives gained popularity at the University of Paris by the time Thomas Aquinas was appointed to fill one of the two chairs reserved for the Dominican Order. The Dominicans were organized to defend the Pope's interests during the Inquisition and Albert Magnus, Aquinas' mentor, had chosen to do so as a scholar, not an inquisitor. Unlike Averroes, Magnus and Aquinas approached Aristotle's works from a background of Church authority and, in the process, Aquinas synthesized Aristotle's philosophy with the Church's faith. The Augustinians condemned Aristotle from the Neoplatonist Christian perspective, defending the Church against reason and science. The Averroists separated faith from reason, opening the door for an attack on Church doctrine. Aquinas reconciled Aristotle with the teachings of the Church—a monumental accomplishment in defense of the Pope! Hence, when secular interpretations of Aristotle emerged in Europe via Averroes in the fourteenth century, the Church had already made preparations to combat them. By reconciling Aristotle with Catholicism, Aquinas' works took some of the steam out of the Aristotelian/Averroist attacks on the political and economic power of the Church developed by Marsilius of Padua in 1324. Both Marsilius and Aquinas interpreted Aristotle during the period from 1256 to 1324. Marsilius used Aristotle's philosophy to attack the Church's temporal power and was condemned by the Pope; his arguments lent credibility to the growing dissent against the papacy. Aquinas reconciled Aristotle and Christianity during a time of severe threat to the Church and became a saint, buying the Church time before the works of Aristotle emerged in secular thought.

References

1. M. Rostovtzeff, *Rome,* trans. J. D. Duff, Elias J. Bickerman, ed. (New York: Oxford University Press, 1960) p. 50. Originally published by Clarendon Press, 1928.
2. Will Durant, *Caesar and Christ* (New York: Simon and Schuster, 1944) p. 108. *The Story of Civilization,* Part III.
3. Ibid., p. 111.
4. See Rostovtzeff, Chapters IX–XIII and Durant, Chapter IX.
5. W. Durant, *Caesar and Christ,* p. 129.
6. *Holy Bible,* King James Version, Leviticus 25:2.
7. Ibid., 25:23.
8. Ibid., 25:25.
9. Ibid., 25:35.
10. Ibid., 25:10, 13.
11. Ibid., Deuteronomy 23:19, 20.
12. Ibid., 15:2.
13. Ibid., 15:3.
14. Ibid., 15:4.
15. Ibid., 15:9.
16. Ibid., 23:24–25.
17. Ibid., Isaiah 5:1–8.
18. Ibid., 32:6–7.
19. Ibid., 55:11.
20. Ibid., Amos 5:11–12.
21. Ibid., Micah 2:1, 2.
22. Ibid., Malachi 3:5–7.
23. Ibid., Matthew 3:3.
24. Ibid., 3:4–7.
25. Ibid., 3:2.
26. Ibid., Mark 14:58–64.
27. Ibid., Luke 23:2–5.
28. W. T. Jones, pp. 296–297. For a description of the mystery cults, see pp. 293–295.
29. Geoffrey Parrinder, ed. *World Religions* (New York: Facts on File, 1983) p. 430.
30. W. T. Jones, p. 345.
31. Quoted by Rosa Luxemburg in "Socialism and the Churches," in *Rosa Luxemburg Speaks* (New York: Pathfinder Press, 1970) p. 139.
32. Ernst Troeltsch, *The Social Teaching of the Christian Churches,* trans. O. Wyon (New York: Harper and Row, 1960) p. 90. Originally published by The Macmillan Company, 1931.
33. Saint Ignatius of Antioch, *Epistle to the Trallians,* quoted in Parrinder, p. 424.
34. Luxemburg, p. 143.
35. Quoted in Luxemburg, p. 141.
36. Joseph R. Strayer and Rushton Coulborn, "The Idea of Feudalism," in *Feudalism in History,* ed. Rushton Coulborn (Hamden, Conn: Archon Books, 1965) p. 7. Originally published by Princeton University Press. 1956.
37. Ibid., p. 9.
38. For detail, see Joseph R. Strayer, "Feudalism in Western Europe." Ibid., p. 22.

Chapter 6
Roman Thought: The Quest for Hope

G. W. F. Hegel said that religion serves as the mode of expression for those people who cannot comprehend philosophy.[1] When religion cannot satisfy the rational mind, people sometimes turn to philosophy—just as when reason falls short of a satisfying answer, people sometimes look to religion. In Chapter Two, we noted the transition from religion to philosophy that characterized Greek thought from Homer and Hesiod through Democritus and Socrates. In this Chapter, we note how philosophy faded back into religion when reason could not rectify the philosophical perspectives of the past with the realities of the Roman Empire. We begin with Epicurus (writing in Greece during the second century B.C.) and conclude with Augustine, writing in North Africa during the fifth century A.D.

Epicurus

Two centuries before the birth of Jesus, there was a house on the outskirts of Athens surrounded by a walled garden. While this villa may have appeared ordinary from the outside, behind its walls, sheltered from the world, lived the final Athenian philosopher to be mentioned in this book—Epicurus. It was from here, seldom venturing beyond its walls in thought or deed, that Epicurus lectured students (including women and slaves), debated philosophy, and wrote numerous treatises. Unlike Plato and Aristotle, he saw no hope for the ideal of the Greek city–state; its time had passed, along with its union of individual and society. What happiness there could be in life was now dependent upon individual, solitary fortitude—as the state was lost to the all-consuming exorbitance of imperialism. From this basis, Epicurus emphasized personal ethics rather than politics, and individual soul rather than the state. He attracted a widespread following, paving the way for Greek and Roman Stoicism.

The tide of imperialism compelled Epicurus to reject both Plato's and Aristotle's theories of knowledge. Seeing the need for a more authentic theory that reflected the true state of affairs, he drew upon the Atomism of Democritus. The universe is made up only of atoms and the void they move in, and everything is a product of the arrangement of atoms in space. Knowledge begins as atoms bombard our senses as perceptions; many perceptions forge atoms into memories; many memories result in the atomic configurations of experience, and sufficient experience gives knowledge. But knowledge, in reality, is nothing more than differing arrangements of atoms in space. Truth, whether Ideals or Universals, does not exist. There is no hope that an ideal state or polity will emerge to aid in our pursuit of happiness. So, to make the best of our situation, we need only be concerned with what is needed to get through life in the best possible manner.

According to Plato, happiness is found in the life of the philosopher-king; according to Aristotle, contemplation creates the good life. Epicurus discards both, as their actualization is dependent upon an active life within the state and society. Certainly happiness is our desire, but it can only be found with regard to the self. The sole responsibility of life is to maximize pleasure and minimize pain, making ethical choice a decision between pleasures. Finally, there is no benefit in subjecting oneself to pain for some future pleasure or good. But Epicurus did not preach the hedonism of an extravagant life as a response to this dismal view of reality. True happiness is found in simplicity; ignorance, emotion and passion keep us from this realization. Reason must rely upon the senses, but emotion and passion interfere in the process, distorting knowledge by altering experience into error or altering desires into vices. To insure wise choice of pleasure, we must be able to control the distorting affects of emotion and passion.

A troubled soul is the source of troubled feelings and the cause of a troubled soul is anxiety, says Epicurus. We are anxious for two unfounded reasons: death and divine intervention. The fear of death is a fear for our soul's afterlife. But the soul does not transcend death—it dies with the body. There is nothing to be done to save our soul, so there is nothing to fear. Divine intervention is founded on the notion that supernatural forces may disrupt or enhance our lives as they carry out our destiny in conjunction with the destiny of the universe. This too is an unfounded fear, as such forces can only be concerned with good and unconcerned with evil. Human life is especially evil, so such forces cannot be concerned with human life; hence, we need not worry about supernatural forces because they do not worry about us. By eliminating these two causes of anxiety, we can seek wisdom and act with prudence.

Nothing is good or bad in itself because there is no fate or transcendent soul to judge goodness and evil. The measure of good and bad is only determined by the degree to which individual happiness is attained. Thus, where Plato and Aristotle held that justice, moderation and knowledge were good in themselves, Epicurus argued that happiness is the only good. Virtue (such as justice, moderation and knowledge) is only a means to happiness because it frees us from physical pain and a troubled soul. Happiness is found in a tranquil soul and passive repose. Truly, Epicurus locked himself away from the world—professing a passive life filled with wisdom and simple pleasures. A similar retreat from the active life was practiced by the followers of Jesus of Nazareth after the crucifixion, as their hopes for immediate salvation were shattered.

Jesus of Nazareth and Early Christianity

If Epicurus' advocacy of withdrawal and resignation can be seen as the result of the destruction of the hope for human improvement associated with the Greek city–state, the dashing of hope for the imminent establishment of the "kingdom of heaven" on earth stimulated a similar reaction among the early Christians. Following the crucifixion of Jesus, all hopes for a Maccabee-style political revolt against Rome were lost and Christianity, which clearly included perspectives that could have been used to support such a revolt, became a system of thought resigned to survival and preparation for future salvation. A brief comparison of the ideas associated with Jesus and his apostles (who kept the faithful organized following the execution of their leader) serves to illustrate this point.

The continuity of immediate social concern and activism between the Old Testament prophets and Jesus has already been established. Matthew, Chapter Five, verses 17 and 18, stress Jesus' links to the earlier social reformers:

> Think not that I am come to destroy the law, or prophets: I am not come to destroy, but to fulfill.
> For verily I say unto you, Till heaven and earth pass, one jot or one tittle shall in no wise pass from the law, till all be fulfilled.

In addition, there are references in Matthew (especially in Chapters Two and Three) suggesting that the Old Testament's prophecies are being fulfilled by Jesus. We are also challenged to seek the perfect life: Be ye therefore perfect, even as your father which is in heaven is perfect; and we are told that fundamental change is imminent: Repent ye: for the kingdom of heaven is at hand.[2]

Jesus' views toward the good life, and his practical prescriptions to attain it, also reflect the anti-materialistic values that we have noted as characteristic of the Old Testament. Throughout Matthew, Chapter Six, we are cautioned against being driven by material desires; clearly, there is more to the human potential than the pursuit of material goods, and we are warned that "where your treasure is, there will your heart be also." And in the following passages, we are given a clearcut guideline for the good life that attacks the accumulation of material possessions. A young man asked Jesus what he could do to live the good life in addition to obeying the commandments. Jesus answers: If thou wilt be perfect, [and we have already been told that we should be perfect] go and sell that thou hast, and give to the poor, and thou shalt have treasure in heaven: and come and follow me.[3] The young man's search for perfection stopped at this point (he had "great possessions"), whereupon Jesus told his disciples: Verily I say unto you, That a rich man shall hardly enter into the kingdom of heaven.[4] Jesus and the Old Testament prophets (along with Socrates, Plato and Aristotle) condemn the uncontrolled drive for material possessions because it leads us away from our proper, truly human, pursuits.

While the Old Testament prophets and Jesus criticized those who lose sight of their proper goals and become dominated by material desire, their most scathing attacks were reserved for those who give lip service to righteousness but act on the basis of desire. Recall Amos' attacks on the hypocrisy of political and religious leaders and John the Baptist's description of the Pharisees and Sadducees, then turn to Matthew, Chapter 23 to read Jesus' rebukes of the scribes and Pharisees, who:

Verse 4	bind heavy burdens and grievous to be borne, and lay them on men's shoulders; but they themselves will not move them with one of their fingers.
Verse 5	But all their works they do for to be seen of men: they make broad their phylacteries, and enlarge the borders of their garments.
Verse 6	And love the uppermost rooms at feasts, and the chief seats in the synagogues.
Verse 13	But woe unto you, scribes and Pharisees, hypocrites! For ye shut up the kingdom of heaven against men. . . .
Verse 14	Woe unto you, scribes and Pharisees, hypocrites! for ye devour widows houses, and for a pretence make long prayer. . . .
Verse 27	Woe unto you, scribes and Pharisees, hypocrites! for ye are like unto whited sepulchres, which indeed appear beautiful outward, but are within full of dead men's bones, and of all uncleanliness.
Verse 28	Even ye outwardly appear righteous unto men, but within ye are full of hypocrisy and iniquity.
Verse 33	Ye serpents, ye generations of vipers, how can ye escape the damnation of hell?

But people do not like to be reminded of their hypocrisy, and those who carry the burden of doing so (Socrates, John the Baptist, and Jesus fit into this category) are likely to be met with persecution.

The strength of Jesus' and Socrates' message is illustrated by its longevity. But just as Socrates' ideas were altered by Plato and Aristotle, Jesus' followers introduced a degree of political quietism and earthly withdrawal into their leader's outspoken attacks on established authority.

Withdrawal from society and its problems gradually became the norm, with the Apostle Peter admonishing the followers to "Save yourselves from this untoward generation."[5] Hence, by pulling inward, away from a society over which they had little control, the early Christians were able to follow the ancient laws of the prophets and minimize the intensity of persecution. The high degree of fellowship and the communal norms practiced within the group is summarized in Acts 2:44–46:

> And all that believed were together, and had all things in common;
> And sold their possessions and goods, and parted them to all men, as every man had need.
> And they, continuing daily with one accord in the temple, and breaking bread from house to house, did eat their meat with gladness and singleness of heart.

But even this withdrawal from society could not mask the underlying tension between the spiritual focus of the early Christians and the increasingly material focus of Rome. The tension was solved by Paul's Epistle to the Romans, with its stress on the separation of the spiritual and physical. Like Plato, Paul's perspectives divided the two realms completely: spritually, we are told to ". . . be not conformed to this world."[6] But in day to day affairs, we should willingly submit ourselves to the authority of the state and accept our physical lot in life:

> Let every soul be subject to the higher powers. For there is no power but of God: the powers that be are ordained of God.
> Whosoever therefore resisteth the power, resisteth the ordinance of God: and they that resist shall receive to themselves damnation.[7]

Hence, a system of thought that was initially highly critical of established authority moved through a stage of withdrawal and culminated in the toleration of the Roman Empire. And ultimately, Paul even justified tolerating the physical abuse of believers:

> Rejoicing in hope; patient in tribulation; continuing instant in prayer;
> Bless them which persecute you: bless, and curse not.[8]

The continuity of potentially revolutionary ideas from the Old Testament through Jesus of Nazareth was broken with Paul, following the practice of social withdrawal introduced by the Apostle Peter. Whereas Plato attempted to resolve the distinction between spirit and matter by establishing spirit's control over matter, Paul kept the two separated. As a result, the foundation was created for the compatibility of Christianity and Rome. Paul's writings suggest that the physical world is a world of pain and suffering, which can only be dealt with by accepting what is and living for the rewards of an eternal, unchanging, and perfect afterlife. There is an answer to the poverty of the human condition, but it lies in the spiritual world and is possible only through the grace of God.

Stoicism

The hope of transforming the social and political ideals of Plato and Aristotle into reality dimmed as the city–state became submerged by the rising tide of imperialism. Epicurus witnessed it in Greece and retreated to the seclusion of his garden. The early Christians saw it in Rome and waited for God's salvation. Both encouraged the passive life of noninvolvement. In sharp contrast, the Stoics attempted to bring the outside world into the havens of Epicurean and Christian withdrawal as they extended their principles of ethics and simplicity to the imperative of an active life. The Stoics considered in this section are Epictetus and Marcus Aurelius. Epictetus (60–138 A.D.) spent his philosophical life in poverty in the Greek city of Nicopolis, while Marcus Aurelius (121–180 A.D.) was born into the Roman patrician class and eventually became emperor in 161 A.D.

Universal Law and the World State

Whereas Epicurus subscribed to Democritus' atomism, the Stoics held that the universe is governed by natural law—a law based on benign rationality, not the chance collision of atoms. As such, natural law determines an objective destiny for individuals and states. Hence, everything has its proper place as everything conforms, through fate, to reason. This interpretation allowed the Stoics to reach back to Aristotle and revive the unique human quality of active reason and its quest for a rational understanding of nature:

> God makes one animal for eating, and another for service in farming, another to produce cheese, and others for different uses of a like nature, . . . but He brought man into the world to take cognizance of Himself and His works, and not only to take cognizance but also to interpret them. Therefore it is beneath man's dignity to begin and to end where the irrational creatures do: he must rather begin where they do and end where nature has ended in forming us; and nature ends in contemplation and understanding and a way of life in harmony with nature.[9]

Through the study of nature we come to recognize norms not only of the natural sciences but also of good human conduct—the rational life supported by such virtues as justice, temperance and fortitude.

As the standards of the universe and human nature become evident, we are led to the conclusion that there must be one universal law—a law from which all things derive their existence. And if it is so for the universe, it must be so for human beings. This law is reason, and it creates a common bond from which we can develop common laws and a common state:

> If our intellectual part is common, then reason also, in respect of which we are rational beings, is common; if this is so, common also is the reason which commands us what to do, and what not to do; if this is so, there is a common law also; if this is so, we are fellow-citizens; if this is so, we are members of some political community; if this is so, the world is in a manner a state.[10]

A life of reason, for the Stoics, creates a common bond among peoples. It is a mutual link that goes beyond artificial political boundaries, manifesting itself politically as the world empire. The Stoics discounted the political ideals of Plato and Aristotle, which were wedded to the city–state, and rejected Epicurus' apolitical posture. Instead, they opted for a rational world-state (cosmopolis), making people citizens of the world.

From the one universal law of nature, we derive natural human rights that provide guidelines for the creation of natural human laws which, in turn, form the basis for specific civil laws. Natural rights must be guaranteed, and natural laws must be followed because they define our moral duty. To insure the likelihood of moral action, states must not interfere with these natural laws because people are obligated to follow them. While it is the duty of individuals to act morally, it is the duty of governments to protect human rights through the creation of civil laws that reflect the laws of nature.

Happiness and Social Duty

The stoic life was guided by the recognition of the rational structure of the universe and acceptance of each person's particular role within the structure. It was at this point that the Athenian philosophers failed, according to the Stoics: in attempting to determine the good and wise, they neglected two prerequisites. First, people rarely control their own destiny; more often than not, they are susceptible to misfortune and sorrow, the causes of which often seem arbitrary. Second, given the first point, the issue of happiness is not to be free from disaster and disappointment, but to be free to accept them. If previous philosophy had admitted these prerequisites, happiness would have been seen as the absence of desire. Without desire for a better life, we can have peace of mind and become indifferent to the course of events.

Stoic resignation allows a person to "rise above" everyday situations (much as the early Christians did), and carry out moral duties and responsibilities. Unlike the city–state, where the citizen–politicians had a direct link to the political process, the world-empire was administered by an army of bureaucrats. These officials should not be corrupted by personal gain, just as they should not be apathetic (in the Epicurean sense) toward their duties. Corruption and indifference had to be tempered by a sense of moral duty:

> Every moment think steadily as a Roman and a man to do what thou hast in hand with perfect and simple dignity, and feeling of affection, and freedom, and justice; and to give thyself relief from all other thoughts. And thou wilt give thyself relief, if thou doest every act of thy life as if it were the last, laying aside all carelessness and passionate aversion from the commands of reason, and all hypocrisy, and self-love, and discontent with the portion which has been given to thee.[11]

The Stoic plea for duty and responsibility was founded upon love of universal humanity and promised little in the way of personal reward, whether material or intellectual.

It was obvious to the Stoics that the vastness of an empire precluded a sense of active union between individual and the state. And, to avoid alienation, the populace must take solace in reduced expectations (at least in terms of the philosophies of Plato and Aristotle) concerning control over its destiny. People must seek the simplicity of Epicurus, yet carry out their social and political responsibilities even though their impact can rarely be felt. The stoic justification is in the divine destiny of objective natural law. Plotinus enhanced this concept of divinity, bringing philosophy to the brink of theology as the course of events in Rome appeared to move rapidly beyond human control.

Plotinus and Neoplatonism

Neoplatonism came of age in Rome during the third century A.D. with the writings and teachings of Plotinus (204–270). As a school of thought, it shifted philosophy away from the rationalism of Aristotle, past the idealism of Plato, and came to rest on the very fringes of Christian theology. Reality is no longer a matter of this world, but of another—whose unlimited boundaries stretch beyond comprehension. And as reason can never grasp reality, it can never determine the good life. We are left in a situation where there is no hope for improvement because the attainment of human happiness in this world is only a myth.

Plotinus' starting point was the inadequacy he saw in the rationalism of Aristotle's philosophy. In his quest for good and happiness, Aristotle emphasized the physical world as the source of truth. In this approach, our ideas of good and happiness are conditioned by the physical. All there is to draw upon is the present world as it exists, and its history as it is written. From this, Aristotle expected reason to reach beyond these evident forms to the form of substance itself—universal knowledge. But ultimate truth stretches over, around, and beyond the physical world, making reason an insufficient tool for its discovery. There is more to truth, just as there is more than the physical world.

The quest for good and happiness, according to Plotinus, must direct us away from the physics of Aristotle to the metaphysics of Plato. Inherent in Plato's Doctrine of Ideas is the recognition that truth is outside of the physical realm. But Plato's Doctrine is not wholly correct. To define ideas as particulars is to underestimate their true form and limit our understanding of them. In fact, no description as to how ultimate truth exists is adequate because words only give rational form, and truth is beyond rationality.[12] But some designation must be given, regardless of deficiencies, so Plotinus suggested various terms, such as Unlimited, One, Intellectual-Principle, God, First, Absolute, Good, and Infinite.

Plotinus again drew upon Plato as he accounted for the relation of the Unlimited to our existence. To see this relationship, we must acknowledge that there are three levels of reality. The ultimate level is that of the Unlimited. From the Unlimited comes the Universal Soul, which contains the individual souls of human beings. In the last level, the Soul links our limited existence with the Unlimited. But for Plotinus, Soul is the vehicle by which humans strive for the Unlimited; it is not a vehicle by which we evaluate and change the physical world. The physical world will always be less than perfect, so our time is better spent trying to fathom the Unlimited than applying imperfect solutions to an imperfect world.

Fundamentally, Plotinus painted a picture of alienated existence. In our limited form we can never be identical with the Unlimited, yet this is our source of good and happiness. We are, by our nature, incomplete and our wholeness is out of reach. What happiness there is for us in this world is found in the contemplative life, not the active life. But reason is an insufficient instrument for reaching good and happiness; instead, we must rely upon vision and inspiration. What happiness that is available to us in this world can only be found in meditative contemplation of the Unlimited. Only then do we come as close as we can to the spiritual existence for which we yearn. Clearly, western philosophy blends with Christianity (note, especially, the similarities with Paul) in this conclusion.

Augustine

Neoplatonism officially crossed the boundary between philosophy and religion in the writings of Augustine (345–430). Living in an Empire that was on the brink of collapse, Augustine tried to make sense of the chaos he witnessed. Disorder prevailed to such a degree that reason could not save it; the only recourse was in illumination from a higher form of existence.

In the beginning there was only God and for six days He created the world that we and all other things of His creation occupy. To conceive of what was created, Augustine borrowed from Plotinus, who borrowed from Plato's Doctrine of Ideas. There are, in God's design, three levels of reality, but the supreme level is different from Plotinus' description, and that necessarily affects the lowest level. At the lowest level, God created humans by giving their bodies souls through which to grasp a foggy scene of His eternal beauty and goodness. Such vision can only be accomplished in the contemplative life, where all distractions are eliminated. It is here that all happiness possible in this life can be realized.

Level	Plato	Plotinus	Augustine
Highest	Ideals	Unlimited	God
Middle	Soul	Soul	Soul
Lowest	Body	Body	Body

If Adam and Eve had not sinned and had not been banished from the Garden of Eden, their lives would have been spent in divine contemplation, i.e., leisure. But they did—so we find ourselves in a world full of devilish temptations which, more often than not, distract us from our true purpose—to know and love God. The root cause of our plight, in addition to the foolishness of Adam and Eve, is God. In His infinite wisdom, which we cannot even begin to comprehend, He has limited our capacity to resist sin and thus be close to Him. Here is the human dilemma—the desire to be at one with God, but limited in our ability to do so. Our imprisonment is a two-fold sentence. First, as natural beings, our souls are bound in union with the body—a marriage that cannot be annulled in this life. Second, and critical to this discussion, God gave each of us various amounts (though no one has enough) of will. The amount of will God has bestowed on us determines our happiness in this life and the possibility of our salvation in the next life.

Augustine reached back to Aristotle's concept of the soul (vegetative, sensitive, cognitive), to specify the role of the will in human life. Our sensitive capacity has but one design (the care of bodily needs), while our cognitive capacity has two responsibilities: in contemplation it seeks God and in reason it deduces moral behavior. Like Plotinus, Augustine considered reason to be merely a tool for solving earthly riddles. Superimposed on the soul is the will as the motivation for all action—physical, sensual and intellectual. It is the will that calls upon our hands to open a book, calls upon our eyes to focus on the page, and calls upon our mind to read. Will, as the stimulant for action and knowledge, is God's gift to us and a manifestation of His goodness. Thus, a willed act has only good intentions and evil must result from a lack of will. When evil tempts us, it is not our will—but the absence of will that causes us to sin. The resulting guilt rests squarely with us because the deficiency is ours. God's gift is will, not the lack of will.

According to the philosophers of Athens, moral virtue was the means of fulfilling our nature because through its exercise we moved closer to perfection. To them, virtue was a habit—and a virtuous person became so through a consistent display of morality. An occasional deviation from the moral path did not necessarily deny virtue. To Augustine, God actualized our nature when He shared His will, so there is no potential for improvement in this life. We are, from the moment of birth, predetermined for heaven or hell. Our destiny is cast by our will and we cannot change our standing in God's eyes regardless of how consistently we attempt to exercise moral virtue. Thus, Augustine held that, in this life, our goal is to avoid evil (a product of a deficient will) rather than do good (a product of God's will). It is evil that reflects our damnation more than good mirrors our salvation.

Augustine's analysis of our relationship with God rests on two perspectives—one from above and one from below. From above, God (as Infinite and Unlimited) looks down on us. He is always present and from this position, He determines our lives. From below, we seem to be in control of our lives by willing good and avoiding evil. It is as though we verify our salvation by testing virtue at every turn. But it is all a mirage; reality is with God, not us, and we can only do what God has determined.

Just as God determined our destiny, He determined the destiny of everything as part of a grand plan. Looking at this plan through the history of social organizations and political structures, we see a city within a city. Inside the earthly city is an external city comprised of faithful Christians:

> The earthly city, which does not live by faith, seeks an earthly peace, and the end it proposes, in the well-ordered concord of civic obedience and rule, is the combination of men's wills to attain the things which are helpful to this life. The heavenly city, or rather the part of it which sojourns on earth and lives by faith, makes use of this peace only because it must, until this mortal condition which necessitates it shall pass away.[13]

The heavenly city, not the earthly city, represents the world–state professed by the Roman Stoics. Only those in the "City of God" can possibly surpass earthly political boundaries and cultural differences:

> This heavenly city, then, while it sojourns on earth, calls citizens out of all nations, and gathers together a society of pilgrims of all languages, not scrupling about diversities in the manners, laws, and institutions whereby earthly peace is secured and maintained, but recognising that, however various these are, they all tend to one and the same end of earthly peace. It therefore is so far from rescinding and abolishing these diversities, that it even preserves and adapts them, so long only as no hindrance to the worship of the one supreme and true God is thus introduced.[14]

Peace, the goal of all societies, can only be found in the eternal city. Only in this city can each member find his or her place, so reason and will can harmonize and love and respect prevail. The earthly city, where people live by the senses and love the material, can never have peace. It will take the love of God, and people living by God's grace, to produce peace—which, in turn, will facilitate our final end: oneness with God.

References

1. Roland N. Stromberg, *An Intellectual History of Modern Europe,* (New York: Appleton-Century-Crofts, 1966) p. 247.
2. *The Holy Bible.* King James Version, Matthew 5:48, 3:2.
3. Ibid., 19:21.
4. Ibid., 19:23.
5. Ibid., Acts, 2:40.
6. Ibid., Paul's Epistle to the Romans, 12:2.
7. Ibid., 13:1–2.
8. Ibid., 12:12, 14.
9. Epictetus, *Discourses,* Book I, Chapter 6. In *The Stoic and Epicurean Philosophers,* Whitney J. Oates, ed., (New York: The Modern Library, 1940) p. 234.
10. Marcus Aurelius, *Meditations,* Book V, Section 4, Ibid., p. 509.
11. Ibid., Book II, Section 5, p. 498.
12. Plotinus, *Fifth Ennead,* Fifth Tractate, 6. In *Plotinus: The Enneads,* trans. S. Mackenna (London: Faber and Faber Limited, 1930) p. 408.
13. Augustine, *City of God,* XIX, Chapter 17, trans. M. Dods (New York: The Modern Library, 1950) pp. 695–696.
14. Ibid., p. 696.

Chapter 7
Thomas Aquinas: Cause, God and Our Ultimate End

The stream of classical philosophy came to an end in the third century A.D. with Plotinus, who based his thought on Platonic ideals shared with early Christianity, and stressed the inadequacy of reason. From the third to the thirteenth century there was little in the way of philosophical contributions—even Augustine's Neoplatonism was not philosophical, but theological. During the twelfth century, the writings of Aristotle filtered from the Muslim world into the European (Christian) world, and by the thirteenth century his philosophical system was challenging the traditional teachings of Christianity. The scholastic debate eventually surfaced at the University of Paris: on one side were those subscribing to Augustinian theology; on the other side, Aristotle's perspective was defended by Thomas Aquinas. The issues revolved around Augustine's doctrine of divine illumination versus Aristotle's universal principles, and Plato's realm of ideas against Aristotle's doctrine of cause. Although Aristotle's metaphysics were weak in their solutions to certain problems (including creation and the immortality of the soul), his physics presented a degree of cohesiveness vastly superior to the fragmented solutions offered by the Church.

Theory of Knowledge

The Greek exposition of knowledge presents us with a feeling of the transcendental. Plato's Ideas and Aristotle's Universals go beyond us, making our imperfection obvious. To both, reason provides the bridge from imperfect to perfect. But Aquinas, true to his Christian intellectual background, widens the rift between mortal being and immortal truth to such an extent that reason cannot bridge the chasm. At the very core of knowledge is God—but before we measure the impact of God upon the philosophy of Aquinas, we must first review his approach to the problem of change.

Problem of Change

Throughout the tradition of western philosophy, the subject of change has been a central concern. You remember that it began with Thales, the first western philosopher, and influenced the thought of everyone who followed. You may also recall that the Athenian philosophers approached the problem of change in light of the necessity for stable human values. Aquinas approached this problem by distinguishing between what he discerned as natural and spiritual change. While not an altogether new approach, as the student of Aristotle will testify, it took a new twist with the underlying concept of Aquinas' entire philosophy—God.

Natural Change. Aquinas, like numerous philosophers before him, acknowledged that natural change is the continual transformation of the universe that is evident to our senses. Its proper description, said Aquinas, is found in Aristotle's Doctrine of Cause. Recall that, according to

Aristotle, there are four causes: Material, Formal, Efficient and Final. To Aquinas, Material Cause is the unchanging potential for form and makes possible the existence of a thing; form is the actual structure given to material; Efficient Cause imposes form on material in a particular way; Final Cause is the purpose actualized by imposing form on material.

Spiritual Change. Aquinas built his system of thought on the proposition that God (as perfection) is the source of truth and reality, and that humans are imitations of God. In our imitation of God, we find our only perfection—and because God is reality and truth, we imitate by pursuing reality and truth. This pursuit is called spiritual change. With the acceptance of this initial proposition, Aquinas asked "How do we change spiritually?" In search of an answer, he concluded that the acquisition of knowledge must be in the mode of Aristotle's epistemology.[1] According to Aristotle, we collect information through our senses and, with continual refinement, we make judgments that eventually connect and coordinate with one another. In the end, we arrive at knowledge of the object and its truth.

As the mind changes, it acquires two forms of knowledge: sense (that of the object) and intellectual (that of truth). The formation of sense knowledge gives rise to an awareness of particular things and is acquired by the impression of the object on "external senses" (taste, touch, smell, sight, hearing) and the reaction of the mind through "internal senses" (lower intellectual powers such as imagination, memory and common sense). By applying higher intellectual powers (judgment and reason) to these sense perceptions, an approximation of truth is gained. Called intellectual knowledge, these approximations give us knowledge of the natural sciences, determine how life should be lived, and bring us nearer to an understanding of God.[2]

Thus far we have considered Thomas Aquinas as a reiteration of basic Aristotelian philosophy, but now we must step into the arena of Aquinas' significant modification. In order to reconcile Aristotle's view of nature with Christian theology, he had to find a place for God in Aristotle's system; or, depending on your point of view, a place for Aristotle in God's system. That place was found in Aristotle's "First Cause," and with it, Aquinas was able to advance past the ancient Greeks (who asked why the universe changes as it does), to question why the universe exists at all.

The Problem of God

The world, to Aristotle, was everlasting: it had no beginning and no end. Aquinas, well aware of this position and its obvious incompatibility with Christianity, sought to reconcile the two. By extending the logic of Aristotle in the light of Christian teaching, he transformed the First Cause into a Creator. And because Aquinas' interpretation was grounded in reason, not faith, it provided both a philosophical and a theological solution.

Aquinas developed five rational proofs for the existence of God. Three of them (unmoved mover, efficient cause and final cause) were derived directly from Aristotle's First Cause; the other two are consequences of the First Cause:

1 "The first and more manifest way is the argument from motion."[3] Change takes place by means of action of some being on something else, yet the cause of change must itself change in the act of causing change. Because the process cannot go on indefinitely, there must be an absolute beginning which is beyond change, "and this everyone understands to be God."[4]

2 The second proof is closely related to the first. It is drawn from the conception of the efficient cause and acknowledges that there neither is, nor can be, a being which is the efficient cause of itself. There must be a first efficient cause: God.

3 The third proof is based on the distinction between necessary and non-necessary beings. Aquinas proposed that non-necessary beings make up all of nature. They are contingent—that is, they may or may not be—so their existence is necessarily dependent on an efficient cause. The opposite is a necessary being which finds its own existence in itself and serves as the efficient cause of the non-necessary. The necessary is God.

4 The fourth proof of the existence of God is based upon the degrees of being. Things exist in various degrees of perfection, as measured by perfection itself. The source of perfection must be God because He is infinite, pure actuality and pure existence. From this argument, Aquinas concludes that if our capacity for existence is the total capacity of our potentialities to become actual, and God (as pure actuality) has no limiting potential, He must be the standard for which we strive. God is the final cause.

5 The fifth proof is found in the consideration of the governance of things. It is impossible for opposites to reconcile, yet we see among all the disparities in nature a certain harmony. Thus, there must exist a being who governs opposites toward an ordered arrangement. That being is God.

God, to be God, must be complete, self-fulfilling and actualized. Why, then, did God create this world if it cannot add to or detract from His pure perfection? Because God could have no reason to do so, He must have created the world in an act of free will. With this conclusion, Aquinas raised the distinction between the role of will and reason; will is the tool of God, while reason is the tool of human beings. In this division, the Neoplatonist focus on the power of good will as the motivation for moral action is retained, while Aristotle's active reason has been preserved. From his theory of knowledge (based upon God as the source of knowledge), Aquinas reinterpreted the idea of the human soul and synthesized Aristotelian contemplation with Augustinian illumination.

Individual, Society and the State

Throughout Part One, we stressed that the philosophies of Plato and Aristotle attempted to unite the individual with society and the state. All were entwined in a mutual dependence based on reason. Both philosophers agreed that good states promote good citizens and good citizens make good states because the virtues of citizen and state mirror each other. But Thomas Aquinas lived and wrote almost 15 centuries later; during this intervening period, both political reality and intellectual perspectives changed in a direction that undermined this unity of individual and state. The critical factors, from Aquinas' philosophical perspective, were a) the recognition of the existence of God as the source of truth, and b) its consequence, the insufficiency of reason in discerning truth. If ultimate truth lies beyond rational recognition, then it can only be ascertained through religious insight. And because God's intention, as ultimate good, cannot be rationally comprehended, then reason cannot serve as the sole determinant for action. There must be another determinant—free will.

Individual

In his theory of knowledge, Aquinas challenged Christian intellectualism (based on the metaphysics of Plato) with the physics of Aristotle. To stretch Aristotle's naturalism to encompass divinely-created human beings, Aquinas again confronted his metaphysically-based adversaries. The point of controversy began with the concept of the soul and was extended to the definitions of morality and virtue. He argued for a soul that determines the species of living things, as well as being a receptacle for divine illumination—and for a definition of virtue that included moral action as well as spiritual vision.

Soul. There is a hierarchy of existence, with God at the top as pure existence and chaos at the bottom as non-existence. Each thing's place on this ladder of being is determined by its proximity in likeness to God. Angels are closer to God than human beings because they exist as spiritual beings; they have no body but do have a soul. Physical objects, such as rocks and books, are further from God than human beings because they have a body but no soul. Between angels and physical objects are living beings (humans, animals and plants). They are living because they have body and soul. Thus, to truly live, says Aquinas, is to properly fulfill the functions of body and soul.

While body and soul act as a unit and cannot function separately, they remain distinct from each other as they each have different qualities. The soul is the substantial form of the body; that is, it determines what a body is (plant, animal, or human), and its species (what type of plant or what type of animal).[5] Unique physical traits (size, color, shape, et cetera) are determined by the body and are called accidental form.[6] So while the soul determines differences between species, the body determines differences within a species. The body, as a physical object, changes in its features and moves in its actions. It is, then, the demonstrative manifestation of morality or immorality. And because the body can change for good or evil, it is viewed as corruptible. The soul, as intellectual, changes spiritually but its change is only for good; thus, it is not corruptible. While the soul always inclines toward good intention, its outward display is bodily actions—and, because the body is corruptible, the soul's intentions are not always realized in human behavior. It is this unity of soul and body, as substantial and accidental form and as incorruptible and corruptible, that combine to form individual human beings.

The human soul is comprised of four parts: vegetative, sensitive, appetitive and intellectual.[7]

1 The vegetative part of the soul insures growth and maintains life.
2 The sensitive part of the soul has the power to accumulate sense knowledge.
3 The appetitive part is the desire for good and includes emotions and will. In the exercise of emotions and will, there is no rational vision of what is right; emotion and will are simply instincts inclined toward good. Emotions direct us toward perceived particular goods and away from particular evils. The will is the drive for universal good, which affords us the opportunity to rise above particular circumstances. To this extent, will power is the source of freedom—but it can be obscured by such physical sentiments as hope, despair, pleasure and pain—which can corrupt an act of free will.
4 The intellectual part of the soul represents the degree of human perfection. The virtue of the intellectual part is reason, that which converts the potentially intelligible into the actually intelligible.[8] And, with the aid of the other parts, it makes up that portion of us that is truly human.

Where the body and soul combine to form individual life, the actual functioning of both brings about living, as the body changes physically and the soul changes spiritually. But in this arrangement, the body is meaningless except to the extent that it facilitates the soul by maintaining life and moral actions. True humanness is found in the soul through the use of reason in knowing God as truth. The result is an inner harmony, which brings "peace of mind."

Human Being

Body	Soul
accidental form	substantial form
physical change	spiritual change
corruptible	incorruptible

Morality and Virtue. Spiritual change is incorruptible because it is a dimension shared with God, but physical change can be good or evil. It is physical change, as behavior, that is the subject of morality and it is spiritual and physical change that is the subject of virtue.

Morality is reflected in our intention and choice of action. Aquinas listed three kinds of intentions: moral (such as "to assist someone in need"), immoral (such as "to appropriate to oneself what belongs to another"), and amoral (such as "to go for a walk or to pick up a straw").[9] Moral intention is the first and primary requisite of a good life and insures morality, regardless of the eventual consequences. For example, the moral intention of feeding starving people may have immoral ramifications when, unknown to the donor, the donated food is tainted and causes illness in the recipients. Regardless, the donor still is considered moral. The second aspect of morality is moral choice. Aquinas argued (as did the classical Greek philosophers) that when goodness is evident, a person will act rightly. In this case, there is no question of moral choice. But we live in a world of particular concrete things—all of which have limited amounts of goodness; thus, what is good is not always evident. It is here that moral choice becomes critical and consistent good choice is called virtue.

There are, as Aquinas echoed the words of Aristotle, two types of virtue: intellectual and moral. Intellectual virtue (wisdom and prudence) is contemplative, as wisdom considers truth, and prudence suggests ways to apply wisdom to daily life: Prudence is the *right reason of things to be done.*[10] Prudence serves as an intermediary between wisdom and the moral virtues by comparing what is morally right with what is morally feasible, in order to seek the best possible moral course. Moral virtue is the habit of good action, and to consistently make moral choices, we must rely upon reason.

The purpose of the human being is found in the exercise of wisdom rather than moral virtue, just as it is found in the soul rather than the body. But, as the soul needs the body to facilitate purpose, so wisdom needs moral virtue. Moral virtue begins with moral intention—where we must first desire to do good; then, with knowledge, we determine what good is; prudence then ascertains what amount of good can be accomplished under the given circumstance (by setting parameters it becomes the substantial form of moral virtue); and, lastly, we display moral action by employing the virtues of justice, temperance and fortitude inside the limits set by prudence.[11]

Ideally, the intellectual virtues of wisdom and prudence should be identical; but for inhabitants of a practical world, imperfection taints everything. This situation places responsibility upon society and the state to insure the best possible conditions for bringing prudence and wisdom into practice.

Society and the State

It is a fact that people live in society for certain political, economic, and social advantages. All of these advantages point toward the ultimate justification of the state: the promotion of individual good. The duty of the state is to actively promote good within its citizens and, in so doing, promote the common good. From this premise, Aquinas reconciled the Christian ideal of common good with the politics of Aristotle. His ideal of the state was based on a flexible system of government that conforms to the diversity and capacities of its citizens; when such conformity is present, harmony will be achieved—as common good and individual good reinforce each other. Aquinas, then, echoed Aristotle by suggesting that various types of governments are proper, given the aspirations and desires of society. Aquinas identified three types: Polity, Aristocracy and Kingship.

1 The best state is a Polity, where the whole of society is involved in its governance. The corrupted version of a Polity is a Democracy, where "power is wielded by the common masses at the expense of men of property."[12]
2 An Aristocracy is the next best form of government, where power is in the hands of a few enlightened, trusted rulers who govern for the common good. An Oligarchy is the corrupted form of an Aristocracy, where a few rulers oppress the general populace for their own economic benefit.
3 The third is a Kingship, where one person rules for "the common good of the people and not his own private profit."[13] Its distortion is found in the Tyranny, where a tyrant rules by force and for personal gain.

Individuals live by morals, just as the state governs by laws; and because individuals can be fallible in their assessment of what is right, so can the state—for laws are conceived, designed and enforced by people. Laws devised by humans seldom reflect exact right, but a norm of right.[14] There are three types of laws: divine, natural and human.

1 Supreme laws are the divine laws dictated by God and serve as the true source of natural and human laws.
2 Natural laws are those which are the same for all the universe for all time. They provide the basis for the axioms of science and prescribe guidelines for human behavior. The natural laws which provide the means to measure proper human action are not always self-evident, but will always follow the precepts of practical reason—just as scientific natural laws will always follow theoretical reason.
3 When these natural human laws require legislation by the state, they become human laws. The closer human laws are to their divine source, as portrayed through natural laws, the better a state can enhance the individual ends of its citizens.

Aquinas presented a dualism in his discussion of society and the state. There is an ideal of the state in the form of a Polity (essentially, participatory democracy), but it is only possible when its citizens have, collectively, sufficient intellectual and moral virtue to establish human laws that are derived from true natural laws. In absence of this ideal, the best possible harmony is achieved by structuring a state where only the most qualified rule so that human laws are still reflective of their natural counterparts. This dualism carries over to the ends of the state and the ends of individuals, as ends vary depending upon the collective and individual level of intellectual and moral virtue. But there is an ultimate end which can only be fully realized in the true Polity. The ultimate goal of society, the state, and human laws, is the ultimate end of the individual—the contemplative life.

Implications for Leisure

Because every human action has an intended end, we say that, ideally, intention is the cause and result of action. Aquinas extended this statement to encompass all change when he defined Aristotle's First Cause as God. God is the first intention (unmoved mover) and the ultimate end (final cause) of the universe. As intention, God is potential and as the ultimate end, God is actual. Because human beings are created by the will of God, our goal in life (our ultimate end) is to know God. Hence, our entire lives must focus on this goal if we are to be fully human. Our unique human capacity requires us to subordinate our time and energy to our ultimate end. Clearly, through contemplative leisure, we fulfill our ultimate purpose in life.

True human happiness, as the realization of our ultimate end, can only be found by striving to actualize God's intention. Aquinas argued that disagreements over definitions of human happiness are rooted in ignorance and greed. In reality, there are four conditions of happiness:

1 Happiness is not compatible with evil.
2 Happiness is self-sufficient, leaving nothing to be desired.
3 Happiness results in no harm.
4 Happiness comes from within, not from without.

In the search for happiness, humans have always looked in two areas, material and abstract. The material world is not the source of true happiness (and, consequently, not our ultimate end) because it can only bring fortune, fame, power and honor—none of which can satisfy the conditions of happiness.[15] Aquinas concluded that happiness is found in the abstract, as either the appetitive or intellective part of the soul. The appetitive cannot provide true happiness because it is directed, as a willed act, toward the ultimate end; thus, it cannot be the ultimate end.[16] The intellective part of the soul is divided into speculative and practical, of which only speculative thought (contemplation) generates true happiness. Aquinas gave three arguments to support his position:

1 True happiness must be found in the highest operation or function. "Now man's highest operation is that of his highest power in respect of its highest object, and his highest power is the intellect, whose highest object is Divine Good, which is the object not of the practical, but of the speculative intellect."[17]
2 Contemplation is sought for its own sake, making it self-sufficient, while practical knowledge is sought for the sake of something else.
3 Aquinas notes that "in the contemplative life man has something in common with things above him, namely, with God and the angels, to whom he is made like by happiness."[18]

Speculative thought is divided into two types—that which focuses upon God (as contemplation of the Divine) and that which focuses upon nature (as the speculative sciences). True happiness is a product of the contemplation of God.[19] But the speculative sciences can produce a degree of happiness to the extent that nature (lower order) partakes in God (higher order).

Perfect happiness excludes every evil and fulfills every desire. "But in this life every evil cannot be excluded. For this present life is subject to many unavoidable evils; to ignorance on the part of the intellect, to inordinate affection on the part of the appetite, and to many penalties on the part of the body."[20] Because of these limitations, perfect happiness is not possible in this life. But what true happiness there is can only be found in contemplation—our ultimate end.

Major Philosophical Points

Thomas Aquinas' scholarly life was devoted to reconciling Aristotelian philosophy with Christian intellectualism. His major intellectual accomplishment, then, was his synthesis of Aristotle's concepts and Christian teaching that had been influenced by Plato. He proposed a naturalist theory of knowledge (as natural truth rested in natural first principles) and a theory of nature and human nature defined by four causes: Material, Formal, Efficient, and Final. Aristotle's only failure was not having accounted for the Christian version of God in his philosophy—a forgivable sin, given the fact that he lived 300 years before the birth of Jesus. To "update" Aristotle, Aquinas replaced the First Cause with God, making the ultimate purpose of human beings the contemplative life—to be pursued by the individual through the exercise of virtue and by the state through the enactment of true natural laws.

- Natural change can be explained through the Doctrine of Cause.
- God is the First Cause.
- The body and soul are mutually dependent.
- There are four parts of the soul: vegetative, sensitive, appetitive and intellectual.
- The free will is a "blind" drive for good.
- The steps to morality are intention and choice.
- The proper state is a product of practical reason and is measured by the extent to which it promotes the common good.
- Leisure, as the contemplation of the Divine, is our ultimate end, or purpose in life.

References

1. Thomas Aquinas, *Summa Theologica,* I.P.Q.84.a.1., in Anton C. Pegis, *Basic Writings of Saint Thomas Aquinas,* Vol. 1, (New York: Random House, 1945) pp. 793–795.
2. Ibid., I.P.Q.75.a.2., pp. 684–686.
3. Ibid., I.P.Q.2.a.3., p. 22.
4. Ibid.
5. Ibid., I.P.Q.76.a.1., pp. 697–698.
6. Ibid., I.P.Q.76.a.4., p. 708.
7. Ibid., I.P.Q.76.a.3., pp. 705–706.
8. Ibid., I.P.Q.79.a.8., pp. 758–759.
9. Ibid., I-II.Q.18.a.8., pp. 758–759.
10. Ibid., I-II.Q.57.a.4., p. 435.
11. Ibid., I-II.Q.61.a.2., p. 468.
12. Thomas Aquinas, *Summa Theologica,* I-II, Q.95.a.4., Vol. 2, p. 788.
13. Ibid.
14. Ibid., I-II, Q.97.a.1., pp. 800–801.
15. Thomas Aquinas, *Summa Contra Gentiles,* III, Chapters 28–31, pp. 53–56.
16. Ibid., Chapter 26, pp. 47–51.
17. Thomas Aquinas, *Summa Theologica,* I-II.Q.3.a.5., in St. Thomas Aquinas, *Summa Theologica,* Vol. 1, Trans. Fathers of the English Dominican Province, (San Francisco: Benziger Bros., Inc., 1947), p. 599.
18. Ibid., I-II.Q.3.a.5., p. 599.
19. Ibid., I-II.Q.3.a.6., p. 600.
20. Ibid., I-II.Q.5.a.3., p. 610.

Part II Conclusion

The sense of tragedy associated with the fall of Athens is deepened by adding the historical experiences recounted in the *Old Testament*, along with the rise and fall of Rome, to the Athenian experience. Again, greed and pride seem to be the dominant motivating forces in all of these societies. In addition to the similarities in their problems, we are struck by the obvious affinities in the themes of the social critics. The continuity of ideas from Isaiah through Jesus is indisputable. And in Rome, the essentially Homeric guidelines of reason, moderation and balance continually resurfaced as a beacon for the wise individual to follow in order to resist the perversion of the human spirit and avoid social chaos.

For Epicurus, the world had become so unpredictable and uncontrollable that hope for a good society was out of the question. Pulling inward, he denied the political prescriptions developed by Plato and Aristotle—but retained their personal ethics of a simple, contemplative life. The aspirations of the early Christians for a quick movement into the Kingdom of Heaven were also thwarted by the power of Rome, and they reacted to this environment in a similar manner, by pulling inward away from any notion of political responsibility. Their society became defined by the criterion of belief in future salvation (made possible by the resurrection) and they attempted to remain aloof from the secular power of Rome. The early Christians developed rituals and sacraments to separate themselves from other religious groups and strengthen their unity—a predictable reaction to a hostile world. Hence, the awesome power of Rome stripped the Athenian philosophies and Christian theology of their initial political concerns—paving the way for their integration into the Empire.

Given the widespread feeling of helplessness among those who compared the realities of Rome to the ideals associated with earlier intellectual traditions, we should not be surprised at the tendency to salvage what they could from the past. The Stoics drew from Aristotle in their attempt to synthesize social and political duty with the Epicurean recognition that it probably wouldn't change anything. Nevertheless, they envisioned a world-wide community governed by a state that deduced its civil laws from nature and stressed personal responsibility. Plotinus found Plato's metaphysical approach irresistible, but concluded that the Athenian had placed too much hope in the role of human reason. For Plotinus, vision and inspiration are at the bottom of our limited ability to know what we can about the Unlimited (or God, Good, the Absolute, et cetera). We will never be satisfied or happy because the physical world is far too removed and imperfect to provide a connection to the Unlimited. The Christian stress on human sin (in contrast to God's perfection) and the Neoplatonist acceptance of an imperfect world (in opposition to the Unlimited) became intertwined during the decline of the Roman Empire, through the writings of Saint Augustine.

Augustine developed his views in this intellectual environment of frustration and withdrawal as Rome was being destroyed. For him, the Judeo-Christian God replaced Plato's search for Ideals and Plotinus' concept of the Unlimited. Good, then, became personified in the Creator—and human reason became a tool to (merely) solve earthly riddles. As humans, our uniqueness and goal in life became the quest to know and love God, and any hope of improving ourselves and our societies in this sin-ridden world became absurd.

Like Aristotle and Plato, Augustine argued that different parts of our soul provide us with capacities to do different things. The sensitive part of the soul drives us to satisfy our material needs, while the cognitive part allows us to deduce moral behavior through reason and, through contemplation, seek God. Like the Athenians, Augustine viewed the good life as a life of contemplation, and he warns us to avoid the sinful (desire and passion) earthly pleasures. Our uniqueness lies in our soul—a gift from God—and our time and energy should be subordinated to the contemplation of His goodness. Any other priorities, clearly, lend themselves to evil.

Like Plato, Augustine strictly limited the number of people who could be expected to actually accomplish their goal as human beings. By providing humans with various amounts of will, God has predetermined our capacity to avoid sin and pursue His goodness. With humans defined as inherently sinful, Augustine challenged us to live our lives in contemplation of God, but he recognized that few could and, ultimately, no human being can completely transcend the material body and its temptations until death—when the soul is freed to become one with God. Hence, while we are challenged to live our lives in contemplative leisure, there has been a significant alteration of our essence. For the Athenian philosophers, contemplative leisure as essence-pursuit was designed to promote the good life here on earth, and while the human capacity to actually accomplish this ideal was plagued by our animalistic drives, there were varying degrees of optimism concerning our ability to achieve this goal. For Augustine, the earthly, animal drives are also our weakness and the contemplation of God is our goal. But the alteration is obvious when Augustine slams the door on our ability to achieve any goodness on this earth. The spiritual afterlife (made possible by the sacrifice of Jesus) holds our rewards—and there is no way to improve an inherently evil material world. The "earthly city" is destined to be sinful, chaotic and violent.

With personal harmony and social peace impossible in this life, Augustine meshes the Stoics' concept of a world-wide community with Christianity to form the "city of God"—a community of believers to provide unity and fellowship that transcends political and cultural distinctions. In contrast to the total sin and chaos of the outer world, the community of believers provides us with what little peace and harmony we can look forward to before our deaths.

The religion of withdrawal faced an entirely new environment as it was gradually accepted by Rome and, then, found itself as the strongest organization still intact amid the ashes of the Empire. The community of believers became a highly bureaucratized and essentially Platonic structure that expanded to replace the Roman Empire with a "Catholic Christian" Empire, attempting to dominate Europe through the papacy. The spiritual leaders' involvement in secular affairs caused tension and contributed to numerous conflicts between Rome and political leaders throughout Europe. These tensions were exacerbated by internal accusations of corruption, the growth of secular culture and a number of scientific discoveries that discredited the Church's teachings. By the thirteenth century, the tension had reached crisis proportions.

In this environment (which can be viewed as a reemergence of the debates between Plato and Aristotle in the context of Roman Catholicism), Thomas Aquinas attempted to reconcile the competing factions. He synthesized Aristotle's Doctrine of Cause with Roman Catholicism by making God the First Cause of nature. As a result, the tension between science and religion was eased by suggesting that nature, as God's creation, offers a divinely-inspired system to be studied. Human reason (as opposed to Augustine's "will") also is a divine gift, so humans are obliged to improve their lives and societies—by rising above the shadowy cave of ignorance and sin. Hence, optimism for our earthly potential is reestablished, based on Aristotle's philosophy adapted to the Christian concept of God. The contemplation and understanding of nature, then, takes on religious overtones and secular life holds some meaning if we rationally act to improve it. Unlike God's other creations, we humans are blessed with the ability to understand our environment through active reason. We are constantly tempted by our lower drives but we have been provided with the capacity (reason) to rise above them.

In reestablishing the role of reason as a unique human capacity, Aquinas also stressed the need for a positive and active role of the state by arguing (along with Plato and Aristotle) that a proper state is needed to enhance the likelihood of personal and social improvement. But with all of this concern for earthly activity, Aquinas never strayed from his focus on God. Our ultimate goal of perfection awaits us in an afterlife, when the soul is united with God. In the meantime, our highest and truly human capacity is the contemplation of God's perfection. Again, the good person will devote all of his time and energy to leisure—our "ultimate end"—the contemplation of God.

Aquinas' remarkable synthesis maintained classical leisure as the primary human activity while altering the focus of contemplation from ourselves and nature to God. By separating, or alienating, us from the source of our perfection, an important twist was introduced into the classical legacy that became fully pronounced after the British Empiricists eliminated God from the realm of philosophy. With classical leisure altered to the point that the focus on God replaced the focus on humans, it became meaningless when God's existence was called into question: the importance of the distinctions between philosophy and theology are again clarified when we recognize that our theological separation from God (or Good) creates the tendency to stress human depravity and sin. Aquinas reconciled such negative perspectives with Aristotle's positive view of the human potential. But the sinful human as desire-driven economic animal reemerged with a vengeance during the course of the Protestant Reformation and the rise of capitalism.

Part III
Essence Denied: The Creation of Economic Man

> Practical men, who believe themselves to be quite exempt from any intellectual influences, are usually the slaves of some defunct economist. Madmen in authority . . . are distilling their frenzy from some academic scribbler of a few years back.
>
> John Maynard Keynes

Upon reflection, you may question the necessity of devoting so much time and space to such ancient and "impractical" views. And, without doubt, even the quickest survey of current attitudes toward leisure in our society suggests that if such views were ever important, their significance has been destroyed in our present social milieu. With the recognition that a) these ancient views were not only important but, in fact, critical dimensions of the western tradition, and b) they sound foreign (indeed, alien) to the modern ear, the significance of the following three chapters becomes clear. In them, we will attempt to clarify factors contributing to the destruction of the classical view of leisure, and clarify the dominant attitudes and values that came to replace it in the course of modern history.

To achieve this goal, we must discuss the myriad of changes generally associated with the making of the modern world. In short, factors involved in the changes that undermined the significance of classical leisure include some of the most important economic, religious, political, philosophical, and social changes that the world has ever experienced. Much of modern social science can trace its origins to the attempt to explain the complexities of the growth of the market economy and industrialization. And while we will note its impact on numerous dimensions of social reality, the destruction of the ideals associated with classical leisure serves as our primary focus. The following three chapters, then, delineate the development of the antithesis, or opposing perspective, to classical leisure.

A striking illustration of the inherent tension between the values of classical thought and those associated with the market economy can be seen in the contrast between the following quotations from Aquinas and Benjamin Franklin. Ask yourself how likely it would be that capitalism would flourish in a culture based on Aquinas' views. Then reflect on the impact of Franklin's perspectives on the values associated with classical leisure:

Aquinas: Properly speaking, commerce is the exchange of money for goods with a view to gain. . . . It is justly condemned, for it encourages the passion for money (*cupiditas lucri*) which is without limit and almost infinite. Therefore commerce, considered in itself, has something shameful about it.[1]

Franklin: Remember, that time is money. He that can earn ten shillings a day by his labour, and goes abroad, or sits idle, one half of that day, though he spends but sixpence during his diversion or idleness, ought not to reckon that the only expense; he has really spent, or rather thrown away, five shillings besides.

Remember this saying, The good paymaster is lord of another man's purse. He that is known to pay punctually and exactly to the time he promises, may at any time and on any occasion, raise all the money his friends can spare. This is sometimes of great use. After industry and frugality, nothing contributes more to the raising of a young man in the world than punctuality and justice in all his dealings; therefore never keep borrowed money an hour beyond the time you promised, lest a disappointment shut up your friend's purse forever.

He that idly loses five shillings' worth of time, loses five shillings, and might as prudently throw five shillings into the sea.[2]

It is difficult to imagine a more obvious conflict of perspectives. True to his philosophical origins, Aquinas was reflecting the classical tradition delineated in the preceding chapters. The fall of Athens and Rome was, to a high degree, precipitated by the "passion for money," just as the tribes of Israel were humiliated and enslaved when the ancient covenants were broken. Franklin, then, is turning his back on the advice and perspectives of both the ancient philosophers and the prophets: time, labor, and ethics seem, to him, to be completely subordinated to the accumulation of wealth. This focus on material desire as the driving force in life is, according to Max Weber's classic study, the essence of the capitalist "spirit." And as a result, virtually every dimension of human life—including knowledge, social standing, and leisure time—became subordinated to work and the pursuit of wealth.

In *The Protestant Ethic and the Spirit of Capitalism,* Weber stresses the importance of viewing the accumulation of wealth as an end in life itself. According to Weber, modern capitalism could never have flourished as long as the pursuit of material well-being was subordinated to any other goal, or value. Hence, the concepts of classical leisure developed by Plato, Aristotle and Aquinas, had to be attacked if capitalism (with its focus on the accumulation of wealth as the end, or goal, of life) was to flourish. Weber and his successors, notably R. H. Tawney, stress the importance of this subordination of all activity to economic pursuits as a critical distinction separating modern western societies from other cultures.

From Plato's perspective, then, modern society has permanently sealed the exit from the cave by stressing the importance of activity within it, and desire replaces reason in control of the chariot. Aristotle's and Aquinas' contemplation of higher forms would appear as merely "sitting idle," or wasting time.

Weber identifies attitudes associated with Protestantism (and, in particular, Calvinism) as the primary stimulant influencing the growth of modern capitalism. And while numerous critics have challenged his total focus on religious ideas, their criticism does not affect the conclusion that Calvinism played an important role. Tawney summarizes the role as follows:

It is the change of moral standards which converted the natural frailty of greed into an ornament of the spirit, and canonized as economic virtues habits which in earlier ages had been denounced as vices.[3]

This critical change in attitudes produced the following results:

> Religion has been converted from the keystone which holds together the social edifice into one department within it, and the idea of a rule of right is replaced by economic expediency as the arbiter of policy and the criterion of conduct. From a spiritual being, who, in order to survive, must devote a reasonable attention to economic interest, man seems sometimes to have become an economic animal, who will be prudent, nevertheless, if he takes due precautions to assure his spiritual well being.[4]

Tawney's overview sets the stage for the following three chapters, and moves us from the classical to the modern world—where economic considerations have replaced religion and philosophy as guides for human activity. Chapter Eight focuses on the key dimensions of economic, social and political change that laid the basis for the industrial revolution. Chapter Nine traces the corresponding patterns of thought from Martin Luther through John Locke. Chapter Ten begins with David Hume (after Hume's devastating critique of religion, taking "due precautions to assure spiritual well-being" also became a waste of time) and traces the progression of ideas through the French *philosophes* and Adam Smith. Witness, then, the contributions of theologians, philosophers and social scientists to the systematic destruction of the classical ideal of leisure.

References

1. Thomas Aquinas, *Summa Theologica,* IIa, IIae, quaest. LXXVII art. 4, quoted in Eugene Rice, Jr., *The Foundations of Early Modern Europe* (New York: W. W. Norton, 1970) p. 54.
2. Benjamin Franklin quoted in Max Weber, *The Protestant Ethic and the Spirit of Capitalism,* trans. Talcott Parsons (New York: Charles Scribner's Sons, 1958) pp. 48–50.
3. R.H. Tawney, Foreward to Weber, Ibid., p. 2.
4. R. H. Tawney, *Religion and the Rise of Capitalism* (Gloucester, Mass.: Peter Smith, 1962) p. 279. Originally published by Harcourt, Brace and World, 1922.

Chapter 8
The Market Economy and the Nation State

> No mistake about it, the travail was over and the market system had been born. The problem of survival was henceforth solved neither by custom nor by command, but by the free action of profit-seeking men bound together only by the market itself. The system was to be called capitalism. And the idea of gain which underlay it was so firmly rooted that men would soon vigorously affirm that it was an eternal and omnipotent attitude.
> The idea needed a philosophy.
>
> Robert Heilbroner

While Aquinas' synthesis of Aristotle and Catholicism might have bought the Church some time, it was not able to stop the tide of increasing secularization that swept through Europe in the fourteenth, fifteenth and sixteenth centuries. Marsillius of Padua was not alone in his Aristotelian/Averroist attacks on the temporal power of the Church. While the Dominicans were defending the papacy, the Franciscan Order in England was developing doctrines that, ultimately, led to the excommunication of many friars. The Franciscans' vow of poverty irked the papacy. In the thirteenth century, Roger Bacon stressed the importance of scientific experimentation to discover truth. In the fourteenth century, William of Occam denied the temporal power of the pope, criticized the doctrine of transubstantiation and openly defended the Franciscan vow of poverty. He was called to Rome and excommunicated—but he fled to Bavaria, where he and Marsillius joined forces in defense of the Emperor against the Pope. Hence, while Aquinas did his best to thwart the spread of rational and scientific attacks on the papacy by introducing the authority of Aristotle to support Rome, his accomplishment did not stop such attacks. And, as Bertrand Russell notes, his works may have actually undermined his goal:

> Plato's temperament was more religious than Aristotle's, and Christian theology had been, almost from the first, adapted to Platonism. Plato had taught that knowledge is not perception, but a kind of reminiscent vision; Aristotle was much more of an empiricist. Saint Thomas, little though he intended it, prepared the way for the return . . . to scientific observation.[1]

Our goal in this Chapter is to discuss the dimensions of the scientific, economic, political, and religious change that altered the course of human history and created the modern world. The period under consideration extends from the twelfth century to the eve of the French Revolution of 1789; it includes scientific and technological change, the growth of the market economy, the rise of the nation state and the Protestant Reformation. We will stress that these occurrences were intimately interrelated and key components of the destruction of the classical concept of leisure. Due to the complexity of the relationships between these changes, we will discuss each one separately, and then consider how they merged to contribute to the mosaic of the modern world; note that we are merely scratching the surface of a very complex series of events. For reasons that will become clear, we will focus on England as a case study of the intermingling of these factors. Following Russell's lead, we begin with the growth of scientific approaches to understanding.

The Scientific and Technological Revolutions

The resurgence of science in the Middle Ages can be viewed as both cause and effect in the transition to the modern world. The growing conflicts between secular and clerical authority, and increased tensions within the Church itself, triggered the search for alternative explanations that challenged the existing norms. These explanations, in turn, increased the previous conflicts and tensions. Fascination with the relationship between the earth and the heavens has served as a stimulant for both science and religion: recall that Thales was an astronomer, and the Babylonian preoccupation with celestial movement served as the basis of astrology. Thales argued that the earth is flat and floats on water. His view concerning the shape of the earth was generally accepted by the Babylonians and Egyptians but was challenged by the Pythagoreans and Aristotle—who argued that it is a sphere. But Aristotle also supported the common wisdom of his day and the empirical illusion that the earth is the center of the universe (the geocentric view). By the third century B.C., Aristarchus of Samos argued for a heliocentric view of the heavens (that the sun is stationary and the earth revolves around it), but this concept "was too far in advance of the time to receive general assent."[2] Hence, while there was disagreement on the shape of the earth, empirical observation and common sense convinced most observers that the earth was the stationary center of the universe. This view fit nicely with the concept of divine creation of the earth, and Claudius Ptolemy's arguments in support of the geocentric view were accepted by the Church.

Aristarchus (who was from Samos—the birthplace of Pythagoras, and it is interesting to note that some Pythagoreans believed that the earth circled around a great fire) developed his position at the great library, or museum, at Alexandria. Nearly 500,000 volumes of ancient Indian, Egyptian, Greek and Roman works were stored there, and the list of scholars associated with the library includes Euclid, Archimedes and Ptolemy. In addition to these mathematicians and natural scientists, the study of literature, physiology, anatomy, philosophy and geography flourished. The accomplishments of one geographer, Eratosthenes, are remarkable—given the limited amount of information available in the third century B.C.:

> He held the earth to be spheroidal and calculated its circumference by estimating the latitudes and distances apart of Syene and Meroe, two places on nearly the same meridian. . . . Eratosthenes argued from the similarity of the tides in the Indian and Atlantic Oceans that those oceans must be connected and the world of Europe-Asia-Africa an island, so that it should be possible to sail from Spain to India round the south of Africa. It was probably he who conjectured that the Atlantic might be divided by land running from north to south and inspired Seneca's prophecy of the discovery of a new world. Posidonius later rejected this idea, and, underestimating the size of the Earth, said that a man sailing west for 70,000 stades would come to India. This statement gave Columbus confidence.[3]

The growing power of the Ottoman Turks in the fifteenth century renewed interest in the works of ancient astronomers and geographers. The Turks put pressure on the overland trade routes that united Europe with southern Asia, threatening the importation of precious metals and spices. In this context, science became increasingly associated with techniques of practical application (Eratosthenes argued that the oceans were connected; Columbus took action on this proposition to discover a westward way to the east) and the basis was created for our modern focus on technological accomplishments.

Navigation

Arab influence in southwest Europe began to decline in the early fifteenth century, following the Portuguese victory at Ceuta (in North Africa, south of Gibralter); by the end of the century, Ferdinand and Isabella succeeded in uniting Spain, further weakening Arab influence. With Turkish pressure on the trade routes growing, and with port facilities adjacent to the Atlantic, Portugal and Spain embarked on a process of maritime expansion and exploration. Henry the Navigator, a Portuguese prince, became the patron of geographers and astronomers throughout Europe. With a new observatory and the remnants of the ancient geographers' works at their disposal, the resident scientists developed increasingly sophisticated charts and maps. In addition, a more precise compass was produced, new navigational techniques were introduced, and a new type of rigging was invented that enhanced the speed of European ships.

The Azores were discovered in 1419; Vasco de Gama sailed around the Cape of Good Hope (thereby avoiding the Turks) to India in 1497; in 1511 the Portuguese established a base on the Malay Peninsula; by 1513 they had pushed on to China. In 1491, Ferdinand and Isabella sent Columbus west to find the east and, in 1519, Magellan left Spain with five ships; nearly three years later, one returned after completing the first circumnavigation of the earth. Clearly, the earth was not flat.

The arrogance of imperialism is illustrated by the Treaty of Tordesillas in 1494, whereby Spain and Portugal created an imaginary north-south line and divided the entire world between them. Cortez conquered Mexico in 1521 and Pizarro took Peru in 1538. The discovery of the Americas prompted other countries to follow suit: John Cabot landed in Newfoundland in 1497, flying the English Flag, and the Frenchman Jacques Cartier was exploring the Saint Lawrence Seaway while Pizarro was conquering the Incas.

Gunpowder

A compass and a chart might allow for the creation of an empire, but they are of little help in maintaining it. Scholars have traced the origins of gunpowder in military technology to China in the tenth century, and while it is not well-established that Europe imported it from China (there were many technologies imported from the east, including paper-making), it is clear that the Europeans were more efficient in its military applications.[4] The cannon aboard the Europeans' ships opened the seas to their explorations and made it virtually impossible for people without such firepower to stop them. In 1513, a Portuguese naval captain wrote that "at the rumour of our coming the [native] ships all vanished and even the birds ceased to skim over the water."[5] And when Portugese ships arrived in Canton in 1517, a Chinese official noted that:

> The *Fo-lang-ki* are extremely dangerous because of their artillery. No weapon ever made since memorable antiquity is superior to their cannon.[6]

If the Chinese (who had previous experience with gunpowder) were intimidated by the Europeans' firepower, imagine the terror felt by the peoples of the Americas and Africa, who had never known its capacity for destruction.

The development of firearms also had an impact on the internal politics of Europe by contributing to the decline of feudalism. Recall that protection from invasion was a critical dimension of feudalism, and that the mounted knight and fortress were mainstays of the system. Members of the feudal nobility justified their rights based on the fact that they and their knights monopolized this military function. But the development of increasingly sophisticated weaponry made their castle walls vulnerable to attack—and a peasant, equipped with a musket, could blow the knight off his horse. With firearms, then, the realities of warfare began to change. Instead of a relatively small number of knights fighting comparatively limited battles, the outcome of conflicts was increasingly determined by large conscript or mercenary armies.

Centralizing Monarchs and the Commercial Classes

The changes in military techniques brought about by the introduction of new weaponry corresponded to the growth of centralizing monarchs in western Europe, who were in the process of extending their power over the lower nobility. Their task became easier as the state (as opposed to the feudal lords) began to monopolize military activities. But by abolishing the system of vassalage, the kings had created a new problem: financing their armies. Under feudal arrangements, it was the responsibility of the lower nobles to train and supply knights for service to their superiors. With the feudal bonds breaking down as a result of the kings' actions to centralize power, the nobility responded by attempting to rid themselves of their ancient obligations. Money, not personal obligations, was needed to finance the armies and navies of the emerging nation states. Hence, the monarchs' search for revenue began in earnest and an increase in direct taxes was needed. Meanwhile, other technological improvements—including the water wheel and windmill—were contributing to the efficiency of production and, hence, the growth of profits as a source for state revenue:

> In England the revenues of the Crown grew from about 140,000 pounds a year around 1510 to about 860,000 pounds a year around 1640. In France the revenues of the Crown rose from about 4 million livres around 1500 to about 31 million around 1610.[7]

These technological, economic, and political changes encouraged alliances between the centralizing monarchs and the commercial class. As commoners, merchants and manufacturers enjoyed little social status or political influence in feudal societies: the early capitalists were not the pillars of society, but the outcasts.[8] This new alliance promoted both the further development of the state and the growth of capitalism because the kings needed money and the commercial classes had it. Both kings and commercial interests desired to rid themselves of the ancient feudal norms that limited their power, and capitalism provided them with the opportunity to do so:

> With the share received as a stockholder in Sir Francis Drake's voyage of the *Golden Hynd,* Queen Elizabeth paid off all England's foreign debts, balanced the budget, and invested abroad.[9]

To the degree that the Church was associated with the feudal past (recall Aquinas' attack on commerce and greed, as well as the continued attempts by the Church to assert its political influence), it became an enemy of this alliance.

Science and Humanism: The Renaissance

With the expanding commercial interests and the increasingly powerful political forces added to the well-established line of critics of the Church (a line that included Martin Luther by the early sixteenth century), the challenges to Rome gained momentum. Nicolaus Copernicus added to this momentum in the sixteenth century when he reestablished Aristarchus' view of a heliocentric solar system. Initially encouraged to pursue his studies by Rome, he was probably fortunate that his conclusions were not fully published until shortly before his death. Galileo Galilei picked up where Copernicus left off and, with the aid of the newly-discovered telescope, he supported the heliocentric view. In addition, his observations suggested that the heavenly bodies were much like the earth—from Jupiter's moon, to "our own" moon's mountain ranges. From the Church's perspective, this was heresy; in 1633 the sale of Galileo's books was forbidden, he was tried by the Inquisition (he was 69 years old) and confined to his house for the remainder of his life. Later in the seventeenth century, refinements of the telescope allowed Tycho Brahe and Johannes Kepler to firmly establish the reality of a heliocentric system and explain patterns of planetary motion. During the same period, Isaac Newton combined his interest in gravity with Kepler's laws to argue that planetary orbits are maintained by gravity. He then invented an even more powerful telescope.

In fighting against the growth of astronomy, the Church seriously undermined its credibility. Beginning in 1616, when Copernicus' works were declared contrary to Holy Scripture, Rome denied the validity of the heliocentric view and suppressed those who advocated it (Kepler joined Brahe in Prague to avoid persecution by the Inquisition). Then, in 1757, the Church recanted its position and accepted what it had previously condemned as heresy. Again (recall Russell's suggestion), the tensions presented by the growth of science served to undermine the influence of the Church.

Leonardo da Vinci (1452–1519) personified the ideals of his time, due to his accomplishments in science, art, and engineering. To improve his art, he studied human anatomy and mathematics; to enhance his own understanding of the impact of art, he studied optics and the human eye. Leonardo, then, is generally considered to be the epitome of the well-rounded Renaissance man, and it is notable that the Greek word *arete,* meaning virtue, or excellence, serves as the root for this ideal. Building on Roger Bacon (circa 1214–1292) and anticipating Francis Bacon (1561–1626), Leonardo stressed the significance of empirical observation as the basis for properly understanding reality:

> Those sciences are vain and full of errors which are not born from experiment, the mother of all certainty, and which do not end with one clear experiment.[10]

The obvious message to those (like Aquinas) who deduced their thought from the writings of secular or clerical authorities was to test the knowledge inherited from the past instead of merely accepting it. Francis Bacon (lawyer, politician, philosopher of science, and advisor to English monarchs) extended this line of argument to attack the credibility of revealed theology and stress the significance of scientific inquiry into the observable reality of the material world.

The underlying tone of the Renaissance, then, was one of critical thought, science, and belief in the human potential. Science and reason emerged (or re-emerged from the ancient world—"Renaissance," literally translated, means "re-birth") as the dominant approaches to problems of the human condition, and an extremely positive attitude toward the human potential was established. The following quotations from some of the literary masters of the age illustrate this faith in the capacity of humans:

Man is rightly both called a great miracle, and judged a wonderful being indeed. Let a certain holy ambition invade our souls, so that, not content with the mediocre, we shall pant after the highest, and (since we may if we wish) toil with all our strength to follow it.

Pico della Mirandolla (1463–1494)

What a piece of work is man! how noble in reason! how infinite in faculty! in form and moving how express and admirable! in action how like an angel! in apprehension how like a god! the beauty of the world! the paragon of animals!

William Shakespeare (1546–1616) [11]

These themes suggest that the emphasis was shifting away from the worship of a supreme being toward the worship of the human potential, and the lines between the "City of God" and the "City of Man" were becoming blurred. Other influential writers were even more explicit in their attacks on the Church:

After the same manner a monk; I mean those lither, idol, lazy monks, doth not labour and work, as do the peasant and artificer; doth not ward and defend the country, as doth the man-of-war; cureth not the sick and diseased, as the physician doth; doth neither preach nor teach, as do the Evangelical doctors and school-masters; doth not import commodities and things necessary for the commonwealth, as the merchant doth. Therefore is it, that by and of all men they are hooted at, hated and abhorred.

Francois Rabelais (1495–1553)[12]

The growth of secular literature, then, can be identified as another factor that challenged the credibility of the Catholic Church and, hence, the feudal structures of Europe. By the middle of the fifteenth century, the development of movable type provided for the growth of the printing industry, making books available to a previously unimaginable number of readers.

Early Capitalism

To clearly identify the specific social changes that contributed to the rise of capitalism is a complex undertaking, due to the fact that:

There was no single massive cause. The new way of life grew inside the old, like a butterfly inside a chrysalis, and when the stir of life was strong enough it burst the old structure asunder. It was not great events, single adventures, individual laws, or powerful personalities which brought about the economic revolution. It was a process of internal growth.[13]

This process took place from the twelfth to the seventeenth century, as Europe's economic status changed from a supplier of raw materials (especially iron, timber and pitch) to the east, to an exporter of textiles, glass, paper, soap, and increasingly sophisticated manufactured goods.[14]

Sometime in the latter part of the twelfth century, much of Europe surpassed subsistence agriculture, i.e., a combination of factors (including the invention of a new type of plow) contributed to increased agricultural production, which provided for a surplus of goods. Surplus food supplies stimulated the growth of the market economy, as peasants sold their excess crops.[15] This increase in commerce (as a secondary focus of economic activity for the farmers) contributed to the growth of cities. The availability of sufficient food supplies to allow a growing number of people to work full time in non-agrarian occupations made the extension of manufacturing possible. The cities grew as centers of trade and manufacturing, with those adjacent to the major trade routes

94

(and, especially those with access to the sea and good port facilities) benefiting the most, due to their ability to expand both the internal and external market.

The growth of the European cities, which reached unprecedented levels in the thirteenth century, provided an alternative way of life for the peasants, who negotiated their way out of feudal obligations (or escaped them) for the excitement and opportunities of the new urban centers. The cities allowed for greater social mobility than was possible in the feudal countryside, and the class lines that did exist were less pronounced:

> The town was to the people of Europe from the eleventh to the thirteenth centuries what America was to Europeans in the nineteenth century. The town was the "frontier," a new and dynamic world where people felt they could break their ties with an unpleasant past, where people hoped they would find opportunities for economic and social success . . . and where there would be ample reward for initiative, daring, and industriousness.[16]

Hence, commerce prompted urbanization and urbanization brought about further advances in commercial activity. Capitalism could not have developed without a work force, and to the degree that the feudal nobility maintained its traditional powers (which included control over the peasants' movement), the process of economic development was delayed. Where feudal prerogatives broke down, peasant mobility was enhanced. Finally, the growth of urbanization was accompanied by a noticeable expansion of the population, providing even more potential merchants and manufacturers for the growing cities of Europe.

The Hanseatic League and Venice

Urban and economic growth stimulated the development of compacts and confederacies to further enhance trade. The Hanseatic League was chartered in 1158 to organize commercial activity among the cities on the Baltic Sea and the German river systems. By the fifteenth century, 160 cities were associated in the League, and trade was extended from Novgorod (Russia) to London, and from Sweden south into Germany. Meanwhile, Venice was becoming the increasingly dominant European power in the Mediterranean Sea. Forced to trade because of its peculiar location (built on and around a number of tiny islands, it had to import everything—including drinking water), Venice had influenced the southern flank of European commerce for several centuries. Venetian ties with the Byzantine Empire and southern Asia provided the major link between east and west. In the late thirteenth century, Venice defeated Genoa, its ancient commercial rival, and became the primary economic power in southern Europe. With the city government actively supporting every dimension of trade and Venice linking Europe with Asia, commerce, manufacturing and banking flourished. By the early fifteenth century, Venice "firmly controlled all the major commodity trades in the Mediterranean—pepper, spices, Syrian cotton, grain, wine and salt."[17]

By the beginning of the sixteenth century, the power of Venice was declining. The Turks' seizure of Constantinople in 1453 was a direct threat not only to the eastern trade routes, but to Venice's overseas possessions. The Venetians fought to maintain their influence but, in 1508, the Kings of France and Spain, along with the Pope and the German Emperor, united to strip Venice of its possessions in the western Mediterranean. Under attack from both sides, Venice was overpowered. The Hanseatic League also declined during this period, the victim of increased national consciousness among its members, and its lack of political unity. In 1478, the power of Muscovy was extended to Novgorod and Ivan III eliminated this northeastern link from the League. The growth of Swedish power gradually extended through the northern Baltic, and the Dutch fleet began to control the western portions. By 1630, most of the members had renounced the League, undermining the fledgling economic unity of northern Europe. Meanwhile, economic and political unity was on the rise in western Europe. Hence, while the original innovators of European capitalism were losing their power, their position was being filled by upstart capitalists in the northwest.

The sixteenth century is stressed by virtually all economic historians when they trace the realignment of economic power in Europe. Spain was able to hold out for another 100 years, but by the mid-seventeenth century, the declining supply of riches from the Americas was being funneled through Spain to purchase manufactured goods from northwest Europe:

> about this precious metal which comes to Spain from the Indies, the Spaniards say not without reason that it does on Spain as rain does on a roof—it pours on her and flows away.[18]

Much of the flow found its way to Holland and England, the two countries that, in turn, pushed the development of capitalism beyond its previous limits. If the growth of capitalism is approached geographically and chronologically, we can see that its focal point shifted from southern to northwestern Europe during the sixteenth and seventeenth centuries. In this new environment, which included the early commercialization of agriculture, sympathetic political leaders and Protestant attitudes toward work, the ground was prepared for the industrial revolution. Before turning to this second phase of the development of capitalism, we will note the impact of the Protestant Reformation.

The Protestant Reformation

The Protestant Reformation clearly deserves consideration as one of the most significant events in the history of Europe. We suggest that the importance of Luther and his successors is derived primarily from the fact that their attacks on the Catholic Church (which, as we have stressed, were certainly not unique) came at a time when both capitalism and secular political power were on the rise in western Europe. We have mentioned the long history of attacks on the Church, but they were made prior to the growth of these economic and political forces. Hence, a sort of "critical mass" emerged in the sixteenth century, when capitalism, secular power, and Luther's public condemnation of the papacy coincided. Venice is a clear illustration that the Church's critiques of capitalism were not always binding. Profit was the driving force in Venice, enabling its inhabitants to make the logistical arrangements for the Fourth Crusade, and manufacture and export lamps for Islamic mosques, complete with "pious Koranic inscriptions."[19] But Venice was a small city state with a limited population. Hence, it was fundamentally different from the nation states of western Europe, especially after the Reformation provided their inhabitants with a) a full-fledged attack on the credibility of the Catholic Church, and b) a theological basis to justify their economic pursuits.

We have already stressed the historical conflicts between the German emperors and the popes. Each side claimed to be the rightful heir to the Roman Empire, and continuous struggles occurred as a result. The attempt to maintain the ghost empire actually served to weaken the power of the German emperors, who spent so much time and effort trying to dominate central Europe and the Church that they were unable to unite their own people. Hence, while England and France had established nation states by the sixteenth century, Germany was still a combination of ghost empire and feudal society. As early as the twelfth and thirteenth centuries (when England and France were moving from feudalism toward the nation state) Frederick Barbarossa and Frederick II took steps to unite central Europe, but the diversity and size of the Empire worked against them. Hence, the ghost empire impeded the development of German political and economic unity until the early nineteenth century, when Napoleon abolished it.

In the early sixteenth century, the area that was to become Germany was highly fragmented politically and economically. Cities in the north and west belonged to the Hanseatic League and shared cultural and economic views with western Europe, while feudal systems in the rural areas maintained their ancient customs. As late as 1799, the area "consisted of 314 states and 1,475 estates, making a total of 1,789 independent and sovereign powers."[20] Martin Luther lived and studied in several of these diverse areas.

The actions of the popes during the early sixteenth century were bound to irritate Luther, who joined a monastic order in 1505 (at the age of 21) and vowed to devote his entire life to theological study and denial of worldly pleasures. From 1503 to 1513, Pope Julius II, who probably resorted to bribing the cardinals to become pope, pursued temporal power (recall the war against Venice in 1508) and used Church funds to hire artists, including Raphael and Michelangelo, to beautify the Vatican. His successor, Pope Leo X, was a member of the wealthy and politically influential Medici family and was involved in political conspiracies, the expansion of the college of cardinals, and the further expansion and adornment of the Vatican. These projects were not inexpensive:

> The income of the Pope rose from 170,000 ducats of "spiritual revenues" and 120,000 ducats of "temporal revenues" in 1480 to 202,000 ducats of "spiritual revenues" and 220,000 ducats of "temporal revenues" in 1525.[21]

The Church's economic status was guaranteed by a number of medieval traditions. In addition to the expected tithe of ten percent, an annual assessment was levied on every household. Church positions were sold, the Church's wealth was not taxable (significantly, this included land, and nearly one-third of the land in Germany was owned by the Church), and indulgences guaranteed that a steady flow of money would move out of northern Europe to southern Europe. It is obvious that in a context where secular powers were searching everywhere for revenues and the commercial classes were criticized as too greedy by an organization that did not contribute to alleviating their growing tax burden, forces hostile to the medieval traditions were growing. And as power increasingly shifted toward the commercial interests, the nobility began to eye the Church's land.

Luther's critiques of Church practices rapidly escalated into a full-scale attack on the Pope's credibility. His arguments in favor of the spiritual equality of all believers were interpreted by social reformers as a justification of temporal equality, setting the stage for longstanding social tensions to surface. In 1522 the impoverished lower nobility began seizing Church lands in Germany. The higher nobility and the Church united, and their armies crushed the revolt. In 1524 an even greater threat emerged from the peasants when they used the concept of spiritual equality to demand social equality. We will discuss the significance of Luther's reaction to these revolts in Chapter Nine. At this point, we will simply note that while Luther's argument stressed spiritual equality, he was vehemently opposed to any attempt to extend this view into the temporal realm.

The Reformation spread like wildfire. Anabaptists, interpreting the *Bible* to mean absolute equality of social status among believers, swelled the ranks of the peasant revolts. Ulrich Zwingli led another Protestant movement in Switzerland and was successful in establishing the practice that each local nobleman would determine the religion in his area. In 1530, the people of Geneva (a thriving commercial city) revolted and established a Protestant haven that attracted John Calvin, who had been forced to flee France. Calvinism spread quickly to France (Huguenots), England (Puritans), the Netherlands (Reformed Church) and Scotland (Presbyterians). By 1619, political and religious factors combined to split Europe into two camps, and the Thirty Years War devastated central Europe. In 1648, the Treaty of Westphalia ended the War, on the basis that each nation state would have a dominant state-chosen religion. Northwestern Europe became Protestant, while southern Europe remained Catholic; in Germany, each local prince retained the power to determine religion in his area. Hence, while the Reformation served to reinforce national identity in most of Europe, it was added to the historical factors that continued to undermine the unity of Germany.

The Netherlands

Like Venice, the Netherlands (a confederation of several small states divided into northern and southern regions) was surrounded by the sea, and was incapable of producing enough food to feed its inhabitants. Hence, commerce was necessary for survival, and the realities of geography and nature had a crucial impact on further development. The scarcity of land necessitated actions to increase crop yield, including crop rotation and the early use of fertilizer; windmill technology was developed to drain the soggy ground. The fact that half the country's grain supply had to be imported led farmers to grow cash crops (such as flax, hemp, hops and dye-plants), stimulating the early commercialization of agriculture.[22] The Dutch, then, were highly dependent on commercial activity as early as the sixteenth century, and the widespread commercialization of agriculture brought the majority of the society into the growth of commerce. Commercial activity tended to shift from the south (Bruge and Antwerp) to the north (Amsterdam) during the sixteenth century. Amsterdam's population grew from around 15,000 in 1500 to 180,000 in 1700.[23] The seventeenth century was the Netherlands' century in European commerce, due primarily to the fact that its inhabitants began to serve as the middlemen for world trade.

The Netherlands participated in the Hanseatic League until the mid-fifteenth century, when the Dutch moved to establish themselves as the dominant commercial power in the Baltic. The focus of trade included exports of fish, salt and wine, and imports of grain, timber, wool and flax.[24] Manufacturing and international trade grew hand in hand, as imports of raw materials were turned into manufactured goods and exported. These commercial traditions made the Netherlands a haven for refugees escaping the religious wars of the seventeenth century. The Dutch were staunch Protestants, mostly Calvinists, and prided themselves on their commercial expertise; from Weber's perspective, they tended to view the accumulation of wealth as an end in life. Reinforced by an influx of religious refugees and entrepreneurs, the situation was ripe for the emergence of modern capitalism:

> Amsterdam became the international market where one could find goods from all over the world—Japanese copper, Swedish copper, Baltic grain, Italian silk, French wines, Chinese porcelain, Brazilian coffee, oriental tea, Indonesian spices, Mexican silver. Amsterdam, in fact, became the main world market for a variety of products—from guns to diamonds, from sugar to porcelain—and the price quotations on the Amsterdam market dictated the prices on the other European markets.[25]

This remarkable extension of Dutch commerce was enhanced by the creation of the Dutch East India Company, which was organized in Amsterdam in 1587 and chartered by the government in 1602. The Portuguese also established an East India Company in 1587 but, by 1640, they had been totally overwhelmed by the commercial vitality and military strength of the Dutch. With the government-granted monopoly guaranteeing the East India Company control over Asian trade (along with military and civil power to enforce its decisions), the Dutch rapidly colonized southern Africa, defeated the Portuguese in Asia, and dominated Europe's trade with the east. From our perspective, the rise and decline of the Dutch and Portuguese East India Companies is a clear illustration of Weber's argument: the Catholic countries of southern Europe (where the process of European Empire began) could not compete with the Protestant north when virtually the entire Dutch society united around the pursuit of commerce. In short, remnants of feudalism stifled modern economic growth in southern Europe, opening the door for other societies to build the structure of modern capitalism. But the will and unity of a society could only spearhead the process until it was confronted by a society of equal will, combined with greater military and political power. Hence, while the Netherlands extended the Venetians' foundation of early capitalism into modernity, England rose to power in the late seventeenth century and overtook the Netherlands. The key to this process, it seems, lies in the fact that the English were motivated by attitudes similar to those in the Netherlands—but these attitudes were incorporated into the policy of a modern nation state in England. These commercial attitudes, combined with the support of the nation state, contributed to England's economic growth and made it the leader in capitalist development by the late seventeenth century.

The English East India Company was chartered by Queen Elizabeth I in 1600 and, whereas the continuity of the Dutch Company waivered in the eighteenth and nineteenth centuries, the English version continued intact until 1874. While the Company's political power over the colonies was gradually transferred to the government in the nineteenth century, its economic power was unchallenged. By 1654, English power in Asia was sufficient to weaken Dutch interests. Ten years later, the English extended their power in north America, seizing New Netherland and changing its name to New York. By 1801, the military conflicts between the Netherlands and England that began in the seventeenth century culminated in defeat of the Netherlands, and England established its dominance over the world economy.

England

In retrospect, England in the sixteenth century appears to have been ready made to lead Europe into modern capitalism. Politically, the nation state was well-established and the House of Commons provided a political institution for the commercial classes to express their economic interests. Feudalism had been gradually undermined, and the Catholic Church never enjoyed the degree of power that it held on the Continent. The commercialization of agriculture was well-established and manufacturing was widespread. During the reigns of Henry VII (1485–1509), Henry VIII (1509–1547) and Elizabeth I (1558–1603), these factors converged to lay the basis for English commercial power. There were setbacks and readjustments in the process of establishing the political dominance of the commercial interests but, by the late seventeenth century, most remnants of feudalism were weakened and the government was increasingly dominated by commercial interests.

Historical Setting

England's geographical location, size, and generally poor soil can be seen as important natural factors influencing its social and economic history. England was conquered by the Romans in

43 A.D. but, due to its distance from the center of the Empire, it was never as completely controlled as were areas on the Continent. Roman legions were withdrawn in 407, leaving the country open to invasions by Angles, Saxons and Jutes; in addition, the Danes, Vikings and Normans invaded the British Isles. The Norman conquest of 1066 marks a crucial turning point in English history. William the Conqueror established a system of government in which the feudal lords were subordinated to the king's power, thereby establishing an embryonic form of the modern nation state. In addition, he introduced primogeniture—a practice that allowed only the eldest sons of the nobility to inherit the family's title and estate. These practices set English feudalism apart from the Continent's norms in that a) the early establishment of a centralized monarchy weakened feudal practices, and b) primogeniture forced the younger sons of noble families to support themselves, and many of them gravitated toward commercial endeavors. The relatively poor soil of England necessitated the importation of food and, just as in Holland, this situation encouraged the early commercialization of agriculture.

The Political Setting

The monarchy established by William faced numerous challenges from the eleventh to the fifteenth centuries. Norman Barons revolted against William's rule in 1075, but they were defeated. In the twelfth century, Henry II came into conflict with the Church and Thomas Becket (the Archbishop of Canterbury) was murdered by the King's knights. In 1173, the monarch suppressed another revolt by the feudal nobility. The thirteenth century brought a weak King and increased influence of the Church and nobility; King John's struggle with Pope Innocent III resulted in the temporary establishment of papal supremacy in 1213 and three years later, the barons and archbishop forced concessions, via the Magna Carta, from the King. Significantly, one of the concessions was the limitation of the king's right to tax without the agreement of the barons. On at least two occasions during the thirteenth century, the barons refused to allocate money to pursue foreign adventures. Hence, from a background of a strong central monarch, England moved toward a system of checks on the kings' power. In 1295, the Model Parliament (including both nobility and commoners summoned from the countryside and towns) met to approve funds to finance a war against France. During the fourteenth century, Parliament's influence grew to the point that it became the established institution to check the arbitrary power of the monarchy. The division of Parliament into House of Lords (nobility and Church) and House of Commons was highly significant for the growth of capitalism: the commercial interests among the commoners had their own political institution.

Conflicts between the papacy and the monarch continued through the sixteenth century. In 1296, Edward I openly defied Pope Boniface VII and, in 1353, Parliament and the Monarch issued the Statute of Praeminure, which limited the influence of the Church in the king's affairs. The reign of Henry IV (1339–1413) included more feudal revolts, but they were suppressed. In 1410, Parliament attempted to strip the Church of its wealth and influence, but the King did not cooperate. Parliament's early attack on the Church illustrates a critical dimension of the unique situation in England: the commercial interests were not political outsiders attacking a strong feudal edifice; instead, they had their own institution through which they pursued their political, social, and economic objectives. The House of Commons gained increased influence in the late fifteenth century when a succession crisis caused the nobility to take sides against each other in the Wars of the Roses. Without a recognized monarch, and with the nobility destroying itself, the House of Commons remained intact, further establishing its legitimacy. Henry Tudor (Henry VII) defeated his rivals in 1485. He sponsored Cabot's voyage to north America, and reestablished the power of the central monarchy—a relatively easy accomplishment, given that the nobility had severely weakened itself during thirty years of fighting.[26]

The Social and Economic Setting

While primogeniture served to blur the distinctive class lines between nobility and commoner, it also required the second and third, et cetera, sons of the nobility to support themselves. Many of these disinherited nobles chose textile manufacturing as an occupation, which coincided with their elder brothers' control of landed estates on which sheep were raised. The wool trade, then, became the dominant focus of English economic development—with the wool produced on the estates and processed into cloth in the towns. Unlike other parts of Europe, where the nobility viewed commercialization as a threat, the economic interests of the nobility and commercial classes tended to coincide in England. Hence, the tension between the feudal countryside and the commercial towns was eased by this commonality of interests:

> Thus in England the chief carriers of what was eventually to be a modern and secular society were at this time fundamentally men of commerce in both the countryside and the towns.[27]

In 1348 the plague, or Black Death, reduced England's population by one quarter to one-third. Entire villages were depopulated, and some of the surviving nobility took advantage of the situation to extend their sheep runs. The massive decline in population put labor at a premium and many small farmers left the countryside to work as laborers in the towns. The availability of laborers was critical for the development of manufacturing, and the plague contributed to its growth: the nobility was released from its feudal ties to the peasantry, more land was available to raise more sheep and produce more wool, the manufacturers found workers to process the wool, and the nobility could temporarily hire the workers back when they were needed to shear the sheep. The plague did not destroy feudalism, but when added to the other factors in England, it contributed. During the fifteenth century, the practice of enclosing (fencing) common areas and turning agricultural land into sheep runs increased.[28] As a result of these enclosures (which continued through the nineteenth century), small farmers were increasingly forced off the land and into the towns to seek work wherever they could find it.

In addition to the plague, the fourteenth century included an important movement for religious reform, led by John Wycliffe. Wycliffe led an attack on the temporal power of the papacy and suggested that all Church authorities be subordinated to the monarchy. He denied the Church's right to tax, and went so far as to suggest that the Church's property be seized and distributed among the poor. He challenged the Church to return to its origins of simplicity and faith, stressed predestination, and challenged the sacramental practices (especially transubstantiation) of the Church. In short, he anticipated Luther by more than a century, and Luther acknowledged his influence. Just as Luther's ideas triggered a revolt by the peasants, Wycliffe's teachings became associated with the peasant revolt of 1381 in England. Like Saint Paul and Luther, Wycliffe's temporal loyalty was tied to the existing power structure and he refused to support the peasants' demands for equality—demands that he had helped to promote. The revolt was suppressed, but Lollardry (as Wycliffe's religious movement was called) went underground.

The Sixteenth and Seventeenth Centuries

Upon coming to power in 1509, Henry VIII ruled over a society with the following characteristics: 1) the monarchy was strong and the feudal nobility weak 2) the commercialization of agriculture and basic manufacturing were well established 3) the House of Commons represented the interests of the commercial classes 4) relations between Church and state had generally been resolved in favor of the monarchy, and a century-old religious movement had already delineated the basic arguments that would soon trigger the Protestant Reformation. The House of Commons was openly critical of papal influence, the Church's exemption from taxation, and the fact that the Church owned around 25 percent of the land.[29] The King's interest in an annulment of his marriage coincided with the interests of the commercially active segments of the society to trigger the break with Rome. Parliament debated and approved the ousting of the papacy in 1534, and:

> By 1550 nothing was left of the English monasteries and their immense estates. Not only were their lands confiscated and sold, but their furniture, silver, libraries, jewels, and other holdings were also dispersed.[30]

Henry got the first in a series of new wives and was declared the Supreme Head of the Church of England. The commercial interests got new lands for sheep runs and, hence, more raw material for the extension of the textile industry. "Between 1500 and 1550, the exports of 'short cloths' from the Port of London increased by 170 percent."[31] By the latter part of the century, significant exports were expanded to include glass, iron, and lead: The blast furnaces of England and Wales produced some 5,000 tons of iron ore per annum around 1550 and 18,000 tons per annum around 1600.[32]

While the break with Rome was complete by 1550, Henry VIII did not advocate religious toleration; he was as likely to burn radical Protestants as he was to execute defenders of the papacy. Gradually, in the course of the sixteenth century, a compromise emerged that temporarily mitigated the violence associated with the three dominant religious factions (Anglicans, Puritans, and Catholics). During the reign of Edward VI (1547–1553), the *Book of Common Prayer* was written to provide religious unity for the Anglicans. But Mary, his successor (1553–1558), attempted to move the society back toward Catholicism. Elizabeth I (1558–1603) forged a religious compromise by broadening the *Prayer Book* to allow for virtually all religious factions to interpret it as they pleased, and she reformed some of the Anglican practices to reflect the Puritan attacks on the Catholic remnants in the Church of England. This delicate balance continued through the reign of James I (1603–1625). Although James was somewhat sympathetic to Catholicism, he walked a fine line to maintain the religious compromise. The opposition to James I, then, was more political than religious, as the House of Commons was moving to strengthen its position by arguing that its traditional power of legislating was being threatened. But the possibility of religious and economic conflict overlapped this political tension, given that the issue used to attack the Monarch was taxes, and the House of Commons was increasingly dominated by Puritans:

> a large, able, and noisy minority . . . a minority that enlisted much of its support from the laity including many squires . . . and a large number of merchants and weavers.[33]

These political, economic and religious tensions burst forth during the reign of James' son, Charles I (1625–1642), culminating in his execution at the hands of the Puritan army in 1649.

The Civil War and Puritan Revolution

Unlike his father, Charles I was openly supportive of Catholicism and hostile to Calvinism. In addition, he led England into wars with France and Spain, necessitating the extension of taxes (referred to as "tonnage" and "poundage"). Hence, given the historical role of the House of Commons in financial affairs and its large Puritan membership, the mutual antagonisms between the Monarch and Parliament triggered civil war. In 1626, the Commons attacked the King by attempting to impeach Buckingham, his chief minister, and Parliament was dissolved. During the following three years, tensions grew as Parliament was repeatedly summoned and dissolved, Buckingham was assassinated, and the King continually demanded revenues. The King, again, ordered the House of Commons to adjourn on March 2, 1629—but its members refused to disperse. Instead, they passed the following resolutions (that clearly illustrate the overlap of religious, political and economic conflicts)—then they adjourned:

1 Whosoever brought in innovations of religion or favoured Popery . . . should be considered capital enemies to the kingdom.
2 Whosoever should advise the taking and levying of tonnage and poundage without parliamentary consent should likewise be considered capital enemies.
3 Any merchant who paid tonnage and poundage thus levied should be deemed a traitor to the liberties of England.[34]

Charles I was able to rule without Parliament for 11 years but, in 1640, he was forced to convene Parliament to raise funds to put down a rebellion in Scotland. This fatal mistake was the result of the King's attempt to formalize religious practices in Scotland—where a successful Calvinist (Presbyterian) revolt, led by John Knox, had established religious toleration for radical Protestants as early as 1560. Charles I tried to turn back the clock on 80 years of such toleration, and the Scots revolted. The Calvinist-dominated House of Commons refused to approve the taxation to support the King, and Parliament was dissolved again. With the Scots now invading northern England, the new Parliament escalated its attacks on the monarchy and, after failing in his attempt to have the parliamentary leaders arrested, Charles evacuated London in 1642. Parliament then raised its own army to fight against the King, and created a formal alliance with the Scots against the Royalists the following year. The Royalists were defeated in 1646, and parliament became the sole ruler of England. Calvinist discipline was rigid, and non-Puritans were persecuted. By the following year, Parliament was coming under increased attack by soldiers in the Puritan army, who were ordered to disband without receiving their back wages. The Second Civil War, or Puritan Revolution, began in 1648—when the army declared war on Parliament. In 1649, the monarchy and House of Lords were officially abolished by the House of Commons (which was controlled by the army) and Charles I was executed. Cromwell established a military dictatorship and pursued wars against the Scots and Dutch until his death in 1658. A non-military Parliament was restored in 1660, along with Stuart rule under Charles II (1660–1685). The King pursued the wars with the Dutch, allied England with Catholic France, and proceeded to alienate Parliament by the 1680s: Between the Roman Catholic atmosphere of the Court and the anti-papal fury of Parliament lay a deep gulf.[35] The commercial classes were on the verge of another parliamentary revolt when Charles II died. James II (1685–1689) continued the previous policy, strengthening the alliance with France and attempting to reestablish Catholic influence throughout England. By 1688, Parliament was sufficiently outraged and powerful to invite William of Orange to come to England from the Netherlands to become king. James II fled in December, 1688 and William and Mary were placed on the throne the following month. The traditional rule by the monarch and parliament had been restored, but with a critical twist: Parliament was sovereign and the king served at its request.

The commercial classes, supporters of the monarchy when the Tudors were defending commercial interests, had grown sufficiently strong to assert their power. With the commercial interests now dominating the political system, and Catholic influence eliminated, the economy expanded rapidly—preparing the way for the growth of the British Empire and the industrial revolution:

> Around 1640 re-exports had made up circa 18 percent of total exports. At the end of the century they were about 31 percent, and in 1773, about 37 percent.[36]

The significance of this expansion is further clarified when Britain's foreign trade is compared to other European countries:

Per Capita Foreign Trade, in £ Sterling

	1720	1750	1800
Great Britain	1.9	2.8	6.2
Holland and Belgium	1.3	1.7	3.2
Germany	.7	1.1	2.0
Portugal	1.0	1.1	1.2
Spain	1.3	1.6	1.1
France	.3	.5	1.1
Russia	.6	.7	1.0
Italy	.3	.4	.6[37]

France in the Eighteenth Century

The significance of these changes in England was recognized by observers throughout Europe, especially in France. Unlike England (with its traditions of limited monarchy, widespread commercialization of agriculture, weak nobility, and successful Reformation), France was ruled by an absolute monarch and extensive bureaucracy; commerce was rigidly controlled by the state; the nobility was politically weak but maintained medieval economic rights; the Catholic Church was economically powerful and supportive of the monarchy. Due, in part, to Huguenot (French Calvinists) support for England in the wars of the seventeenth century, religious toleration was suspended in 1685 and the Huguenots fled the country. France, then, is a classic illustration of feudal social norms reinforced by an absolute monarchy in the context of a nation state. As a result, bureaucratic inefficiency prevailed, manufacturing and commerce were hampered, and the state and Church became increasingly separated from the perspectives and demands generated from the society over which they ruled.

The tension between the old regime and society was enhanced by the events in England—events which were, clearly, the culmination of a social, political, and economic process that had developed over several centuries and, in retrospect, appear to be unique to the English experience. The groundwork, then, had not been laid in France; hence, when the seventeenth century revolutionary storm swept across the English Channel in the eighteenth century, it confronted different social, political, and economic realities, and we will return to the discussion of France in Chapter 11.

References

1. B. Russell, p. 478.
2. W. C. Dampier, *A History of Science,* 4th ed. (New York: Cambridge Univ. Press, 1971) p. 44.
3. Ibid., pp. 47–48.
4. John A. Garraty and Peter Gay, eds. *The Columbia History of the World* (New York: Harper and Row, 1972) pp. 323–324.
5. Carlo M. Cipolla, *Guns, Sails and Empires* (New York: Pantheon Books, 1965) p. 137.
6. Ibid., p. 108.
7. Carlo M. Cipolla, *Before the Industrial Revolution,* 2nd ed. (New York: W. W. Norton, 1980) p. 47.
8. R. Heilbroner, p. 13.
9. Ibid., p. 21.
10. Leonardo da Vinci, quoted in W. C. Dampier, p. 105.
11. Mirandolla's *The Dignity of Man* is reprinted in R. Warnock and G. K. Anderson, eds. *Centuries of Transition,* Book 2 of *The World in Literature* (Chicago: Scott, Foresman and Co., 1950) pp. 292–293. Shakespeare is quoted in Garraty and Gay, p. 504.
12. Rabelais, *Gargantua and Pantagruel* in R. Warnock and G. K. Anderson, p. 321.
13. R. Heilbroner, pp. 20–21.
14. See C. Cipolla *Before the Industrial Revolution,* pp. 220–221.
15. Fernand Braudel, *The Perspective of the World,* trans. S. Reynolds, Vol. III of *Civilization and Capitalism* (New York: Harper and Row, 1984) pp. 94–96.
16. C. Cipolla, *Before the Industrial Revolution,* p. 146.
17. F. Braudel, p. 123.
18. C. Cipolla, *Before the Industrial Revolution,* p. 252.
19. Ibid., p. 222.
20. Koppel Pinson, *Modern Germany,* 2nd ed. (New York: Macmillan, 1966) p. 5.
21. P. Patner, "The Budget of the Roman Church in the Renaissance Period," in E. F. Jacob, ed., *Italian Renaissance Studies,* quoted in Cipolla, *Before The Industrial Revolution,* p. 47.
22. F. Braudel, pp. 178–179.
23. C. Cipolla, *Before the Industrial Revolution,* p. 303.
24. Ibid., p. 265.
25. Ibid., p. 268.
26. For elaboration, see G. M. Trevelyan, *A Shortened History of England* (Baltimore, Md.: Penguin Books, 1959). For a quick reference, see the Chronological Outline, pp. 561–586. Originally published in 1942, Longmans, Green and Company.
27. Barrington Moore, Jr., *Social Origins of Dictatorship and Democracy* (Boston: Beacon Press, 1966) p. 13.
28. Ibid., pp. 9–10.
29. C. Cipolla, *Before the Industrial Revolution.* p. 57.
30. Ibid., p. 58.
31. Ibid., p. 279.
32. Ibid., p. 282.
33. Maurice Ashley, *England in the Seventeenth Century,* 3rd ed. (Baltimore, Md.: Penguin Books, 1961) p. 26.
34. Ibid., p. 64.
35. Ibid., p. 135.
36. R. Davis, "English Foreign Trade 1700–1774," in W. E. Minchinton, ed. *The Growth of English Overseas Trade in the Seventeenth and Eighteenth Centuries,* quoted in C. Cipolla, *Before the Industrial Revolution,* p. 292.
37. W. W. Rostow, *How It All Began* (New York: McGraw-Hill, 1975) p. 128.

Chapter 9
Economic Man: The Calling, Natural Rights, and Labor

The new economic forces that were changing the social and political structures of northern Europe were antithetical to the values of medieval society. To justify the rise of these forces, a new moral perspective had to be formulated—and John Locke, building on the background of the Protestant Reformation, rose to the occasion. We have chosen four important individuals—Martin Luther, John Calvin, John Locke and Bernard de Mandeville—to illustrate the gradual unfolding of the new morality.

In the early years of the sixteenth century, Martin Luther led a spiritual revolution in Germany that contributed to the process by undermining the credibility of the Catholic Church—the primary intellectual defender of medieval norms. Luther's attack on the papacy undermined the authority of Rome to defend anything. John Calvin's followers turned the spiritual revolution into a material revolution by associating the values of capitalism with God's grace. John Locke, closely associated with the Glorious Revolution in 1688, replaced God's grace with human reason and natural law, and argued that labor determines value. Bernard de Mandeville took these perspectives to their crass, but logical end: the state and society exist for the benefit of the wealthy. Hence, the accumulation of wealth became the driving force in life, and the classical concept of leisure was relegated to a meaningless and unproductive past, as economic man gradually replaced contemplative man.

The Protestant Reformation

The Roman Catholic Church created a unity between individual and state upon the propositions that people strive for good and that spiritual well-being takes precedence over material well-being. With these suppositions, it developed a hierarchy of authority to interpret scripture and administer sacraments. But, by the thirteenth century, this hierarchy appeared to be more concerned about its own material comfort than about the spiritual well-being of its followers. As criticism mounted, the Church instituted the Inquisition—yet accusations continued, fueled both by papal abuses and changes in the secular sphere of life. The flowering of the Renaissance, new scientific discoveries and technological inventions, the rise of capitalism, growing nationalism, and the spread of literacy compounded to jeopardize not only the credibility of the Catholic Church, but the entire medieval structure. Finally, these pressures found a focal point—the Protestant Reformation.

Martin Luther

Germany's conflict with the Roman Church was a historical reality; initially based on tensions between the emperors and the popes, this conflict had spread through many segments of society.

In the early 15th century, John Huss of Bohemia (following the example of John Wycliffe in England) urged the Church to reform its ways or else the secular faithful would take matters into their own hands. In response, the Church burned both Huss and his writings, causing a revolt in Bohemia. Concerned but undaunted, the papacy continued its policies, and 16 years later Bohemia returned to the fold. By the eve of Martin Luther's spiritual revolution there was widespread popular resentment toward Church claims of clerical immunity from civil legislation, exemption from taxation, and authority over emperors. In addition, the Catholic Church in the area that is now Germany was the richest in Europe—possessing nearly a third of the land.[1]

One day, during the summer of 1505, Martin Luther was knocked to the ground by a bolt of lightning. As the story goes, this experience frightened him so much that he became an Augustinian monk—devoting himself completely to monastic discipline and study of the scriptures. Unlike most of his monastic brothers, Luther's educational background was in a secular environment— he received his masters degree in February 1505, and was studying law at the time of his brush with lightning. This secular background might have stimulated his theological interest in William of Occam's arguments which, as we have noted, were highly critical of the temporal power of the papacy and the elaborate sacraments of the Church. In 1507 Luther was ordained a priest; in 1512 he received his doctorate in theology and became professor of biblical theology at the University of Wittenberg.

Like Paul and Augustine before him, Luther subscribed to the theological belief that predestination, rather than good works (fasting, pilgrimage, prayer, indulgences, et cetera), was the determinant of salvation. Hence, no amount of good behavior could influence a person's destiny to go to heaven or hell. But Luther was troubled about the uncertainty of salvation. As a pious monk and priest, he found release in St. Paul's Epistle to the Romans: The just shall live by faith.[2] Luther recalled his breakthrough as follows:

> I greatly longed to understand Paul's Epistle to the Romans and nothing stood in the way but that one expression, "the justice of God," . . . My situation was that, although an impeccable monk, I stood before God as a sinner troubled in conscience, and I had no confidence that my merit would assuage him. . . .
> Night and day I pondered until I saw the connection. . . . Then I grasped that justice of God is that righteousness by which through grace and sheer mercy God justifies us through faith.[3]

Through faith in God's justice, people receive God's grace and love. Hence, faith (as opposed to the good works associated with practical virtue) is the mark of a good person, and Luther condemned Aquinas for accepting reason and trying to harmonize Christianity with the philosophy of Aristotle.

Luther's reliance on faith is essential when considering the disparity between human beings and God. All virtue, truth and goodness belong to God, and all vice, falsity and evil belong to human beings. God is strong and we are weak and depraved; the intellect is blind to God's truth; the human will is free only to choose between degrees of sin. We are powerless and insignificant when compared to God, and we can only find relief in total submission.

The influence of Paul and Augustine can also be seen in Luther's views toward authority; secular authority is supreme regarding temporal matters, and the *Bible* is supreme regarding spiritual matters. From this position he undermined the authority of the papacy in two ways. First, he recognized the autonomy of the German nobility. Second, he made each Christian a priest because each has the right to interpret scripture in his or her own way. Another important aspect of his position is the Christian "calling," which restrains a person's worldly activity to his or her "station" in life. Founded in God's predetermined universal plan and His infinite (but incomprehensible) justice, the calling tends to justify existing political and social structures.

Luther openly confronted papal authority in 1517 when Pope Leo X sold a high position to the German Prince of Brandenburg. To raise money to pay for the position, the practice of indulgences was extended to allow redemption for future sins, as well as redemption for souls already in purgatory. Entering Wittenberg, the indulgence vendor sang, "As soon as the coin in the coffer rings, the soul from purgatory springs."[4] Luther responded to this crass practice by posting his Ninety-Five Theses to the door of the castle church in Wittenberg. Immediately there was popular support for this bold step and the sale of indulgences declined. Sentiment in favor of the Church suggested that Luther disseminated "Bohemian Poison," a reference to Huss. Friction grew and the Church arranged for an ecclesiastical trial. Demanding that Luther recant several points of his Ninety-Five Theses, the Church defended the righteousness of its position:

> The treasury of the Church from which the Pope grants indulgences . . . is not this of Christ and the saints because these always and without the Pope bring grace to the inward man and the cross, death and hell to the outward man?[5]

Under guarantee of safe conduct, Luther appeared at the trial but he refused to recant. In 1520 he was excommunicated; he retaliated by publicly burning the papal bull and books on scholastic theology. Declared an outlaw by the Emperor and a heretic by the Papacy, Luther found refuge in Saxony, where he was protected by a number of princes.

Luther's zeal for spiritual equality was interpreted by the peasantry as sanctioning social equality. In 1524, peasants in Central Europe united, refusing to pay taxes to state, church and feudal princes; in addition, they circulated articles demanding their freedom. In pursuing religious reform, Luther lent credibility to a social and political revolution aimed, in part, at the princes who were protecting him. The peasant revolts were widespread and bloody, but not as violent as the reaction against them. The revolts were suppressed by 1525, with Luther (a religious rebel) condemning the political rebels of central Europe. His response to the peasants reveals his contempt for their demands for earthly equality:

> That is making Christian liberty an utterly carnal thing. Did not Abraham and other patriarchs and prophets have slaves? . . . Therefore this article is dead and against the Gospel. It is a piece of robbery by which every man takes from his lord the body, which has become the lord's property. . . . This article would make all men equal, and turn the spiritual kingdom of Christ into a worldly external kingdom.[6]

The nobility's success was complete, and Luther managed to close the floodgates that he had opened—but the idea of spiritual equality remained to stimulate demands for social equality throughout the following centuries.

The lower nobility of Germany was attracted to Luther because he distrusted commercial activity and was content to preserve an agrarian society. The nobles' world had lost its predictability, as they watched the economic forces of early capitalism grow. In desperation they turned to Luther, seeing in his theology a way to arrest the breakdown of medieval order and secure their status as their calling. Unlike the English nobility, which tended to participate in the commercialization of agriculture (the first step in the development of capitalism), the German nobility attempted to maintain feudal social and economic practices.

John Calvin

John Calvin's parents lived in Noyon, France, at the time of his birth in 1509. His father, a clerical worker, encouraged his son to study theology and, in 1523, the young Calvin enrolled at the University of Paris. After receiving a master of arts degree in 1528, he abandoned theology for the study of law. During the course of his studies at Orleans, he was introduced to Luther's ideas. After receiving his law degree he devoted himself to studying language and literature while he continued to circulate among scholars and clerics sympathetic to Luther. By 1534, Calvin's associations raised the suspicions of Church and civil authorities, and he was forced to flee Paris. During that same year he had a "sudden conversion" to the Protestant faith and began his active role in the Reformation. In 1536, Calvin wrote *Institutes of the Christian Religion*—a plea for the acceptance of Protestant teachings throughout Europe. Later that year, while on a journey from Paris to Strasbourg, he was diverted to Geneva—where, without warning, he was chosen to lead the Reformed Church.

Like Luther, Calvin's theology rings with the sound of Paul and Augustine. He rejected the contemplative life, the purity of reason, and ignorance as the cause of sin. Instead, he proposed that we are predestined for heaven or hell, and that no amount of good works can affect one's salvation. The cause of our predicament is rooted in the original sin of Adam and Eve. Satan tempted Eve, Eve tempted Adam, and their disobedience, for Calvin, demonstrated the evil of human nature and the loss of free will. But God is merciful and has chosen some human beings to be saved, giving them faith in their redemption.

The opposite of human depravity is God's greatness, an almighty mystery that governs all the universe for all time. In comparison to God, human existence is insignificant. Nothing is left for us but to submit to God's will, which is to glorify Him in this world by pursuing our calling: the Lord enjoins each one of us, in all the actions of His life, to have regard to His own calling.[7] The human mind is restless and can lead a person into "folly and rashness;" only by following God's will can such confusion be avoided. God, then, has assigned each of us a "mode of life," or "vocation." "Each man's mode of life, therefore, is a kind of station assigned to him by the Lord, that he may not be driven about at random all his life."[8] And to the degree that each person fulfills his or her Christian calling (being industrious and useful in the affairs of everyday life), unity between individual and society is established.

Just as Augustine distinguished between the earthly city and eternal city, Calvin distinguished between the visible and invisible church. Those elected to heaven (whether still unborn, alive or dead) represent the invisible, true church—while the visible includes all living church members (elected and damned).

When Calvin entered Geneva in 1536, he carried the belief that God had a grand scheme for His chosen people. And when Calvin accepted the commission to lead Geneva, he believed that God's plan could be realized there. His task was to create the "City of God," inhabited by God's elected. Seeing how tolerance of differing religious beliefs fragmented communities in the past, Calvin unified church, state and education under the banner of the Reformed Church. He gave the church the power to discipline immoral behavior, excommunicate, and force nonmembers out of the city. Moral and religious infractions were first punished by reprimand, then fines, then imprisonment, and then banishment. Serious moral violations (such as adultery, blasphemy, heresy and idolatry) could result in exile or death. The Genevans were to be dedicated to the glory of God; to assist them, every aspect of life was regulated—from the color of clothing to the number of dishes permissible at a meal.

Calvin's views toward economics reflected his religious views. The economy of Geneva was as regulated as its religious and social life. While he recognized the necessity of capital, credit, banking and finance, he instituted strict laws to regulate their use. As a further deterrent to excessive greed, he sanctioned the virtues of diligence, frugality, sobriety and thrift. These economic dimensions of Calvinism appealed to the small merchant and constituted one more step in the direction of the modern economy.

Protestantism was already established in Geneva when Calvin arrived; thus, the implementation of his religious doctrine was a peaceful process. When John Knox (a Scottish Protestant) fled to Geneva in 1554, the city had the appearance of an ideal Christian community. Taken by the accomplishments of Calvin, he decided to emulate them in his native Scotland. But Scotland was Catholic, prompting Knox to preach violent revolution as a means to religious freedom. Knox and his followers considered themselves among the elect, and Catholicism composed of the damned. In 1559 Knox returned to Scotland to help lead the revolt; the Scottish Monarch sought aid from Catholic France, and Knox enlisted assistance from Protestant England. The Protestants won and, in 1560, the first General Assembly of the Reformed Chruch was held in Edinburgh. Significantly, John Knox's open rebellion made revolution a religious duty when papal interests dominate society.[9]

The Calling

One of the critical views introduced by Luther and Calvin was the importance they placed upon work. Termed the calling, it refers to the role God has chosen for each of us in this world. Weber defines the calling as "a life-task, a definite field in which to work."[10] Seeing no equivalent concept in either classical Greece or medieval Catholicism, he suggests that its source comes from Protestant *Bible* translations, "through the spirit of the translator, not that of the original."[11] The calling directs morality toward worldly activity rather than religious contemplation or rigid monastic life. Although, at least in Calvin's notion, a semblance of monkish self-denial appears to have been retained.

Martin Luther condemned the monastic life because it avoided secular responsibilities. People can only satisfy God's will by fulfilling worldly duties, and anything else is selfishness. For him, the true Christian calling is found in labor—but it is restricted to the satisfaction of personal needs. Like St. Paul, he considered any additional material gain (accumulated at the expense of others) a testimony to the lack of grace. True to Catholic tradition, he remained opposed to usury and interest. For Luther, each of us has a station in life, prescribed by Divine providence, and our duty in life is to pursue it with our utmost ability.

Essentially, Luther's calling offered no assistance to those interested in changing economic and social conditions. His tie to the nobility and authority supports forgiveness, contrition, and negotiation as a means of solving social and religious conflicts. Only peaceful resolution coincides with God's will, and rebellion should be suppressed with the sword. Human depravity must be regulated by government, laws and punishment; he imagined only complete chaos if the peasant revolts succeeded. While he was, possibly, sympathetic to the horrid conditions of German peasant life, earthly conditions were insignificant in comparison to questions of eternal salvation. Unlike the architect of Geneva's reformation, Luther's preaching retained many medieval Catholic traditions (such as emphasis on the after-life, repentance for sins, and individual spontaneity).

John Calvin turned away from Catholic tradition and focused his attention on the secular world where, he believed, atonement for sin was impossible. To guarantee moral conduct, life must be governed by social and religious regulation, and individual self-control. From Calvin's perspective, the world exists for the glorification of God. Human labor and moral living, not spiritual mysticism, demonstrate brotherly love and God's glory. The problem, though, lies in the fact that "the mind of man is so completely alienated from the righteousness of God that it conceives, desires, and undertakes everything that is impious, perverse, base, impure, and flagitious."[12] To bring human behavior in line with its true earthly task, Calvin instituted strict moral codes to govern domestic activity and sanctioned punctuality, industriousness and frugality to promote consistency in work. The goal was to mold methodical, impersonal, objective people striving for moral and material success as a means of controlling our inherently evil and chaotic human drives.

John Locke

John Locke was born in 1632, seventeen years before Charles I was beheaded. His father, a Puritan attorney, instilled in his son the traditional Calvinist virtues and the political idea of popular sovereignty. Locke attended Christ College, Oxford, receiving a B. A. in 1656 and an M. A. in 1658. After a time of tutoring and lecturing, he took up the study of medicine and obtained employment with the Earl of Shaftesbury—a leader of the Whigs—who represented the commercial interests in Parliament. Immediately, Locke found himself in the midst of English politics. As strain between the Parliament and Catholic King (Charles II) intensified, Shaftesbury was arrested. Fearing for his own welfare, Locke sought refuge in Holland in 1683.

Theory of Knowledge

While in Holland, Locke finished his *Essay Concerning Human Understanding*—culminating twenty years of work. Published in 1690, it suggested that all knowledge is the product of experience. There are, says Locke, three levels of knowledge. The lowest level (sensitive) is merely a personal opinion about how things affect us (for example, water may be pleasurably soothing or painfully cold, but water, in itself, is not pleasure or pain). At the second level (intuitive) there is no disagreement regarding truth (for example, the perception that a circle is not a square, or two is more than one); such knowledge is self-evident. The highest level (demonstrative) is reached when the relationship between a series of intuitions and sensations can be verified.

For Locke, the mind is a blank tablet where experience writes ideas. There are two types of ideas: simple and compound. Simple ideas (primary and secondary) comprise the sensitive and intuitive levels of knowledge. Secondary simple ideas reflect the object's ability to produce sensation (for example, water's ability to cause pain) and refers to qualities such as color, sound and taste. Primary simple ideas reflect those qualities which belong to the object (namely solidity, extension, shape, motion and number). Within simple ideas we distinguish between reality and appearance, and knowledge and opinion; if an object appears to have color (secondary simple idea), in reality it has no color; but if an object appears to have shape (primary simple idea), it really has shape. Simple ideas relate together to form a compound idea; for example, the compound idea of a tree is the result of many simple ideas (shape, solidity, color, et cetera). Demonstrative knowledge, then, is comprised of compound ideas which are formed by simple ideas.

In Locke's theory, the classical notion of "innate ideas" is rejected, and with it, the tradition of Platonic ideals. Reality and truth are of this world, not dependent on another realm. The mind is simply a container for ideas, having no inherent faculties (such as creative thought or free will). God exists and He has a design for the universe, but it cannot be ascertained through religious contemplation or spiritual vision. Contemplative thought, as any thought, is only a combination of ideas derived from experience. While there are objective, natural laws to explain the world and guide our behavior, they are known from experience. The year before his *Essay* was published, Locke hastened back to England; the "Glorious Revolution" had taken place.

Individual, Society and the State

While Locke was in Holland he enjoyed the companionship of other English exiles, creating an atmosphere that probably reinforced many of his views on human nature. People in their primitive, true state of nature, says Locke, are unencumbered in their calling to labor and free to exercise their natural rights of life, liberty and property. Such a condition is the law of nature; for "God, who hath given the World to Men in common, hath also given them reason to make use of it to the best advantage of Life, and convenience."[13]

Limits to Human Reason. According to Locke, an all consuming desire to accumulate and use property dominates human rationality. When property becomes scarce, such desire will ignore the law of nature and threaten natural rights. "For though the Law of Nature be plain and intelligible to all rational Creatures; yet Men being biased by their interest . . . are not apt to allow of it as a law binding to them."[14] Human nature, then, cannot be trusted to curb selfishness and abide by natural law; for Locke, reason is a tool of self-interest, not a mechanism to control desire. In view of this predicament, rational people form political states to protect their right to property. This is as it should be, states Locke, because God wills that the "Industrious and Rational" should benefit from the use of their property:

> God gave the World to Men in Common; but since he gave it them for their benefit, and the greatest Conveniences of Life they were capable to draw from it, it cannot be supposed he meant it should always remain common and uncultivated. He gave it to the use of the Industrious and Rational, (and *Labour* was to be *his Title* to it;) not to the Fancy or Covetousness of the Quarrelsom and Contentious.[15]

Right of Appropriation. When Locke arrived in England after the revolution, he was anxious to defend the expulsion of James II by Parliament. His *Second Treatise of Government,* published in 1690, argues that "Government has no other end but the preservation of Property."[16] Serving as the means to express human creativity, and the original justification for the state, property is at the very core of Locke's thought: the right of property precedes both society and state. God gave the earth and its fruits to human beings for their support and comfort. And to benefit from God's gift, an individual must be able to appropriate it. Rightful appropriation is determined by an individual's labor, says Locke:

> Though the Earth, and all inferior Creatures be common to all Men, yet every Man has a *Property* in his own *Person.* This no Body has any Right to but himself. The *Labour* of his Body, and the *Work* of his Hands, we may say, are properly his. Whatsoever then he removes out of the State that Nature hath provided, and left it in, he hath mixed his *Labour* with, and joyned to it something that is his own, and thereby makes it his *Property.* It being by him removed from the common state Nature placed it in, hath by this *Labour* something annexed to it, that excludes the common right of other Men. For this *Labour* being the unquestionable Property of the Labourer, no Man but he can have a right to what that is once joyned to, at least where there is enough, and as good left in common for others.[17]

Limits to appropriation. To protect the right of appropriation there are three traditional moral limitations: 1) an individual appropriation "must leave enough and as good for others," 2) an individual must not produce more than can be consumed before it spoils, and 3) "the rightful appropriation appears to be limited to the amount a man can procure with his own labour."[18]

Locke observed that in societies where money is not used, these limitations are obviously valid because there is always unappropriated land. But, wherever money has come into use, there ceases to be unappropriated land and, as a result, traditional moral limits are no longer applicable. Yet, Locke argues, this does not mean that such societies are living outside of natural law. The reason for limits on appropriation was to ensure that others could procure life's necessities. The invention of money justifies appropriation beyond initial limits, because commercialization increases productivity, enhancing the living conditions of everyone in society. The spoilage limitation does not apply to money since, unlike produce, it will not spoil; but the intention of its acquisition should be to supply capital for economic growth, not to hoard or spend extravagantly. Locke recognized that the concentration of land and money creates, of necessity, a wage-earning class. But if people's labor is considered their property which can be freely and morally sold—and if the labor sold becomes the property of the buyer, then both buyer and seller (capitalist and worker) are justified in procuring its fruits:

> Thus the Grass my Horse has bit; the Turfs my Servant has cut; and the Ore I have digg'd in any place where I have a right to them in common with others, become my *Property,* without the assignation or consent of any body. The *Labour* that was mine, removing them out of that common state they were in, hath *fixed* my *Property* in them.[19]

Capitalists (employers), then, may rightly benefit from more than just their individual work, because they can appropriate the labor of others as their property.

Locke attempted to take the moral limits which governed accumulation in feudal society and apply them to a market economy. By reinterpreting these limits (property, spoilage, labor), which previously restricted capitalism, he circumvented the traditional belief that the earth and its fruits were given to all people for common use, providing a moral foundation for the commercial interests. His mission accomplished, Locke retired to a career of government service and continual revision of his manuscripts.

Qualification of Natural Rights. Inherent in John Locke's political theory is a division between people in terms of natural rights, which is ultimately manifested in a class separation. In the beginning, where common property is abundant, each person has equal natural rights and is the sole proprietor of self. Over the course of time, property is appropriated by rational people, leaving the non-rational and depraved propertyless. Because of this inequity, the propertyless necessarily become dependent upon the propertied. At this point, the state arises to protect the possessions of the propertied class and, in so doing, perpetuates a class distinction based on unequal possessions. Essentially, the function of government is to act as a police agency to protect the propertied interests ("Industrious and Rational") from the remainder of society ("Quarrelsom and Contentious").

The propertyless comprise the working class, and since they are necessary members of the state, they fall within its jurisdiction. Yet because they are non-rational and depraved, they should not be granted full citizenship. In addition, because they are lazy and corrupt, any idle time will result in thoughts of revolution (Locke seems to reserve the right of rebellion for the commercial class). Thus, their wages should be no more than what is needed to provide minimum subsistence, "the labourer's share [of the national income], being seldom more than a bare subsistence, never allows that body of men, time, or opportunity to raise their thoughts above that."[20] Living hand to mouth, they will not be able to think about anything but getting by. On the other hand, the propertied commercial class, in providing for the workers' subsistence, is justified in acquiring land and generating profits to an unlimited degree. In this class distinction, there is a similarity to Calvin's recognition of the elect and damned: laborers appear to be equivalent to the non-elect because they lack the virtue of industriousness, and are unable to achieve material success. The propertied class is identified with the elect because it follows the law of nature (or God) in its rational, industrious behavior.

Locke's qualification of natural rights and class distinction is clearly a product of 17th century English views. Unemployment was a sign of moral degeneration, not a result of economic conditions. The unemployed were viewed as burdens to the state and neglectful of their duty. Much labor had to be forced and workhouses were concentrations of "sweated—labour." Based upon this commonly held perception, Locke did not hesitate to espouse different rights for different classes of people.[21]

Bernard de Mandeville

Where John Locke warranted class distinctions based upon qualified natural rights, Bernard de Mandeville considered class distinctions necessary for economic efficiency. Mandeville, a London physician, published a short pamphlet in 1705, entitled *The Grumbling Hive*. Originally consisting of a 400 line poem comparing a bee hive to human society, it was later expanded and, in 1714, reprinted under the title *The Fable of the Bees*. Mandeville's story of a beehive shows how individual greed improves the welfare of society. The luxurious living of the wealthy promotes economic growth and civilization. Replace luxury with austerity and industry will collapse, reducing human existence to mere savagery. Private vices, says Mandeville, are public virtues:

> Thus vice nursed ingenuity Which join'd with time and industry, Hand carry'd life's conveniences, It's real pleasures, comforts, ease, To such a height, the very poor Lived better than the rich before; And nothing could be added more.[22]

Possibly inspired by Isaac Newton's laws of motion, Mandeville proposed that religious moralists prevented human behavior from gravitating toward true social harmony, because they deemed greed and opulance vices, and moderation and frugality virtues. Eliminate the tamperings of theology, and the natural desire for wealth and possessions will take over; the commercial class will become rich while the working class will remain poor; the wealthy will live luxuriously while the poor will remain ignorant. This is nature at work, according to Mandeville:

> It would be easier, where property is well secured, to live without money than without poor; for who would do the work? . . . As they ought to be kept from starving, so they should receive nothing worth saving . . . in a free nation, where slaves are not allowed of, the surest wealth consists in a multitude of laborious poor; for besides, that they are the never-failing nursery of fleets and armies, without them there could be no enjoyment, and no product of any country could be valuable. To make the society happy and people easier under the meanest circumstances, it is requisite that great numbers of them should be ignorant as well as poor; knowledge both enlarges and multiplies our desires, and the fewer things a man wishes for, the more easily his necessities may be supplied.[23]

While knowledge only increases desire for possessions, extreme poverty produces desperation; and anything more than minimum subsistence results in insolence and laziness. If the commercial class can effectively maintain a poor, ignorant working class, society will have the efficiency of a beehive and the harmony of Newton's universe.

Martin Luther and John Calvin justified work on religious and moral grounds. John Locke, through the labor theory of value, provided capitalism with moral vindication through natural laws. To Bernard de Mandeville, work and capitalism were warranted on the basis of efficiency and natural order.

Implications for Leisure

In the classical and medieval world, leisure was viewed as the most important human activity: for Plato, Aristotle and Aquinas, it was a necessary condition enabling the pursuit of the human potential. In the 16th century, this idea was attacked in the writings and preachings of Martin Luther and John Calvin and, in the 17th century, a new definition of human potential materialized in the writings of John Locke. Luther and Calvin argued that life's outcome (salvation or damnation) cannot be affected, regardless of a person's actions. Their notion of predestination eliminates any purpose to life, other than the glorification of God; there is no other human potential to be actualized. John Locke conceived human potential as actualized through labor and accumulation; those not so inclined, or limited in their ability to pursue wealth, are viewed as morally depraved, with little hope for improvement.

According to Plato and Aristotle, the good life was reached through a unity of individual and state based on a mutual commitment to peace and leisure. While such a unity was never accomplished in ancient Greek, Roman, or Medieval times, the idea always loomed in the background as a plausible reality and a goal of life. Martin Luther, a spiritual reformist, held to the idea of a unified individual and state; in Calvinism the view becomes strained. Not only does Calvin alienate the non-elect, he alters the relationship of citizen and state. Because citizens have no potential to influence their status in God's eyes, the state's role is to enforce moral and industrious behavior. The state serves as an overseer of God's glory, not a facilitator of secular human potential. Where Calvin views the state as an instrument of God, John Locke holds that the state is an instrument of property owners. Locke separates individual and state and undermines the prerequisite to leisure (economic self-sufficiency) when he equates God's will with natural law. As people are divided into two classes (commercial and laboring), the state becomes the protector of capitalist interests—a justified role of the state because only the "Industrious and Rational" have a potential (accumulation of land and capital), while the "Quarrelsom and Contentious" are depraved and corrupt. While Locke recognizes the interdependency of capital and labor, it is not a unity for mutual enhancement; the working class can never achieve economic security and the wealthy capitalist class (dominated by desire) can never exercise temperance and moderation. Neither class can be satisfied; the poor will never have enough and the wealthy will never be content with what they have.

A decisive component in the classical concept of the good life is the ability of reason to control desire, allowing the human being to transcend greed and exercise the intellectual virtue of wisdom. Called practical virtue, it is important only as a means to intellectual virtue. But Luther, Calvin, Locke and Mandeville denied intellectual virtue and focused almost exclusively upon practical concerns. The Christian calling emphasized the secular life and, in the case of Calvin, frugality, diligence, thrift and sobriety reflect morality and virtue. Locke, influenced by Calvin, modifies the classical perspective to a point that reason guides activity toward desire's end. Unbridled desire, with the aid of reason, is free to pursue material success—the emblem of the "Industrious and Rational."

References

1. Will Durant, *The Reformation* (New York: Simon and Schuster, 1957) p. 329. *The Story of Civilization,* Part VI.
2. *Holy Bible,* King James Version, Epistle to the Romans, 1:17.
3. Roland H. Bainton, *The Age of the Reformation* (New York: Van Nostrand Reinhold, 1956) p. 97.
4. Ibid., p. 28.
5. Ibid., p. 100.
6. Martin Luther quoted in Eugene F. Rice, Jr., *The Foundations of Early Modern Europe* (New York: W. W. Norton, 1970) p. 150.
7. Albert-Marie Schmidt, *John Calvin and the Calvinistic Tradition,* trans. Ronald Wallace (New York: Harper and Brothers, 1960) p. 144.
8. Ibid.
9. G. H. Sabine, p. 370.
10. M. Weber, p. 79.
11. Ibid.
12. John Calvin quoted in W. Durant, *The Reformation,* p. 463.
13. John Locke, *Two Treatises of Government,* intro. Peter Laslett (New York: The New American Library, 1965) p. 328. Originally published by Cambridge University Press, 1960.
14. Ibid., p. 396.
15. Ibid., p. 333.
16. Ibid., p. 373.
17. Ibid., pp. 328–329.
18. C. B. Macpherson, *The Political Theory of Possessive Individualism* (New York: Oxford University Press, 1964) p. 201.
19. J. Locke, p. 330.
20. J. Locke quoted in C. B. Macpherson, p. 223.
21. Ibid., pp. 222–223.
22. Bernard de Mandeville, quoted by Edwin Cannan, Introduction to Adam Smith, *An Inquiry into the Nature and Causes of the Wealth of Nations* (New York: Modern Library, 1937) p. liii.
23. Bernard de Mandeville, quoted in Karl Marx, *Capital,* ed. Frederick Engels (New York: Modern Library, 1906) pp. 673–674.

Chapter 10
Efficient Economic Man: Utility, Reason, and Material Self-Interest

With the sixteenth and seventeenth centuries viewed as the historical context that produced the ideas associated with economic man, the eighteenth century introduced a degree of evaluation and alteration of the concept. Locke was condemned by David Hume for failing to pursue his empiricist origins and falling back on metaphysics. Several French intellectuals praised Locke, attacked the corruption and inefficiency of their society, and argued that a utopian future awaited rational man if only the proper form of government could be created. Others organized a search to discover a social counterpart to Newton's law of gravity which, if found, could be used as a basis to "naturally" regulate society—thereby diminishing the need for a government. Finally, Adam Smith developed a sweeping view of the historical process that attempted to reconcile virtually all of these perspectives under the auspices of efficient economic man.

The century began with Hume's skepticism and concluded with systems of thought steeped in optimism for the future. After all was said and done, a glorious future was on the horizon, and economic man was destined to enjoy it. But to do so, he would have to make way for his mature relative: efficient economic man, who became even further removed from the classical concept of leisure.

David Hume

David Hume was born in 1711. He was raised in Edinburgh, Scotland, where he entered the local university at the age of twelve and was introduced to the ideas of Isaac Newton. He left the university before he was 16 to pursue law studies, but he became increasingly interested in philosophy. After reading Locke, he jettisoned his belief in religion and, eventually, discarded the idea of a law career. His *An Enquiry Concerning Human Understanding* was published in 1752, and western philosophy would never be the same.

Theory of Knowledge

Hume attacked western philosophy by arguing that its traditional position concerning two kinds of knowledge (opinion—resulting from sense perceptions—and truth, resulting from reason) is false. There is only one kind of knowledge, and it is derived from sense perception. All understanding is built upon our immediate sensations and emotions, which initially enter the mind as impressions. These impressions, which can be as simple as the color of an object or as complex as a city skyline, become ideas when recalled or thought about. Ideas, then, are copies of impressions and can be of two types—simple and complex, corresponding to the two types of impressions.

All ideas flow from impressions, and any idea conjured by imagination is meaningless (an obvious reference to the notion of innate ideas). Hence, Hume rejects the ideas of substance and substantial form (Aquinas) on the grounds that we have no such impressions. All we can have are impressions and ideas about the qualities (Aquinas' accidental form) of the objects and events we experience. Finally, we can never verify that our impressions are identical to the objects of experience. Calling into question the existence of substance and the validity of experience, Hume raises doubts about our ability to know anything; the extent of knowledge seems to be confined to opinion.

What is commonly referred to as knowledge is merely the association of ideas. In our minds, ideas connect when they resemble one another, occur closely in space or time, or suggest a cause-effect relationship. Through these methods of association, the mind reasons—developing so-called explanations about the world and events in it. According to Hume, cause-effect relations encourage us to perceive a series of immediate impressions, and from these impressions, our minds generate the idea of cause and effect. Hence, we can never be certain that natural laws exist.

Hume's forceful arguments challenged the power of reason to determine the validity of scientific inquiry, as well as the existence of God. Science rests not on fact, says Hume, but on faith. There is no certainty that a natural event (such as an ocean tide or a sunset) will occur. Natural laws are supported by repeated past impressions, but that does not mean they will be valid in the future. Hume is saying that even though the sun has unfailingly set on the horizon in the past, there is no way for reason to demonstrate that it will set on the horizon tomorrow. And because reason cannot prove a fact, we must reject all rational proofs for the existence of God (Aquinas). Finally, because all ideas come from impressions, we cannot argue that God or natural laws are innate ideas. We can have faith in God's existence, just as we can have faith in natural laws; but we cannot prove that either exists.

Individual, Society and the State

The role of human reason is to compare ideas (such as in mathematics) and to attempt to verify facts about the world (such as in experimentation), but it cannot make moral judgments about what it compares or verifies. Extending the role of reason to moral behavior, Hume reverses the traditional notion that reason controls our desire (practical virtue). Reason can only gather, compare and verify facts about moral choice; it cannot make a moral choice. Our passions (love, hate, anger, ambition, envy, pride, et cetera), says Hume, determine moral behavior. In the end, morality is determined by feelings of approval and disapproval, and pleasure and pain. Social customs and civil laws determine morality, not an inward rational principle or external objective natural law.

If reason is the servant of emotional desire (Hume's passion), then philosophical and religious morality is non-existent. In the past, it had been assumed that individual reason could rise above particular circumstances and direct behavior according to a higher principle (God's will or natural law). Such a belief saw in human beings a potential to be more than a reaction to their desires: by actualizing rationality, individuals could strive for higher goals. Hume's arguments undermined this view and, ultimately, weakened the concept of self-identity.

All ideas are products of impressions; thus, the idea of self must also be a product of impressions. And as impressions of ourselves vary (joy, pain, dissatisfaction, pleasure, grief, et cetera), so will our idea of self. There can be no consistent idea of the self that stands apart from our variable impressions of its qualities and states:

> If any impression gives rise to the idea of self, that impression must continue invariably the same, thro' the whole course of our lives; since self is suppos'd to exist after that manner. But there is no

impression constant and invariable. Pain and pleasure, grief and joy, passions and sensations succeed each other, and never all exist at the same time. It cannot, therefore, be from any of these impressions, or from any other, that the idea of self is deriv'd; and consequently there is no such idea.[1]

Hume can make this startling proposal because he considers reason to be a slave of the passions, not a faculty of the mind that can control passion and make our lives orderly and consistent. We have no self-identity; all we have regarding ourselves are impressions of ourselves. We have no more potential than what we are at the moment.

Hume's attack on traditional morality and the role of reason is not only directed at Greek and Medieval philosophy but also at John Locke—his empiricist predecessor. While Locke's moral system was governed by desire, it was grounded in a natural law visible to rational people. Hume's arguments reveal the inconsistencies of Locke's theory. If the empirical assumption (that the mind is a blank tablet and all knowledge is derived from experience) is accepted, then Locke's conceptions of natural rights and law must be rejected. Hume's philosophy also counters John Locke's political theory. Governments were not formed out of an alliance of people for the protection of their natural right to private property, because there are no natural rights to uphold. The state evolved because it was a useful device for managing complex arrangements between people; governments are not guided by reason, but by history and custom. While hereditary succession, divine right of kings and social contract all claim legal governmental authority, they are all a facade. History shows that force and violence legitimize rule and that loyalty and obedience are ensured only to the degree that the state is useful to society.

Hume was influenced by Isaac Newton, who developed laws of motion that appeared to explain the harmonious relationship of planets. Newton argued that the universe was the result of matter and motion, not the product of a higher form of consciousness. And while gravity served as a force, it was not the result of any rational first principle. Hume attempted to apply this view to humans and societies. Ideas move about in the mind until, by association, they form opinion. Individuals, following their personal desires, are encouraged or restrained by social custom and civil law. Hence, Hume suggests that we study the origins and development of traditions, customs, and civil laws in order to enhance our understanding of society.

Hume pursued such studies, contributing to the growth of history as an independent discipline. And while he was highly critical of Locke's metaphysical leap into natural rights doctrine, he accepted the labor theory of value: everything in the world is purchased by labor, and our passions are the only cause of labor.[2] In the end, then, the labor theory of value was one of the few existing concepts in western thought that emerged intact after Hume's devastating critiques.

The French Enlightenment: *Philosophes* and Physiocrats

Whereas Locke's ideas were initially generated by historical conditions in Britain, their appeal was sufficiently strong to promote their spread to other areas. In France, they lost their reformist, pragmatic dimensions and became rigid critiques of the corrupt and inefficient Bourbon Monarchy. In England, Charles I was accused of subverting the ancient constitution; in France, there was little historical ground to justify the legitimacy of the commercial revolution, as illustrated in Louis XIV's famous statement "I am the State." Hence, the French commercial interests and their intellectual defenders had a more difficult battle to fight than their British counterparts, and the tone of their arguments reflects this increased tension. The *philosophes* and Physiocrats were far from united in their views; their identity as a school of thought is derived from their direct and indirect attacks on eighteenth-century French society—attacks that fanned the flames of Revolution in 1789.

Seventeenth-century French philosophy was dominated by the ideas of René Descartes, who was educated at the Jesuit College La Flèche. Descartes' critical observations of his formal education led him to reject all the knowledge he learned and begin to search for understanding by doubting everything. From this point of departure, he deduced the existence of God and laws of nature, knowable to humans through the soul and the mind. In addition, he drew a sharp contrast between these higher human faculties and daily bodily actions. On the physical plane, we share the attributes of other animals, driven as we are by bodily desires. Our goodness and uniqueness, then, is derived from exercising our higher mental and spiritual powers. As dualistic beings, our future is up to us, depending on which dimension of our being we choose to follow. The *philosophes* tended to adopt Descartes' deductive method, but they rejected his spiritual dimensions. For them, reason provided all the tools necessary for the improvement of the human condition.

Louis XIV's revocation of the Edict of Nantes in 1685 served as a pivotal event stimulating the *philosophes'* thought. With the suspension of religious toleration, the Catholic Church's power was reinforced, and the monarchy also moved to suppress political criticism. In this environment, Fontenelle (1657–1757) published a popular work on Copernican astronomy in 1686, which was read as an attack on the Church:

> All now turns round the sun, the earth herself goes round the sun, and Copernicus, to punish the earth for her former laziness, makes her contribute all he can to the motion of the planets and heavens. And now stripped of all heavenly equipage with which she was so gloriously attended, she hath nothing left her but the moon, which still turns around about her.[3]

This secular tone also underlies Pierre Bayle's writings. Deprived of his teaching position and forced to flee from France due to persecution of Protestants, Bayle's skepticism ultimately overtook his religious inclinations, and he came under attack by Protestants in the Netherlands, who had originally offered him sanctuary. Bayle stressed logic and empirical reality as the basis of all knowledge. He attacked the hypocrisy of both Catholics and Protestants, and argued:

> that morality depended in no way upon religious principles . . . even a society of atheists could be more moral than a society founded on religious fanaticism.[4]

These early Enlightenment views were extended during the course of the eighteenth century by some of the best known figures in modern western thought. There were far too many *philosophes* to include them all in this brief summary, but we will note the contributions of some of the most important French thinkers. Their similarities include the following perspectives— 1) Stress placed on science and reason, as opposed to faith, 2) firm belief in the unlimited potential for human progress, 3) through the proper application of reason, government could move society toward human perfection on earth, 4) major changes were necessary to improve French society.

Voltaire

While Voltaire's works strike the modern reader as entertaining and witty, his style conceals a biting attack on eighteenth-century French society. Born a commoner in 1694, he was educated with the sons of the nobility by the Jesuits. His satires of the Bourbons and the Church caused him to be exiled from Paris on several occasions, and during these periods of exile (in England,

Holland and Prussia), he developed his literary skill—just as he did during his two terms of imprisonment in the Bastille. Hence, while Voltaire is commonly recognized as one of the most important carriers of Locke's ideas to France, his relationship to the existing power structure was far different than Locke's.

In 1726, at the age of 30, Voltaire was released from his second prison term and exiled to England. He studied the social, economic and political realities there during the next three years, creating the basis for his *Letters Concerning the English Nation.* The work was written as if it was a compilation of letters written from England, although it was not actually put together until Voltaire was back in France in 1732. It was translated and published in England during the following year—but the French censors banned it, burned it, and (again) ordered Voltaire's arrest. The official reaction to these descriptions of English life suggests that the French government and Church had become desperate in their attempts to maintain the status-quo. A brief look at the thrust of the *Letters* illustrates both Voltaire's attacks on France and his clever style.

In one of four letters entitled "On the Quakers," Voltaire recounts time spent trying to understand the followers of this religion. He presents them as odd, somewhat confused, but kind people. His host (a retired merchant) is a generous (though narrowminded) person who, while describing the Quaker Church, becomes a mouthpiece for an attack on the Catholic Priesthood:

> "Haven't you any priests?" I asked.
> "No, friend," said the Quaker, "and we do very well without them. God forbid that we should presume to ordain anyone to receive the Holy Ghost on Sunday to the exclusion of the rest of the faithful. By God's grace we are the only ones on earth to have no priests. Would you deprive us of so happy a distinction?"[5]

Voltaire's appeal for religious toleration is mixed with the admiration for the dynamics of English commercial activity in the Sixth Letter. Note his observation concerning the true outcasts of English society:

> Go into the Exchange in London, that place more venerable than many a court, and you will see representatives of all the nations assembled there for the profit of mankind. There the Jew, Mahometan, and the Christian deal with one another as if they were of the same religion, and reserve the name of infidel for those who go bankrupt.[6]

The Ninth Letter, "On Government," stresses the political power of the House of Commons in relationship to the House of Lords and relates this power to the thriving economy and political liberty. The Tenth Letter extends these accolades to the flourishing trade and, once again, draws a stark contrast between the English norms and the feudal remnants of French society:

> Yet I don't know which is the more useful to a state, a well-powdered lord who knows precisely what time the king gets up in the morning and what time he goes to bed . . . or a great merchant who enriches his country . . . and contributes to the well-being of the world.[7]

In addition, Voltaire commented on Locke, saying: Perhaps there has never been a wiser and more orderly mind, or a logician more exact, than Mr. Locke.[8]

Voltaire's comments on Locke are focused on the latter's *Essay Concerning Human Understanding.* And while Voltaire lends a degree of credence to Locke's views on the origins of government, he does not advocate a totally unregulated market and the "policeman" role of government. Voltaire argues that "Every man in the depth of his heart has the right to consider himself equal to other men," but stresses that it is impossible for men to be equal, due to their "violent propensity for domination, wealth and pleasure."[9] Hence, the role of enlightened government is to formulate good laws to govern society in a rational manner for the benefit of all:

> luxury is a necessary consequence of property, without which no state can subsist, and of a great inequality in wealth, which is the consequence, not of the right of property, but of bad laws. Luxury arises then from bad laws, and good laws can destory it.[10]

With this last statement, we identify Voltaire's movement toward the concept of a positive role of government to alter social abuses, regardless of their origin. Whereas Locke argued that because the original role of government was to protect property, government should maintain the interests of propertied individuals, Voltaire is willing to use the government to limit the aspirations of the rich. Voltaire put these principles into practice on a modest scale after 1758, when he used his wealth to purchase a chateau at Ferney:

> As benefactor of Ferney he built more than a hundred houses, gave the town a church, a school and hospital, improved the land, established a watch factory and a silk stocking mill, and planned an ideal village at Versoix where complete toleration was to reign, with Catholic and Protestant churches facing each other.[11]

Montesquieu

Like Voltaire, Montesquieu began his career with satire, publishing the *Persian Letters* in 1721. Ostensibly written by a Persian traveler visiting Paris, the letters are obvious critiques of French society. The French King and Pope are referred to as "magicians," (Letter 24), the nobility is described as conceited and arrogant (Letter 74), and Christians are described, essentially, as hypocrites (Letter 75).

Montesquieu also spent time in England, and his experiences there had a major impact on his monumental work *The Spirit of the Laws,* published in 1748. While the book is primarily a sociological study, admiration for English law and customs is apparent. Montesquieu held up the English system as a model of good government, with the monarchy, aristocracy, and commoners each having their own political institution to check the power of the other interests. His ideas provided guidelines for the writers of the Untied States' Constitution and, again, suggested that the French political system was seriously out of step with the times.

The Concept of Utility

The critique of French society was combined with Hume's world view to produce further suggestions for altering the conditions in France. Attempting to view human behavior and morality in terms of Newtonian physics, other *philosophes* set out to discover a social counterpart to the law of gravity. For the anatomist La Mettrie, humans are mechanical objects: Let us conclude boldly then that man is a machine, and that in the whole universe there is but a single substance with various modifications.[12] He concluded that metaphysics and theology are "childish weapons" and that the future lies in the scientific study of the human machine, guided by those trained in such techniques.[13]

Like Hume and Locke, Helvetius argued that the human machine is motivated by self-interest. Society, then, is made up of atom-like individuals, whose lives center around the desire to maximize pleasure and minimize pain. This creates an inherently chaotic society, because of our tendency to think only of our own well-being. Governments, however, have the ability and responsibility to create laws that will integrate the private interests of competitive individuals into a social order conducive to harmony and, ultimately, perfection. This optimistic view of the future was not based on any arguments concerning human morality. Instead, it accepted self-interested desire as the motive force of all humans, and challenged governments to introduce sufficient reforms to reconcile the conflicts within society:

> The ideas of good and evil that men form depend wholly on what circumstance, or in a broad sense education, make pleasurable or the reverse; the inferiority or superiority of a nation's morals results chiefly from legislation. Despotism brutalizes while good laws make a natural harmony of individual and public interests.[14]

This harmony of public interests was to be created by legislation promoting the "greatest happiness for the greatest number" in society.

Whereas Helvetius sought solutions to the problems in France through enlightened government, another group of critics argued that government action was the problem, not the solution. Agreeing with Helvetius that humans are motivated by the pleasure-pain principle, the Physiocrats extended this view into economics. They argued that "natural" laws control economic activity and that state-imposed regulations on such activity distort the natural process. With land and agriculture viewed as the source of all wealth, the Physiocrats argued that taxation on non-agricultural activity was unfair. Echoing Locke and Mandeville (and prefacing Adam Smith), the Physiocrats concluded that the scope of government activity should be reduced to a minimum, allowing desire-driven individuals to pursue their economic self-interest without interference.

Optimism: The Heavenly City

While the attacks on French society and government were highly diverse, in retrospect we can identify several common themes. Clearly, the entire past was bankrupt and offered no valid guidelines for the future. The remnants of medieval society limited and distorted the drives of enlightened individuals, thereby working against nature and holding humans back from fulfilling their unlimited potential for improvement. Human misery and degradation resulted from centuries of ignorance and the domination of society by those who perpetuated the past. But science and history was in the process of moving beyond this intolerable state of affairs, and new leaders were needed to awaken society and guide its members into the future.

For the *philosophes,* the capacity of human reason to promote this change was accepted without question. Whereas Hume's skepticism demanded reevaluation and testing of all such assumptions, the *philosophes* accepted human reason as their point of departure. And whereas Hume called upon scholars to study the past to discover their origins, the *philosophes* focused on the future. As Carl Becker notes:

> What difference does it make, they seem to be saying, how society came to be what it is? There it is for all men to see, obviously irrational, oppressive, unjust, obviously contrary to the essential nature of man, obviously needing to be set right, and that speedily. What we seek to know is how it may be set right; and we look to the past for light, not on the origins of society, but on its future state.[15]

In his classic study of the *philosophes,* Becker argues that while they marched under the banner of science, the eighteenth-century French thinkers were, in fact, similar to their religious predecessors in that they worked extremely hard to reconcile facts with their assumptions of human nature. These assumptions are described as "The essential articles of the religion of the Enlightenment," and listed as:

1. man is not natively depraved;
2. the end of life is life itself, the good life on earth instead of the beatific life after death;
3. man is capable, guided solely by reason and experience, of perfecting the good life on earth;
4. the first and essential condition of the good life on earth is the freeing of men's minds from the bonds of ignorance and superstition, and of their bodies from the arbitrary oppression of the constituted social authorities.[16]

In addition to their tendency to blur the lines that divide empiricism from deductive philosophy, the *philosophes* were inclined to place the responsibility for social change in the hands of the educated and wealthy middle class. Hence, just as their critique of the traditional religion concealed a new religious view, their critique of the medieval class structure (dominated by the nobility and Catholic Church) laid the basis for the development of a new class to dominate society. Holbach's candid discussion of the concept of "people" clearly suggests the importance of wealth as the crucial factor in determining social and political status:

By the word people I do not mean the stupid populace. . . . Every man who can live respectably from the income of his property and every head of a family who owns land ought to be regarded as a citizen. The artisan, the merchant, and the wage-earner ought to be protected by a state which they serve usefully after their fashion, but they are not true members until by their labor and industry they have acquired land.[17]

Note that "labor" and "industry," the essential features of "economic man," again surface as dominant factors. Hence, in a roundabout way, French thought meshed with Locke in its quest to identify leaders for the future society. Rational economic man emerges as the heir to history, with the rights and responsibilities of leading society into a glorious future that includes the possibility of heaven on earth. Science served to stimulate the early *philosophes,* but their drive for social change and their optimism for the future led them away from its skeptical basis.

British Political Economy: Adam Smith and the Laws of Economic Man

While the *philosophes* pursued their dreams of the heavenly city, British scholars were building upon Hume's legacy by analyzing the origins and functions of capitalist economics. With the concept of material self-interest firmly established as the human counterpart to Newton's law of gravity, the early economists attempted to discover the mechanisms that allowed self-interested economic men to live together in harmony.[18] In the works of Adam Smith, most of the Enlightenment's optimism concerning the future was maintained.

The changing focal point of Adam Smith's intellectual interests suggests the increasing power of the concept of economic man during the eighteenth century: as professor of moral philosophy at the University of Glasgow in 1759, Smith argued that sympathy serves as the motive force of morality. In 1776, his *Inquiry into the Nature and Causes of the Wealth of Nations* was published, and sympathy was replaced with unlimited economic self-interest as the basic human drive. Viewed as the culmination of a century-long debate over economic self-interest versus traditional values, Smith's work attempted to reconcile individual economic drives with social harmony, wealth and progress. Viewed as the beginning of modern economic theory, the book set the parameters for discussion and debate for, at least, the following century. Through this process, economic man was able to add social science to the theological and philosophical foundations that had been established by the Calvinists and Locke.

Smith's admiration for his friend David Hume can be seen as a factor influencing his decision to study the historical origins of the wealth of nations. His association with leading Physiocrats and *philosophes* during his two year stay in France from 1774 to 1776 appears to have reinforced his views and encouraged a degree of optimism that, again, is not to be found in Hume's works. The tension between Hume's skepticism and French optimism occasionally comes through in *The Wealth of Nations,* but the overall thrust is highly optimistic and, in many ways, reminiscent of Mandeville's arguments concerning the meshing of self-interest and social well-being:

> As every individual, therefore, endeavors as much as he can both to employ his capital in support of domestic industry, and so to direct that industry that its produce may be of the greatest value; every individual necessarily labours to render the annual revenue of the society as great as he can. He generally, indeed, neither intends to promote the public interest, nor knows how much he is promoting it. By preferring the support of domestic to that of foreign industry, he intends only his own security; and by directing that industry in such a manner as its produce may be of the greatest value, he intends only his own gain, and he is in this, as in many other cases, led by an invisible hand to promote an end which was no part of his intention. Nor is it always the worse for the society that it was no part of it. By pursuing his own interest he frequently promotes that of the society more effectively than when he really intends to promote it.[19]

In addition to economic self-interest as the atom of society, Smith's world was based entirely on productive labor and commerce as the source of human happiness. And in 63 pages of the highly detailed index to *The Wealth of Nations* (with nearly 1300 entries), there is no citation for "contemplation," or any other value associated with classical leisure.

Individual as Self-Interested Laborer

There can be no doubt that the alteration of classical ideas that we have associated with the rise of capitalism served as Smith's point of departure. The unique quality of human beings is defined as "the propensity to truck, barter, and exchange one thing for another."[20] And this quality, clearly, is based on individual self-interest:

> In almost every other race of animals each individual, when it is grown up to maturity, is entirely independent, and in its natural state has occasion for the assistance of no other living creature. But man has almost constant occasion for the help of his brethren, and it is vain to expect it from their benevolence only. He will be more likely to prevail if he can interest their self-love in his favor, and show them that it is for their own advantage to do for him what he requires of them. . . . It is not from the benevolence of the butcher, the brewer, or the baker that we expect our dinner, but from their regard to their own interest. We address ourselves, not to their humanity but to their self-love, and never talk to them of our own necessities but of their advantage. Nobody but the beggar chuses to depend chiefly upon the benevolence of his fellow-citizens.[21]

Note that, from the outset of the book, the lines are being drawn that separate humans from animals, and good humans from beggars. The underlying logic suggests that if self-interest and economic pursuits are natural, then those who are not motivated by (or not successful in) these drives are, somehow, less-than-human. Smith does, however, give us an option if we find this conclusion repugnant:

> Whether this propensity be one of those original principles in human nature, of which no further account can be given; or whether, as seems more probable, it be the necessary consequence of the faculties of reason and speech, it belongs not to our present subject to enquire.[22]

Because economic drives are a necessary consequence of reason, we are left with two options: the lack of self-interest and economic motivation suggests that a person is either a) less-than-human, or b) not fully rational. Reflect on how Plato, Aristotle and Aquinas would respond to this argument.

Like Locke and Hume, Smith viewed labor as the source of value. But he notes that because the value of labor is often difficult to determine, money tends to replace it as a measure of worth. Labor, then, is the human activity that produces money, and money becomes the means to purchase the "necessaries, conveniences, and amusements of human life."[23] In the world of efficient economic man in a capitalist society, even barter (let alone labor) is too cumbersome to serve as a measure of value:

> It is more natural and obvious to him, therefore, to estimate their value by the quantity of money, the commodity for which he immediately exchanges them, than by that of bread and beer, the commodities for which he can exchange them only by the intervention of another commodity; and rather to say that his butcher's meat is worth threepence or fourpence a pound, than that it is worth three or four pounds of bread, or three or four quarts of small beer. Hence it comes to pass, that the exchangeable value of every commodity is more frequently estimated by the quantity of money, than by the quantity either of labour or of any other commodity which can be had in exchange for it.[24]

For the sake of utility, then, the amount of money involved in an exchange of commodities tends to become associated with their value. As a result, the worth of a commodity is not necessarily determined by the amount of labor put into it; instead, the price tends to be set by the amount of money that someone is willing to pay.

With the growth of wage labor in the eighteenth century, we should not be surprised that Smith included labor in the category of commodities—something to be bought and sold, depending on the amount of money that someone is willing to pay. Hence, the value of labor becomes different to different people: for the employee, it is absolute, or real; for the employer, it is relative, or nominal:

> But though equal quantities of labour are always of equal value to the labourer, yet to the person who employs him they appear sometimes to be of greater and sometimes smaller value. He purchases them sometimes with a greater and sometimes with a smaller quantity of goods, and to him the price of labour seems to vary like that of all other things.[25]

Smith suggests that drawing distinctions between real value (labor) and nominal value (wages) "is not a matter of mere speculation, but may sometimes be of considerable use in practice."[26] If the significance of the word "mere" does not strike you immediately, we suggest that you review that part of the Introduction that discusses the association of "speculative reason" with the classical concept of leisure, and "practical reason" with modern society. Can you imagine someone you know saying "that is merely practical?"

With labor established as the real, or continuous determinant of value (because wages vary at different times and places), Smith equates changes in types of labor to human progress. This progress is measured solely in terms of economic growth, leading Smith to draw distinctions between productive labor (that which directly contributes to capital development) and unproductive labor (that which does not). Again, the importance of labor itself tends to be replaced by the importance of that which it produces. Hence, productive labor results in the creation of commodities that continue to exist after the labor has been expended. The less-than-flattering label of "unproductive," then, is applied to virtually everyone on any government payroll (from kings to policemen and the military) because "Their service, how honourable, how useful, or how necessary soever, produces nothing for which an equal quantity of service can afterwords be procured."[27] The value of an individual's labor to society (which, clearly, is equated with the value of the individual to society) determines a hierarchy, based on the level of productivity. Unproductive laborers, or the bottom of the hierarchy, include the following: churchmen, lawyers, physicians, men of letters of all kinds; players, buffoons, musicians, opera-singers, opera-dancers, and c.[28]

The world, then, belongs to competitive, self-interested economic man, and it follows that the diversion of wealth away from capital formation to support "unproductive labourers, and those who do not labour at all" detracts from the vitality and well-being of society.[29]

Society: The Division of Labor as Social Progress

Whereas Hume's study of history was pursued almost by default (having attacked the credibility of moral philosophy and science, there was little left to study), Smith's elaborate economic history presents an entirely different picture. By studying variations in labor over an extensive period of time, Smith attributes meaning to the events recorded in history by suggesting that progress takes place as societies move through various economic stages. Thus, the stages of history and human improvement can be identified and measured—based on their degree of productive efficiency. This efficiency is best measured by noting the degree to which labor is divided into specific tasks. Hence, the division of labor (which arises from the human characteristics that we have just discussed) becomes Smith's key social concept, which promises to promote the good society.

Smith's famous discussion of work in a pin factory stresses the efficiency of production when each worker performs a particular function. He notes that even such a relatively simple operation has been divided into 18 specific functions, and that if even 10 people focused their labor on these specific tasks, they could produce "upwards of forty-eight thousand pins a day."[30] Without such specialization, this level of efficiency would be impossible:

> But if they had all wrought separately and independently, and without any of them having been educated to this particular business, they certainly could not each of them have made twenty, perhaps not one pin a day; that is, certainly, not the two hundred and fortieth, perhaps not the four thousand eight hundredth part of what they are at present capable of performing, in consequence of a proper division and combination of their different operations.[31]

Smith is praising the efficiency of work on an assembly line. And the qualities associated with such division of labor are listed as follows.

Improved dexterity. "Division of labour, by reducing every man's business to some one simple operation, and by making this operation the sole employment of his life, necessarily increases very much the dexterity of the workman."

Saving of time. "The habit of sauntering and of indolent careless application, which is naturally, or rather necessarily acquired by every country workman who is obliged to change his work and his tools every half hour, and to apply his hand in twenty different ways almost every day of his life; renders him almost slothful and lazy, and incapable of any vigorous application even on the most pressing occasions."

Development of machinery. "But in consequence of the division of labour, the whole of every man's attention comes naturally to be directed towards some one very simple object. It is naturally to be expected, therefore, that some one or other of those who are employed in each particular branch of labour should soon find out easier and readier methods of performing their own particular work, wherever the nature of it admits of such improvement."[32]

Stages of Human Progress

Smith integrates all of these points into his view of human progress. The critical dimension of all societies is to be found in their economic structures, and the degree to which the division of labor has been perfected. Societies, then, are classified according to the manner in which they are organized economically, and they are ranked according to their productive efficiency. With this total economic focus, he presents four stages of history and human progress.

Stage 1: Nations of Hunters. People who satisfy their economic needs by hunting constitute "the lowest and rudest state of society."[33] The division of labor is minimal, there is little accumulated wealth and governments, as we know them, are nonexistent.[34]

Stage 2: Nations of Shepherds. The division of labor is slightly more advanced. Increased wealth causes increased disparities throughout the society, introducing "a degree of authority and subordination which could not possibly exist before."[35] Social tension arising from this inequality necessitates the creation of civil government, which is "in reality instituted for the defence of the rich against the poor, or of those who have some property against those who have none at all."[36]

State 3: Agriculture. Increased concentration of property in the hands of a small group of individuals. Laborers totally dependent on power of a feudal nobility. "Wherever there is great property, there is great inequality. For one rich man, there must be at least five hundred poor, and the affluence of the few supposes the indigence of the many."[37]

Stage 4: Manufacturing and Commerce. Market economy gradually grows outward from feudal constraints. Greater division of labor creates greater efficiency and, hence, comfort and progress. "Thirdly, and lastly, commerce and manufactures gradually introduced order and good government, and with them, the liberty and security of individuals."[38]

Smith viewed society as a self-regulating mechanism, with the market and the invisible hand providing the focus to guide it in a progressive direction. Human progress is directly related to productive efficiency, and historical trends are moving societies toward commerce and manufacturing, which are viewed as the apex of progress. This progress appears to be natural and inevitable, stimulating Max Lerner (in his Introduction to *The Wealth of Nations*) to remind the reader that Becker's observations concerning the "Heavenly City" of the *philosophes* also apply to Smith—regardless of his social-scientific origins.[39] Lerner quotes Harold Laski's study, *The Rise of Liberalism,* to summarize the link between Smith's work and the further growth of capitalism:

> The businessmen were delighted. "To have their own longings elevated to the dignity of natural law was to provide them with a driving force that had never before been so powerful. . . . With Adam Smith the practical maxims of business enterprise achieved the status of a theology."[40]

The Limited State: Facilitator for Economic Man

With economic drives presented as the force to motivate individuals and regulate societies, it follows that the state's functions should be limited to those that encourage such "natural" activity. Smith identifies three duties that should be performed by the state:

Protection of the society from other societies. Providing a military to protect a society from outside invasion is a government's "first duty," and Smith engages in an elaborate discussion of how this function has changed throughout history. His major points include the increasing expense of maintaining a military in each stage of history, the social impact of increased sophistication of military technology, and the advantages enjoyed by wealthy societies—because they can afford a large arsenal.[41]

Protecting every member of society from the injustice of every other member. In this discussion, Smith equates the need for government with the accumulation of property. The "avarice and ambition of the rich" and the "hatred of labour and the love of present ease and enjoyment" among the poor necessitates civil government.[42] Echoing Locke, Smith suggests that the primary role of government in domestic affairs is to protect private property: Where there is no property . . . civil government is not so necessary.[43]

Erection and maintenance of public works and institutions. Smith recognizes the necessity of a certain amount of public works, such as roads and canals, to facilitate commerce. In addition, he stresses the government's responsibility to maintain basic educational institutions to prepare everyone to "read, write, and account."[44] The justification of public education is based solely on its utility—"There is scarce a common trade which does not afford some opportunities of applying to it the principles of geometry and mechanics"[45]—and he argues that the public must not bear the entire financial burden to support it. Smith shows a great deal of contempt for higher education—the bastion of classical learning. He concludes that it is, essentially, useless in "the real business of the world."[46]

With all of these points in mind, it may sound odd to suggest that Smith was anything more than an apologist for the interests of the early capitalists. Interestingly enough, though, a close reading reveals numerous critical passages and concepts. Lerner quotes Eli Ginzberg's *The House of Adam Smith* to suggest that "His own personal sympathies were not entirely with the capitalist."[47] And Heilbroner notes that "he was more avowedly hostile to the *motives* of businessmen than most New Deal economists."[48]

From our perspective, Smith was truly attempting to reconcile the common good with the drives of self-interested economic man. Unlike Mandeville, he argued for basic education and high wages for workers, and underlying the entire system of thought is the assumption that the greater the wealth of a society, the better the lives of all of its members. The fact that he had to fall back on such a mystical concept as an "invisible hand" suggests that such an undertaking was not an easy task. Hence, while Smith's work can be seen as an extension of the Calvinist-Lockean views, it also served as a foundation for many nineteenth-century critiques of capitalism—including Marx's. Smith's passages describing the living conditions of the common workers are not unlike those written by Marx, though it must be noted that Marx's moral outrage is lacking in Smith's work. Both Smith and Marx describe government as a tool of an economic elite, and Marx would agree with Smith's definition of profit—as something that is created when the capitalist "shares in the produce of their [the workers] labour."[49] In addition, Smith even suggests that capitalists tend to conspire to keep the wages of the workers as low as possible, and that class conflict between the workers and capitalists is inevitable. To Smith, this conflict will result in victory for the capitalist; to Marx, the workers will ultimately prevail.[50] We will return to several of these points in the discussion of Marx's thought in Chapter 13.

Implications for Leisure

The eighteenth century quest for understanding was profoundly influenced by, and linked to, a myriad of social, political and economic changes. And as the century unfolded, these realities interacted with both the classical legacy and the concept of efficient economic man to produce a variety of interpretations.

For Hume, the elimination of God, innate ideas, natural laws and even the self left little to contemplate, even if economic man was inclined to spend any time thinking beyond the material world. Hence, the classical stress on the uniqueness of humans as contemplative beings was lost and the door was open for the empirical study of the interactions of passion-driven man and nature. Knowledge, then, became knowledge of what has been, with no links to the future. And humans were stripped of any capacity (or reason) to transcend the past as they stumble their way toward whatever may happen beyond this moment.

For some of the *philosophes,* especially Voltaire, "reason" provided the basis for hope, but its definition was so nebulous that we are left wondering what it is we should contemplate in addition to reason itself. Helvetius' pleasure-pain principle seems clear enough as an initial assumption, but its social counterpart of "the greatest happiness for the greatest number" was also too vague to be meaningful until a definition of happiness is established, i.e., whose definition (Plato's Aristotle's, Aquinas', or Locke's) do we use? With Holbach, economic man clearly reemerges, suggesting that Locke's view, after all is was said and done, had successfully supplanted the classical perspectives. Given the diversity of the *philosophes,* it is probably best to conclude that a consistent view toward leisure is difficult to establish. Such is not the case, however, in the British tradition.

The labor theory of value remained intact from Locke through Hume and Smith, and the model of efficient economic man completely dominated Smith's view of humans and his hope for the future. Classical learning and contemplation were replaced by reading, writing and arithmetic at levels designed to promote economic efficiency.

Like virtually everything else in the world, Smith argued that leisure time changed through the stages of human progress. And with these stages based on the historical unfolding of efficient labor, we should not be surprised that human progress and leisure time came to be viewed as opposites: the more leisure, the less progress—the more progress, the less leisure. "A shepherd has a great deal of leisure; a husbandman, in the rude state of husbandry, has some; an artificer or manufacturer has none at all."[51]

References

1. David Hume, *A Treatise of Human Nature,* Bk. I, Part IV, Sect. VI, ed. L. A. Selby-Biggs (Oxford: Clarendon Press, 1967) pp. 251–252.
2. D. Hume, "Of Commerce" *Political Essays* XVI, ed. C. W. Hendel (Indianapolis: Bobbs-Merrill, 1953) p. 135.
3. Bernard le Bovier de Fontenelle, *Conversations on the Plurality of Worlds,* in Normal L. Torrey, ed. *Les Philosophes* (New York: Perigee Books, 1980) p. 22.
4. Ibid., p. 34.
5. Voltaire, *Philosophical Letters,* trans. E. Dilworth (Indianapolis: Bobbs-Merrill, 1961) pp. 8–9.
6. Ibid., p. 26.
7. Ibid., p. 40.
8. Ibid., p. 52.
9. Voltaire, in Torrey, pp. 81–82.
10. Ibid., p. 81.
11. Ibid., p. 233.
12. Julien Offray de La Mettrie, *Man a Machine,* in Torrey, p. 177.
13. Ibid.
14. G. Sabine, p. 566.
15. Carl L. Becker, *The Heavenly City of the Eighteenth-Century Philosophers* (New Haven: Yale University Press, 1932) p. 98.

16. Ibid., pp. 102–103.
17. G. Sabine, p. 570.
18. For a discussion of the development of the ideas of self-interest in British thought, see Milton L. Myers, *The Soul of Modern Economic Man* (Chicago: University of Chicago Press, 1983).
19. Adam Smith, *An Inquiry into the Nature and Causes of the Wealth of Nations,* ed. E. Cannan, intro. M. Lerner (New York: Modern Library, 1937) p. 423.
20. Ibid., p. 13.
21. Ibid., p. 14.
22. Ibid., p. 13.
23. Ibid., p. 30.
24. Ibid., p. 32.
25. Ibid., p. 33.
26. Ibid.
27. Ibid., p. 315.
28. Ibid.
29. Ibid.
30. Ibid., p. 5.
31. Ibid.
32. Ibid., pp. 7–9.
33. Ibid., p. 653.
34. Ibid., p. 653, 669.
35. Ibid., p. 674.
36. Ibid.
37. Ibid., p. 670.
38. Ibid., p. 385.
39. Ibid., p. ix.
40. Ibid.
41. Ibid., pp. 653–669.
42. Ibid., p. 670.
43. Ibid.
44. Ibid., p. 737.
45. Ibid.
46. Ibid., p. 728.
47. Ibid., p. x.
48. R. Heilbroner, p. 54.
49. A. Smith, p. 65.
50. Ibid., pp. 66–67.
51. Ibid., p. 659.

Part III Conclusion

The tension between Aquinas' Roman Catholicism and the demands of the market economy are obvious. If people had devoted their lives to classical leisure in the form of contemplation of God, who would have worked, saved and invested? It is clear that the imperatives of capitalism necessitated a wholesale assault on the entire classical tradition—an assault that, ultimately, was aimed at destroying the definition of humans as contemplative beings. Hence, it was an attack on classical leisure, the human essence and speculative philosophy. From Plato through Aquinas, the material world had been viewed (in varying degrees) as relatively insignificant when compared to the higher capacities associated with our essence. By eliminating this essence, we are left with nothing but the material world and our actions in it. Hence, contemplation gives way to labor as the uniquely human capacity and we are obliged to subordinate our lives to work. Oddly enough, this very secular conclusion can be traced to Luther's theological focus on the "calling." Aquinas argued that, as humans, we are obligated to contemplate God and his creations. As a Calvinist, Locke viewed labor as "an obligation which must be analysed as a component of the calling."[1] Hence, labor fills the spiritual void created by Luther's focus on the Augustinian separation of man and God.

Martin Luther's contribution to the assault on classical leisure was twofold. First, by attacking the credibility of the Roman Catholic Church he was doing his part to discredit the remnants of classical thought. Aquinas' synthesis of Greek and Roman philosophy with Christianity integrated the western intellectual tradition under the banner of Catholicism. Hence, an attack on the Church was also an attack on Plato and Aristotle. The Church leaders were highly corrupt—having succumbed to the same human weaknesses that the ancient social critics repeatedly condemned. In short, the contrast between the Church's ideals and its leaders' realities was as wide as the gaps that we have noted in the Athenian, Hebrew and Roman societies.

The Church's corruption provided a stimulus for Luther's attack but the underlying cause is traceable to the clash between the Augustinian and Thomistic views toward the human potential. Aquinas' optimism was challenged by Luther's Augustinian focus on sin and evil. This resurgence of a totally negative view of the human potential presented a stark contrast to the growing optimism in secular culture associated with the Renaissance. Given that we are sinful and depraved, Luther argued that we must subordinate our time and energy to the pursuit of our calling.

The calling (the second dimension of Luther's attack) became associated with work, or a particular vocation. Its practical application can be seen as a way to keep us occupied so we have less time to sin. If humans are viewed as good, or potentially good, then leisure time provides us with the opportunity to improve—to actualize this potential. But if we are inherently evil, leisure time provides us with the opportunity to pursue our evil and sinful desires. For the Greeks and Aquinas, the human potential for improvement served as the basis for classical leisure—a time to transcend our lower drives. For Luther, the human potential for evil necessitates an environment of total work to avoid idleness and sin.

Calvin extended the calling to its logical conclusion, presenting a view of the world based on a rigid system of predestination. Some are saved and some are damned before we are even born. When combined with the practical values of diligence, frugality, thrift and hard work, we can see that the Calvinist views provided a ready-made justification for capitalism. Luther eliminated the Catholic Church as a credible force. The Calvinists provided a view of the world that both filled the religious void and encouraged the further development of capitalism. The English Calvinists (Puritans) led the assault against the Stuart Monarchy, and Locke's Calvinist upbringing (combined with the realities of power in England that led to the Glorious Revolution in 1688), provide the background for the *Second Treatise of Government*.

Classical thought is based on the argument that contemplation (whether spiritual or speculative) is the only true source of happiness. In contrast, Locke considered happiness to be derived from practical reason rather than speculative reason. Happiness is not a "dwelling in wisdom" or "peace of mind," as Classical thought proposed—but a continual pursuit of practical business concerns. As the rational person is forever industrious toward the appropriation of capital and possessions, it is industrious behavior, more than capital and possessions, that brings happiness. Locke, like Calvin, compelled people toward a life of total work; idleness and enjoyment signify the "Fancy and Covetousness" of the "Quarrelsom and Contentious."

Classical philosophy held reason to be the highest human capacity when manifested in the contemplative life. Locke, likewise, argued that reason is an important human capacity, but only when it serves desire's ends. He reversed the Platonic hierarchy, supplanting reason with desire. Reason is to assist desire in its insatiable drive for possessions. The effectiveness, then, of practical reason is measured by the accumulation of material things. In this way, happiness is dependent upon outside possessions and not generated from within the individual. And because desire can never be satisfied, happiness can never be complete and self-sufficient. Eventually, the appropriation of land in the capitalists' pursuit of happiness must usurp the natural rights of others. From the classical perspective, such usurpation is harmful and evil, denying the purity and goodness of whatever happiness is claimed to be gained in the process. Locke countered this moral indictment by accusing the propertyless of corruption. Whatever harm comes to them is their punishment for not being "Industrious and Rational;" they are impure and evil (for Calvin, the damned), and the commercial class is pure and good (the elect).

Finally, labor was established as the source of all value, and society became structured to reward it with material comfort, social status and political influence. With such pressure, speculative philosophy and classical leisure were engulfed by the quest for practical results and profit. There is no time left for contemplation of our actions and our society. Economic activity as a means to the end of "knowing thyself" becomes the end goal of life, and the "unexamined life" is worth living; in fact, it becomes the only way of life.

The Protestant Reformation opened the door for John Locke's justification of capitalism. By uniting Protestant imperatives with natural laws and rights, Locke gave credence to the commercial interests that were asserting their power in seventeenth-century England. In the spirit of his Puritan contemporaries, he focused all human energy on the secular sphere of life. He replaced intellectual wisdom with material wealth, reason with desire, leisure with work, moderation with greed. Indeed, Locke's influence cannot be overlooked; he deserves credit for establishing a moral basis to justify capitalism. And with this justification, the foundation was created for a new definition of human beings—that of economic animal.

Hume left few stones unturned in his attack on the western philosophical tradition. T. Z. Lavine notes that "He was the most mercilessly destructive of all the British empiricists" and she refers to his arguments as a "wrecking ball" unleashed against philosophy.[2] From this perspective, it is critical that we again stress the fact that Locke's labor theory of value was one of the few concepts in western thought to escape his wrath. Locke's concept fit nicely with Hume's observation of passion-driven humans and, instead of trying to find a way to overcome this condition, Hume was content to strip us of any potential to become something more than we appear to be. Hence, classical leisure, which was intimately associated with speculative philosophy, became as absurd to Hume as nearly everything else in the western tradition.

While the *philosophes'* view of reason as the uniquely human force (as opposed to a merely calculative capacity to make our desire more efficient) initially hints at a return to pre-Lockean approaches, their thought was steeped in practical reason and its application, as opposed to speculative concerns. Voltaire's admiration for Locke, along with Helvetius' pleasure-pain principle and Holbach's contempt for the "stupid populace," suggest that the concept of self-interested economic man had become as deeply ingrained in the mainstream of French rationalism as it had in British empiricism. The Physiocrats' arguments obviously influenced Adam Smith, who also accepted the labor theory of value and equated work with everything positive in human history.

Smith presented industrial society as the culmination of history and insisted that, although the workers live miserable lives, they should be glad to know that their labor is contributing to the wealth of the nation. The concept of efficient economic man served as Smith's point of departure and the goal of history. Guided by an invisible hand, humans could look forward to a future of more wealth, more specialized work and more material possessions, as long as the state did not interfere with our natural economic drives. Finally, Smith argued that the stages of historical progress destroyed leisure, making contemplation and *aretē,* or the "Renaissance man," anachronistic. Through increased specialization of labor, the nation would continue to progress and be able to offer humans more material comforts. In return, all we need to do is work hard to produce material goods, deny any dimensions of our personality that do not contribute to increased efficiency and forget about any potential to be something more than efficient economic animals; in short, forget about classical leisure.

References

1. John Dunn, *The Political Thought of John Locke* (Cambridge: Cambridge Univ. Press, 1969) p. 219.
2. T. Z. Lavine, p. 147, 173.

Part IV
Essence and Existence: The Marxian Synthesis

It is not Communism that is radical, it is Capitalism.
Bertrolt Brecht

It should be clear that the expansion of the market economy necessitated a wholesale attack on the ideal of classical leisure, because the view of human beings as efficient economic animals was incompatible with the earlier concept. In addition, it should be equally clear that this antithesis contributed to the development of previously unimaginable levels of production and the plethora of consumer goods that most of us take for granted. There was, then, a trade involved: something was lost and something was gained.

But to jump so quickly from the origins of the market economy to the modern world of consumer abundance is to dismiss the significance of massive human suffering caused by the demands of early industrialization. The process of efficient manufacturing entailed much more than just building factories and time clocks. The assault on the entire pre-industrial view of the world was accompanied by the destruction of rural communities, families, and countless human beings.

In England, where the process began, the people had decades to adjust to the new realities. The political system was gradually altered throughout the nineteenth century and the dominant values tended to reinforce the process of industrialization. Nevertheless, the daily horrors created by the conditions in which the vast majority of humans were forced to live during the early period of industrialization cause us to reel in disbelief, and they must be recognized as a major stimulant to nineteenth-century socialist thought. Emile Durkheim, an eminent twentieth-century sociologist, refers to socialism as "a cry of grief, sometimes of anger," and even Polanyi's normally detached style suggests an underlying revulsion:

> Before the process had advanced very far, the laboring people had been crowded together in new places of desolation, the so-called industrial towns of England; the country folk had been dehumanized into slum dwellers; the family was on the road to perdition; and large parts of the country were rapidly disappearing under the slack and scrap heaps vomited forth from the "satanic mills." Writers of all views and parties, conservatives and liberals, capitalists and socialists invariably referred to social conditions under the Industrial Revolution as a veritable abyss of human degradation.[1]

The obvious conflict between such degradation and the "heavenly city" optimism so characteristic of eighteenth-century thought produced a number of critics. In fact, much of the intellectual history of the nineteenth century is traceable to the tension between the earlier optimism and the ugly realities.

The goal of the following three chapters is to clarify the arguments developed in the century-long quest to overcome the misery imposed by the advance of industrialization. Chapter 11 outlines specific aspects of the economic, political and social conditions associated with industrial development. Chapter 12 summarizes the perspectives of both socialist and non-socialist critics. In Chapter 13, we will clarify the significance of Marx's attempt to synthesize these critiques with the earlier optimism and, indeed, his remarkable synthesis of contemplative and economic man. With these definitions of human beings at the base of the tension between classical and modern leisure, Marx's attempt to transcend the conflict makes him the master philosopher of leisure in modern western thought.

Like Hume, Marx attacked the abstractions of philosophy: The philosophers have only interpreted the world, in various ways; the point, however, is to change it.[2] As it did for Plato and Aristotle, the classical ideal of leisure played a critical role in his vision of the good society. Significantly, though, Marx was not talking about an ideal—but a reality that the process of history is working toward.

With Marx we identify Aristotle adapted to the nineteenth century, Locke and Plato meshed, and the voices of the prophets speaking in the language of Adam Smith. The democratization of human degradation had created the basis for the democratization of classical leisure. Human labor and reason, both action and reflection, will create the basis (for the first time in history) to actually realize the goals that other philosophers "merely" talked about.

References

1. Karl Polanyi, *The Great Transformation* (Boston: Beacon Press, 1957) p. 39. Originally published in 1944, Rinehart and Co. Emile Durkheim, *Socialism,* ed. A. W. Gouldner, trans. C. Sattler (New York: Collier Books, 1962) p. 41. Originally published in English as *Socialism and Saint-Simon.*
2. Karl Marx, "Theses on Feuerbach," 1845. Robert C. Tucker, ed. *The Marx-Engels Reader,* 2nd ed. (New York: Norton, 1978) p. 145.

Chapter 11
The Contexts of Industrialization

If the starting points differ, how can one expect linear or even parallel developments?

Hans Daalder

The centuries of change in England that contributed to the concept of efficient economic man prepared the society for the industrial revolution. By the 1780s, the economic structures and attitudes that supported Britain's rise to commercial domination of the world were in place.[1] The full significance of the incremental changes in England (as discussed in Chapter 8) is best appreciated with the recognition that the social, political, economic, and intellectual climate was altered over the course of centuries, laying the foundation for industrial development.

In the course of the nineteenth century, Britain's growing power presented other countries that had not experienced similar changes with two options: catch up to Britain or be dominated by it. This dilemma triggered rapid alterations of some societies and the introduction of various political tactics to promote industrialization throughout Europe. These changes tended to exacerbate social tensions between the deeply entrenched medieval power structures and the forces of modernity, sparking political revolutions throughout the century.

As the industrial imperative moved eastward in Europe, economic development became increasingly associated with the state, as opposed to private entrepreneurs. Hence, the gradual extension of political influence and social status outward from a hereditary elite (prompted by the growth of a relatively large and influential commercial class in the west) proved to be the exception, and not the rule, of industrialization. Traditional elites in Germany and Russia succeeded in promoting economic development while suppressing demands for social and political change that were associated with the process in the west. The results included rapid industrialization combined with festering social discontent and political repression that continued throughout the century.

Repression and discontent were also widespread in Britain in the early nineteenth century. But, unlike other European contexts, the medieval system had been sufficiently altered by the commercial interests so that political structures were in place to allow for the gradual integration of the working classes into the system during the course of the century.

The first part of this Chapter is devoted to a discussion of general patterns associated with the process of industrialization in Europe. It is followed by an analysis of the stark differences in social and political realities in selected European countries. The exploitation and human degradation in the early stages of industrialization clearly spurred the growth of modern socialist critiques of capitalism. And it is equally clear that these ideas were influenced, throughout the nineteenth century, by the ways in which different governments reacted to these conditions.

The Stages of Industrialization

With the process of industrialization recognized as one of the most profound changes affecting the modern world, it is not surprising that numerous scholars have attempted to discover consistent patterns associated with it. Given the differences in pre-industrial conditions and the plethora of tactics employed to promote economic development, the search for a pattern has yielded predictably controversial results. One of the most stimulating approaches (in terms of both accomplishments and controversy) was developed by W. W. Rostow in the 1960s. Rostow's attempt to identify commonalities in the process of industrialization by approaching it as a series of five stages that can be applied to all modern economic systems has produced a series of critiques and refinements. For the most part, the critiques have come from economic historians who argue over the specific dates Rostow assigned to various stages in particular countries. In *The World Economy*, published in 1978, Rostow notes these controversies and, in some cases, adjusts his original dates in deference to area experts. For our purposes, the broad outlines of the approach will suffice to illustrate the disparities in the timing of industrialization during the nineteenth century.

Focusing on the stages of economic development from "Traditional" economic systems through those based on high mass-consumption, Rostow identifies three intermediate stages: the Preconditions for Take-off, the Take-off, and the Drive to Maturity. With the scope of this Chapter limited to the nineteenth century (before any system entered into high mass-consumption), the critical stages are briefly summarized as follows:

Traditional: Limited production. Primary focus of economy is agriculture.
Preconditions for Take-off: Sporadic growth in manufacturing and commerce. Growing tendency toward economic expansion.
Take-off: Rapid growth in leading sectors. Economic growth becomes the normal condition.
Drive to Maturity: Economic growth expands from original leading sectors to increasingly complex and technologically sophisticated production.[2]

By applying these stages to selected European societies from Take-off to Maturity, a clear picture of the delay in the process of industrialization from west to east is presented:

```
          1780   1800   1820   1830   1840   1860   1870   1890   1905   1913
Britain         (—Take-off—)  (——————————— Maturity ———————————)
France                        (——— Take-off ———)  (— Maturity —)
Germany                              (Take-off)  (——— Maturity ———)
Russia                                           (Take-off)(———
                                                                        3
```

The obvious delay in the movement into industrialization is also related to a tendency toward a shortening of the Take-off period. Britain's Take-off lasted nearly 50 years, France's lasted 40, Germany's shrunk to 30, and the Take-off in Russia was shortened to a mere 15 years. The fact that each society experienced pronounced revolutionary activity and government repression during its Take-off period suggests the depth of industrialization's disruptive effects on pre-industrial societies. Keep in mind the suggestion that the shrinking of this stage, i.e., the increasing rapidity of the transition from pre-industrial to industrial production, tends to intensify both the degree of social upheaval associated with the early phases of industrialization, and the intensity of governments' reactions to it.

Leading Industrial Sectors

The distinctions between the four countries are further demonstrated by noting the leading economic sectors in their respective Take-offs. The leading sector in Britain was the textile industry, which continued to lead the economy until the 1840s. With industrialization firmly established through the production and export of consumer goods (clothing), the leading sector expanded into heavier, producer-oriented development—beginning with railroads in the 1840s, and steel, electricity, and modern chemical production throughout the remainder of the century.[4]

During the eighteenth century, France's textile industry showed signs of generating a Take-off similar to Britain's, "but it did not match the British after 1760 in generating new technologies and, especially, in bringing them efficiently into the economy."[5] Although Rostow is not directly concerned with our concept of "efficient economic man," note the stress he places on British "efficiency." In addition, he supports Weber's argument concerning the importance of Protestantism to the development of capitalism by noting that the impact of the Revocation of the Edict of Nantes (which outlawed Protestantism in France in 1685):

> helped to dissipate the corps of men who might have performed the acts of invention and innovation which, in the end, most distinguish the British from the French industrial position.[6]

Without "efficiency" in textile production, the French Take-off was delayed until 1830, when coal, iron, and railroads provided the basis for French industrialization.[7] The tendency for capital-intensive production to lead the Take-off became more pronounced as the process was delayed: in Germany and Russia, the Take-offs were spearheaded by railroads, steel and other heavy industries.[8] Unlike Britain, the other countries (and, again, it is important to remember that this tendency is more pronounced as the process moved eastward) moved rapidly from the traditional focus on agriculture to heavy industrial production. In Britain, textiles provided an intermediate stage that allowed a relatively large number of private entrepreneurs to accumulate capital as they expanded their production. In the other areas the state and traditional elites became increasingly involved in entrepreneurial activities, providing the capital necessary for the rapid move from agriculture to heavy industry. The impact of this tendency on social norms and political power was pronounced. In Britain, the middle classes used their growing economic power as a weapon to weaken the remnants of aristocratic-medieval traditions. Where the economic role of middle class entrepreneurs was a less significant force, particularly in Prussia and Russia, medieval traditions (including hereditary political power and inherited social status) often remained intact, undermining the ability of the middle class to limit the traditional powers of the state.

The Role of the State in Industrialization

Perhaps the clearest way to demonstrate the significance of a state's role in the process of industrialization is to clarify different types of state activity. Wolfram Fischer has suggested three categories of state involvement: government as legislator (creating patent, trade, and custom laws), government as administrator (determining fiscal policy and the building and maintenance of roads, bridges, et cetera), government as entrepreneur (playing an active role in mining, industries, banking, insurance, and other institutions of capital formation).[9] In comparing the process of economic development during the nineteenth century in Germany and Britain, Fischer emphasizes the relatively low level of state participation in Britain in all three areas—particularly entrepreneurial activity. He concludes that while the German state (and, especially, Prussia prior to 1871) played an active part as entrepreneur throughout the century, a strong "countervailing tendency" of "private enterprise and entrepreneurship" developed "as the nineteenth century progressed."[10]

Alexander Gerschenkron's analysis of nineteenth-century Russian economic development stresses the extremely high profile of the Czarist state in all aspects of industrialization:

> No one studying the course of economic change in Russia during the period under review can fail to be impressed with the extent and intensity of the government's intervention.[11]

This high level of government intervention is associated with the persistence of a primarily agrarian society into the latter decades of the nineteenth century and a late Take-off. Gerschenkron stresses that Russia "was burdened with the most backward economy among the major countries in Europe."[12] And Talcott Parsons links the likelihood of increased state activity to relatively backward systems attempting to advance rapidly in order to compete with those that started the process earlier:

> The development of industrial economies for the first time had to be independent of predominant government initiative. On the other hand, "catching up" occurs in a situation which puts a strong premium on government initiative, hence a collectivist emphasis, especially where there is a strong sense of urgency involved.[13]

With Britain and Russia illustrating the European extremes in all of these facets of industrialization (timing, leading sectors, and the role of the state), it is clear that France and Germany fell somewhere in between. French and German entrepreneurs repeatedly sought, and received, legislative and administrative support from the state. In Germany, this combination of private and state capitalism produced rapid economic development. In France, the results were not nearly as impressive:

> On the whole, it appears that government activity [in France], both promotional and regulatory, retarded more often than it assisted economic growth.[14]

This point suggests that while concepts such as timing and government involvement can help us begin to distinguish the types of industrialization, they do not tell the full story. Hence, to clarify further the distinctions between the four systems, a brief examination of the pre-Take-off conditions in each society is necessary. The German and Russian cases illustrate the fact that, with considerable effort, governments intent on catching up to Britain could match (and even surpass) its industrial output. However, political institutions, cultural differences and social practices were not altered as easily as levels of production.

The Social and Political Contexts

The centuries of political, social and economic changes in England that were discussed in Chapter Eight did more than provide the basis for industrialization. They also prepared a strong foundation for the development of representative government, derived from the successful battle waged by the middle classes against the power and prerogatives of the hereditary medieval elite. As the process of industrialization moved eastward, it was adapted to societies that had not gone through a preparatory period of social and political change. The revolutionary attacks on medieval society that began in England in the mid-seventeenth century did not reach France until 1789. The German middle classes attempted to assert their power in 1848. In Russia, the closest counterpart to these upheavals did not appear until 1905. Once again, as the process moved eastward, the revolutionary middle classes encountered increasingly powerful opposition, and the extent of their success declined dramatically.

Britain

In the final decades of the eighteenth century, British social and political norms appear to have been nearly perfect for industrialization. The market economy was well established, the political conflicts of the seventeenth century resulted in the supremacy of the commercial class through parliament, and the values of efficient economic man permeated the society. The growth of manufacturing and commerce provided jobs in the cities, but the fluctuations in trade and production brought with them widely varying levels of employment and unemployment. Unable to survive in the countryside due to the continuing enclosures of common land, increasing numbers of people moved to the cities, where they became subject to economic cycles far beyond their control. For the majority, the harsh (though predictable) life in the countryside was replaced by an equally harsh and thoroughly unpredictable life as wage-laborers in the urban industrial centers.

The major population shifts resulting from urbanization served to undermine the legitimacy of the British political system. While the subordination of the monarchy to parliament is recognized as a major step toward representative government, it must be stressed that the process had not advanced significantly since 1688. An elected House of Commons vied for political power with the House of Lords, and the monarchy was increasingly subordinated to parliament. Although these features of political modernity form a stark contrast to other European systems during this period, they are equally removed from modern concepts of representative government. The key distinction is based upon the issue of suffrage—or the number of people allowed to vote for representatives to the elected house. Whereas modern values suggest that voting is a right of people, eighteenth-century British values were shaped by the medieval concept that suffrage was a right of property. Hence, the origins of British electoral districts reflected the pre-industrial agrarian policies, and less than one out of 30 people was eligible to vote.

Such highly restricted suffrage, combined with the existence of an elected house, contributed to social tension. As early as 1769, groups began forming to agitate for electoral reform—including the extension of the suffrage and the alteration of electoral districts to reflect population shifts. John Wilkes, a radical member of the House of Commons, introduced a bill to reform parliament along more representative lines in 1776. He was not successful, but the attempt triggered more agitation and the creation of more groups committed to expanding representation and participation in the political system. Note that Rostow traced the Take-off in Britain to the 1780s, and note that it was precisely during this period that radical organizations (including the London Constitutional Society and the London Corresponding Society) were created. As we will see, this relationship between the early stages of industrialization and widespread political unrest became even more pronounced as the process of economic development moved eastward.

The British government responded to this unrest by enacting highly repressive measures. Beginning with the Treasonable and Seditious Practices Act in 1795 and culminating with the Six Acts of 1819, the government moved to weaken the influence of radical organizations by outlawing public meetings (1795), limiting the radical press (1798 and 1810), repressing reform organizations (1798), and suspending habeas corpus (1817). In addition, the Combination Acts of 1799 and 1800 undermined the fledgling trade unions.[15] However, radical members of parliament were still elected to the House of Commons during this period, keeping the reformist demands alive within the official institutions of government. The fact that even a few dissenting voices were allowed to speak during the period of widespread repression, and that they were able to use the House of Commons as their forum, is quite significant. With hope kept alive during the first two decades of the nineteenth century, the radicals were able to reestablish their organizations in the 1820s, when the repression was eased.

By the 1830s (and note that, according to Rostow, Britain was entering into economic maturity), numerous radical organizations had resurfaced, with demands ranging from increased religious toleration for Catholics to universal suffrage. In 1824, the Combination Act of 1800 was repealed, opening the door to legalized trade union activity. In 1832, a process of electoral reform that was to continue throughout the century began with the extension of the suffrage to the urban middle classes. The adult male urban workers were enfranchised in 1867, and their rural counterparts gained the vote in 1884. We should stress that women and children (who made up a significant part of the work force) were not included in these reforms. Hence, with the recognition that throughout the nineteenth century the right to vote was confined to adult males, the changes still appear to be quite significant when the ratio of voters to population was altered from less than one in 30 before 1832 to one in six after 1884. In addition, measures to alter electoral districts in response to population shifts were passed, and the secret ballot was introduced in 1872. We will return to a discussion of significant political change in Britain during the last decades of the nineteenth century in the Chapter 14.

France

Our brief discussion of change in the British system suggests that political movements based on the demand for equality grew during the nineteenth century—nearly 200 years after medieval political structures and practices were successfully challenged. In France, these two movements coincided in 1789, as forces demanded both an end to the absolute monarchy and the creation of equality. As a result, French society experienced an upheaval far more drastic than Britain's, and the attempt to alter its structure so completely in such a short period of time left a legacy of tensions and unsolved problems. Given this highly unsettled environment, it is not surprising that the drive to economic modernity was hampered.

At precisely the time that the Calvinist-led House of Commons was limiting the power of the English Monarchy, King Louis XIV (1643–1715) was increasing his control over French society. In his quest to extend the power of the central government, he outlawed Protestantism (by revoking the Edict of Nantes) in 1685, undermined the political influence of the nobility, and extended the northern and eastern borders of France through war. The nobility was allowed to maintain its traditional economic privileges (including its exemption from direct taxation) and hereditary feudal status. The Catholic Church also continued to enjoy its traditional privileges and powers (including the power to levy its own taxes), as it provided support for the monarchy. At the bottom of the rigidly hierarchical society, the Third Estate (described by Leo Gershoy as "a legal catch-all" lumping together everyone not included in the "ecclesiastical aristocracy") accounted for 96 per cent of the population.[16]

The persistence of the medieval class structure, Church power, and absolute monarchy aggravated social tensions during the eighteenth century that were further exacerbated by weak and unpopular kings following Louis XIV's death. In addition, the expansion of trade enlarged the commercial middle classes (in French, the bourgeoisie), who were taxed by the Church, nobility, and the state—to finance expenditures that, if given a choice, they would not support. France's traditional legislative body, the Estates General, was not convened between 1614 and 1789—so there was no national institution through which grievances could be formally aired.

By the late 1780s, France's fiscal problems had become compounded by military spending (including aid to the American colonists) and the government was forced to initiate a search for new revenues. Hence, in an environment that included antagonistic middle classes and an increasingly restive aristocracy, Louis XVI (1774–1792) was forced to convene the Estates General to deal with the financial crisis. The timing of this decision proved to be suicidal. The poor harvest of 1788 had exhausted food reserves and created the highest prices in France's history. Impoverished commoners faced famine, and the sharp decline in their ability to purchase manufactured goods contributed to widespread unemployment in the urban areas. In the wake of the coldest winter of the century, rising prices, growing unemployment and the threat of starvation, the newly-elected deputies began demanding changes much more profound than those envisioned by the King.

In the course of the election campaigns for the Estates General, issues arose which extended far beyond the fiscal crisis. The ideas developed during the preceeding decades by critics of French society (discussed in the previous Chapter) provided a dynamic force that encouraged widespread hope for the future and demanded immediate social and political change. In June of 1789, deputies of the Third Estate announced the creation of a National Assembly and promised a constitution. By July, violent revolution spread throughout the country, as the urban and rural commoners vented their pent-up frustrations against the old regime. In late August, the National Assembly (renamed the National Constituent Assembly) produced the Declaration of the Rights of Man and of the Citizen, a document that reflected and institutionalized many of the principles that we discussed in Chapter Ten.

As the title suggests, the Declaration established the rights of citizens in the new regime. The first article combined the doctrine of natural rights with the concept of utility, by stressing natural equality while allowing for "social distinctions" if they contribute to "public utility." Natural rights were defined as "liberty, property, security and resistance to oppression" in the second article, and the sanctity of property was restated in the last of the 17 points. Citizens' consent was established as the basis for government, and traditional censorship was abolished, as "free communication of ideas and opinions" was guaranteed.[17] With the power of the old regime challenged, the fiscal problems were approached in a new manner: property belonging to the Catholic Church was seized and sold to pay the state's debt.

Once the authority of the monarchy was severely limited and the traditional feudal prerogatives of the nobility and Church were abolished, the moderate bourgeoisie controlled the political institutions through the summer of 1792—effectively accomplishing their goal of eliminating the medieval political structure. During this period, Voltaire's thoughts concerning the capacity of reason to improve society, Helvetius' utilitarianism, and Holbach's view of citizenship (as a right of property) meshed to lend support to the regime. But other forces were growing to challenge the newly ascendent bourgeoisie, as those who could not meet the tax or property qualifications to vote questioned the actual degree of equality in the new system. In addition, dispossessed aristocrats conspired to undermine the new regime and, in a pattern that has become commonplace in post-revolutionary societies, they established emigre communities in other countries—encouraging their hosts to intervene in French affairs. Hence, the moderate bourgeoisie found itself caught between the swelling forces on either side and, following the invasion of France by Austria and Prussia, the monarchy was abolished and the Republic was created. The degree of external threat was expanded in 1793, when Britain was added to the growing list of enemies.

Faced with counter-revolution, war and invasion, the radical deputies (Jacobins) aligned themselves with the working classes while the moderates (Girondins) represented the interests of the bourgeoisie. Conflicts between these factions increased in 1793 when the Jacobins insisted on the arrest and execution of Louis XVI. In the Vendee, a royalist-Catholic revolt contributed to the instability of the already precarious system and, again, a poor harvest contributed to domestic unrest. The Jacobins' actions against their adversaries were conducted by the Committee of Public Safety, which instituted a widespread violent attack on those they considered enemies of the revolution. While legally terrorizing the society, the Jacobins found time to create a new constitution that declared the establishment of social and political equality. In addition, they were highly successful in mobilizing the society to defend the revolution against internal and external threats. In late July, 1794, the Jacobin Terror was replaced by the Thermidorian Reaction—an anti-Jacobin (and anti-working class) movement that utilized the same violent tactics against those who had just recently been in charge of the guillotine. In the fall of 1795, still another stage of the revolution began, under the Directory, with the goal of restoring order.

In a mere six years, the French had experienced an upheaval so tumultuous that the growing desire for calm and predictability does not seem at all surprising. The government was dominated by both rural and urban property owners, who vowed to provide a proper environment for the reconstruction of the economy. But while the commercial interests desired a stable environment conducive to economic development, they were caught between the same forces that undermined their moderate predecessors in 1792 and, by 1799, political power had shifted toward a three-member consulate that included the military commander of the Paris garrison—Napoleon Bonaparte. By 1804, Napoleon had manipulated the system and the general populace to the point that he was declared Emperor, and a system of hereditary succession (not unlike that under the Bourbon Monarchy) was created. While certain rights were guaranteed under the Napoleonic Code, the new Emperor was able to dominate the society by appealing directly to the people, who supported the popular general until his renowned military successes were checked by a massive alliance of European countries and Paris was occupied by foreign troops. Early in April, 1814, Napoleon abdicated and by July, the Bourbon Monarchy was restored under Louis XVIII (1814–1824).

The impact of the events from 1789 to 1814 on French society was profound. The attempt to apply the ideals of the *philosophes* to practical politics left a legacy of both hope and frustration that continued to influence, if not dominate, French politics and society throughout the nineteenth century. The moderate monarchy of Louis XVIII was followed by his reactionary brother Charles X (1824–1830), whose policies triggered another revolution in 1830. Louis Philippe ascended to the throne in 1830, reigning until another revolution deposed him in 1848. The Second Republic was declared in 1848, but gave way to the Second Empire under Napoleon III from 1852 to 1870, when still another revolution shook the society and toppled the government. Finally, a measure of continuity was established with the creation of the Third Republic, which lasted from 1870 until 1940.

Given these drastic shifts in government and policy throughout the nineteenth century, which reflected deep divisions within the society, it is not surprising that France's economic development and industrialization lagged behind Britain's. Under Louis Philippe (known as "the bourgeois king") and Napoleon III, tension between the revolutionary and monarchical factions abated long enough to permit the "Take-off" in French industrial development.

In addition to their domestic consequences, the upheavals in France shook the foundations of other European systems. Traditional monarchies and feudal elites throughout Europe were threatened by the revolutionary ideals (liberty, equality, fraternity), as well as by the demonstrated military capacity of Napoleon's armies. The highly motivated citizen army spreading these values throughout Europe evoked varied responses in other societies. The repression of dissident movements in Britain during the 1790s can be traced to the fear that demands for total equality would spread across the English Channel. Western-oriented intellectuals in central Europe and Russia hailed the dawn of a new world, as the *philosophes'* optimism spread eastward to support critiques of other monarchies and feudal societies. Some monarchs committed themselves to repressing these tendencies, while others quietly admired the efficiency and capacities demonstrated by a mobilized society—regardless of the source of the motivation. Two important responses can be identified in the Prussian and Russian systems in the early nineteenth century.

The Confederation of the Rhine

When assessing the impact of the French Revolution of 1789 outside the borders of France, it is clear that central Europe was most directly affected. Austria and Prussia were major forces in the wars against Napoleon, and the areas of southern and western Germany were invaded and occupied early in the conflict. The political fragmentation of what is now Germany (as we noted in Chapter Eight) resulted from its historical diversity and the continued attempts to maintain the Holy Roman Empire. The political focus on empire left de facto political control in the hands of the German princes, serving to reinforce feudal tendencies at the same time that Britain and France were becoming nation states. Attempts to unify the Germans economically (the Hanseatic League) and politically (under Frederick Barbarossa and Frederick II in the twelfth and thirteenth centuries) were not successful, and the Treaty of Westphalia (1648) reinforced the lack of unity by guaranteeing that each of the hundreds of German princes would determine the religion in his domain.

The fall of Louis XVI provoked excitement and hope in several areas of central Europe—especially in the Rhineland, where the Enlightenment's tenets had been well-received. In 1806 the Confederation of the Rhine was created by Napoleon to ally several German states with France. Under the Confederation, the traditional powers of the nobility and churches were undermined, free trade was established and the Napoleonic Code was installed as the basis of government. Koppel Pinson summarizes Napoleon's impact:

> The first semblance of national unification in Germany . . . [was a] combination of the attempt to exploit the country for French interests with the missionary and civilizing aim to bring Germany the benefits of what Napoleon had selected from the revolutionary heritage.[18]

But the Confederation was abolished in 1813, as France's power declined. Meanwhile, the leaders of Prussia recognized the significance of the French experience and took steps to alter their system to avoid similar revolutionary upheavals, while incorporating the illusion of political reform.

Prussia

The establishment of the Prussian state took place in the seventeenth century. Under three leaders—Frederick William, the Great Elector of Brandenburg, (1640–1688), Frederick William I (1713–1740) and Frederick II (Frederick the Great, 1740–1786)—a highly bureaucratized authoritarian system was created. The ability of these leaders (from the Hohenzollern family) to combine the interests of the monarchy with the nobility (the Junkers) led to widespread acceptance of the central government. While the nobility was threatened by the growing power of centralizing monarchs throughout the rest of Europe, the Prussian rulers effectively integrated the Junkers into the new military and civilian bureaucracy, establishing them as the privileged class. As a result of this alliance:

> In Prussia the nobles were the chief champions of the Crown and their historical importance was due to the fact that they were protagonists of a monarchical state ethos that subsequently extended among the middle and lower classes.[19]

The significance of the absence of competition between the nobility and the monarchy cannot be overemphasized. Their unity made it virtually impossible, until the late nineteenth century, for other segments of society to limit the highly centralized power of the Prussian state—creating a legacy for German political thought and action that persisted into the twentieth century. A. J. P. Taylor underscored the importance of the unique combination of "unscrupulous authoritarianism" combined with "a striving after efficiency and improvement" as a key factor in later industrial and political changes in Germany.[20] And Hans Rosenberg supports the point by arguing that:

> In effect, the transition from parochial Junker rule to the centralizing and bureaucratizing Hohenzollern regime further strengthened the repressive structure of the political and social organization.[21]

The repeated military defeats of such a state at the hands of Napoleon's armies (at least allegedly fighting for liberty and equality) were bound to send shock waves through the Prussian government. As early as 1807, Prussian ministers began suggesting that the government institute reforms that would make the society more efficient, increasing its capacity to defend itself against the highly mobilized French. Politically, the reforms included the creation of an elected assembly; socially, the abolition of serfdom was advocated. The reformers were intent on adopting those dimensions of the French revolutionary heritage that fostered the concept of citizen (as opposed to subject)—a concept that appeared to have promoted the efficiency of Napoleon's armies. Genuine reform of the basis of power was never considered, and this tendency in Prussia to create the illusion of reform by introducing controlled political changes from the existing power structure was to become the norm throughout the century. Significantly, however, serfdom was abolished in 1815 and a mobile workforce gradually emerged to provide the labor for industrialization. The movement for political reforms declined, but was rekindled in the 1840s—when the French revolutionary legacy resurfaced in popular movements, igniting revolution throughout Europe.

The German Revolution

The unsettled issues of the 1790s festered in France until February, 1848, when Paris exploded again in revolution. Unlike the previous upheaval, the revolution of 1848 acted as a spark to ignite revolutions throughout central Europe. Like their English and French counterparts, the German middle classes led the movement against the traditional power structures.

While the motives behind the middle class revolutions in England, France and Germany were similar, it should already be clear that the conditions in each society played a crucial role in determining their results. In England, the move to limit the traditional power structures was successful. France faced a more problematical situation, as the drive for social and political equality overlapped the move against the monarchy and feudal elite. In Germany, the middle classes faced the same problems as the French, but an additional factor complicated their movement: there was no national state to limit. Given that virtually all of the middle class arguments in England and France (from Locke through Smith and Voltaire) focused on limiting a centralized monarchical nation state, the German middle classes had little to go on. They were torn between the usual middle class desires to limit the nation state's power (by guaranteeing civil rights and liberties and expanded participation) and the widely perceived need to unite the fragmented German states into a single political entity. Clearly, their task was much more complex than that of their English and French counterparts: they had to create a centralized nation state, and limit it at the same time. This dilemma, combined with deeply entrenched sectional interests, split the German middle classes. Some looked to Prussia for strong monarchical leadership (which they would then limit) to unify Germany. Others viewed Prussia as completely antithetical to their goals. In addition, industrial production in the 1840s (the beginning of the Take-off) had produced a working class more organized and militant than the French middle classes had faced. Class and economic conflicts reinforced ancient sectional differences, creating a myriad of loyalties and goals that, given the best of circumstances, would be difficult to unite.

Beginning as an assembly of volunteers (who, unlike their English and French counterparts, had no national legislative body to legitimize their movement), the Frankfurt Assembly called for general elections for a National Assembly—which met in May, 1848. By December, The Declaration of Fundamental Rights (including freedom of the press, assembly, speech, religion and, of course, the sanctity of property rights) was accepted by the Assembly and in March, 1848, a constitution uniting the German states was completed. Austria was the first of the states to deny the constitution's validity, and others followed suit in refusing to ratify it. The King of Prussia demonstrated his contempt for the Assembly by refusing to accept the document—even though the constitution would have made him emperor of the united Germans. As early as April, 1849, the German states began recalling their deputies from the Assembly. Several radical democrats, republicans and socialists refused to disband and insurrections supporting them flared throughout the German states. By the end of summer, the Prussian military had annihilated the remnants of the revolution.

The political reform movement within the Prussian government that had been stimulated by Napoleon's victories resurfaced during the revolution of 1848, and a constitution was created for the Prussians by King Frederick William IV (1840–1861) and his advisors. With significant modifications through 1850, the Prussian Constitution of 1848 served as the model for the German Constitution of 1871, after Prussia succeeded in uniting Germany through military force. In keeping with the traditional Prussian norms, the Constitution gave the monarch exclusive control over the appointment of cabinet ministers and army officers, as well as emergency powers allowing him to suspend civil rights. In response to demands for increased representation, a bicameral legislature was created. Members of the first house (later named the House of Lords) were elected by men over thirty who could qualify as large property owners; members of the second house (later named the House of Deputies) were originally elected by universal male suffrage, age 25.

In May, 1849, the real power of the lower house was revealed when its members asked the government to accept the Frankfurt Assembly's proposed constitution. The Monarch responded by dissolving the lower house and instituting new election laws to undermine its influence. The three-class suffrage was based on the division of Prussian voters into groups, determined by the amount they paid in direct taxes, i.e., those who paid the most, the least, and a middle group. Each group chose an equal number of electors who, in turn, chose a deputy to the lower house. The result was a highly disproportionate amount of power in the hands of the smallest and wealthiest group. This obvious manipulation of the allegedly representative system by altering the suffrage guaranteed that power in the lower house would be controlled by a small wealthy group. In addition, it discouraged voter turnout among the lower classes:

When for the entire state an average of 132 voters in Class III had the same voting power as 19.1 voters in Class II and as 7.1 in Class I, the masses saw little inducement to express their political opinions by balloting.[22]

An additional revision to the Constitution in 1850 guaranteed the Junkers a vast majority in the House of Lords and gave the upper house veto power over bills submitted by the lower house. Article 45 of the new constitution stated that "Complete authority rests only in the person of the King."[23] Hence, what at first might appear to be the introduction of representative government into the Prussian state was, in reality, merely the introduction of the illusion of change:

> The monarchy with its absolutist tools—the army, bureaucracy, and the ruling Junker class—emerged victorious from the revolution.[24]

The German Empire

Prussia also emerged victorious from the wars of 1866 and 1870, defeating its rivals for German supremacy and creating the German Empire. On the surface, the Constitution of 1871 appears to establish an institutional basis for legitimate political competition throughout the Empire—with a monarch, chancellor, and two legislative bodies; one of these (the Reichstag) was nationally elected by universal male suffrage (age 25) and secret ballot. But in reality, the domination of the Prussian nobility was assured throughout Germany. The federal branch of the legislature (the Bundesrat) represented the 25 German states through 58 voting members. Of the 58, 14 were able to veto amendments to the constitution, and all state delegations were required to cast their votes as a single unit. Prussia's 17 votes, then, guaranteed its veto power over constitutional issues in the Bundesrat. In addition, the hereditary king of Prussia became the German emperor, with sole power to choose the chancellor and other cabinet ministers. Article 15 delineates the relationship between the monarch, chancellor and the two elected houses as follows:

> The presiding chair in the Bundesrat and the conduct of business appertain to the Imperial Chancellor, who is to be appointed by the Emperor.

And the role of the Reichstag is defined in Article 23:

> The Reichstag shall have the right, within the competence of imperial legislation, to present and to pass on petitions directed to it, to the Bundesrat and the Imperial Chancellor.

Article 13 illustrates the close relationship of the Prussian-dominated Bundesrat and the Prussian-controlled executive:

> The Bundesrat and the Reichstag shall be summoned annually. For the preparation of these meetings, the Bundesrat can be summoned without the Reichstag, but the latter cannot be summoned without the Bundesrat.[25]

In addition, the Prussian monarchy and nobility maintained control over the military.

While the significance of the Prussian norms did not become fully evident until 1871, the failure of the German middle classes to alter them appreciably became fully apparent during the 1930s. The legacy of the failed revolution included a fragmented middle class combined with deep cleavages separating the middle and working classes. In Britain, the middle-class radicals led the move for reform of the political system throughout the nineteenth century and the monarchy increasingly tended to support the dominant party in the House of Commons. In Germany, the

Prussian monarchs and nobility were united in their attempt to deny political leadership to anyone outside of their inner circle. In addition, the fact that many middle-class delegates to the Frankfurt Assembly went home when the revolution became violent strengthened working-class animosities toward them—further undermining any potential alliance between the commoners against the traditional Prussian elite:

> In most instances of urban violence during the period in Germany, the people who died on the barricades were workers. . . . But the men who emerged as temporary political leaders were bourgeois liberals, and the issues discussed and measures proposed served the interests of bourgeois liberals. Thus while the revolution as a whole failed, many workers felt that they had been especially sold out.[26]

Under the Constitution of 1871, Germany moved into the phase of economic maturity—successfully merging the concept of efficient economic man with efficient Prussian authoritarianism.

Under the watchful guidance of Chancellor Bismarck and Emperor William I (1871–1888), the economy moved into the stage of "Maturity," stimulated by heavy industry. The results were impressive, and Germany was able to produce 76% of Britain's industrial output in 1900—up sharply from 41% in 1860.[27] This remarkable rise in production was accompanied by Bismarck's ability to manipulate and fragment hostile political and social forces in Germany. The historical lack of unity that characterized the middle classes was extended to the working classes, as the socialist movement inherited the regional diversity and corresponding fragmentation that allowed the traditional Prussian elite to maintain its power after 1848. In addition, Bismarck's capacity to amplify this disunity by manipulating the working classes must be stressed, and it is best illustrated by the Anti-Socialist Laws of 1878 to 1890.

Following an attempted assassination of the Emperor in May, 1878, Bismarck introduced the Laws, but the Reichstag refused to support them. After a second attempt (and, significantly, neither of the unsuccessful assassins was shown to be linked with the Social Democratic Party), Bismarck convinced the Bundesrat to dissolve the Reichstag and actively campaigned against the socialists up to the election of July 30. "The Exceptional Laws Against the Publicly Dangerous Endeavors of Social Democracy" were passed by the new Reichstag in October for a period of two years, and extended four times until they were allowed to lapse in 1890. By outlawing the socialist press and the party organization outside the Reichstag, the Laws crippled the organization and forced the exile of its leaders. However, socialist deputies were not barred from the Reichstag or prohibited from campaigning for office. From 1878 to 1890, while the party was officially outlawed, its percentage of votes increased from 7.6% to 19.7%, which provided for an increase in seats from nine to 35![28] Clearly, Bismarck's goal was to eliminate the leadership, party organization and press—without pushing the rank and file members toward open revolt. During the 1880s, Bismarck attempted to drive more wedges between the socialist leadership and the working classes by introducing highly progressive social legislation (including health, disability, accident and old-age insurance for the working classes) that further undermined the position of the revolutionary party leadership: how could they criticize such a benevolent state?

The impact of the outlaw period on the German Social Democratic Party was dramatic. Many exiled leaders became increasingly radical while others, notably Eduard Bernstein, became more moderate. The exiled leadership was separated from the socialist deputies in the Reichstag, the trade unions, and the rank and file party members; many in the latter group were enticed into adopting the traditional Prussian view of the state as the source of progress in exchange for social welfare and seats in the Reichstag. The electoral success of the party would have been significant in a real parliamentary system. But, given the constitutional power of Prussia over the executive, seats in the Reichstag had little to do with policy. Again, the full significance of these events did not become clear until the twentieth century, and we will return to these issues in Chapter 14.

Russia

From the establishment of the Muscovite state in the fifteenth century, the domination by the czars (Ivan the Terrible, 1533–1584, was the first Muscovite prince to be crowned "czar") was an essential feature of the system. Following the Muscovite conquests of Novgorod and Pskov in 1478 and 1511, the Veche (a traditional local legislative body) disappeared. Ivan III (1462–1505), after ordering the exile or execution of Novgorod's influential citizens, set the tone for Russian political behavior through the early twentieth century: The veche bell in my patrimony, in Novgorod, shall not be . . . and I will rule the entire state.[29] Although the Boyar Duma—a council of nobles—continued to exist, it was subordinated to the power of the czars. Hence, at precisely the time that Tudor monarchs were affirming the legitimacy of the English Parliament by working closely with it, potential opposition to the centralized monarchy was being weakened in Russia.

The autocratic characteristics of the Russian state were reinforced in 1560 when Ivan the Terrible accused the Chosen Council (his hand-picked advisors) of plotting to murder his wife. All of its members were exiled or executed and the Czar's wrath was extended to the entire nobility. Through his secret political police, the Boyars were further subordinated to the Czar. The reigns of Peter the Great (1682–1725) and Catherine the Great (1762–1796) are notable for their reforms of the system; these reforms, however, were intended to increase administrative efficiency—not to extend political influence to other segments of society.

Alexander I (1801–1825) initially responded to the threat posed by the French Revolution and Napoleon in much the same way as his Prussian counterpart—and a series of reforms were proposed by his advisor, Michael Speranskii, from 1807 through 1812. Some of Speranskii's reforms that were designed to increase the government's efficiency were accepted, but those that would have introduced representative government were not. Speranskii was exiled in 1812 and the ideas of Nicholas Karamzin were adopted as the guidelines for the remainder of Alexander's reign:

> Savage people love independence, wise people love order, and there is no order without autocratic power.[30]

Unlike the Prussian military and civil bureaucracy, the young Russian officers who desired reform had little influence on their monarch. Hence, with no legal means of initiating change, a group of officers went underground—as early as 1816—to plan a revolt in order to modernize Russia. As we will see, this conspiratorial response to czarist autocracy became the dominant form of political activity throughout the nineteenth century. The goals of leaders such as Captain Muraviev and Colonel Pestel focused on the need to institute widespread political and social reforms—including the abolition of serfdom, the recognition of legalized competition for political influence and guarantees of civil rights. Alexander I died on December 1, 1825 and, on December 25, the officers made their move. But the Decembrist Revolt was poorly planned, the movement was highly fragmented, and Nicholas I (1825–1855) easily suppressed it. The leaders were exiled or executed and Nicholas moved to extend his power beyond the already significant levels enjoyed by his predecessor. In 1832 (the same year that the electoral reforms began in England), a new codification of the laws articulated the political realities in Russia:

The Emperor of All the Russias is an autocratic (*samoderzhavny*) and unlimited (*neogranichenny*) monarch; God himself ordains that all must bow to his supreme power, not only out of fear, but also out of conscience.[31]

During his reign, Nicholas I strengthened the secret police, instituted strict censorship laws and severely limited the courses (including philosophy and constitutional law) that could be taught in Russian universities.[32] Not surprisingly, underground revolutionary activity escalated sharply during the widespread repression by this "quasi-military dictatorship."[33]

Given this brief description of the political conditions in Russia, the significance of the reforms introduced by Alexander II (1855–1881) is evident. The emancipation of the peasantry, the reform of local and municipal governments and the consideration of a constitution that would have introduced institutionalized political competition all suggest that the long-awaited reform of traditional Russian society finally emerged in the latter part of the nineteenth century. But a closer look at both the source and outcome of these reforms reveals a strong element of continuity with traditional Russian political practices, as well as extremely problematical results. The Czar, not the society, was the source of change and, as later events clearly demonstrate, what the czars gave the czars could take away.

The defeat of Russia at the hands of a poorly organized French and British alliance in the Crimean War provided the immediate context for Alexander II to introduce his reforms. On March 30, 1856 (the day Russia surrendered) the Czar told a group of the Moscow nobility that "it is better to begin abolishing serfdom from above than to wait for it to begin to abolish itself from below."[34] Predictably, the nobility did not share the Czar's perspective—viewing the abolition of serfdom as a direct threat to its political, economic and social status. Without the nobility's support, Alexander planned the emancipation with his advisors and in mid-February, 1861, the statutes were enacted.

The zemstvo reforms of 1864 created institutions that provided an outlet for political representation on the local level. They were never recognized as legitimate sources of demands on the central government: Dmytryshyn stresses the fact that they had no executive power and Riasanovsky summarizes their role as "a junior partner to the central government."[35] The limited nature of the reform of local governments might have established a starting point for heightened political competition if a plan drawn up by Loris-Melikov, one of the Czar's closest advisors, to create a consultative national assembly—with members chosen from the zemstvos—had been pursued. But the reforms stopped with the assassination of Alexander II in 1881 and the ascendence of his reactionary son, Alexander III (1881–1894).

If the reign of Alexander II offered the possibility of meaningful change in Russia, any hope for an alteration of the traditional Russian autocracy was shattered under the new Czar. Immediately after his father's assassination, Alexander III surrounded himself with new advisors, scrapped Loris-Melokiv's plan and issued the Manifesto on the Inviolability of the Autocracy, which stated:

Amidst our great sorrow the voice of God enjoins us to take up firmly the reins of the government, with trust in divine Providence, with faith in the strength and verity of autocratic power, which we have been called upon to maintain and defend, for the good of the people, against all encroachments upon it.[36]

The autocracy moved quickly; further reforms were halted and those that had been initiated were severely curtailed. The potential influence of the zemstvos was limited and, ultimately, they were placed under the power of the nobility. Public and private meetings, along with freedom of the press, were outlawed and detention of suspects without trial became the norm. In addition, the universities and student organizations were affected, with the government assuming total control over the former and outlawing the latter.

The widespread repression of the 1880s and 1890s pushed still another generation of Russians toward violent revolution as the only conceivable means to alter the society. The revolutionaries of the 1830s went underground when they found themselves caught between an autocratic state and an illiterate peasantry. But the industrialization of Russia began under Alexander III (note that the Take-off is dated around 1890) and some of the peasants were being transformed into industrial workers under a powerful mixture of private enterprise, state capitalism and foreign investment. The growth of an industrial working class coupled with the traditional autocratic political norms provided a new source of hope for the revolutionaries of the 1890s. Unlike the Prussian elite, the traditional Russian power structure was confident of its ability to repress (as opposed to manipulate and undermine) challenges to its power, while it encouraged drastic alterations of the society through industrialization. This confidence was disastrous for czardom, as underground movements built their organizations that surfaced in the revolutionary upheavals of 1905 and 1917.

Individuals and Industrialization

While the political conditions in nineteenth-century Europe varied greatly, a degree of commonality was established through the experience of industrialization. Even a cursory glance at the working classes who were sharing this experience discloses the cause of Durkheim's "cry of grief and anger," shedding light on the growth of socialist critiques throughout the century. And the true depth of the tension is revealed when we recall that promises of unlimited improvement and the flourishing of the human potential coexisted with such suffering and abject degradation. Edmund Wilson's chilling summary of conditions in Manchester around 1842, as they were observed by Friedrich Engels, provides a sobering counterpoint to the eighteenth-century optimism:

> He saw the working people living like rats in the wretched little dens of their dwellings, whole families, sometimes more than one family, swarming in a single room, well and diseased, adults and children, close relations sleeping together, sometimes even without beds to sleep on when all the furniture had been sold for firewood, sometimes in damp, underground cellars which had to be bailed out when the weather was wet, sometimes living in the same room with the pigs; ill nourished on flour mixed with gypsum and cocoa mixed with dirt, poisoned by ptomaine from tainted meat, doping themselves and their wailing children with laudanum; spending their lives, without a sewage system, among the piles of their excrement and garbage; spreading epidemics of typhus and cholera which even made inroads into the well-to-do sections.
>
> The increasing demand for women and children at the factories was throwing the fathers of families permanently out of work, arresting the physical development of the girls, letting the women in for illegitimate motherhood and yet compelling them to come to work when they were pregnant or before they had recovered from having their babies, and ultimately turning a good many of them into prostitutes; while the children, fed into the factories at the age of five or six, receiving little care from mothers who were themselves at the factory all day and no education at all from a community which wanted them only to perform mechanical operations, would drop exhausted when they were let out of their prisons, too tired to wash or eat, let alone study or play, sometimes too tired to go home at all.[37]

This passage clearly demonstrates the fact that, by the nineteenth century, we are no longer dealing with Calvinist merchants who consciously chose to pursue wealth. Instead, we are observing the results of the total institutionalization of the Calvinist through Locke and Smith view of the world. And while members of the economic elite chose to deny classical leisure as a way of life, the system they created guaranteed that no such choice would be presented to the vast majority of society. The former group willingly sacrificed its potential leisure to the quest for greater profit; the latter group was forced to surrender its time and energy to dehumanizing labor just to stay alive. Recall that Aristotle's support of slavery was justified as a necessary condition to allow some people to pursue classical leisure. During the early stages of industrialization, this new form of slavery was painted as freedom by the commercial classes—and justified as a necessary condition to enhance profit.

A more personal glimpse into the daily lives of the working classes was presented as evidence to a committee of the British Parliament in 1832. At the age of 28, William Cooper had already spent 18 years laboring in textile factories. At the age of 10 he worked from 5:00 A.M. to 9:00 P.M. with one 40 minute break. At the age of 20, his daily regimen was as follows:

> When I was only a gigger I went at five o'clock on a Monday morning, and had half an hour at breakfast and an hour at dinner, and half an hour at drinking; then went on till nine on Monday evening, and stopped half an hour; then went on to twelve at midnight, and stopped half an hour; then went on to half-past four on Tuesday morning, and stopped half an hour; then went on again from five to eight, and stopped half an hour; then went on till twelve, and stopped an hour; then went on again from one to five, and stopped half an hour; then went on again to nine o'clock at night, then we went home.[38]

During the hearing a physician was called to testify on the impact of such conditions, and his observations lend themselves nicely to the theme of this book:

> The reflecting or spiritual mind gradually becomes debased . . . the being is necessarily ruined, both for the present and for the future life.[39]

The physician concluded that during his experience on a West Indies slave plantation, "I never saw nor heard of such inhumanity."[40]

The significance of the disparitites in political conditions from Britain to Russia is accentuated by the recognition that the working classes throughout Europe shared William Cooper's lifestyle during the early years of industrialization. The critical question, then, hinges on the availability of political means to improve their plight. In Britain, the House of Commons gradually responded to working class demands for legislation to alleviate this misery in the latter part of the century. And, because the House of Commons had the power to do something about these demands, significant reforms were instituted. In Germany, the working classes were provided with progressive insurance programs and representation in the Reichstag, but the Prussian-dominated state successfully limited and fragmented their political influence. Under the Russian autocracy, there were no political institutions available to permit the pursuit of legal change.

References

1. The Act of Union of 1707 integrated the Kingdoms of England and Scotland into the "United Kingdom of Great Britain," referred to hereafter simply as Britain.
2. W. W. Rostow, *The Stages of Economic Growth,* 2nd ed. (New York: Cambridge Univ. Press, 1960) pp. 4–16.
3. W. W. Rostow, *The World Economy* (Austin, Texas: Univ. of Texas Press, 1978) pp. 383, 400, 407, 437.

4. Ibid., p. 383.
5. Ibid., p. 394.
6. W. W. Rostow, *Politics and the Stages of Growth* (London: Cambridge Univ. Press, 1971) p. 85.
7. W. W. Rostow, *The World Economy*, p. 400.
8. Ibid., p. 407, pp. 427–428.
9. Wolfram Fischer, "Government Activity and Industrialization in Germany," *The Economics of Take-off Into Sustained Growth*, ed. W. W. Rostow (New York: St. Martin's Press, 1965) p. 84.
10. Ibid.
11. Alexander Gerschenkron, "The Early Phases of Industrialization in Russia: Afterthoughts and Counterthoughts," Ibid., p. 158.
12. Ibid., p. 153.
13. Talcott Parsons, "Characteristics of Industrial Societies," *The Transformation of Russian Society*, ed. Cyril E. Black (Cambridge: Harvard Univ. Press, 1967) p. 39.
14. Rondo E. Cameron, "Economic Growth and Stagnation in France, 1815–1914," *The Experience of Economic Growth*, ed., Barry E. Supple (New York: Random House, 1963) p. 338. Reprinted from *The Journal of Modern History*, xxx, 1 (1958).
15. G. D. H. Cole and A. W. Filson, ed. *British Working Class Movements, Select Documents* (New York: St. Martin's Press, 1965) pp. 74–77.
16. Leo Gershoy, *The Era of the French Revolution* (Princeton, N.J.: Anvil, Van Nostrand, 1957) pp. 14–16.
17. Declaration of the Rights of Man and Citizen, *Readings in Western Civilization*, ed. George H. Knoles and Rixford K. Snyder (Chicago: J. B. Lippincott Co., 1954) pp. 528–529.
18. K. Pinson, *Modern Germany*, 2nd ed. pp. 31–32.
19. Otto Hintze, "The Hohenzollern and the Nobility," *Historical Essays of Otto Hintze*, ed. Felix Gilbert (New York: Oxford Univ. Press, 1975) p. 62.
20. A. J. P. Taylor, *The Course of German History* (New York: Capricorn Books, 1962) pp. 29–30.
21. Hans Rosenberg, *Bureaucracy, Aristocracy, and Autocracy* (Boston: Beacon Press, 1958) p. 42.
22. Eugene N. Anderson, *The Social and Political Conflict in Prussia* (New York: Octagon Books, 1968) p. 414.
23. Louis Snyder, ed. *Documents of German History* (New Brunswick, N.J.: Rutgers Univ. Press, 1958) p. 191.
24. Hajo Holborn, *A History of Modern Germany* (New York: Alfred A. Knopf, 1969), Vol. III, p. 79.
25. L. Snyder, p. 230.
26. Gary P. Steenson, *Not One Man! Not One Penny!* (Pittsburgh, Pa.: Univ. of Pittsburgh Press, 1981) p. 3.
27. B. R. Mitchell, *European Historical Statistics*, 2nd ed., revised (New York: Facts on File, 1981) p. 335.
28. Thomas T. Mackie and Richard Rose, *The International Almanac of Electoral History* (New York: The Free Press, 1974) pp. 148–155.
29. Nicholas Riasanovsky, *A History of Russia*, 2nd ed. (New York: Oxford Univ. Press, 1969) p. 115.
30. James H. Billington, *The Icon and the Axe* (New York: Vintage Books, 1970) p. 68.
31. Lothar Schultz, "Constitutional Law in Russia," *Russia Enters the Twentieth Century*, ed. Erwin Oberländer (New York: Schocken Books, 1971) p. 35.
32. Thomas G. Masaryk, *The Spirit of Russia*, 2nd ed., trans. Edin and Cedar Paul, 3 vols. (New York: Macmillan, 1955) vol. I, pp. 111–112.
33. Basil Dmytryshyn, *A History of Russia* (Englewood Cliffs, N.J.: Prentice-Hall, 1977) p. 346.
34. George Vernadsky, ed. *A Source Book for Russian History from Early Times to 1917*. 3 vols. (New Haven, Conn.: Yale Univ. Press, 1972) vol. III, p. 589.
35. Dmytryshyn, p. 367. Riasanovsky, p. 416.
36. Vernadsky, vol. III, p. 680.
37. Edmund Wilson, *To the Finland Station* (New York: Farrar, Straus and Giroux, 1972) pp. 159–160.
38. Minutes of Evidence from the Sadler Report, *Sessional Papers*, 1833, vol. 123, ed. 706. Reprinted in Knoles and Snyder, p. 567.
39. Ibid., p. 586.
40. Ibid.

Chapter 12
Beyond Economic Man: The Quest for Community

While the concept of efficient economic man served to support the drives of the commercial classes and justify the growth of industrialization, it left others searching for an alternative perspective. Some went back to the *Old Testament* and early Christianity, while others looked to modern science as the solution to society's ills. Many longed for the relative simplicity and communal norms of the agrarian village, while others sought a way to humanize industrial production. Despite their divergent approaches, these critics shared the hope for future improvement. Focusing on the Enlightenment's legacy of unlimited optimism, the critics challenged their predecessors' proposed means to accomplish the end of heaven on earth. They argued that the atomistic view of humans was antithetical to social harmony. They challenged the justifications of private property and laissez-faire economics when they compared its results to its theory. They viewed economic self-interest as a weakness, rather than a virtue, and they condemned the system of thought that used the idea of natural equality to justify massive social, political and economic inequalities.

The obvious clash between the "heavenly city" optimism of the eighteenth century and the abhorrent conditions resulting from nineteenth-century industrialization would have been enough to provoke criticism and reevaluation. But in addition, a new source of tension emerged as the scientific imperative drove economists to analyze specific dimensions of the market economy. Whereas Adam Smith was able to reconcile his empirical analysis with optimism for the future, other economists painted a gloomy—and even terrifying—picture. As early as 1798, Thomas Malthus made his famous proposal concerning the relation of food supplies to population that predicted widespread starvation as the human destiny. Because food supplies grow arithmetically while population grows geometrically, Malthus predicted a future where population growth would outstrip the species' ability to feed itself. This overall tendency would be hastened to the degree that the working classes were paid higher wages because the corresponding improvement in their standard of living would encourage them to have more children and more food would be consumed. In 1817, David Ricardo's studies concluded that any increase in wages (for the working classes) or profits (for the commercial classes) would be nullified by corresponding increases in prices and rents. So much for optimism.

While tension between hope, ideals, reality and economic theories created a common ground for the critiques of "efficient economic man" throughout Europe, two distinct views emerged. The defenders of the dominant eighteenth-century doctrines focused on science and reason, insisting on a precise (often mathematical) definition of humans and society. Individuals were defined as self-interested hedonists and society was viewed as a mechanical construct that could be taken apart and rearranged, guided by the proper scientific principles. Locke, Hume, La Mettrie and Voltaire provided the intellectual foundation for the movement. On the other side, critics of these views flocked to the romantic movement, stressing sentiment and feeling (instead of reason) as the solution to social ills. Individuals were viewed as complex spiritual and empathetic beings, and society was perceived as an organic culmination of the past. Science was condemned as arrogant and anti-spiritual, and its focus on material reality (and the economic preoccupation with material things) became the object of attack. Nature was to be revered—not exploited and manipulated for economic gain. The process of economic development and industrialization was regarded as inherently anti-human, and its supporting ideal of efficient economic man (referred to by Thomas Carlyle as "the pig philosophy") was viewed as the ultimate insult to humanity.[1]

Throughout the nineteenth century, advocates of these competing orientations battled to influence the ideas and, hence, the future of the species. By the latter part of the century cultural and historical factors seem to have elevated variations of one or another focus to a dominant position in almost every western society. In Britain, the scientific and practical approach established by Locke, Hume and Smith emerged from its conflict with romanticism as an empirical and pragmatic form of socialism. In France, the rationalist tradition of Descartes and the *philosophes* provided the basis for one strain of socialist thought, while the Physiocrats' empiricism inspired still another. In Germany, romanticism permeated society and socialism inherited the historical preoccupation with a strong centralized state that dominated other currents of nineteenth-century German thought. In Russia, the total power of the autocratic state was echoed in the authoritarian voices of virtually all critics.

Marx's primary intellectual accomplishment was his merging of the two competing traditions. In addition, he both integrated and denied the national characteristics of socialist thought while relying on empirical analysis of economic trends to support (as opposed to his fellow-economists, who tended to deny) the eighteenth-century optimism. Finally, he provided an extremely optimistic view of the future (with strong romantic overtones) and argued that it would actually be created by the process of industrialization. His attempted synthesis united the ideals of economic man and contemplative man, thereby creating the basis for the democratization of classical leisure. As the nineteenth and twentieth centuries unfolded, the strength of pre-Marxian intellectual patterns undermined his attempt to unify the entire western intellectual tradition and his attempted synthesis crumbled. We will return to these points in Chapters 13 and 14.

France: Romanticism versus Technocracy

The origins of Romanticism are generally traced to the early works of Jean-Jacques Rousseau, who was born in Geneva in 1712 and died in 1778. Rousseau lived in France for several years and was well acquainted with the views of the *philosophes,* which he condemned in his *Discourse on the Moral Effects of the Arts and Sciences* in 1750. Whereas the majority of his contemporaries applauded science and longed for the day when its proper application (combined with the expansion of reason) would open new vistas for human beings, Rousseau argued that it was impossible to derive any hope from the progress of arts and sciences because they were antithetical to, and destructive of, virtue. In this rather disjointed critique of the Enlightenment, Rousseau expounded his major themes of simplicity versus abundance and nature versus science—themes that served as the foundation for the Romantic movement. Rousseau posited a natural state of simplicity as our original (and happiest) form of existence:

> Behold how luxury, licentiousness, and slavery have in all periods been punishment for the arrogant attempts we have made to emerge from the happy ignorance in which eternal wisdom had placed us.[2]

The State of Nature: An Alternative Perspective

By 1753, Rousseau had developed a more coherent critique of the Enlightenment—published as the *Discourse on the Origin of Inequality*. Explicitly denying the relevance of historical fact, he presented an idyllic "state of nature," in which humans had existed as benign animals prior to the creation of society. Rousseau adopted this technique (in order to identify the most basic of human drives) from Thomas Hobbes and Locke.

Writing in the midst of the tumultuous seventeenth century in England, Hobbes had argued that the natural state of humans included fear, self-interested competition for scarce resources, and "a restless desire of power."[3] Total chaos is the predictable result of such natural drives, and humans were viewed as capable of summoning enough rationality to realize that this unrestrained conflict would be detrimental to their survival. The creation of the Sovereign, then, was an extension of the instinct of self-preservation:

> as if every man should say to every man, *I authorize and give up my right to governing myself, to this man, or to this assembly of men, on the condition, that thou give up thy right to him, and authorize all his actions in like manner.* This done, the multitude so united in one person, is called a COMMONWEALTH, in Latin CIVITAS.[4]

Hobbes' concern about the chaos triggered by man's natural egotistical drives caused him to argue for a state in which power would be concentrated in the hands of the sovereign, and the criteria by which the sovereign would be evaluated were based on its success in creating harmony out of natural chaos. Hence, it follows that the sovereign's power to establish order could (and should) not be limited in any way—and here we identify the massive differences between the arguments of Hobbes and Locke. For Hobbes, total power included the sovereign's right to determine the proper distribution of property. He reminded us that the distribution of property among the children of Israel, upon entering the promised land, was not the result of egotistical competition; instead, it was divided among the tribes according to established principles:

> In this distribution, the first law, is for the division of the land itself: wherein the sovereign assigneth to every man a portion, according as he, and not according as any subject, or any number of them, shall judge agreeable to equity, and the common good.[5]

Beginning with the need to create social order out of natural chaos, Hobbes concluded that any method of doing so is justified, including the Sovereign's power over property arrangements. As we stressed in Chapter Nine, one of Locke's major goals in *The Second Treatise* was to deny governments the power to place restrictions on private property. Locke's "state of nature" produced distinctions in wealth and the decision to create a political entity to govern the society was stimulated, in part, by the desire to protect this wealth (by guaranteeing the sanctity of private property) against both the "quarrelsome and contentious" and state regulation. While Hobbes sought stability at any cost, maximum stability combined with unquestioned property rights summarizes Locke's alternative.

Rousseau agreed with Hobbes and Locke that reason enters into the decision-making process to enforce goals previously established by passion, or desire. But he introduced a startling (and critical) twist by arguing that basic, pre-rational human drives include compassion for others, as well as concern for self. In addition to *amour propre* (egoism), he asserted that humans are motivated by *amour de soi* (self-respect). Rousseau claimed that we cannot respect ourselves unless we respect others; hence, it is clear that the egotistical calculation of the competitive individual presented by Hobbes, Locke, Mandeville and Smith as "natural" is actually "an unnatural and perverted condition."[6] In developing his argument that compassion is a crucial part of human nature, Rousseau cited the "golden rule," then altered it to read, "Do good to yourself with as little evil as possible to others."[7]

The Impact of Private Property

Having defined humans as a natural mixture of concern for self and others, Rousseau searched for the origin of social conflict. He concluded that a particular economic custom has caused us to deny our innate compassion and perceive ourselves as the individualistic, competitive atoms that others mistook for our natural condition. And in imagery reminiscent of the *Old Testament* prophets, Rousseau identified the institution of private property as the source of our downfall:

> The first person who, having fenced off a plot of ground, took it into his head to say *this is mine* and found people simple enough to believe him, was the true founder of civil society. What crimes, wars, murders, what miseries and horrors would the human race have been spared by someone who, uprooting the stakes or filling in the ditch, had shouted to his fellow-men: Beware of listening to this imposter; you are lost if you forget that the fruits belong to all and the earth to no one![8]

The fire and brimstone admonitions of the prophets are absent—but Marx would add them in the following century.

Whereas Locke and Smith argued that the origins of human progress and civil society can be traced to private property, Rousseau suggested that it moved us away from our true humanity. In a fascinating passage discussing this process, he noted that in the transition from solitary hunter toward family and community, humans discovered that their collective energies made satisfaction of their needs less time-consuming. For Rousseau, humans faced a critical turning point:

> The simplicity and solitude of man's life in this new condition, the paucity of his wants, and the implements he had invented to satisfy them, left him a great deal of leisure, which he employed to furnish himself with many conveniences unknown to his fathers: and this was the first yoke he inadvertently imposed on himself, and the first source of evils he prepared for his descendents. For, besides continuing thus to enervate both body and mind, these conveniences lost with use almost all their power to please, and even degenerated into real needs, till the want of them became far more disagreeable than the possession of them had been pleasant. Men would have been unhappy at the loss of them, though the possession did not make them happy.[9]

The significance of this passage should strike anyone who has thought about the classical concept of leisure. The decision to use discretionary time to accumulate material objects was a fatal decision, and the use of such time in this manner resulted in enslavement to these possessions. In addition, such activity weakened the mind and body, whereas the classical view of leisure was designed to strengthen them.

We cannot avoid suggesting (and we suspect that Rousseau might agree) that a focus on the values of classical leisure might have at least buffered the blind quest for these possessions—possessions that, in the last analysis, are far less satisfying than the accumulator thought they would be. Less satisfying is one thing, but a yoke limiting freedom and distorting humanity is an even more disturbing prospect. Marx developed this argument in depth through his early philosophical writings, and we will return to the discussion in the following Chapter. At this point, we suggest that Rousseau prepared the groundwork for what is, perhaps, the most haunting point in the critique of efficient economic man: the more you have, the less you are.

The General Will

While it may seem that the *Discourses* succeeded in challenging virtually every aspect of Enlightenment thought and efficient economic man (note that Voltaire scorned The *Discourses* as an attack on the human race), Rousseau was not finished. In 1762, he published his primary political work, entitled *The Social Contract,* in which he delivered the final blows. Building on the ideas established in his *Discourse on Political Economy* (in which he challenged Locke and Smith by arguing that "It is . . . one of the most important functions of government to prevent extreme inequities of fortune"), Rousseau insisted that social and communal considerations are, at least, as important as any individual.[10] The community, then, is viewed as totally responsible for establishing and determining the validity of rights, including those of private property.

Building on his concept concerning innate human sociability, Rousseau argued that the role of government is to enhance this natural inclination. He also challenged the suggestion that freedom should be viewed as the elimination of restraints on human activity by reviving the (essentially Platonic) argument that true freedom is self-imposed restraint. Rousseau envisioned a force he called the General Will as necessary to hold such a system together. In stressing the General Will, he was (again) attacking the suggestion that the good society will emerge out of individual competition and self-interest. The good society can exist only when humans use their rational capacity to reinforce their innate compassion and sociability (instead of their egotism) and collectively pursue their future as a community.

Rousseau took one last jab at the Enlightenment by questioning its optimistic view of the future. Ultimately, Rousseau stressed the importance of tradition as a cohesive social force, linking his thought with the conservative reaction that we will discuss below. And as for the Enlightenment's hope for the future based on the proper functioning of government and good laws, Rousseau's comment reveals a deep pessimism: If Sparta and Rome perished, what State can hope to endure for ever?[11] Hence, while the concept of innate sociability could (and did—for others) provide a basis for hope, Rousseau concluded his political writings on a strong pessimistic note: the title of the chapter that includes the above quote is "The Death of the Body Politic" and it is immediately preceeded by a chapter entitled "The Abuse of Government and its Tendency to Degenerate." Again, so much for optimism.

Saint-Simon: The Scientific Solution

While Rousseau's search for a solution to social ills led him to stress emotions, Saint-Simon (1760–1825) relied on science to provide guidelines for improvement. Having lived through the tumultuous events in France, Saint-Simon recognized that the cohesive force of the Catholic Church had been irreparably damaged and would not totally recover. Hence, society would become increasingly chaotic unless new forces developed to replace the medieval power structure.

Referring to his ideas as "The New Christianity," Saint-Simon pictured a society in which reason would dominate through the rule of educated, enlightened technicians. The new Christianity, then, would replace religious dogma with rational planning and the new leaders would be those who could apply scientific principles to social problems:

> The scientific opinions formulated by these philosophers should then be clothed in forms which make them sacred, in order that they can be taught to the children of all classes and the illiterate, whatever their age.[12]

Unlike Rousseau, Saint-Simon did not see "efficient economic man" as a problem. He did, however, call for the subordination of egoism and economic activity to the rule of enlightened technocrats.

Saint-Simon and his followers were reacting to the revolutionary years in France by attempting to create a new society that would bring order out of chaos. Their solution included economic, as well as social and political order because they viewed the unregulated competition of the market economy as the economic equivalent of anarchy. Hence, the degree to which they deserve to be called socialists is due to their critique of unregulated economic competition:

> Let us now add that this fundamental principle, *laissez-faire, laissez passer,* presupposes a personal interest that is always in harmony with the general interest, a supposition that innumerable facts tend to refute.[13]

The ideas of Rousseau and Saint-Simon resurfaced in French thought throughout the century. From Gracchus Babeuf through Pierre Proudhon, Rousseau's basic arguments provided the foundation of French socialist thought:

> Babeuf (1797): By its origins, the land belongs to no one, and its fruits are for everyone.[14]

> Proudhon (1840): What is property? It is theft.[15]

Saint-Simon's assistant, August Comte, continued the search for a scientific basis for social improvement but, as the century progressed, Comte's ethical concerns gave way to an increased stress on scientific observations. As a result, positivism was led away from ethics and the link between science and socialism was broken—at least in French thought.

Germany: The Challenge to Empiricism

Far away from the tumult associated with industrialization and political revolution, a middle-aged professor at the University of Konigsberg began developing a series of arguments that were designed to introduce a "Copernican revolution" into philosophy. Immanuel Kant (1724–1804) was born, lived and died without ever leaving the quiet university town in East Prussia. His simple and highly disciplined lifestyle is noted by virtually all commentators, and it may sound odd to suggest that, in his own way, this quiet professor of physics and moral philosophy prompted a revolution in thought as profound as the better-known economic and political changes of the eighteenth century.

As a deeply religious (though he avoided organized religion) scientist, it is not surprising that Kant was shaken by Hume's attacks on science and morality. Even more problematical was the fact that Kant concluded that Hume's arguments could not be refuted, and he recalled that Hume forced him to awake from his "dogmatic slumber."[16] Kant was also impressed by Rousseau's arguments concerning equality, and influenced by his suggestion that reason should be a tool for moral and ethical concerns. We have noted the significance of the general will in Rousseau's thought: it provided a cohesive force to unite humanity. But Rousseau failed to develop this concept in sufficient detail to allow such a force to be clearly defined and developed. Kant's accomplishments include the formulation of a "categorical imperative" to provide a rational basis for judging morality. But before discussing Kant's ethics, we must note his theory of knowledge—the basis for his revolution.

The empiricist's view of the human mind as a blank tablet that merely records sensory data had a profoundly devastating effect on the concept of morality. In addition, Hume's suggestion that reason is a slave to passions further undermined the human capacity to live by any moral standards. Kant was particularly troubled by these arguments and, in addition, his scientific inclinations seemed to conflict with his concern for morality: if the universe is governed by laws based on cause-effect relationships, how could humans ever be free? In short, the inherent determinism of Newtonian physics, when applied to human actions, causes us to question whether we actually have any freedom—including the freedom to make moral decisions.

Kant responded by denying the blank tablet view and proposing a way to overcome these apparent dilemmas. For Kant, sensory data (the content of experience) interact with structures of the mind (the forms of experience) to produce the natural world. These structures of the mind are the perceptual forms of space and time, twelve concepts or categories of understanding including quantity, causality and substance, and finally the laws of reason itself. They exist prior to, and independent of, the things that we sense and understand. Because "nature" means the totality of those things, the mind and its structures transcend the natural world. Hume failed to find evidence for causal necessity and therefore couldn't justify science because he looked for causality in the content rather than in the forms of experience. It was Kant's genius to suggest that if we suppose causality and the other structures to be the forms which experience and understanding inevitably take because of the nature of the mind, we can explain how Hume went wrong and, at the same time, justify fundamental scientific notions about the quantitative, material, and causal aspects of nature.

Rather than the mind's being within nature, then, nature is "within" the mind, which imposes on it its spatial, temporal, quantitative, material and rational order. It was this inversion of the usual conception of the relation between the mind and the world that Kant was alluding to when he called his discovery a "Copernican revolution" in philosophy. Natural objects and events are causally determined, but the mind is free of such determinism, so morality no longer need be threatened by science. Kant has made room for freedom and morality by limiting the scope of science, but in so doing he has made it impossible to attain any scientific understanding of the mind or "transcendental ego," which transcends nature. It may not sound as significant as the steam engine or Napoleon, but Kant's suggestion altered the course of western thought.

In addition to being prior to and independent of experience, these *a priori* structures, Kant argued, are universal. They provide a common bond linking all human minds, and the most fundamental of them, the laws of reason, unite all rational beings—human and, possibly, non-human—in a community of beings all of whom, by the very fact that they are rational, are subject to the same laws. If these laws of reason could be shown to imply a moral law, a universal morality would not only be possible, it would be established with all the certainty of other rational disciplines like mathematics and logic. This is the task Kant set for himself in the second of his famous *Critiques*. He argued that the fundamental principle of morality is as necessary to rational thinking as the principle of non-contradiction and that it has always been part of sound moral thinking. It needs only rational philosophical analysis to make it explicit. We all know that a person is moral or immoral not just because of *what* he does but because of *why* he does it. Kant understood that human beings always act either out of inclination, or out of duty. To act from inclination is to act from feelings, desires, or emotions. While Locke, Hume and Smith accepted inclination as the only motivation for human action—considering reason to be its slave—Kant taught that inclination should be subordinated to duty, which is a child of reason. Our inclinations are subjective;

they divide us—so to act from inclination is to act selfishly, in ways based not on what we share but on what separates us from each other.

Duty, on the other hand, is based on reason—on what unites us all as rational beings—and to act rationally is to be objective rather than subjective, unselfish rather than selfish. To choose to act is to will, and Kant argued that the morally good person is the person of "good will" who wills rationally and unselfishly. How far this is from the idea that the good person is the efficient and egotistical producer of things that satisfy desires!

Kant's definition of "good will" initially sounds similar to Rousseau's definition of the "general will," as a force to overcome social tension. But Kant goes further—and identifies the single foundation upon which good will and all morality is based. Whereas Rousseau looked to historical examples of rules that had an impact on the innate sociability of humans, Kant pressed further to discover the principle upon which all truly moral rules are based. This principle—the categorical imperative—is an innate, *a priori* precept that is part of the rationality that all human minds are equipped with. In the same way that the forms and categories create a meaningful physical world, it provides a basis for the universal standards of morality which make possible a meaningful moral world.

Kant argued that, to be free, we must deny that we are determined by any outside forces—whether nature (biological determinism) or our inclinations (Hume's passions). And just as the understanding orders nature, reason establishes morality:

> Everything in nature works according to laws. Rational beings alone have the faculty of acting according *to the conception* of laws—that is, according to principles, that is, have *a will*. Since the deduction of actions from principles requires *reason,* the will is nothing but practical reason.[17]

The significance of the universality of *a priori* concepts is clear when we expand this suggestion (to be rational is to act according to principle) to the conclusion that to be moral is to act in accordance with a universal principle.

The categorical imperative—the universal principle of morality—is defined as: I am never to act otherwise than *so that I could use also will that my maxim should become a universal law.*[18] Hence, an action is moral if the principle it is based on could be a governing principle for all actions by everyone. The test of the morality of our actions, then, is to ask: could a world exist in which the principle of my decision became a law that governed everyone's actions? The obvious challenge to rampant self-interest lies in Kant's insistence that no one make exceptions to this imperative in his or her own case. Kant referred to the imperative as "a compass" that allows everyone to determine the morality of an action.[19]

Kant removed morality from any standard of empirical measurement by stressing the importance of the motive behind the decision: an action is moral only when it is based on a decision derived from the categorical imperative. We can identify three types of actions: 1) *immoral*—or doing the wrong thing for the wrong reason; 2) *legal*—or doing the right thing for the wrong reason; 3) *moral*—or doing the right thing for the right reason. Hence, obeying laws because you will be punished if you do not may be legal, but it is not moral because the motive behind the action is fear—as opposed to good will. With this suggestion, we identify the source of Kant's aversion to organized religion, which is far more legal than moral due to the coercive rules that replace true morality with fear.

The pursuit of morality is a deeply personal endeavor that is made possible by the shared rationality of humans. This mixture of personal and collective concerns may at first sound similar to the utilitarian views proposed by Helvetius. Kant, however, separated morality from general notions of happiness. In short, our reward for moral behavior is morality itself—and the dignity intrinsic to acting freely rather than as slaves to our desires. There is no link between it and any empirical state of happiness. Clearly, Kant's "compass" offers little that would guide efficient economic man. Finally, Kant cautioned us not to expect anything approaching certainty in our pursuit of morality because we can never be absolutely certain of the motivation behind our own, and others', actions.

Kant's contributions (and critique of "economic man") should be obvious. To be motivated by inclination is, essentially, to deny one's humanity. In addition, to act in such a manner is to deny the significance of other human beings. Kant stressed the importance of treating others as "ends in themselves," not as objects to be manipulated (i.e., means) for our individual selfish interests. The view of humans as atomistic, egotistical calculators was replaced with a universal community drawn together through reason and common *a priori* knowledge. Reason is the bond that unites humans and allows us to transcend individual self-interest in a "kingdom of ends," in which the good of rational individuals is united with the moral community. But, like Rousseau, Kant is more cautious than his "heavenly city" predecessors, and he concluded by admitting that there are limitations to our ability to understand and act morally. While reason provides a bond capable of uniting the diverse interests of humanity, it is useless in any endeavor to push beyond the *a priori* concepts in order to comprehend their source. *A priori* ideas, through the mind, bring order to the world—but we can never know the ultimate source of the mind and these ideas:

> It is just the same as if I sought to find how freedom itself is possible as the causality of a will. For then I quit the ground of philosophical explanation, and I have no other to go upon. I might indeed revel in the world of intelligences which still remains to me, but although I have an *idea* of it which is well founded, yet I have not the least *knowledge* of it, nor can I ever attain to such knowledge with all the efforts of my natural faculty of reason . . . there is more beyond it; but this something more I know no further.[20]

Kant developed an entirely new way of understanding the world, the mind, and their relationship. The moral imperative allows us to identify what ought to be done and implies that what ought to be done can be done—thereby establishing the foundation for freedom and morality. We are free when we will moral action, and we can no longer consider ourselves as victims of circumstance or determined by animalistic passions. We have the duty to transcend circumstance and selfishness by willing the dictates of reason. In the end, though, Kant reminds us that human reason and morality cannot guarantee happiness—a shocking conclusion to people who have become accustomed to expecting happiness as a reward for proper behavior. Finally, he recognized that there are limitations on the knowledge our reason can provide. This was not necessarily a pessimistic conclusion, but it did open a door for those who chose to comprehend deeper questions—questions that Kant concluded were "incomprehensible."

G. W. F. Hegel: Reason as Spirit

G. W. F. Hegel (1770–1831) was formally educated in theology and was teaching at the University of Jena in 1806 when the city was conquered by Napoleon. In 1818 he was invited to the University of Berlin, where his lectures drew standing-room-only crowds. His essentially theological perspectives, his dialectical method and his political conclusions serve as the focus of our brief discussion. Noting his theological background should help you grasp the deeply religious undertones in his thought. Recognizing the significance of the dialectical method is crucial in preparing to understand Marx's thought. Hegel's views on the relationship between the individual, society and state take us a long way toward clarifying his popularity in the capital of the Prussian state. Hegel was an extremely complex thinker—possibly due to the fact that he set out to explain what Kant concluded was "incomprehensible," i.e., the source of all knowledge as it has manifested itself throughout history. Hegel's thought is a straightforward attack on the Enlightenment. The assault began with the separation of reason from the realm of what is essentially human and its elevation (or degradation—depending on your perspective) into the realm of metaphysics. Without reason, humans are left as self-serving, narrow-minded egotistical individuals; that should sound familiar.

Whereas Kant was devoted to establishing human reason as a foundation for moral activity, Hegel denied reason as a human quality—opting, instead, to look outside of humanity for a guiding moral force. This moral force is referred to as the "Absolute"—or the "Idea"—and is associated with divinity. This divine force is responsible for manipulating passion-driven humans through history, creating order out of competitive chaos. In addition to theology and Kant's arguments concerning the importance of the human mind in all understanding, Hegel was influenced by Adam Smith and the political economists—and it seems entirely possible that he was integrating German philosophy, Smith's "invisible hand," and Judeo-Christian convictions. In the process, he created a profoundly conservative philosophy of history that immediately stimulated an equally profound revolutionary adaptation that viewed the past as the midwife for the future.

The Conservative Reaction

Hegel was not alone in his conservative reaction to the Enlightenment. With Hume's skepticism serving as the catalyst, numerous critics attacked the ideas of the *philosophes* and the actions of the French revolutionaries. They challenged atomistic individualism, questioned the source of the "Rights of Man" and argued that such ideas would inevitably lead to total chaos and the destruction of European civilization. Edmund Burke's *Reflections on the Revolution in France* attempted to replace atomism with traditional concepts of community, individualism with collective effort, and the notion of equality with an argument for a natural aristocracy. According to Burke, societies have gradually evolved from the past, and their customs, traditions and laws should not be taken lightly just because one or two generations do not find them appealing. Burke's concept of "the nation" links generations past, present and future—and he was convinced that long-standing laws and traditions should be sacrosanct because they are the only bonds holding self-interested individuals together in a society:

> Society is indeed a contract. . . . It is a partnership in all science; a partnership in all art; a partnership in every virtue, and in all perfection. As the ends of such a partnership cannot be obtained in many generations, it becomes a partnership not only between those who are living, but between those who are living, those who are dead, and those who are to be born. Each contract of each particular state is but a clause in the great primeval contract of eternal society, linking the lower with the higher natures, connecting the visible and invisible world. . . . The municipal corporations of that universal kingdom are not morally at liberty at their pleasure, and on their speculations of a contingent improvement, wholly to separate and tear asunder the bands of their subordinate community, and to dissolve it into an unsocial, uncivil, unconnected chaos of elementary principles.[21]

Burke's religious tone was shared by other conservatives, including DeMaistre in France and Hegel in Germany. Recall that Saint-Simon also concentrated on religion—but he had concluded that traditional religion would not recover from the challenges, and a "new religion" of science was needed to restore order.

The Cunning of Reason

Hegel's view of the world was a far cry from the "heavenly city" faith in the human potential. The basis of Hegel's thought is "Idea," described by Robert Hartman as "the logical power of the divine;" humans are viewed as mere tools of this divine force that "enters and guides, through mortal men, the scene of historical struggle."[22] From a Judeo-Christian perspective, this sounds familiar: humans are greedy and self-centered, requiring a metaphysical force to overcome conflict and establish unity. Like Hobbes, Hegel viewed basic human drives as selfish and violent. Our goal, according to Hegel, is not only to control and defeat all other objects we encounter—but to negate them; that is, to totally deny, or eliminate, them in our unending struggle to conquer everything around us. Fortunately for us, there is a rational force in the cosmos that needs us as much as we need it. History is an account of the Idea manipulating human beings to actualize its goal of ultimate fulfillment:

> the Idea is in truth the guide of peoples and the world; and the Spirit, its natural and necessary will, guides and always has guided the course of world events.[23]

Hence, regardless of how absurd events in history may appear, they are all pieces of a rational mosaic crafted by the Idea, as it moves toward its fulfillment. Ultimately, the goal of this force is to perfect humans and unite them with self-fulfilled Idea.

With humans lacking any tendency toward morality and behavior that would naturally assist the Idea in this process, it is necessary that the Idea separate from itself, or alienate itself from its metaphysical realm in order to influence our behavior. Hegel argued that the great leaders in history were great precisely because Spirit chose to infiltrate their minds in order to guide them. These "world historical individuals" are not even aware of the mission they accomplish: reason uses them—it motivates their personal desires in the direction that it wants history to move—and then allows them to be destroyed when they have accomplished their tasks. There is no relationship between historical significance and happiness—as the lives of Alexander the Great, Julius Caesar and Napoleon demonstrate. In fact, there is little happiness to be found in all of human history; Hegel argued that "the periods of happiness are blank pages in it."[24]

With the natural human drives viewed as destructive, Hegel developed a strict hierarchy of forces that combine to create order and move history toward its goal. These forces are 1) Idea, 2) world historical individuals and the states they rule, 3) culture—or tradition. As pure Spirit, Idea cannot move humanity toward its ultimate goal. Therefore, it alienates itself from pure thought to manipulate change in the world through the ruler of a particular state. Any attempt to limit the power of the state would, then, be an affront to the divine force of the universe. Again, recall that Prussia was preparing to make its move to unify the German states in the 1820s—and recognize that Hegel's popularity can be seen as the result of his philosophy meshing with the practical political interests of the Prussian elite. For Hegel, the nation state was the highest form of political development—the ultimate stage in world history. It reflected the commands of Idea in the physical world. As a manifestation of divine will, the nation state was totally rational and, therefore, completely good. Hegel was convinced that Germany's destiny included the creation of a powerful political entity to lead the world into its final stages of historical struggle.

Freedom as Subordination

Given Hegel's radically negative view of humans, it is not surprising that he also denied the Enlightenment's definition of freedom. Rather than dismantling the traditions and laws that regulate individual activity, Hegel reasserted their importance. True freedom, to Hegel, is the total acceptance of one's cultural and political traditions. The culture and the state define ethics and values and he argued that the proper role for individuals is the complete internalization of the "spirit" of their society (*Volkgeist*). The height of human alienation is to be at odds with your culture and state, and freedom is possible only when you willingly submit to these constraints on individualism. Society and the state exist as gifts from the divine force to limit the greedy and violent drives of individuals. For Hegel, accepting this insignificant role is the closest that most of us can come to unity with the Idea.

Like his conservative counterparts, Hegel perceived the atomistic view of society as absurd—arguing, instead, for a broad organic perspective. In fact, he claimed that humans are best understood as cogs in the wheels of culture. In short, there is no human freedom. Freedom belongs to the realm of the divine force and although we may think that we exercise freedom through our choices, these choices are actually determined by our culture:

> And so while you are going about pursuing your own desires, buying the foods and clothes and electronics that you like, building the career you have chosen, what you do is channeled into the ongoing manufacturing, marketing, financial, and educational functions of your nation, and so helps to sustain the nation, although you did not intend this or even understand it when you did these things . . . your desires themselves are sustained or determined by the society. Your choice of clothes or a career is determined by the various options which your culture has developed and made available for you to desire and to choose.[25]

With this assertion, we really begin to apprehend the depth of conflict that underlies Hegel's view of the world. Far from the "onward and upward" Enlightenment approach to linear progress, Hegel's perception stressed constant tension in virtually every realm: between Idea and nature, between Reason and desire, between individual drives and the state, between state and state, and between freedom and cultural determinism. Everything in the world appears as a conflict of opposites—opposites that are, ultimately, reconciled through dialectical movement.

The Divine Dialectic

The dialectical movement of history is a crucial part of Hegel's thought. We have developed this book from a dialectical perspective, focusing on the tension between views toward leisure time. Parts I and II established the thesis, or starting point of western thought. Part III described the emergence of the antithesis (efficient economic man), and we are currently working toward Marx's attempt to synthesize these competing views. We have suggested that this "process of philosophy" is the result of changing material conditions (economic, political and social) challenging existing philosophies that were established during an earlier period. From our point of view, tension between ideas and material reality stimulate the process of philosophy, as noted in our Introduction. Hegel posited the inverse relationship: philosophy is driven not by material reality, but by the divine Idea. Tension, then, results from Idea's drive toward a higher stage of its fulfillment and material reality. Human minds, far from being the source of ideas, are merely conduits through which the Idea manipulates physical action.

Kant's emphasis on the importance of the human mind was adapted by Hegel to the latter's (essentially theological) argument. But the human mind is subordinated to, and motivated by, a divine force. Hence, our ideas are not totally our own and thought is seen as important only to the degree that it brings us closer to the spiritual force of the world: The purest form in which the Idea manifests itself is Thought itself.[26] Hence, with humans defined as incapable of developing their own ideas (again, our motivations are greed and conquest), Hegel viewed philosophies as divinely inspired.

Hegel's dialectic begins with the thesis as a particular stage of the Idea's development. Its opposite (antithesis) is civil society. The thesis is pure reason, the antithesis is pure chaos. Tension between the two eventually produces a synthesis, as reason manipulates humans to move history a step closer to the fulfillment of Idea. History, at any given point in time, is exactly what the Idea required it to be during that period. And understanding the dominant philosophy of any period is the closest that we may come to grasping that particular stage of Idea's development:

> The insight then to which . . . philosophy should lead us is that the actual world is as it ought to be, that the truly good, the universal divine Reason is the power capable of actualizing itself. This good, this Reason, in its most concrete representation, is God. God governs the world. The actual working of His government, the carrying out of His plan is the history of the world.[27]

Reason, then, is much more than a mere human capacity—and there is no humanly-created philosophy (for, according to Hegel, all thought is a manifestation of Idea) that influences the world. Instead, the most that we can hope for is to comprehend what the divine force is creating.

Hegel might have deemed these conclusions optimistic. But when we compare them to the Enlightenment's faith in the human potential, his philosophy reinforced the pessimism that we have identified growing out of the other contexts. We are reactors, not actors; we are destructive competitors, not social beings; we are culture carriers, not culture creators; we are recipients of divine reason, not the source; we participate in the actualization of Idea's potential, not our own; true freedom lies in subordination of individuals to an unlimited state. Again, so much for optimism.

Ferdinand Lassalle

Ferdinand Lassalle (1825–1864) combined Hegel's insistence on a strong state with concern for the working classes in Germany. Lassalle's flamboyant mixture of aristocratic and revolutionary perspectives led him from the highest echelons of Prussian society to prison, and his influence on the German socialist movement was at least as profound as that of Marx. He began his political career in 1861 with the Prussian Progressive Party, an organization that attempted to forge an alliance between the workers and the middle classes. In 1863, Lassalle concluded that this coalition was ineffective and he began to advocate the creation of a new alliance between the workers and the Prussian state. From his perspective, the frightful conditions of industrial society could be altered only by introducing universal suffrage (to give the workers political influence) and worker-owned cooperative industrial enterprises. Lassalle actually met with Bismarck to promote these changes that are best summarized as state socialism:

> Only by making the workers owners of the means of production could a change be accomplished, and to this end he proposed the founding of "workers production cooperatives." The capital needed for such cooperatives was large and could only come from the state.[28]

Lassalle's synthesis of working-class agitation and the Hegelian view of the state provided the ideological guidelines for Prussia's first socialist political organization, the General German

Workingman's Association. Formed in 1863, the Association was highly centralized—reflecting the norms of Prussian society. Other German socialists, including Marx, were extremely critical of Lassalle's authoritarian organization and his courtship of the Prussian state. In general, socialism advocated workers' control of the state, as opposed to a cozy relationship with the traditional elite. But for Lassalle, Hegelian statism was not to be challenged:

> From his earliest youth he had regarded the idea of the State as the realization of morality, right, and reason. His enthusiasm for this idea, and his belief in the destiny of the State, not only as protective force, but also as positive stimulus to right and culture, runs through all his writings.[29]

Lassalle's views continued to influence large segments of the German working class throughout the nineteenth century, and his perspective must be recognized as a significant factor in the intellectual milieu that contributed to the rise of Nazism.

Britain: The Greatest Happiness for the Greatest Number

Hume's critique of Locke's natural rights doctrine provided the foundation for utilitarianism. As we noted in Chapter 10, the concept of utility was expanded in France by Helvetius, who accepted individual egoism (for Helvetius, "self-love") as a given and concluded that humans are driven by the goal of maximizing pleasure and minimizing pain. Combined with Adam Smith's economic arguments, these ideas were refined into a "school" of philosophy in Britain by Jeremy Bentham (1748–1832) and widely publicized by James Mill (1773–1836). The reader who is still a little mystified by the intricacies of German thought can draw comfort from the absence of metaphysics in utilitarianism, which is characterized by "a love of the particular and concrete, and a wholly English dislike of abstract general principles."[30]

With self-interested economic man accepted as a given, Bentham attempted to develop a guideline to measure pleasure and pain. Equipped with this "hedonistic calculus," he hoped to provide a mathematical standard to measure and evaluate the impact of laws on individual activity. This approach clearly reflected the strong individualist focus so prevalent in British thought from Locke through Smith:

> The community is a fictitious *body,* composed of the individual persons who are considered as constituting as it were its *members.* The interest of the community then is, what?—the sum of the interests of the several members who compose it.[31]

Given this atomistic view, the proper role of government is described as follows:

> It has been shown that the happiness of the individuals, of whom a community is composed, that is their pleasure and security, is the end and sole end which the legislator ought to have in view.[32]

Bentham went on to identify 13 sources of pleasure (including wealth and power) and 12 sources of pain. His conclusions seem sufficiently straightforward: the good government will create laws that enhance individual pleasure. There is, then, a positive role for government to play in the day-to-day lives of its subjects or citizens, and with this point we begin to identify the growth of a subtle tension between this view and the legacy of Locke and Smith:

In the judgement of the classical liberal, the state is always suspect, for it possesses power, and power corrupts. Consequently, that state is the best which governs least. Government, as the instrument of the state, rarely intervenes; it "interferes." Government functionaries rarely act; they "meddle." They rarely err; they "blunder."[33]

To be sure, there are large remnants of this view in utilitarianism. But there is also a perceptible shift toward expanding parameters of acceptable government activity. Through the movement of ideas from Locke through Bentham, we can identify the following stages: 1) for Locke, the government exists to protect property; 2) for Smith, government exists to protect property and enhance the natural development of commerce, i.e., the wealth of the nation; 3) for Bentham, the government should promote both of these goals and enhance the greatest happiness for the greatest number.

The key to the tension seems to lie in the definition of the "greatest number." If this concept is limited to property owners (recall Locke's, Mandeville's and Holbach's contempt for the "Quarrelsome and Contentious," the "Grumbling Hive" and the "stupid populace"), then utilitarianism justifies the political power of the propertied commercial interests. If, however, ALL humans are defined as part of the "greatest number" (and the working classes far outnumbered their employers), then utilitarianism lays the groundwork for laws to alleviate the human misery created by early industrialization and begins to sound decidedly socialist. This tension is clearly illustrated in the ideas of reformers such as Robert Owen and the platforms of working-class movements such as Chartism.

Robert Owen

"Socialist utilitarianism" provides a convenient description of the reformist views advocated by Robert Owen (1771–1858). As a successful factory owner who had struggled his way out of the working class, Owen established a model manufacturing community at New Lanark, Scotland. His practical reforms (including limitations on hours of work and child labor, and the creation of decent housing facilities) were based on the assumption that humans are conditioned by their environment—and by changing environments, people can be changed. His vision of the future included the extension of manufacturing communities based on the New Lanark model throughout Britain and the world, combined with major reform of education to facilitate social responsibility, as opposed to egoism:

> Will it not, then, tend to the welfare and advantage of this neighborhood, to introduce into it such a practical system as shall gradually withdraw the causes of anger, hatred, discord, and every evil passion, and substitute true and genuine principles of universal charity and of never-varying kindness . . . and of an ever-active desire to benefit to the full extent of our faculties all our fellow creatures, whatever may be their sentiments and habits.[34]

Owen also became active in the movement to organize trade union activity into a viable political force. But his Grand National Consolidated Trade Union lasted only a year, as the divisions among the workers undermined a united front. By 1840, Owen's contributions were overshadowed by a new movement for the "People's Charter."

The Chartists

The Chartist petitions of 1839, 1842 and 1848 were addressed to the members of parliament and requested major political reforms. The following passage from the Charter of 1842 is representative of the critical, and yet deferential approach:

That your honourable House, as at present constituted, has not been elected by, and acts irresponsibly of, the people. . . .

That notwithstanding the wretched and unparalleled condition of the people, your honourable House has manifested no disposition to curtail the expenses of the State, to diminish taxation, or promote general prosperity.[35]

There was no challenge, then, to the existing political institutions. In fact, each Charter emphasized that "none but peacable means shall be employed."[36] A final illustration of the continuity between utilitarianism and working-class reform movements can be found in the closing passages of the 1842 Charter:

That your petitioners, therefore, exercising their just right, demand that your honourable House do remedy the many gross and manifest evils of which your petitioners do complain, do immediately . . . pass into law the document entitled "The People's Charter," which embraces the representation of male adults, vote by ballot, annual Parliaments, no property qualification, payment of members, and equal electoral districts.

And that your petitioners, desiring to promote the peace of the United Kingdom, security of property, and the prosperity of commerce, seriously and earnestly press this, their position, on the attention of your honourable House.[37]

Parliament did not accept the petitions, and the Chartist movement declined after 1848. Some of its leaders began to establish the foundations of a working-class political party that formally emerged in the 1890s. And we should note that, by 1918, five of the six demands (all but the call for yearly elections to parliament) became law.

James Mill

The challenge presented to the political status quo by organized workers, turning utilitarianism into a call for improvements in factory conditions and expanded political influence, shook the foundations of British thought. One option was to view the workers as fully human and respond to their demands in order to promote "the greatest happiness." Another option was to fall back on the well-established connection between property owners and true human beings. James Mill's attempt to bridge the gap between wealth and suffrage by suggesting that the wealthy should rule and the people should vote is nicely summarized in an article from the *The Westminster Review* in July of 1830. Recall that agitation for electoral reform was growing, and note Mill's attempt to link the past with this context:

Our opinion, therefore, is that the business of government is properly the business of the rich, and that they will always obtain it, either by bad means, or good. Upon this every thing depends. If they obtain it by bad means, the government is bad. If they obtain it by good means, the government is sure to be good. The only good means of obtaining it are, the free suffrage of the people.[38]

John Stuart Mill

James' son, John Stuart Mill (1806–1873), clearly synthesized British thought and socialism. Raised in a rigid utilitarian environment, the younger Mill began to criticize Bentham as early as 1838:

Mankind needed "binding forces," including a fixed principle or an institution, and feelings "of sympathy or common interest among those who live under the same government." In its true and healthy state, Mill concluded, society was a community of shared values, principles, and loyalties.[39]

These views were expanded in his *Autobiography,* published in 1873. Accepting the utilitarian goal of the greatest happiness for the greatest number, Mill concluded that it could only be accomplished by moving beyond the egotistical individualism of his predecessors. The following passage illustrates a critical turning point in British thought: the recognition that the workers deserve to be treated as equals:

> our ideal of ultimate improvement went far beyond Democracy, and would class us decidedly under the general designation of Socialists. While we repudiated with the greatest of energy that tyranny of society over the individual which most socialistic systems are supposed to involve, we yet looked forward to a time when society will no longer be divided into the idle and the industrious; when the rule that they who do not work shall not eat, will be applied not to paupers only, but impartially to all; when the division of the produce of labour, instead of depending, as in so great a degree it now does, on the accident of birth, will be made by concert on an acknowledged principle of justice; and when it will no longer either be, or be thought to be, impossible for human beings to exert themselves strenuously in procuring benefits which are not to be exclusively their own, but to be shared with the society they belong to.[40]

In the following passages, Mill argued that the "deep rooted selfishness" in his culture "is so deeply rooted only because the whole course of existing institutions tends to foster it."[41]

The gradual alteration of these institutions, especially the system of education, was viewed by Mill as the logical approach to improving the likelihood of the new society. And the following quote clearly suggests an attempt to reconcile utilitarianism's concern for the individual with socialism's emphasis on the collective. In addition, it is notable that Mill refused to establish a specific goal. Concrete prescriptions for the "final aim of socialism" did not enter into Mill's system of thought:

> We had not the presumption to suppose that we could already foresee, by what precise form of institutions these objects could most effectually be attained, or at how near or how distant a period they would become practicable. We saw clearly that to render any such social transformation either possible or desirable, an equivalent change of character must take place both in the uncultivated herd who now compose the labouring masses, and in the immense majority of their employers.[42]

It is clear that John Stuart Mill challenged the dual set of standards that had dominated British thought since the Puritans and Locke. And yet, in a typically English manner, Mill's socialism was pragmatic and reformist, based on gradual movement toward a better society sometime in the future. This view provided the basis for the flowering of the democratic socialist movement in the last decades of the nineteenth century and its institutionalization in the British Labor Party. The willingness to accept the basic foundations of the existing system, while working to gradually reform it, has continued to the present day.

Russia: The Origins of Revolutionary Populism

While John Stuart Mill was gradually adapting utilitarianism to the realities of industrial society in Britain, the Russian Populists were charting a very different course. Their quest for community focused on the communal village of the peasantry, their political conclusions demanded violent revolution and they expressed little hope for any meaningful reform under the Czarist autocracy. Alexander Herzen (1812–1870) summarized his environment as follows:

> What a painful epoch is ours! Everything around us is in a state of dissolution, of an agitation which recalls a dizzy spell or a malignant fever.[43]

This tone permeated Russian Populism, which became increasingly desperate in the latter part of the century.

A clear indication of this desperation—and the extremes to which the Populists were willing to go to transcend it—can be perceived in Herzen's interpretations of Hegel as a revolutionary. We discussed Hegel's thought as a profoundly conservative reaction to the Enlightenment; for Herzen, it was "the algebra of revolution."[44] By focusing on the Hegelian view of history as progressive movement, Herzen interpreted Hegel's thought from a relative perspective, concluding that history must have a better future in store for Russia. Herzen's influence on nineteenth-century Russian thought is acknowledged by virtually all scholars of the period, with Franco Venturi suggesting that his views provided the foundation for the Russian revolutionary tradition:

> The fundamental elements of Russian Populism—distrust of all democracy; belief in a possible autonomous development of Socialism in Russia; faith in the future possibilities of the *obshchina;* the need to create revolutionaries who would dedicate themselves to the people—these were the principles Herzen clung to after his experiences in 1848, the ideals he had created for the next generation.[45]

We will return to the discussion of the second generation of Russian Populists in Chapter 14.

The reactions to "efficient economic man" were as diverse as the environments that produced them. They range from romanticism and French Positivism through German Idealism, revolutionary Russian Populism, and reformist British socialism. Some of the critics looked to an idealized past for a model on which to base a new society, while others turned to the future. Some looked to religious sources for guidance, while others insisted on empirically verifiable laws that determined human behavior. With a few exceptions, much of the "heavenly city" optimism was lost in the course of the nineteenth century. Marx's thought provides us with one of these exceptions, and we are finally ready to discuss his synthesis of numerous dimensions of the western intellectual tradition—including its conflicting concepts of leisure time.

References

1. Thomas Carlyle quoted in R. N. Stromberg, p. 212.
2. Jean-Jacques Rousseau, *The First and Second Discourses,* ed. Roger D. Masters, trans. R. D. and J. R. Masters (New York: St. Martin's Press, 1964) p. 46.
3. Thomas Hobbes, *Leviathan,* ed. Michael Oakeshott, intro. Richard S. Peters (New York: Crowell-Collier Publishing Co., 1962) p. 80.
4. Ibid., p. 132.
5. Ibid., p. 186.
6. G. D. H. Cole, Introduction to Jean-Jacques Rousseau, *The Social Contract and Discourses,* trans. G. D. H. Cole (New York: E. P. Dutton and Co., Inc., 1950) p. xlix.
7. J.-J. Rousseau, "A Discourse on the Origin of Inequality," in G. D. H. Cole, ed. p. 227.
8. J.-J. Rousseau, "Discourse on the Origin and Foundation of Inequality Among Men," in R. D. Masters, ed. pp. 141–142.
9. J.-J. Rousseau, "A Discourse on the Origin of Inequality," in G. D. H. Cole, ed. p. 240.
10. J.-J. Rousseau, "A Discourse on Political Economy," in G. D. H. Cole, ed. p. 306.
11. J.-J. Rousseau, "The Social Contract," in G. D. H. Cole, ed. p. 87.
12. Henri de Saint-Simon, "Introduction to the Scientific Studies of the 19th Century," in *Social Organization, the Science of Man and Other Writings,* ed. and trans. by Felix Markham (New York: Harper and Row, 1964) p. 20. Originally published in 1952 by Basil Blackwell, Oxford, England.
13. Saint-Amand Bazard, "Exposition of the Doctrine of Saint-Simon," in Albert Fried and Ronald Sanders, eds. *Socialist Thought: a Documentary History* (Garden City, N.Y.: Anchor Books, 1964) p. 116.

14. Gracchus Babeuf, "Babeuf's Defense," Ibid. p. 63.
15. Pierre Proudhon, "What is Property," Ibid. p. 201.
16. Immanuel Kant, *Prolegomena to Any Future Metaphysics,* trans. James W. Ellington (Indianapolis: Hackett Publishing Co., 1977) p. 5.
17. Immanuel Kant, *Fundamental Principles of the Metaphysics of Morals,* trans. T. K. Abbott (Indianapolis: Bobbs-Merrill, 1949) p. 30.
18. Ibid., p. 19.
19. Ibid., p. 21.
20. Ibid., p. 79.
21. Edmund Burke, *Reflections on the Revolution in France,* ed. Thomas H. D. Mahoney (Indianapolis: Bobbs-Merrill, 1955) p. 110.
22. Robert S. Hartman, Introduction to G. W. F. Hegel, *Reason in History,* trans. Robert F. Hartman (Indianapolis: Bobbs-Merrill, 1953) p. ix.
23. G. W. F. Hegel, *Reason in History,* trans. R. F. Hartman (Indianapolis: Bobbs-Merrill, 1953) p. 10.
24. Ibid., p. 33.
25. T. Z. Lavine, pp. 232–233. We should add that we consider Lavine's discussion of Hegel to be the clearest introduction available.
26. G. W. F. Hegel, p. 22.
27. Ibid., p. 47.
28. H. Holborn, Vol. 3, p. 284.
29. George Brandes, *Ferdinand Lassalle* (New York: Bergman Publishers, 1968) p. 36.
30. Guido de Ruggiero, *The History of European Liberalism,* trans. R. G. Collingwood (Boston: Beacon Press, 1959) p. 98.
31. Jeremy Bentham, *The Principles of Morals and Legislation* (Darien: Conn.: Hafner Publishing Co., 1970) p. 3.
32. Ibid., p. 24.
33. Harry K. Girvetz, *The Evolution of Liberalism* (Toronto: Collier-Macmillan, 1946) p. 66.
34. Robert Owen, "An Address to the Inhabitants of New Lanark," in A. Fried and R. Sanders, p. 167.
35. D. Douglas, ed., Vol. XII, Part 1, pp. 444–446.
36. G. D. H. Cole and A. W. Filson, ed., p. 375.
37. D. Douglas, ed., Vol. XII, Part 1, p. 449.
38. C. B. Macpherson, *The Life and Times of Liberal Democracy* (Oxford: Oxford Univ. Press, 1977) p. 42.
39. Stanley Pierson, *Marxism and the Origins of British Socialism* (Ithaca, N.Y.: Cornell Univ. Press, 1973) p. 42.
40. John Stuart Mill, *Autobiography* (Indianapolis: Bobbs-Merrill, 1957) pp. 148–149.
41. Ibid., p. 149.
42. Ibid.
43. Hans Kohn, ed. *The Mind of Modern Russia* (New York: Harper and Row, 1962) p. 158.
44. Franco Venturi, *The Roots of Revolution,* trans. Francis Haskell (New York: Alfred A. Knopf, 1960) p. 15.
45. Ibid., p. 35.

Chapter 13
The Transcendence of Economic Man

Karl Marx was born in the quiet Rhineland town of Trier in 1814 and died in the teeming city of London in 1883. Virtually everyone who has written about him notes the contrasts, ironies and paradoxes associated with his life and work, and we cannot resist including some of these points at the outset of our discussion. One of Marx's daughters remembered him as "the cheeriest, gayest soul that ever breathed" and as a "delightful playfellow" and "unrivalled storyteller."[1] And yet the tone of his works suggests the dour seriousness and intolerance of a vicious social critic. He was a meticulous scholar; yet he is primarily known for his contributions to the decidedly unconventional scholarly activity of promoting violent revolution. He attacked all forms of religion; yet he has become the cornerstone of the twentieth century communist trinity that includes Engels and Lenin. His Ph.D. dissertation compared the classical ideas of Epicurus and Democritus; yet his life's work centered on the study of industrial capitalism.

His normal workday began at seven in the morning and concluded 19 hours later at two the following morning; yet he had supper at home and always reserved Sundays for what we now call "quality time" with his family. While his workweek was devoted to scouring government documents that detailed the conditions of industrial society, his Sundays meant reading Shakespeare, Goethe and Aeschylus with his children. Despite these cultured interests and the grueling hours of studying and writing, the majority of his life was spent in abject poverty. He viewed his work as a catalyst for social revolution and human fulfillment—insisting that philosophy be applied to the task of improving the world. And yet, when his followers attempted to apply his thought in various social and political contexts, he was highly critical of their approaches. After a life dedicated to developing his system of thought, he recognized that it was being interpreted and applied in ways that he had not intended—prompting him to note "that whatever else he might be, he was certainly not a Marxist."[2] But underlying the ironies and apparent contradictions there is a remarkable degree of continuity and consistency in Marx's thought. In the end, it may well be that the paradoxes are not a consequence of deficiencies in Marx's system—but instead, a result of the task that he chose to pursue: the synthesis of much of the western intellectual tradition—including the conflicting concepts of contemplative and economic man.

Karl's father, Heinrich Marx, was a successful attorney of Jewish ancestry (his father and grandfather had been rabbis) who adopted the secular optimism of the Enlightenment as his faith. The integration of Trier into the Confederation of the Rhine by Napoleon temporarily created institutional support for Heinrich's views and provided the opportunity for Jews to become fully assimilated into the mainstream culture. Following Napoleon's defeat, the Congress of Vienna allocated Trier to the Prussians and shortly thereafter rigid limitations on Jews were introduced. Heinrich responded pragmatically by converting to Lutheranism and swearing loyalty to the Prussian system. Karl was born a year after his father's conversion and, although he did not inherit his father's accommodating disposition, he was influenced by Enlightenment thought:

It seems certain that the father had a definite influence on his son's intellectual development. The elder Marx believed with Condorcet that man is by nature both good and rational, and that all that is needed to ensure the triumph of these qualities is the removal of unnatural obstacles from his path.[3]

At the age of 17, Karl entered the law school at the University of Bonn. All evidence suggests that, like many freshmen, his academic concerns were subordinated to his social life—which included normal rowdiness and even a trip to jail. In 1836 he transferred to the University of Berlin, the bastion of Hegelian philosophy. This move marked a turning point in Karl's life. His frivolity gave way to a deep and brooding seriousness stimulated both by the conditions he observed and his reactions to them:

> He was sobered by the tense and tragic atmosphere in which he suddenly felt himself, and with his accustomed energy began at once to explore and criticize his new environment.[4]

In a letter to his father a few months after his arrival in Berlin, he noted that a recent illness was due, in part, to the pervasiveness of Hegel's thought in the new environment, forcing him "to make an idol of a view that I hated."[5]

To overcome this annoyance, Karl sought the company of a group of radical students and faculty who chose to deny Hegel's conservative orientation while preserving some of his underlying concepts. The "Left," or "Young Hegelian" approach grew from the acceptance of Hegel's concern for meaning in the historical process and his dialectical method—combined with the Enlightenment's focus on the importance of the individual human being.

Marx's reaction to the Berlin environment molded his future. After receiving his doctorate in philosophy he began editing a radical socialist newspaper in Cologne. Within a year the paper was banned by the government and Marx moved to Paris in 1844 where he began formulating his views in the *Economic and Philosophical Manuscripts*. His work continued in Brussels after he was expelled from France in 1845. The revolution of 1848 drew him back to Cologne but he was banished in 1849. He made his way back to Paris and then to London, where he lived until his death. He met Friedrich Engels, a student of British political economy, in 1844. Engels became his collaborator, friend, patron and literary executor. Engels' writings probably had more to do with popularizing "Marxism" than Marx's own works—a fact that turned out to be the fatal flaw in an otherwise satisfying partnership. This defect had serious ramifications, and we will return to this point at the end of this chapter.

The Young Hegelians

Hegel's view of history rested upon the notion of the progressive unfolding of Reason (or Spirit, or God) in time. He denied the apparent duality of Spirit and matter by asserting that matter was simply one of the forms in which Spirit manifested itself in the process of becoming self-conscious. This claim flowed out of the idea that to become self-conscious Spirit would have to see itself in relation to an "other"; something outside which would enable it to be aware of 'self' as over against that which was *not* it. Matter was, in a sense, the means which Spirit had chosen to use in order to become conscious of itself. Hegel posited that Spirit was developing through history by gradually transforming the material world into its own image. This process of transformation occurred dialectically as Spirit separated or alienated itself from its existence as pure Idea to manipulate men and nature in accordance with its purpose: unifying or synthesizing Spirit and matter to recreate its likeness in the objective world. Movement toward this goal was incremental and after each intervention in the world Spirit recognized a closer, yet imperfect approximation of itself. Spirit's awareness of the continued estrangement provoked renewed intervention, and hence it was this dynamic which propelled history. All history, then, revealed the growth and development of Spirit and all matter, including humanity, was merely the means which Spirit employed to make itself perfectly manifest in the world. By reproducing itself in the material realm, thus objectifying itself, Spirit would become fully self-conscious. Thus the dialectical interaction of Spirit and matter which shaped history permitted Spirit to attain fulfillment through self-understanding and awareness. Hegel concluded that the culmination of this process in the unity of Spirit and matter in history was manifested in the nation state.

Ludwig Feuerbach, one of the Young Hegelians, revived the claim that reality is material and thus challenged Hegel's essentially theological orientation in his *Essence of Christianity*, published in 1841. Relying on the empiricist tradition, Feuerbach argued that matter is the basis of reality. Hence, instead of humans being manifestations of God, God is a result of the self-alienation of human beings. Human beings, frustrated by their inability to become what they think they ought to be, have separated or alienated their own potential from themselves and projected it into a transcendent dimension. This projection is God, an abstract image of man's own abilities which have been turned into an external object. Because man does not realize that God is but an image of his own potential he is alienated from himself and his possibilities—trapped by the illusion that goodness is outside, beyond him. Feuerbach concluded that man must overcome this deceptive illusion and reappropriate his own potential in order to escape the alienation from himself caused by Christianity.

With these thoughts in mind, we can identify the roots of Marxism, or Hegel's system "stood on its head." While Hegel claimed that man was but an alienated unit of God, Feuerbach argued that God was an alienated image of man. The relationship of thinking and being is reversed: Hegel's notion that thinking precedes being is inverted with Feuerbach's assertion that it is being which shapes thinking. Thus although history is a process of alienation, it is not the alienation of Spirit but of human beings, and it must be understood that alienation has its roots in the material world—not in some mysterious realm of Ideas. Such estrangement was not confined to religion or thought, but was extended throughout the human experience. Political organizations (especially Hegel's nation state) should be viewed as a manifestation of man's separation from his power of social self control. But the ultimate form of alienation can be found in economic activity.

In his Preface to the *Economic and Philosophical Manuscripts of 1844,* Marx characterizes his work as that of an empirical political economist while acknowledging the theoretical influence of Hegel and Feuerbach. This mixture reintroduced the importance of the human being in the context of a meaningful and progressive theory of economics and history. The intellectual promise of this synthesis still contributes to the significance of Marx's thought. By 1859, he summarized this first synthesis as follows:

> It is not the consciousness of men that determines their being, but, on the contrary, their social being determines their consciousness.[6]

With this proposition, Marx was prepared to move toward his synthesis of economic animal and contemplative man as the product of the full development of capitalism. The historical process was, in fact, progressive and meaningful—holding in store the transcendence of all human alienation, once the pre-history of people (economic animals) gave way to a society based on economic abundance. Such a society would open the door to true human history—the history of economically secure beings who could finally discover and pursue their unlimited creative potential.

In order to untangle the intricate threads of Marx's thought, we will discuss his basic views toward the individual, society and the state. We will then attempt to clarify his integration of these concepts into a coherent radical philosophy of history that holds staggering implications for leisure. Before proceeding, however, we should note some of the problematic aspects of "Marxism" which became evident following the publication of the early philosophical writings from 1927 through the 1930s. By this time, widely-varying "Marxist" ideologies had been developed by individuals who did not even have access to the early philosophical works that provided the foundation for Marx's later (and more publicized) writings. In short, many "Marxists" and non-Marxists were shocked by the realization that the Marxian synthesis was much more profound than anything they had decided "Marxism" should be. For most "Marxists," the shock came with the recognition "that much of what traditionally passes for Marxism is directly contradicted by some of Marx's own writings."[7] For non-Marxists (who generally consider themselves to be anti-Marxists), the jolt came with the realization that:

> Marx's philosophy is rooted in the humanist Western philosophical tradition . . . the very essence of which is concern for man and the realization of his potentialities.[8]

Erich Fromm extends this initial observation by linking Marx to the social concerns of the Old Testament prophets, early Christianity, Aquinas and the Renaissance.[9] Other scholars have made similar arguments, with the Biblical links repeatedly mentioned and the image of an outraged and revolutionary Moses invoked in tandem with Marx.[10]

In short, the availability of Marx's early philosophical works—long after most of the world had decided what "Marxism" was—revealed the presence of strong connections between the nineteenth-century radical political economist and several historical figures closely associated with the classical concept of leisure. By adding Aristotle's fundamental concern for *potentiality* to this lexicon of ancient philosophers and prophets, we are ready to begin our discussion of Marx's writing—in which he suggests that most people, throughout history, have *actually* been the debased and animalistic creatures that the empiricists claimed we are: economic man. But economic animals are *potentially* true human beings: contemplative man. The prerequisite for this *actualization* of the human potential is in the satisfaction of material needs—the transcendence of economic scarcity and its replacement with economic abundance. The key to the realization of the historical movement toward real human freedom, then, lies in the efficiency of capitalist production which, for the first time in history, is capable of transcending scarcity and creating the basis for the fulfillment of the human potential.

The Early Writings: Alienation versus Human Potential

The *Economic and Philosophical Manuscripts* and the *Critique of Hegel's Philosophy of Right,* begun in 1844, provide the nucleus of Marx's entire system of thought. The *Manuscripts* focus on human alienation and the role of society in perpetuating it. The *Critique* attacks Hegel's view of the nation state in much the same way as Feuerbach had attacked Hegel's theology. By viewing humans as potentially God-like, Feuerbach criticized Christianity because it preserves the illusion of God's existence and thus prevents man from becoming conscious of the fact that this deity is nothing more than an image of his own potential. By perceiving humans as capable of acting as social beings, Marx criticized the nation state because it alienates us from our capacity to cooperate with each other in social harmony. From these beginnings, Marx's works moved through three identifiable stages: (1) a focus on the causes and consequences of human alienation; (2) a transition period from the late 1840s to the early 1850s, as the concept of economic class emerged as the collective expression of alienated individuals; (3) the development of an elaborate study of political economy that allegedly discovered "scientific laws" of capitalist development which would magnify human alienation to an intolerable point—paving the way for the transcendence of industrial capitalism, private property, the nation state and all forms of human alienation. While the later works might superficially appear to be more economics than philosophy, the nucleus of alienation unites Marx's ideas from beginning to end. In short, Marx's "laws of capitalist development" were different from the "laws" identified by other economists precisely because they were conditioned by the goal of transcending human alienation. Although the reader of *Capital* might occasionally be distracted from Marx's critique of economic man by the statistics and footnotes, underneath the empirical analysis there lurks both the logic and the youthful outrage at the degradation of human potential that was well-established in the 1840s:

> Marx's later writings merely articulate the conclusions at which he arrived at this early stage of his intellectual odyssey. The various economic, social and historical studies undertaken by Marx are but a corollary of the conclusions he drew from his immanent critique of Hegel's political philosophy.[11]

And given the degree to which Hegel was actually attempting to systematically approach Adam Smith's concept of the "invisible hand" as the guide of human history, Marx's critique of Hegel had serious ramifications for the concept of efficient economic man.

Essence versus Existence: The Alienated Individual

For Marx the tragedy of the human condition is rooted in the inherent conflict between the pursuit of the human essence—defined as "creative," "free," "conscious activity"—and the biological requirement of satisfying the needs of our existence.[12] We human beings long to be not only creative and free, but also to be conscious and active participants in the creation of our historical destiny:

> The animal is one with its life activity. It does not distinguish the activity from itself. It is its activity. But man makes his life activity itself an object of his will and consciousness. He has a conscious life activity.[13]

Thus consciousness, or the capacity to contemplate our lives and activity, and our unique ability to posit a goal and deliberately pursue it, elevate us above non-conscious animals. The influence of Aristotelian thought should be obvious in Marx's point of departure: the potentiality of true humanity lies in our conscious activity that creates awareness of ourselves and our surroundings. Kant's concept of the active mind is also present, but from Marx's perspective this potential is just that—potential—because our biological needs take precedence over our ability to pursue our unique human capacity.

The needs of existence limit our ability to actualize our essence, giving rise to human alienation. Labor power, or the individual's creative energy, should provide us with the opportunity to reach our uniquely human potential; instead, it degenerates into a means of fulfilling biological needs. As a result, the product of our labor actually becomes an "alien being" because it is an objective manifestation of labor—an objective, material thing that represents the denial of our essence.[14] The product of our labor represents energy and time spent producing something in order to exist—instead of producing something in conjunction with the pursuit of our human potential. Our alienation is further intensified when we sell this product of our creative time and energy in order to survive. The product of our labor, as an objective manifestation of human creativity, is really a part of us—the result of our labor. Losing this manifestation leaves us with trinkets, metal coins or paper money in its place—a poor substitute for the material evidence of our creativity.

In addition to being alienated from our essence as fully creative human beings (because our labor power is devoted solely to existence), as well as the product of our labor, Marx argued that the market economy enhances our alienation from other human beings—our species. The concept of "species-being" suggests that our past, present and future is intimately intertwined with other humans. In addition, it is derived from the fact that we tend to view ourselves as the personification of the species:

> Man is a species-being not only in the sense that he makes the community . . . his object both practically and theoretically, but also . . . in the sense that he treats himself as the present, living species, as a universal and consequently free being.[15]

Once again, we are alienated from our potential when species-activity, or "conscious life activity," is replaced with individual egoism—the motive of animals. But even animals share some sense of community, recognizing bonds within their species; for Marx, this capacity is stripped from us as we are forced into rigid competition by capitalism.

The final characteristic of humans, and the one that we share with animals, is defined by Marx as our "natural being." This concept refers to "natural" activities, including eating, sleeping, procreating and roaming. This most basic part of our being prompts spontaneity and focuses on objects outside of ourselves. We know of no better summary of this concept than Bertell Ollman's:

> As a natural being, Marx claims, man is like an animal in being 'identical with his activity'. At this level, man is as he does, because he is unable to distinguish himself in his imagination from what he is doing. He is a 'person' without intellectual abilities or self-awareness. His faculties operate only to secure his physical needs, only to realize what have been called his natural powers. As such, he produces only his physical self, adding to his weight, stature and offspring and improves his health; but, according to Marx, he cannot reproduce nature or create things of beauty. His actions are 'spontaneous' rather than 'voluntary', which is a way of stating that man is completely controlled by natural forces rather than the reverse.[16]

For Marx, then, our history is actually the account of pre-human activity characterized by alienation. Beginning with the original conflict of essence versus existence, the drive to secure the material necessities of life led to the division of labor to enhance efficiency. While efficiency was increased, the division of labor alienated man from the product of his labor, as individual producers became merely component parts in the process of production. By stressing unfettered competition among all individuals, man became further alienated from his species and, hence, the social part of himself. Finally, even animalistic spontaneity was stifled by the strict regimentation of the entire society that had become accustomed to time clocks, productive efficiency and unconscious performance of boring tasks on the assembly lines of industrial capitalism. Again, so much for optimism. But underneath these lamentations about the human condition, Marx was working toward one of the most optimistic conclusions in the western intellectual tradition. Economic scarcity serves as the historical root of all of these dimensions of human alienation. And while capitalism was in the process of intensifying alienation by stripping away all of the camouflage that had disguised it in the past, it was also creating—for the first time in history—economic abundance, i.e., the capacity to transcend scarcity that would open the door for the transcendance of all forms of human alienation. By transcending economic scarcity, people would be free, for the first time in history, to utilize their consciousness to discover their truly human potential and coordinate their unalienated labor to pursue it. Essence-pursuit as a way of life—classical leisure—would be available to all and *human history* would begin.

The Economic Infrastructure, Class and Society

Given the recognition that the effort to supply the requisites for existence supercedes the pursuit of human essence, it follows that organizations develop as a consequence of the imperatives established by the struggle for survival. Hence, societies come into being because of their superior ability to supply the requirements for existence: a community can function far more efficiently than any of its solitary members could be operating individually. We are, therefore, members of a society by virtue of the fact that the division of labor within the social unit increases our productivity and thus promotes survival. Whatever innate sociability we share with animals is completely subordinated to the pragmatic recognition that a professional carpenter is a more efficient builder than the amateur, and the professional farmer is a more efficient food producer than the novice, et cetera. Modern society emerges not out of a social contract designed to institutionalize our innate sociability—but out of economic expediency, based on the division of labor as a mechanism to boost efficiency:

> Social relations are intimately connected with the forces of production. In acquiring new forces of production . . . they change all their social relations.
>   The same men who establish social relations in conformity with their material power of production, also produce principles, laws and categories of conformity with their social relations.[17]

Because society insures our survival, it is absolutely necessary to preserve it; hence, the mode of production in any given society creates and perpetuates specific attitudes, values and institutions for a single purpose—to support and reinforce the economic system. In the Preface to Volume I of *Capital*, Marx summarized his life's work as the study of "a process of natural history" of "the evolution of the economic formation of society."[18]

Modern society, then, is organized to perpetrate a particular system of values and practices that reinforce the economic, productive infrastructure. Departures from these norms is intolerable because widespread deviations would undermine the capacity of the society to mold behavior suited to the end of guaranteeing survival. Consequently, the illusion of individual freedom promulgated in classical political economy disguises the rigid constraints that shape individuals into the functionaries that societies require:

> the whole of *civil society* is only this mutual conflict of all individuals who are no longer distinguished by anything but their *individuality*. . . . In the modern world, every individual participates *at the same time* in slavery and in social life. But the *slavery* of *civil society* is, *in appearance,* the greatest *liberty,* because it appears to be the realized *independence* of the individual . . . a manifestation of his own liberty, when in reality it is nothing but the expression of his absolute enslavement and of the loss of his human nature.[19]

Like Hegel, Marx contended that society and culture impose constraints on human freedom. For Hegel, this was a positive accomplishment because men were defined as destructive egotists whose actions must be controlled and whose anti-social behavior must be curbed. For Marx, these social and cultural shackles severely undermine our capacity to transcend alienation. To the extent that culture insidiously perpetrates alienated labor, destroys true sociability, and restricts our spontaneity, it is a second tier in the barrier obstructing progress toward human freedom.

By now, Marx's remarkable skill in turning the basic premises of earlier arguments against the conclusions they once supported is both evident and impressive. By positing that men are inherently social (species-beings), Marx completely inverts the Hegelian view of culture and society; because humans are capable of cooperation, civil society based upon competitive, antagonistic social relations is a serious impediment to human fulfillment—not a support. Obviously human fulfillment is Marx's goal—as opposed to the fulfillment of Spirit, or God, in Hegel's system. Hegel assumes that the human capacity to alter the material world through labor makes us important participants in the process of history primarily because our skills can be conveniently manipulated by Spirit to complete its projects. For Marx, our labor (as activity that alters nature) is also the source of our uniqueness—but the movement of history is driven by our material needs, not by the needs of an abstract Spirit. This view of humans as laborers who alter nature begins to link Marx with Smith and Locke. But, unlike the creators of economic man, Marx argued that this labor is not fulfilling—it is alienating. With alienated labor at the foundation of Marx's thought, whatever improvements or benefits that may come out of labor actually produce anti-human results.

Adam Smith viewed the division of labor as the key to economic abundance and the wealth of the nation. Marx agreed, but adds that it separates us from the possibility of fulfilling labor—further enhancing our alienation. Smith divided history into stages, based on the efficiency of production, and concluded that capitalism is the culmination of economic history. Hegel argued that the nation state represents the highest form of human evolution. Marx combined their approaches and asserted that neither had gone far enough. History holds still another stage: the positive transcendence of private property, the division of labor, and the nation state (each of which deepens alienation) into a realm of hitherto unknown human fulfillment, defined as communism. For Marx, communism represents the ultimate reconciliation of man with his creative labor, his species, the product of his labor, his natural spontaneity and his capacity for social self-control. Communism:

> is the definitive resolution of the antagonism between man and nature, and between man and man. It is the true solution of the conflict between existence and essence, between objectification and self-affirmation, between freedom and necessity, between individual and species.[20]

Class and Ideology: Distorted Consciousness

After establishing the basis for his system of thought in the early manuscripts, Marx began to develop the concept of alienation in greater detail. Having presented people as alienated from their humanity, he expanded his approach to include social class as the collective expression of the alienated individual. Beginning in 1845 in *The Holy Family* and *The German Ideology* (1845–46), and continuing through the Preface to Volume I of *Capital,* the industrial working class, or proletariat, was portrayed as the collective expression of alienated individuals—a picture which should not surprise anyone who read the final pages of our previous Chapter. In *The Holy Family,* Marx and Engels justify this transition:

The possessing class and the proletarian class represent one and the same human self-alienation. But the former feels satisfied and affirmed in this self-alienation, experiences the alienation as a sign *of its own power,* and possesses in it the *appearance* of a human existence. The latter, however, feels destroyed in this alienation, seeing in it its own impotence and the reality of an inhuman existence. To use Hegel's expression, this class is, within depravity, an *indignation* against this depravity, an indignation necessarily aroused in this class by the contradiction between its human *nature* and its life-situation, which is a blatant, outright and all-embracing denial of that very nature.[21]

And again, in his Preface to Volume I of *Capital,* Marx reminds us of this transition:

But here individuals are dealt with only in so far as they are the personifications of economic categories, embodiments of particular class relations and class interests.[22]

It is clear that in shifting his focus to economic classes Marx maintained his initial concern with human alienation—while providing himself with an additional tool for analyzing and attacking the social (or in human terms, anti-social) basis of exploitation. For Marx, social history is an account of conflict between economic classes. Class distinctions result from the apportionment of the control over a society's production. Every society that is based on private property produces an economic elite—or ruling class—as its oppressors. Adam Smith shared this view, including the recognition of class-based exploitation. But while Smith accepted the degradation of the working class as a necessary condition for the "wealth of the nation," Marx concluded that it was an intolerable affront to potential human beings.

After accepting the economists' class-based structure of civil society as the reality in a pre-human world, Marx highlighted the role of conflict between economic classes throughout history. Viewed as the force behind the dialectical movement of history, class conflict can be recognized in Athens (commercial interests and oligarchs), Rome (aristocratic landowners, dispossessed small farmers and slaves), feudal Europe (monarch, nobility, Church and peasants), and nineteenth-century industrial society (bourgeoisie and proletariat). One of the major results of the successful bourgeois revolution in England was the simplification of the complex class system associated with feudal societies and a corresponding concentration of the once dispersed tension between classes on a single conflict between capitalists and workers:

The modern bougeois society that has sprouted from the ruins of feudal society has not done away with class antagonisms. It has but established new classes, new conditions of oppression, new forms of struggle in place of the old ones.

Our epoch, the epoch of the bourgeoisie, possesses, however, this distinctive feature: it has simplified the class antagonisms. Society as a whole is more and more splitting up into two great hostile camps, into two great classes directly facing each other: bourgeoisie and proletariat.[23]

This dramatic separation of the rulers and the ruled extends far beyond its basis in economic power—into the realm of ideas and politics.

Ideology as Alienation

Of all the obstacles that economic necessity and class-based society have placed in our path toward discovering and pursuing our true humanity, the most insidious hindrance is in the distortion of our own consciousness. Marx argued that, along with the social institutions that develop to buttress the modes and relations of production, certain attitudes, values and definitions of ourselves as people limit our true humanity: a slave has lost any hope for freedom when he sees himself as a slave—when he, in his own consciousness, accepts his identity as a slave. The dominant ideas of any period in history reflect the values and needs of the material basis of a society. It follows that the greatest insult to humanity is our willingness to accept a definition of ourselves as anything less than spontaneous and creative social beings.

For Marx, the concept of economic man was a fabrication of the dominant economic interests (recall Locke's intimate association with the Whigs) in England during the early stages of capitalism. It was elaborated upon by Smith (via Hume) and improved the efficiency of production by stripping us of any consciousness of ourselves as something more than egotistical economic animals and laborers. Dominant ideas are consequently also manifestations of particular forms of economic production—as opposed to Hegel's definition of them as a manifestation of Spirit's progress. They are created and perpetuated by the economic elite and their spokesmen (recall Aristotle's acceptance of slavery) in order to completely control society:

> The ideas of the ruling class are in every epoch the ruling ideas: i.e., the class which is the ruling material force of society, is at the same time its ruling intellectual force. . . . The ruling ideas are nothing more than the ideal expression of the dominant material relationships, the dominant material relationships grasped as ideas; hence of the relationships which make the one class the ruling one, therefore, the ideas of its dominance.[24]

Ideology—which is the particular consciousness of the ruling class defined as general consciousness for the entire society—is, therefore, a deceptive illusion that leads potential humans away from their essence. In addition, it serves to justify the political power of the economic elite.

The State: Institutional Defender of Alienation

The final factor obstructing the path to human fulfillment is the class-based state. With economic power at the foundation of civil society, the state exists to enforce dominant class interests. All political struggles are extensions of the class struggle; the control by the dominant class over state policy adds the illusion of legality to the suppression of human potential:

> The centralised State power, with its ubiquitous organs of standing army, police, bureaucracy . . . and the judicature . . . [are] organs wrought after the plan of a systematic and hierarchic division of labor.[25]

The state acts as a final bastion of alienation to coerce those who, somehow, have slipped through the net of economic, social and intellectual impediments to human fulfillment.

The significance of Marx's view of the state is easily perceived through a discussion of political reform. The conflict between radical communists and reformist social democrats grew out of this pivotal issue and fragmented the European left by the latter part of the nineteenth century. Marx contended that movements to reform the state are a useful tactic for the working class because its members will learn organizational skills and, in the long run, such efforts to reform political systems enhance the proletariat's revolutionary class consciousness. For the social democrats in western Europe, reform of the state became the final goal of socialism. John Stuart Mill concluded that gradual reform of the social and political system would bring about change and improvement. Mill believed that society and state are independent entities that can be reshaped by reform. In contrast, Marx claimed that because the state is merely an extension of class-based society, the destruction of the foundation of alienation, i.e., private property and the classes that it has produced, would be necessary. Given this perspective, Marx was convinced that political reform is an illusion that cannot produce meaningful economic and social change—but the proletariat will not recognize this until it has exhausted the possibilities for reform and, in the process, come face to face with the class-based realities of political power.

To transform the environment that produced, increased and perpetuates human alienation, every remnant of bourgeois society must be destroyed by the proletariat's seizure of the state's coercive apparatus. After gaining control the working class will be able to employ the state's power to create a community that supports the realization of the human potential instead of stifling it. Thus, in another clever move, Marx has reintroduced the Greek's positive view of the state as facilitator of the human potential.

While it may seem contradictory to claim that the most degraded and dehumanized people in history have the power to carry the society into hitherto unknown realms of human accomplishment, Marx showed how it was possible by using the dialectical conflict of opposites with unprecedented skill. Such deprivation is precisely the key to the transcendence of human alienation. The development of industrial capitalism that causes this degradation also generates the material conditions and revolutionary class consciousness among the workers that is required to destroy and transcend it. Capitalism's unique historical contribution is its efficiency—its ability to create economic abundance which will permit economic animals to become human. While perfecting the means to overcome scarcity, the bourgeoisie inadvertently welds the workers into an army that, upon recognizing the source of its collective abasement will rise up and overthrow its oppressors. Capitalism creates its "own gravediggers" out of the formerly complacent illiterate masses of society:

> Masses of labourers, crowded into the factory, are organized like soldiers. As privates of the industrial army they are placed under the command of a perfect hierarchy of officers and sergeants. Not only are they slaves of the bourgeois class, and of the bourgeois State; they are daily and hourly enslaved by the machine, by the over-looker, and, above all, by the individual bourgeois manufacturer himself.[26]

The general pessimism of the nineteenth-century political economists (especially Ricardo and Malthus) is applied by Marx to the conditions of industrial production. But by applying the dialectic of material history to this situation, Marx emerges with an optimism for the future which exceeds even the vision of the "heavenly city" developed by Enlightenment philosophers. The political revolution carried out by the proletariat against the bourgeoisie would usher us into the world of de-alienated species-being and create a truly human society deliberately designed to promote the realization of the human potential. Creative freedom leading to self-realization would no longer be denied by economic necessity and the future society would emerge as an idyllic environment out of the alienated past:

> the division of labor offers us the first example of how . . . man's own deed becomes an alien power opposed to him, which enslaves him instead of being controlled by him. For as soon as labor is distributed, each man has a particular, exclusive sphere of activity which is forced upon him and from which he cannot escape . . . in communist society . . . each can become accomplished in any branch he wishes, society regulates the general production and thus makes it possible for me to do one thing today and another tomorrow, to hunt in the morning, fish in the afternoon, rear cattle in the evening, criticize after dinner, just as I have a mind, without ever becoming hunter, fisherman, shepherd, or critic.[27]

By nearly any definition, this glimpse of the future community is utopian, if for no other reason than its retreat into pre-industrial imagery. But what sets Marx apart from his "utopian socialist" and romantic predecessors is his attempt to ground the inevitability of such a vision becoming reality in the empirical observations of the political economists—in "immutable laws of history." To accomplish this, Marx extended his initial philosophical concepts into the empirical study of the development of capitalism.

The "Laws" of Capitalist Development

Surplus value is the key to Marx's economic thought. With it, Marx used the Labor Theory of Value—which Locke had used to justify private property—to attack bourgeois society. If all value is created by the individual's labor, how can the owner of the factory who has not directly participated in this process have any claim on the manufactured goods? Marx suggested that surplus value is the value created by the workers above that which they are paid for. This unpaid labor is siphoned by the capitalist as profit, allowing him to increase his wealth by, in effect, stealing labor from the workers. As surplus value grows and is turned into working capital, the exploitation of the proletariat is compounded because more jobs are being created and more individuals are being sucked into the process as workers. The surplus value created by these workers' labor will, in turn, augment the existing store of capital and allow for more workers, extending the exploitation. As capitalism unfolds, the expanding proletariat will eventually create enough surplus value for the capitalist to procure ever more sophisticated machinery, which will make the large proletariat superfluous:

> When viewed as a transaction between the capitalist class and the working class, it makes no difference that additional labourers are employed by means of the unpaid labour of the previously employed labourers. The capitalist may even convert the additional capital into a machine that throws the producers of that capital out of work, and that replaces them by a few children. In every case the working class creates by the surplus-labour of one year the capital destined to employ additional labour in the following year. And this is what is called: creating capital out of capital.[28]

Marx's moral outrage is undeniable as labor (the potential means to individual self-realization) is perverted to create great wealth for the capitalist class, as alienation is increased among the workers.

Because capitalism tends to constantly expand, the size of the proletariat grows while, at the same time, the constant advancements in more sophisticated machinery lead to fewer and fewer jobs. Keen competition, and the introduction of a system of credit, lead to the inevitable concentration of capital in fewer and fewer hands. Monopolies are created and additional technological improvements further decrease the demand for labor:

> The labouring population therefore produces, along with the accumulation of capital produced by it, the means by which itself is made relatively superfluous, is turned into a relatively superfluous population; and it does this to an always increasing extent. This is a law of population peculiar to the capitalist mode of production.[29]

Thus, Marx presents an inverse relationship between the efficiency of capitalist production and the number of workers employed. As production grows, fewer and fewer workers will be able to find means of subsistence, let alone self-fulfilling labor; the "industrial reserve army" will expand and discontent will grow.

The growth of this reserve force of workers is guaranteed by another "law" based on the industrial cycle, which goes through the steps of (1) average activity, (2) high production, (3) crisis,

(4) stagnation.[30] Through this alternate expansion and contraction, understood to be as inevitable as the motion of "heavenly bodies," the hoard of unemployed workers will be kept in a state of constant uncertainty and agitation, while being reduced to "a mass of human material."[31]

The result of these "laws" of the increasing superfluousness of the working class and the inevitability of ever-greater crises is the "absolute general law of capitalist accumulation": that as the capitalist class shrinks and becomes wealthier, the proletariat constantly grows and becomes more destitute—all of which is the consequence of inevitable economic laws:

> At a certain stage of development, it brings forth the material agencies for its own dissolution. From that moment, new forces and new passions spring up in the bosom of society; but the old social organization fetters them and keeps them down. It must be annihilated; it is annihilated.[32]

These concluding statements at the end of Chapter 32 of *Capital,* Volume I, are among the most well-known passages written by Marx. We are told that "immanent laws of capitalist production" created bourgeois society, and then laid the basis for its destruction:

> Along with the constantly diminishing number of the magnates of capital, who usurp and monopolise all advantages of this process of transformation, grows the mass of misery, oppression, slavery, degradation, exploitation; but with this too grows the revolt of the working-class, a class always increasing in numbers, and disciplined, united, organised by the very mechanism of the process of capitalist production itself. The monopoly of capital becomes a fetter upon the mode of production, which has sprung up and flourished along with, and under it. Centralisation of the means of production and socialisation of labour at last reach a point where they become incompatible with their capitalist integument. This integument is burst asunder. The knell of capitalist private property sounds. The expropriators are expropriated.[33]

And finally, "Capitalist production begets, with the inexorability of a law of nature, its own negation. It is the negation of the negation."[34]

This negation of private property (which, itself, was the negation of pre-capitalist communal property) will, in most cases, necessitate violence. But for Marx (and for Hume and Hegel) all historical change is violent. The communist revolution would grow out of the tension between new productive forces in conflict with institutions that were created to support old forces of production—just as the bourgeois revolution had earlier destroyed feudalism when the traditional society impeded the interests of the commercial class. But the communist revolution would be both less protracted and less violent than the bourgeoisie's attack on the feudal order and, for the first time in history, social and political transformation would be democratized:

> The transformation of scattered private property, arising from individual labour, into capitalist private property is, naturally, a process, incomparably more protracted, violent, and difficult, than the transformation of capitalistic private property, already practically resting on socialised production, into socialised property. In the former case, we had the expropriation of the mass of the people by a few usurpers; in the latter, we have the expropriation of a few usurpers by the mass of the people.[35]

These passages clearly unite the early focus on alienation, Hegelian epistemology "turned on its head," and empirical indicators of economic development in order to support the inevitability of the destruction of capitalism. Because capitalism has become so efficient in the mechanical production of goods, scarcity will be abolished and man, for the first time, will no longer be required to spend the bulk of his time supplying the needs of existence. Old forms of individual private property, destroyed in the process of capitalist development, will not be reintroduced. Instead, the social nature of production, introduced and perfected by the bourgeoisie, will be expanded to the distribution of goods also—and all will benefit instead of the few. "Cooperation and possession in common of the land and the means of production" will be the norm.[36] Indeed, the utopian goal will be realized due to the "laws" of capitalist development. The final upheaval will herald the arrival of the classless society—free of the exploitation, alienation and suffering that have dominated the history of natural man. Real humanity, i.e., Species-Man, will emerge and real human history will begin—providing all human beings with the opportunity to discover and pursue their potential.

Afterthoughts: Marx's Legacy

Marx's synthesis of so many dimensions of the western intellectual tradition in a humanistic response to the horrors of early capitalism was a staggering accomplishment. But, as any practitioner of the dialectic will note, the strength of something also conceals its weakness. If one needs to be conversant with all of the currents in the western intellectual tradition in order to fully appreciate Marx, the likelihood of the laboring masses being able to grasp the full significance of the Marxian synthesis is questionable. The three authors of this book have had the opportunity to study Marx for many years and, sometimes, we feel that we barely know him. What chance would Mr. William Cooper (whose testimony to the Sadler Committee we recounted at the end of Chapter 11) have to fully grasp the Marxian synthesis?

Marx was able to argue for the inevitability of communist revolution and, hence, the actualization of the human potential because his empirical analysis of capitalism supported his philosophically-established goal of transcending human alienation. The equation, then, begins with economic and social conditions of advanced capitalism (material reality) prompting the growth of revolutionary proletarian class consciousness (ideals). The dialectical tension between the two makes revolution "inevitable"—precisely because Marx, like Hegel, denied any duality between mind and matter. As George Lichtheim, an eminent scholar of Marxism has noted:

> For Marx, as for Hegel, the idealist emphasis upon the discrepancy between things as they are and things as they ought to be, is the mark of a shallow and trivial incomprehension of the ultimate identity of mind-matter. There are no "ideals" that cannot be realized, for the emergence of new aims is itself an index to the presence of forces which make for their realization.[37]

The underlying link between Hegel and Marx, then, emerges in the idea of praxis, or the unity of theory and practice. It connects the dialectical interaction between material conditions, proletarian class consciousness, and revolutionary change. Granted, capitalism establishes the material base for transcending scarcity and creates the proletariat; its contradictions then create the material conditions conducive to sparking the working classes into forming a revolutionary organization. Such organization encourages the proletariat to realize that it is an exploited class and, hence, develop a revolutionary consciousness. This consciousness becomes an active force in the creation of the new material reality, i.e., the revolution and apocalyptic change. From this perspective, we can also identify Marx's role as revolutionary: by delineating the contradictions of capitalism and contributing to the proletariat's recognition of its historical role, Marx's works can be viewed as enhancing the likelihood of revolution through his "critical theory":

> The understanding of existing reality is therefore a necessary condition for the possibility of revolutionizing it. . . . Hence a theoretical analysis of the structure of the capitalist economy is undoubtedly the revolutionary praxis par excellence.[38]

A major problem in all socialist organizations, however, has been the development of revolutionary class consciousness—and the socialist experience supports the assertion that it does not inevitably arise from contradictions inherent in capitalism. The link between Marx and Hegel is therefore vitally important. Any attempt to put Marxism into practice which does not emphasize this Hegelian aspect fails to come to grips with the question of how proletarian, i.e., revolutionary, class consciousness develops.

The centrality of these points becomes clear with the recollection that it was the later, empirically-based works of Marx and Engels which were popular prior to the publication of Marx's early works. Thus "Marxism" in the late nineteenth century did not include the early writings, which clearly establish the link with Hegel. And without this link, distinctions between mind (revolutionary ideas) and matter (material conditions of capitalism) became more likely.

The suggestion that Engels was the first to open this gap has been made by several scholars of Marxism, and his direction took Marx's ideas away from their link with Hegel. Robert Tucker relates an incident in which Alexis Voden, after Engels had published Marx's "Theses on Feuerbach," suggested that the remainder of the early works should be made available. Engels' response indicates that he recognized the Hegel-Marx link, but seemed to denigrate it:

> He reported afterwards that Engels showed embarrassment when the subject was raised, and answered that 'Marx had also written poetry in his student years, but it could hardly interest anybody'. Was not the fragment on Feuerbach 'sufficient'? And ought he not continue work on Marx's unfinished economic writings rather than publish 'old manuiscripts from publicistic works of the 1840s'? Besides, Engels concluded, 'in order to penetrate into that "old story" one needed to have an interest in Hegel himself, which was not the case with anybody then, or to be more exact, "neither with Kautsky nor with Bernstein." '[39]

Tucker also notes that Marx himself did not encourage publication of the early works.[40] But without the earlier emphasis on the unity of mind and matter, the original system of thought would not be complete.

Engels' contribution to the system of thought is undeniable. He and Marx cooperated on numerous works and Engels edited Volumes II and III of *Capital*. The important point, however, is that Engels' influence during the twelve years between his death and Marx's had a decisive impact on "Marxism." Lichtheim notes that:

> We therefore start from the well-nigh unchallengeable proposition that as a coherent system 'Marxism' came into being during the dozen years which separate the death of Marx (1883) from that of Engels (1895).[41]

Yet this "Marxism," he suggests, was much different from Marx's thought, as it combined a positivist approach and a mechanistic twist which went "far beyond anything that he [Marx] can have envisaged.[42]

The irony here is that the major growth of "Marxist" organizations took place during the years from 1890 to the beginning of World War I—after Marx's death. In addition, Lichtheim argues that Engels' works, notably *Anti-Duhring, Socialism: Utopian and Scientific,* and *The Origin of the Family, Private Property and the State* served as the primary theoretical basis for the movements during this time period:

> It was from them, rather than from *Capital* (not to mention Marx's early writings, which were still largely unknown), that most socialists drew their mental picture of the world.[43]

Hence, if we want to understand why Marx became increasingly disillusioned by the way "Marxism" was being interpreted and applied, we must recognize that the necessity of popularizing his complex system of thought—and Engels' willingness to do so—probably started the process of its fragmentation.

Lichtheim stresses the profound alteration of praxis, arguing that Engels was responsible for pushing the system of thought in a mechanistic direction:

> Once the crucial vision of a "critical theory," which would transform the world by exposing its inner contradictions, had been exchanged for the far less exciting notion of a science of causal evolution, the ancient cleavage . . . between factual understanding and normative judgment—was back in full force.[44]

Avineri also argues that Engels began the process of distorting the Marxian synthesis. Echoing Lichtheim's suggeston that Engels pushed the system of thought away from Hegel and toward an overly materialist position, he concludes that this approach (that humans are totally manipulated by outside material forces) opens itself to Marx's critique of eighteenth-century materialism:

> Such a view, considering only the objective side of historical development and not its subjective elements, is open to all of Marx's criticism in his *Theses on Feuerbach*. Such a view ultimately sees in man and in human will only an object of external circumstances. . . . Both the cruelty and harshness of Bolshevism and the intellectual wastelands of Social Democracy grow directly from this mechanistic twist Engels gave to Marxism.[45]

We will return to this point in Chapter 14, with a discussion of the widely varying interpretations of "Marxism" that dominated the socialist movement in Russia (Lenin), Germany (Karl Kautsky) and England (Eduard Bernstein).

Implications for Leisure

Through Marx's synthesis of Hegel's view of history as a meaningful process, the empirical analysis of economic development and the essentially Aristotelian concept of actuality and potentiality, the classical ideal of leisure was rescued from the assault by economic man. Granted, the history of the species is a history of conflict, egotism and economic self-interest—just as Hume and Smith claimed. But the historical record is based on economic scarcity and our actions, the growth of economic classes, ideologies and states, are manifestations of the struggle to survive. While the political economists tended to accept this view as a given of the past, present and future, Marx argued that just because we have been economic animals in the past does not mean that we are destined to continue as pre-human beings.

Our potential to become truly human—to be united with our species, our labor and its products, and nature—awaits actualization in the future. Prior to communism, people (as economic animals) are actually living in pre-human conditions. Hence, empirical observations of the past and present can never reveal the unlimited capacity for creativity and cooperation that post-revolution human history will introduce. The few glimpses Marx provides into the future *human* society hold the promise of the transcendence of all forms of alienation through the resolution of the conflict between essence and existence, i.e., between contemplative and economic man. With this reconciliation the traditional dichotomy between thought and action, or contemplation and labor, fades into obscurity—as the material and ideal world merge into a unity of non-alienated, creative labor and truly human consciousness. Hence, contemplation as a luxury reserved for the non-laboring economically self-sufficient few can, for the first time in history, be replaced by the democratization of leisure as essence-pursuit.

While the entire process of history is viewed as paving the way for democratized classical leisure, human consciousness is a critical element in this process. The part played by revolutionary class consciousness (as the intervening variable between material conditions and messianic change into a totally new and fulfilling environment) stresses the pivotal role of our awareness of the conflict between our *actuality* (economic animal) and our *potentiality* (true humanity). This potentiality is the product of thought—the contemplation of the past, present and future. Hence, the goal of transcending human alienation can only be achieved through the collective expression of active, contemplative minds recognizing, like Kant, that it is possible to will our fulfillment.

Our leisure time, then, provides us with the opportunity to become totally free if we choose to be truly human and actively strive to overcome our own alienation. It is not merely time to rest from alienating labor, or consume the products of other people's alienated labor, or escape from the reality of the human condition. It is time to confront the tension between the past and the future and actualize our potential to form the world into a decent place for humans to live. For Marx, our *"categorical imperative"* is to recognize our capacity *"to overthrow all those conditions* in which man is an abased, enslaved, abandoned, contemptible being."[46] To spend our time in any other manner impedes the historical movement toward true humanity.

Major Philosophical Points

Marx's synthesis of German idealism and British empiricism grounded Hegel's progressive view of historical development in the material reality of the actions of people struggling to exist. The productive efficiency of advanced capitalism creates the material capacity to transcend the historical conflict between existing and the human essence of creative freedom, thus preparing the foundation for the history of true humanity—as opposed to the pre-history of economic animals. His vision of the communist future was derived from the synthesis of the Athenian ideal of classical leisure and its antithesis, efficient economic man. By positing the ability of humans to mesh these hitherto opposite perspectives, Marx democratized the classical concept of leisure as essence-pursuit.

- The dialectical interaction of material reality and the ideas it stimulates link mind and matter.
- The human essence is totally free, creative, responsible and social.
- The need to survive has focused human attention on existence throughout history—thereby forcing us to deny our essence.
- The struggle to survive creates private property and, hence, the alienation of our sociability.
- Ideas and institutions develop from existing economic relationships to maintain the power of a small economic elite.
- The industrial proletariat under capitalism is the collective expression of human alienation.
- The productive capacity of capitalism creates economic abundance—a necessary condition if human alienation is ever to be transcended.
- Capitalism intensifies human alienation by eliminating the disguises that have made it tolerable in the past. The contradictions of advanced capitalism lay the basis for its own destruction.

- The tension between the bourgeois nation state and the industrial working class will intensify as capitalism develops, due to a corresponding growth in the proletariat's consciousness of itself as a revolutionary class.
- The revolution by the proletariat will be a continuation of the liberating force of the previous middle class revolution against the feudal elite.
- The revolution will socialize the means of production and distribution. With productive capacity at its historical peak, the socialization of the distribution of material goods will free man from the degradation of wage-labor. Labor will become a self-fulfilling expression of creativity.
- Thus freed from the subordination of essence to the needs of existence, people will emerge from the pre-history of humanity. By transcending the historical conflict between existence and essence we can transcend all forms of alienation and pursue our creative social potential.
- Communism will democratize the Athenian ideal of leisure time as essence-pursuit.

References

1. Eleanor Marx-Aveling, "Karl Marx, A Few Stray Notes," reprinted in Erich Fromm, *Marx's Concept of Man,* (New York: Frederick Ungar Publishing Co., 1966) p. 248, 249.
2. Isaiah Berlin, *Karl Marx: His Life and Environment* (New York: Time Incorporated, 1963) p. 221.
3. Ibid., p. 24.
4. Ibid., p. 28.
5. Robert C. Tucker, ed. *The Marx-Engels Reader,* 2nd ed. (New York: W. W. Norton and Company, Inc., 1978) p. 8.
6. Karl Marx and Frederick Engels, Preface to "The Materialist Conception of History," in T. B. Bottomore and Maximilian Rubel, ed. *Karl Marx: Selected Writings in Sociology and Social Philosophy,* trans. T. B. Bottomore (New York: McGraw-Hill, 1964) p. 51.
7. Shlomo Avineri, *The Social and Political Thought of Karl Marx* (Cambridge: Cambridge Univ. Press, 1968) p. 1.
8. E. Fromm, p. v.
9. Ibid., p. 68.
10. See E. Wilson, p. 246, 360, 374 and I. Berlin, p. 6, 180. For a recent argument viewing Moses as the archetype for modern revolutionary leaders, see Michael Walzer, *Exodus and Revolution* (New York: Basic Books, 1985).
11. S. Avineri, p. 5.
12. K. Marx, *Economic and Philosophical Manuscripts,* in E. Fromm, p. 101.
13. Ibid.
14. Ibid., p. 95.
15. Ibid., p. 100.
16. Bertell Ollman, *Alienation: Marx's Conception of Man in Capitalist Society* (Cambridge: Cambridge Univ. Press, 1971) pp. 82–83.
17. Karl Marx, *The Poverty of Philosophy,* in T. Bottomore and M. Rubel, ed. p. 95.
18. Karl Marx, *Capital: A Critique of Political Economy,* ed. Frederick Engels (New York: The Modern Library, 1906) p. 15.
19. Karl Marx and Frederick Engels, *The Holy Family,* in T. Bottomore and M. Rubel, ed. p. 219.
20. K. Marx, *Economic and Philosophical Manuscripts,* in Fromm, p. 127.
21. K. Marx and F. Engels, *The Holy Family,* in R. Tucker, ed. pp. 133–134.
22. K. Marx, *Capital,* in Lewis S. Feuer, ed. *Marx and Engels: Basic Writings in Politics and Philosophy* (Garden City, N.Y.: Anchor Books, 1959) pp. 136–137.
23. K. Marx and F. Engels, *The Communist Manifesto,* Ibid., p. 8.
24. K. Marx, *The German Ideology* in R. Tucker, ed. pp. 172–173.
25. Karl Marx, *The Civil War in France,* in David Caute, ed. *Essential Writings of Karl Marx* (New York: Collier Books, 1970) p. 183.

26. K. Marx and F. Engels, *The Communist Manifesto,* in D. Caute, p. 132.
27. K. Marx, *The German Ideology* in Feuer, p. 254.
28. K. Marx, *Capital: A Critique of Political Economy,* p. 638.
29. Ibid., pp. 692–693.
30. Ibid., p. 694.
31. Ibid., p. 693.
32. Ibid., p. 835.
33. Ibid., pp. 836–837.
34. Ibid., p. 837.
35. Ibid.
36. Ibid.
37. George Lichtheim, *Marxism: An Historical and Critical Study,* 2nd ed. (New York: Praeger, 1965) p. 239.
38. S. Avineri, p. 149.
39. Robert C. Tucker, *Philosophy and Myth in Karl Marx,* 2nd ed. (New York: Cambridge Univ. Press, 1972) p. 173.
40. Ibid.
41. Lichtheim, p. 235.
42. Ibid., p. 238.
43. Ibid., p. 241.
44. Ibid., p. 240.
45. Avineri, p. 144.
46. Karl Marx, *Economic and Philosophical Manuscripts,* in D. Caute, p. 54.

Part IV Conclusion

The settlement of the political conflicts between the traditional elites and the commercial forces in England during the seventeenth century created an environment that spurred industrialization in the 1780s. In response to the abhorrent conditions forced upon the workers, agitation for greater political equality grew and, after a period of repression, the working classes were gradually integrated into the system. All three of these major movements that initiated the modern world (the limitation of the power of traditional elites and institutions, the industrial revolution and the demand for greater equality) were compressed into the hundred year period from the 1780s to the 1880s in other European societies. As a result, the social tensions that emerged during the course of a 200 year period in England blossomed on the Continent in half the time. In France, the move to limit the Bourbon Monarchy and Church merged with the demands for social and political equality in 1789—setting in motion a cycle of revolution and reaction that lasted nearly 100 years. In Prussia (and, after 1871, in Germany) the traditional elite was able to maintain most of its power, enabling it to influence the course of industrial development and manipulate the forces of equality. The traditional elite in Russia maintained its power, relied on a mixture of private, foreign and state capital to initiate industrialization in the last decade of the nineteenth century, and attempted to suppress movements for greater equality.

Tension between the eighteenth-century optimism concerning the prospects for human fulfillment and the nineteenth-century realities in these societies was sufficiently pronounced to cause serious reevaluations of the ideas associated with efficient economic man. From Rousseau's romanticism through the French Positivists; from Kant's emphasis on the creative role of the human mind through Hegel's divine dialectic; from John Stuart Mill's pragmatic search for a better industrial society to the Russian Populists' focus on the peasant village and violent revolution, the reactions were all bound by a common theme that centered on the importance of community. Some looked back to the communal norms of medieval society for a model that existed prior to the development of the market economy. Kant turned human reason against self-centered materialism, challenging its subordination to the atomistic egotism that gave birth to economic man. Hegel's hope rested entirely on divine reason as the guiding force to overcome the inevitable conflicts among passion-driven humans. Mill expanded the definition of human beings to include the working classes as part of "the greatest number" that deserved to anticipate "greater happiness" in the future. Meanwhile, the Russian Populists concluded that violent revolution was necessary to move Russia toward its historical destiny and that the Russians might even be able to skip the stage of self-centered economic man by linking the communal past with a communal future.

Had Marx merely synthesized all of these competing approaches, his dialectical skills would have been impressive. Had he synthesized all of these critiques of efficient economic man with the original concept, his accomplishment would have been extremely important. The fact that he did all of this by linking the nineteenth century with its forgotten past—by reconciling the human essence of unlimited creativity with the exigencies of efficient economic man—makes his thought a staggering intellectual accomplishment.

With the "laws of capitalism" discovered by other economists (notably Ricardo and Malthus) presenting an extremely pessimistic view of the future, Marx's "laws" merely prefaced the opportunity for people to burst beyond economic necessity and establish a qualitatively different world. His optimism was based on the transcendence of efficient economic man into the realm of absolute human creativity, made possible precisely because economic man had become so efficient as to create fully-developed capitalism. With advanced machinery accounting for the bulk of productive capacity, all people (not just Plato's Philosopher-Kings and Aristotle's slave-owners) could become truly human by discovering and actualizing their unique potential. The tension between passion-driven economic animals and rational, creative, sociable human beings would be reconciled through a quantum leap into democratized classical leisure, where the pursuit of the human essence would no longer be confined to a tiny group.

Marx's attempt to transcend the conflict between speculative contemplation as essence-pursuit (associated with classical leisure) and the practical energy to alter the earth for a more comfortable existence (associated with economic man) can be traced to a critical assumption about people. Underlying his entire work we can identify an essentially classical perspective: if given the opportunity to choose between (a) continued enslavement to perceived needs of existence and (b) the opportunity to discover and pursue our unique potential to become more than history suggests humans are, we would opt for the latter. Obviously, this assumes that we have the ability to view ourselves as capable of becoming something more than efficient economic animals. Under conditions of economic scarcity, such a realization, if possible at all, was reserved for the few who owned enough land and slaves to provide them with the needs of existence. With material needs guaranteed, they were able to pursue their essence. Again, we are reminded of the Athenian philosophers, who stressed essence-pursuit as contemplative leisure, but reserved true humanity for the few—leaving the rest to labor for the good of the society.

Our experience with this material suggests that those who are attracted to the concept of classical leisure find the inherent acceptance of inequality associated with Athenian thought nearly as repugnant as the idea of passion-driven efficient economic animal. Marx attempted to overcome this tension by replacing slaves with advanced machinery. Part of the uniqueness of capitalism (for both Marx, who attacked it—and Smith, who defended it) can be traced to its constant push to find more efficient ways to produce things. With this tendency contributing to the satisfaction of the needs of existence, and a definition of ourselves as something more than economic animals, then a time would come when our society's ability to produce would match our wants—freeing us from the monotonous labor that, throughout history, has kept people from becoming truly human. For Marx, the technological imperative combined with human self-actualization would allow, for the first time in history, all people to actualize their potential and become true human beings, i.e., open the door for the democratization of classical leisure.

If we accept the logic of this suggestion—and, from our point of view, it makes Marx the pivotal thinker in this book—then we can easily identify obstacles to this goal. One obstacle to the democratization of classical leisure would be a halt in the increase of productive efficiency that would throw industrial (and post-industrial) society back to the struggle for existence. Another problem would be the strength and depth of the widespread perception of ourselves as economic animals. In short, to the degree that we define ourselves primarily as passion-driven egotistical accumulators of material goods, we can never say "I have enough" and begin to think about actualizing our potential to become something more. Again, we can identify the importance of Kant's "Copernican Revolution" to Marx's thought. Ultimately, it seems that Marx's entire synthesis is based on the expectation that, given the proper material conditions, all of us (like Kant) will refuse to allow ourselves to be defined by the seventeenth-century concept of economic animal. Instead, the full development of capitalism will allow us to view ourselves as active, creative participants in the historical process. If we accept the definition of humans as amoral, passion-driven animals that merely react to outside stimuli (as Kant refused to do), then the most we can ever hope for is to become efficient workers and efficient consumers. But if we insist that we are something more than this, an entirely new world is at our fingertips—and our decision not to accept Locke's and (especially) Hume's definition of us becomes a radical, liberating act. We may not receive many rewards and honors from a society that is geared toward the acceptance of humans as economic animals, but our horizons will be expanded beyond the unending search for material possessions. Like the goose in Kierkegaard's story, we may have to fly off alone.

For Marx and the ancient Greeks, flying alone was not sufficient. The pressures of a backward-looking society ruled by an economic elite that, in order to maintain its power, *must* convince us that we are merely economic animals (producers and consumers) is too great to allow for human fulfillment without a total restructuring. The political superstructure derived from the historical infrastructure based on economic scarcity will constantly impede the social forces growing from abundance. And, according to Marx, this tension will necessitate revolution because, just as the middle classes had to fight violent revolutions against the institutions and elite of feudal societies, the new social forces must struggle against their oppressors. Locke viewed the bourgeois revolution in seventeenth-century England as a necessary means to alter a political system that was interfering with human progress. Marx made the same point 200 years later.

For Marx, the development of capitalism (enhanced by the bourgeois revolution and justified by Locke) provided the material basis to transcend the historical conflict between essence and existence. A bright future awaited humanity once the tensions between the nation state (a creation of early capitalism) and new social forces (creations of advanced capitalism) were destroyed and transcended. This future offered the opportunity to democratize classical leisure—opening the door to the discovery and pursuit of a truly *human* future. The dialectical tension between ideals and reality would culminate in a heaven-on-earth environment that utopian philosophers had "merely" talked about. In short, the Enlightenment's promises could be fulfilled by linking its focus on rational active economic man with the Greeks' concern for rational contemplative man.

Marx began his intellectual odyssey by using Hegel's dialectical method to critique Hegel's conservative, metaphysical idealism. He concluded by using the techniques of British political economy to critique the British political economists. He attempted to reaffirm the Enlightenment's optimism within the generally pessimistic tone of nineteenth-century thought by relying on "scientific laws" of capitalist development that would lead to the transcendence of human alienation. Through this transcendence, the Athenian ideal of classical leisure would be realized for all people. In his dialectical method, the human mind provides the link between material conditions and the future actualization of the human potential. Eliminate the active mind that holds the ideal of unfettered essence up to the realities of the material world and the unity of his thought crumbles. Eliminate the human mind, and its capacity to contemplate, and you are left with a Darwinian-type view of humans as mere reactors to outside stimuli: passion-driven economic animals struggling to survive at the whim of material reality. In short, eliminate the creative role of the human mind in its quest for essence-fulfillment through contemplative leisure and you are left with economic man.

Marx died in 1883 and, by the beginning of the twentieth century, his attempted synthesis had crumbled. Focusing entirely on empirical reality, the British socialists stripped the synthesis of its utopian promise, opting for the gradual reform of capitalism. With the acceptance of efficient economic man, their tactics focused on getting a bigger piece of the monetary pie. In Russia, Lenin denied the empirical dimensions of the legacy (the link between capitalism's ability to guarantee the needs of existence and the fulfillment of the human potential) and adapted Marx to a backward agrarian society to enhance the appeal of his drive for revolution. In Germany, many socialists continued to pay lip-service to the unity of his thought while, in practice, they opted for gradual reform of the existing system.

In all three cases, passion-driven economic man emerged victorious. He thrived in the British welfare state, proud of the fact that the sun never set on his country's Empire. In Germany, he supported Hitler's state capitalism, quietly accepting any means necessary to pull his nation out of the depression and avenge the Treaty of Versailles. In Russia, he emerged as a Soviet commissar—utilizing state-terrorism to force the Russians to rapidly adopt the requirements of efficient industrial production. Hence, Marx's ideals lost in their struggle with twentieth-century realities and, with this defeat, the classical concept of leisure again faded into obscurity.

Part V
The Synthesis Crumbles:
The Twentieth Century

Although the past may not repeat itself, it does rhyme.

Mark Twain

Upon reaching the twentieth century, you might feel relieved because we are finally focusing on the contemporary world. But while the events of this century may be more familiar, most serious observers feel a deep anxiety rather than a sense of relief when surveying the contemporary world. Hence, what little comfort we can derive from familiarity tends to fade with any discussion of issues such as overpopulation, nuclear warfare, toxic waste, and the wholesale pollution of the natural environment.

While some of these problems are unique to the twentieth century, our ways of responding to them seem to mirror responses to earlier crises. One option, exercised by the romantics (and traceable to the Epicureans) is to deny the current problems by "going back" to an idealized, simplified, and less hectic life-style. Another option, which has its origins in the Enlightenment (and, in turn, reflects Aristotle's science), is to place all of our hope in the soundness of technological solutions to our current problems (ironically, many of these problems resulted from earlier technological solutions to earlier problems). Obvious examples of this popular approach include nuclear waste (by the time it becomes a "real" problem, we will have discovered a way to dispose of it safely) and thermonuclear weapons (if we can just perfect "star wars," they will no longer be a threat). A third option is to dull the senses and the mind with drugs, alcohol, or fantasy. And the obvious historical tendency to seek relief from a confusing and hostile reality by opting for utopian visions of the future (Marx, Christianity and Plato) presents still a fourth option. Nearly everyone we know, to some extent, has incorporated one of these options into his or her life.

Throughout this study we have tried to stress the apparent relationship between widespread social change and the significant contributions to western thought. For the most part, our consideration of the profound impact of such change on individual human beings has been implicit. Now that we are discussing issues that every reader can easily relate to, it seems appropriate to emphasize the unsettling (and often devastating) psychological effects of rapid change. Psychological tension—anxiety, or stress—is compounded when a person's values (developed during one period of time) are challenged by new values and practices associated with another period. A clear illustration can be drawn from the native American (hunter) response to demands that an agricultural life style be adopted, essentially, overnight:

You ask me to plow the ground! Shall I take a knife and tear my mother's bosom. Then when I die she will not take me to her bosom to rest. You ask me to dig for stone! Shall I dig under her skin for her bones? Then when I die, I cannot enter her body to be born again. You ask me to cut grass and make hay and sell it, and be rich like white man! But how dare I cut off my mother's hair?[1]

While such conflict can be seen as a major stimulant for the process of philosophy, its tendency to disrupt, if not destroy, individuals and societies should be clear. Unemployed industrial workers and independent farmers who are losing their land in the United States are being forced to recognize the impact of post-industrial realities on the value of their skills—and, in light of such reflection, the plight of former hunters should be more understandable.

The significance of this disruptive dimension of what we generally define as progress is particularly critical in the twentieth century, due to the unprecedented rapidity of change; reflect, for a moment, on human flight. Prior to this century, humans could only fantasize about flying, and evidence suggests that they have done so for thousands of years. But in less than 100 years (hardly a speck in the history of the species) we have developed the means to not only clear the ground, but to send humans on extended flights into space. Increasingly rapid advancements in science and technology are major characteristics of the twentieth century. Think about the increasing complexity of the following discoveries, then contemplate the significance of the decrease in lag time from discovery to application:

Photography	1727–1839	112 years
Telephone	1820–1876	56 years
Radio	1867–1902	35 years
Radar	1925–1940	15 years
Television	1922–1934	12 years
Atomic bomb	1939–1945	9 years
Transistor	1948–1953	5 years
Integrated Circuit	1958–1961	3 years[2]

This rapid march of technological change has contributed to expansion of communication, the eradication of numerous diseases, and a vastly more comfortable life-style. But numerous observers are asking if we can adapt our individual psyches and societies to the new conditions created by such rapid change. One obvious outcome of the rapidity of technological change is a chronic uncertainty concerning the goals of individuals and societies. George Orwell summarized the dilemma in *Coming Up For Air;* significantly, he is referring to life in England before World War I—when the pace of change had barely begun to accelerate:

It's quite true that if you look back on any special period of time you tend to remember the pleasant bits. That's true even of the war. But it's also true that people then had something that we haven't got now.

What? It was simply that they didn't think of the future as something to be terrified of. It isn't that life was softer then than now. Actually it was much harsher. People on the whole worked harder, lived less comfortably, and died more painfully. . . . And yet what was it that people had in those days? A feeling of security, even when they weren't secure. More exactly, it was a feeling of continuity. All of them knew they'd got to die, and I suppose a few of them knew they were going to go bankrupt, but what they didn't know was that the order of things could change. Whatever might happen to themselves, things would go on as they'd known them. . . . Individually they were finished, but their way of life would continue. Their good and evil would remain good and evil. They didn't feel the ground they stood on shifting under their feet.[3]

From all accounts, David Hume was able to function in a world without traditional morality and predictability—but what about the rest of us?

Standards of morality and degrees of predictability have changed in the past, but the rate of change has never been so fast. The transition from hunting and gathering societies to agrarian societies can be measured in thousands of years, following the domestication of animals and the use of planting seed. The transition from agrarian to industrial society was much faster, measured in hundreds of years, triggered by the development of the steam engine. The transition to post-industrial, or information-based, society has taken place in only decades, prompting Robert Heilbroner to note:

> There is a question in the air, more sensed than seen, like an invisible approach of a distant storm, a question that I would hesitate to ask aloud did I not believe it existed unvoiced in the minds of many: "Is there hope for man?"
> . . . the brooding doubts that it arouses have to do with life on earth, now, and in the relatively few generations that constitute the limit of our capacity to imagine the future. For the question asks whether we can imagine that future other than as a continuation of the darkness, cruelty, and disorder of the past; worse, whether we do not foresee in the human prospect a deterioration of things, even an impending catastrophe of fearful dimension.[4]

In Chapter 14, we discuss some of the significant historical factors that not only stimulated this headlong rush into uncertainty and anxiety, but also caused the Marxian synthesis of western thought to crumble. In Chapter 15, we discuss the existentialist response, focusing our attention on the ideas of Jean-Paul Sartre.

References

1. James Mooney, "The Ghost-Dance Religion and the Sioux Outbreak of 1890," *Annual Report of the Bureau of American Ethnology,* XIV, 2 (Washington, 1896), pp. 791, 724. Cited in Mircea Eliade, *Shamanism* (New York: Pantheon Books, 1964) and Robert S. Ellwood, Jr. *Many Peoples, Many Faiths* (Englewood Cliffs, N.J.: Prentice-Hall, 1976) p. 54.
2. Jean-Jacques Servan-Schreiber, *The American Challenge,* trans. Ronald Steel (New York: Avon, 1969) pp. 80–81.
3. George Orwell, *Coming up for Air* (New York: Harcourt, Brace and World, 1939) pp. 124–126.
4. Robert Heilbroner, *An Inquiry Into the Human Prospect* (New York: Norton, 1975) p. 13.

Chapter 14
The Triumph Of Economic Man

> Men make their own history, but they do not make it just as they please; they do not make it under circumstances chosen by themselves, but under circumstances directly encountered, given and transmitted from the past. The tradition of all the dead generations weighs like a nightmare on the brain of the living.
>
> Karl Marx

The variations in political practices, economic development and social norms in Britain, Germany and Russia created the circumstances that molded the first decades of the twentieth century. By the time Engels died (1895) the Marxian synthesis was crumbling, as competing interpretations emerged throughout Europe in response to widely varied contexts. While Marx's thought rested upon the legacy of centuries of social criticism, the "practical" socialists tended to focus on tactical considerations associated with acquiring political power. As a result Marx's link between speculative reason and practical action—embodied in the concept of revolutionary praxis—was weakened. Ultimately the system of thought crumbled when the bond connecting the empirical analysis of capitalism, proletarian class consciousness and revolutionary change into a future of non-alienation broke down into the component parts. In Britain the concern with empirical reality led most socialists to deny the need for revolution. In Russia the perceived need for revolution led Lenin away from the empirical focus, i.e., the necessity of the full development of capitalism as a precondition for revolution. In Germany the goal of revolution was maintained as a future ideal while the socialists quietly opted for reform. With the disintegration of the Marxian synthesis, passion-driven economic man emerged triumphant—equipped with a previously unimaginable capacity to destroy himself.

Britain: Working Class Reformism

Following the suppression of Chartism in 1848, the working-class movement splintered. Several disenchanted leaders abandoned political agitation and chose to concentrate on social issues, including educational reform. Those who remained politically active concluded that the working class was not sufficiently strong to transform society alone. The alliance between the middle-class radicals and the workers during the 1830s—an alliance that crumbled when the workers attempted to influence parliament by themselves—seemed to have provided what few gains were made. Hence, by 1852, Ernest Jones—who had been the staunchest advocate of working-class solidarity—had "accepted the necessity for a policy of class compromise, that endeavored to work for reform in association with the middle class and Radicals."[1] The alliance between the working class and the middle-class radicals had dissolved during the late 1830s when the middle class agitated for the repeal of the Corn Laws—a remnant of trade protectionism that maintained artificially high prices for food. While the Chartists were suppressed the Anti-Corn Law League succeeded in its demand for repeal in 1846. The success of the League, combined with the failure of Chartism, provided the impetus for the reestablishment of middle and working-class cooperation for political reform.

The lessons of the 1840s were not lost on those who sought to organize the working class. In 1860 the London Trades Council was formed to unite the trade union movement and promote political reform. Led by Robert Applegarth, a carpenter, the Council established a close working relationship with several radical members of parliament—including the Christian Socialists. The Council organized the Manhood Suffrage and Vote by Ballot Association, which appealed to the workers to organize for political activity:

> We do not wish you to relax one iota of your efforts in reference to the amelioration of our social condition.
> Nor do we wish to turn our trade societies into political organizations, to divert them from their social objects; but we must not forget that we are citizens, and as such should have citizens' rights . . . by obtaining these rights we shall be able more effectually to secure our legitimate demands as unionists.[2]

Applegarth also contributed to the establishment of the Reform League in 1865, which agitated for electoral reform and supported parliamentary candidates who promised to defend the interests of the working class. The group of middle-class radicals elected to the House of Commons in 1865 included John Stuart Mill.

By 1868 the Manchester and Salford Trades Council succeeded in organizing a national trade union that included the London unions by the following year. Much of the unionists' time was spent lobbying parliament for reform bills to improve the condition of the working class and, as the suffrage was expanded, the workers' support became more important to candidates seeking seats in the House of Commons. During the final decades of the century trade union membership expanded rapidly, rising from 118,000 in 1868 to nearly 2,000,000 in 1899.[3] These numbers, combined with the increasingly sophisticated organization of the unions and their willingness to work with the progressive middle class, resulted in impressive labor legislation:

Master and Servant Act: (1867)	Workers allowed to give evidence on their own behalf in disputes with employers.
Trade Union Act: (1871)	Trade unions acquired legal status.
Employers and Workmen Act: (1875)	Status of workers equal to employers under law in civil contracts.
Nine Hours Act: (1878)	Maximum 56 1/2 hour work week for women and children.
Factories Act: (1891)	Government regulation of safety and health conditions in factories.[4]

Britain's first avowedly Marxist organization was founded by Henry Hyndman in 1881. Originally named The Democratic Federation (the name was changed in 1883 to The Social Democratic Federation), the reformist thrust of the movement was undeniable. According to Hyndman, "The difference between us and the [middle-class] radicals is merely one of time and opportunity."[5] The primary concern of the Federation was agitation for the eight-hour day and unemployment relief. The S.D.F. maintained no official ties with the Trades Union Congress, yet managed to establish over 40 branches throughout Britain by 1888 with more than 1,000 members.[6] In 1885 the Socialist League was formed as an offshoot of the Federation. Influenced by the romanticism of William Morris, the League sought to educate the public on the virtues of socialism and uphold the future socialist utopia as an ideal. At its peak, the league counted 1,000 members.[7]

The Progressive Association was organized in 1882 by a group of well educated, influential citizens. Its goal, according to George Bernard Shaw, was to "bring about the moral awakening which is itself the occasion for all political and social improvement."[8] By 1883 the group split into a faction which viewed utopian thought as a means of personal growth and another which advocated social reform. The group devoted to metaphysical awareness and personal development called themselves The Fellowship of the New Life; the social reformers called themselves The Fabian Society.

Under the auspices of the Labor Representation Committee of the Trade Unions Council, representatives from all of these organizations came together in 1899 to form a political party to represent the interests of the working class. The Social Democrats' resolution to "recognize the class war" was soundly defeated, and the conference resolved to establish:

> a distinct labour group in Parliament . . . which must embrace the readiness to co-operate with any party which for the time being may be engaged in promoting legislation in the direct interests of labour.[9]

Along with representatives from the Independent Labor Party (which we will discuss below), these groups formed the first broad-based political organization of the working class, officially adopting the name British Labor Party in 1906. The goals of the Party were based on the reformist ideas generated by the Fabian Society.

Fabian Socialism

The Fabians' position on social issues evolved from John Stuart Mill's gradual acceptance of democratic socialism. And while several Fabians began their quest for social justice from a Marxian perspective, they gravitated toward the empirical dimensions of the theory (which Marx derived from British thought) and concluded that the dialectic between empirical reality, proletarian class consciousness and revolutionary change was nonsense. George Bernard Shaw's attitudes illustrate the Fabian position—an orientation that stressed reform, not revolution; linear progress, as opposed to dilectical tension; and the denial of class conflict. While denying virtually all of Marx's important concepts, Shaw concluded that Marx's work was admirable because "It knocked the moral stuffing out of the bourgeoisie, and made an end forever of middle-class self complacency and optimism."[10]

Hence, in Britain, the Marxian synthesis was reduced to a mechanism that was useful to the reformers because it attacked industrial capitalism, but Marx's projected solution was denied. The Fabians eliminated the concept of surplus value, the class struggle, the dialectical interaction of material conditions and revolutionary consciousness and, finally, the need for revolution. Like Mill, the Fabians' evolutionary perspective denied the need to alter the productive infrastructure of society and concluded that piecemeal reform of the existing system promised greater benefits for the working class. As a result, Marx's objective of transcending human alienation by democratizing classical leisure was rejected. The Fabian leaders:

> viewed socialism as the enlightened consciousness of society as a whole. It found expression not through the material strivings of the working classes but through the rational capacity of political and administrative leaders.[11]

This approach should sound familiar: it represents the final step in the British transition from utilitarianism to socialism. The Fabians concluded that socialism is "merely individualism rationalised, organised, clothed, and in its right mind."[12]

Eduard Bernstein

The Fabian denial of German dialectics and the concommitant need for revolution was a consequence of the British intellectual tradition and the immediate political environment. The House of Commons was extending its influence during the latter part of the nineteenth century and the working class had gained the right to participate in elections, raising the hope for legal reform. The power of the House of Commons to create the executive (through action of the party holding a majority of the seats) provided the possibility of the working class eventually gaining control of the government and pursuing its program through legal means. This situation, combined with the unquestionable intellectual power of the Fabians, had a significant impact on the ideas of the German Marxist Eduard Bernstein when, after being exiled from Germany under Bismarck's Anti-Socialist Laws, he went to London and mingled with the Fabians. The British socialists were never really considered Marxists by their counterparts on the Continent. But Bernstein was a major figure in "orthodox" social democracy, and his Fabian-inspired revisions of the Marxian synthesis sent shock waves throughout the socialist movement.

While there are indications that Bernstein was moving toward an essentially reformist position prior to his exile in 1878, his years in London (1888 to 1901) are recognized by numerous scholars as a major juncture in "Marxist" thinking:

> his denial that he learned a great deal from the Fabians, and from the English in general, will not stand up. When, during the 1898 controversy, Bebel accused him of applying English conditions to Germany, Bernstein disagreed: "I haven't become THAT English. . . ." But surely Bernstein underestimated the impact of his dozen years of residence in Britain . . . the Fabian philosophy, a typical example of the reformist spirit, was a major influence that acted on him during his English years.[13]

Like the Fabians, Bernstein approached the Marxian synthesis from a rigidly empirical perspective and focused his attack on the elements of Hegelian influence in Marx's thought. Although the position adopted throughout *Evolutionary Socialism* is an obvious assault, Bernstein presented it as an attempt to save Marxism from its detractors by adjusting the concepts to fit "reality." The way to accomplish this, and the stated goal of the work, was to:

> reject certain remains of Utopianism which adhere to Marxism, which are the cause of the contradictions in theory and practice which have been pointed out in Marxism by its critics.[14]

Thus, by 1899 "scientific socialism" had fallen under attack for its utopian aspects, and Bernstein's work was an attempt to re-evaluate and purge them. The way to do so, he argued, was to determine "whether it rightly represents the real facts of the case today, or whether the picture has not another side"; this, to Bernstein, was the "only question."[15]

Using the empirical thrust of Marx's work to attack its conclusions, Bernstein construed the economic "laws" as testable propositions, which produced a devastating critique of the purportedly scientific nature of Marxism. Just as Marx had criticized Hegel's abstract, non-empirical system of thought, Bernstein attacked the credibility of the Labor Theory of Value. He then went on to test the "scientific laws of capitalism," focusing primarily on conditions in England.

Continually emphasizing the need to study empirical reality—"A scientific basis for socialism or communism cannot be supported on the fact only that the wage worker does not receive the full value of the product of his work"[16]—Bernstein tested, and found wanting, all three of the "laws." Far from the conditions of the average man worsening as capitalism developed, he argued that they were actually improving. That economic crises are an inevitable part of capitalist development was not denied by Bernstein; that they are cyclical and of increasing intensity, however, was. The key to his argument is that while overproduction is unavoidable, there is no reason to suppose that it will occur in anything more than a few industries at any one time, and "overproduction in single industries does not mean general crisis."[17] Thus, Marx's last law was questioned and Bernstein's conclusion is clear:

> If the universal crisis is the inherent law of capitalist production, it must prove its reality now or in the near future. Otherwise the proof of its inevitableness hovers in the air of abstract speculation.[18]

The result of this exclusive focus on the empirical aspect of the legacy was the denial of any need for the revolutionary destruction of capitalism. Like the Fabians, Bernstein concluded that the good society was one of "organized liberalism," that is, "a social condition where political privilege belongs to no one class as opposed to the whole community,"[19] with the suppression of government controlled by any one class, though not the suppression of classes.[20]

Instead of a great social upheaval brought about through the contradictions within the system and a corresponding growth of the workers' conception of their historical role, socialism could come about through gradual reforms, i.e., through the evolution of the political system toward greater participation and freedom. With this point added to the general line of reasoning, it is obvious that Bernstein denied the clash of opposing forces inherent in the dialectic. His view of history, as a linear development, is reminiscent of the "ever onward and upward" orientation of the Enlightenment, as opposed to the struggle necessitated by the dialectical conflict of opposites. Following this line of thought, Bernstein noted that cooperative societies (his word for socialism) are most likely to arise in areas "where the soil is prepared for them."[21] And finally, he argued that it would be "utopian to imagine that the community could jump into an organization and manner of living diametrically opposed to those of the present day."[22] The "jumps" resulting from the dynamic movement of the dialectic, were consequently viewed as utopian holdovers in Marx's thought.

Having thus denied the need for revolutionary change, Bernstein's strategy shifted to the reform of existing social, economic and political systems for the benefit of the working class. Socialist tactics, then, concentrated on the reform of existing institutions through parliamentary and trade union activity. Marx's stress on heightened proletarian class consciousness precipitating revolution and bringing the transcendence of human alienation through the democratization of classical leisure was supplanted by an evolutionary view of capitalism's capacity to satisfy the working class materially, while slowly integrating its members into the existing system. Economic man became democratized while the classical ideal of leisure was forgotten, and the reform-oriented British Labor Party had an evolutionary system of thought to justify its policies.

The Labor Party's "readiness to co-operate" stripped it of any radical (let alone Marxian) identity. It became part of the existing system—chipping away for gradual reform and the welfare state—while accepting the foundations of the economic, class, ideological and political relationships in Britain. With the outbreak of World War I, many pacifist Laborites protested against the War—including the Party's leader, J. Ramsey MacDonald. MacDonald resigned from parliament in protest, but such a diverse organization had no trouble replacing him with someone willing to support the War. In 1924 the Labor Party, with support from the Liberals, formed its first government. But Liberal backing was withdrawn when MacDonald (who had returned to lead the party) introduced a treaty with the Soviet Union and he was forced to resign within the year. The 1929 election brought Labor back to power but, as the international depression consumed Britain, even the pursuit of social welfare was subordinated to the need to maintain a semblance of order. By 1931, as the economic crisis deepened, MacDonald again resigned from the party. But instead of returning to pacifism, he defected to the Conservatives and formed a new government with their support. In the end, "readiness to co-operate" with pro-labor officials meant "readiness to co-operate" with anyone—including the aristocratic Conservative Party.

The Elite's Reaction

While the middle-class radicals had been soliciting working-class support throughout the century, the two dominant political parties began to follow suit with the extensions of the franchise in 1867 and 1884. The Liberal Party sponsored three working-class candidates in 1865. By 1885, "no fewer than eleven 'Lib-Lab' candidates—six of them miners—were elected, and after the general election of 1886 there were still nine."[23] In 1893, James Keir Hardie, one of the workers elected with Liberal support in the previous year, bolted from the Liberals and created the Independent Labor Party. The avowedly socialist position of Hardie and the ILP ran counter to the reformist approach of the trade unions and, by the time the Labor Party was organized, the moderate influence of the Fabians and trade unionists had eliminated the revolutionary fire from the ILP's original platform.

On the domestic scene, the elite's willingness to respond to working-class activism illustrates the uniqueness of the British experience in contrast to Germany and Russia. But the response entailed much more than merely sharing influence in domestic politics. The growth of organized working-class activism correlated with the massive expansion of European imperialism from the 1870s through 1914.

Virtually all accounts of European imperialism stress the links between expansion of economic activity and the heightened sense of national purpose which served to unite societies that appeared to be splintering from class tensions. Hannah Arendt's analysis takes this logic a step further by noting that while imperialism was considered to be an economic necessity, it actually diminished the viability of the nation state. She argues that the nation state, which was originally built on the alliance of capital and state, was undermined when capitalist-based imperialism was extended throughout the world. The demand for a limited state was replaced by the insistence on a strong, active, militarized state capable of protecting foreign investment. Expediency, which had always governed economic activity, was extended into politics—crippling the notion of the rule of law. The diverse domestic social and economic interests, which had provoked conflicts between the middle and working classes, were reconciled through an aggressive nationalistic claim to racial and cultural superiority. In short, twentieth-century totalitarianism had its roots in nineteenth-century imperialism, as the elite's reaction to economic cycles and class tension pushed Europe toward expansion:

> Half consciously and hardly articulately, these men shared with the people the conviction that the national body itself was too deeply split into classes, that . . . the very cohesion of the nation was jeopardized.[24]

Arendt traces modern imperialism to two factors. First, economic expansion had reached its domestic limits by the last decades of the nineteenth century, leaving the commercial interests with two options: either accept national limitations on growth, or find new markets, sources of inexpensive labor and natural resources in other areas throughout the world. Given that the bourgeoisie was driven by the imperative of constant growth, international expansion was the favored option. In addition to providing capitalism with a temporary economic solution to incessant crises and imminent stagnation, imperialism became a mechanism capable of uniting the society. National unity, as opposed to class identity, was strengthened within European societies by fostering an adversarial attitude in relation to the rest of the world. Cecil Rhodes, the exemplary imperialist (he lamented that he could not colonize the planets), summarized this view most succinctly:

> Yesterday I attended a meeting of the unemployed in London and having listened to the wild speeches which were nothing more or less than a scream for bread I returned home convinced more than ever of the importance of imperialism . . . the great idea in my mind is the solution of the social problem. By this I mean that in order to save the forty million inhabitants of the United Kingdom from a murderous civil war the colonial politicians must open up new areas to absorb excess population and create new markets for the products of the mines and factories. I have always maintained that the British Empire is a matter of bread and butter. If you wish to avoid civil war then you must become an imperialist.[25]

Hence, imperialism was perceived as an answer to the problems that Marx had predicted would plague capitalism. But this solution created new problems—problems that eventually precipitated a wholesale attack on the limited nation state. In its quest to alleviate domestic economic and social tensions the bourgeoisie began to support principles and actions that were directly opposed to everything that its limited nation state had represented:

> Imperialism was born when the ruling class in capitalist production came up against national limitations to its economic expansion. The bourgeoisie turned to politics out of economic necessity; for if it did not want to give up the capitalist system whose inherent law is constant economic growth, it had to impose this law upon its home governments and to proclaim expansion to be an ultimate political goal of foreign policy.[26]

Once again, desire and passion outstripped reason's capacity to control them. The denial of Aristotle's insistence on a self-sufficient society—and even Smith's stress on a limited state—led Europe into a race to control the world, setting the stage for World War I.

The shift from a national to an international economic system destroyed the concept of the limited state and introduced attitudes and practices that laid the groundwork for twentieth-century totalitarianism. The rule of law gave way to expediency, whereby all principles were subordinated to the acquisition of unlimited power for the sake of economic growth. Class conflicts were minimized by promoting racism to unite domestic classes against Asians, Africans, et cetera. Excess wealth was pumped into overseas investments, while the casualties of capitalism (the unemployed, downwardly-mobile masses) could vent their aggressive hostility against colonized peoples through state service, rather than attacking the elite in their own societies.

This alliance between the "mob and capital" circumvented the class war that Marx predicted and, instead, extended the tensions of capitalism outward, curbing domestic revolution while inciting international conflict.[27]

From Arendt's perspective, the uniqueness of Britain's case lies in the fact that this gutting of the principles and practices of the limited nation state was confined to the colonies, and did not seep back into the domestic political arena:

> The so-called hypocrisy of British policies was the result of the good sense of English statesmen who drew a sharp line between colonial methods and normal domestic policies, thereby avoiding with considerable success the feared boomerang effect of imperialism upon the homeland.[28]

In Germany and Russia, Hitler and Stalin built upon the practices that had originated with European imperialism in its colonial affairs—but they applied them to their relations with other Europeans and their own societies. Economic and political expediency, racism, the alliance of the mob and capital, and the increase in the arbitrary power of the state reached a peak in the 1930s in Nazi Germany and Stalinist Russia—as the boomerang came back to batter Europe and the world.

Germany: Reform or Revolution?

Whereas in Britain the working class was able to forge alliances with the middle-class radicals, the failure of the German middle classes to wrest power away from the Prussian nobility produced an extremely complicated context for the development of working-class organizations. The middle classes were deeply fragmented—torn between the drive to limit the Prussian-dominated state and the desire to enjoy the economic opportunities that Bismarck's unification of Germany had created.

The environment that had successfully divided the German middle classes contributed to the same results among the working classes during the latter part of the nineteenth century. After two years of cooperating with the middle classes to forge an alliance against the Prussian state, Ferdinand Lassalle concluded that middle-class support was meaningless, and he organized the General German Workingmen's Association in 1863. Viewing increased economic independence as the goal of the working class, Lassalle promoted universal suffrage as the socialists' primary political strategy. In addition, Lassalle accepted Ricardo's conclusion that no amount of trade union activity would help the working class rise above its degradation. Hence, in addition to the drive for political equality, Lassalle advocated the creation of workers' cooperatives to be established and supported by the Prussian-dominated state. Disgusted with the politically-impotent middle classes, Lassalle propounded an essentially Hegelian brand of German socialism in which the workers would ally themselves with the state against the interests of the bourgeoisie.

William Liebknecht and August Bebel, the future leaders of the "Marxist" wing of German social democracy, also began their political activity in alliance with the middle classes. Unlike Lassalle, however, they did not sever their alliance with the South German liberals until the 1890s. As late as 1868, Marx and Engels were "exasperated" with their socialist position, the latter suggesting that there was "Nothing but hidden South German federalism" in Liebknecht's views.[29] Liebknecht had been active in the revolution of 1848 and after the Prussian defeat of Austria and Saxony in 1866, he was instrumental in founding the Saxonian People's Party—an organization that preserved the 1848 demands while rallying South Germans around an anti-Prussian banner. In 1866, Liebknecht stated that "Democratic and socialist are for me identical terms"—implying that his primary concern was still the issues of 1848. Thus while the Social Democratic Worker's Party, led by Liebknecht and Bebel and established in 1869, supported the principles of the First

International, it was strongly influenced by the reformist goals of the staunchly anti-Prussian South Germans. In addition, nearly one-third of the delegates to the first meeting (held in Eisenach, hence the label "Eisenachers" was applied to the organization) had defected from Lassalle's organization, and come over to the South Germans because they disliked the authoritarian structure of Lassalle's group. But dislike of the organization's authoritarianism did not sway the defectors commitment to its goals, and the Eisenacher program included several Lassallean concerns.[30]

The merger of the Eisenachers and the Lassallean organization at Gotha in 1875 that created the Socialist Labor Party of Germany (SPD) was a compromise between the two groups. Marx was furious that the program preserved Lassallean and South German reformist perspectives, and his *Critique of the Gotha Program* is a virulent attack on the remnants of German bourgeois attitudes masquerading as socialism.

By 1878 Bismarck's Anti-Socialist Laws succeeded in further splintering the SPD, that originated as a tenuous coalition of diverse organizations. The exile of the leadership left the rank and file members to chart their own course. Some opted for reform and participation in the Reichstag. A few became radicalized. The majority settled back into a life made more comfortable by Bismarck's social welfare programs, pursued trade union activity (that was severed from party guidance by the Anti-Socialist Laws) and cast their votes for SPD candidates for Reichstag seats. During the Outlaw Period, electoral support grew dramatically. But the large membership and electoral successes masked the underlying reality of a socialist party that was hopelessly at odds with itself over the tactics and goals it should pursue.

One wing began to advocate immediate violent revolution as a reaction to the Anti-Socialist Laws. Significantly, their primary support came from Berlin—where the repression against the SPD was by far the most severe.[31] By the mid-1880s, these ultra-radicals were purged, but the Copenhagen Congress of 1883 resulted in the declaration that the SPD was now a "revolutionary party."[32] Hence, while Bernstein was formulating his purely reformist program in England, activists who were exposed to Prussian repression became increasingly radicalized. Again, the majority of the workers were enjoying their social welfare programs while supporting the party at election time.

The conflict between the fading ideal of revolution and the reality of reform was exacerbated by the growing tendency of the activists to lean toward the former while the working-class electorate tended to opt for the latter. A classic illustration of this tension can be seen in the party's position on Bismarck's plan to provide government subsidies for steamship production in 1884. The "radicals," led by Bebel, argued that the subsidy was tantamount to supporting imperialism because the ships would be used to expand overseas trade and power: the party's deputies in the Reichstag, then, could not possibly vote for it. The moderates, led by Ignaz Auer, contended that the subsidy would provide jobs for unemployed workers, many of whom had voted for the party with the expectation that it would support their interests. The radicals attacked the moderates' willingness to accept Bismarck's state capitalism, while the moderates criticized the radicals' insistence on a unified stand:

> The Socialist Workers' Party is not a sect in which the members are sworn to the letter, but a political party in which there is room, as there must be, for different opinions on subordinate points.[33]

In the end, the SPD deputies did not vote for the plan, but the debate clearly shows the split between the "theoreticians" and the "practical politicians." This split provided the context for the first congress held after the Anti-Socialist Laws lapsed in 1890. The Erfurt Congress of 1891 attempted to integrate the increasingly radical position of much of the exiled leadership and the "practical" concerns of the reformists.

Karl Kautsky: The Class Struggle

The most important theoretician to emerge during the Outlaw Period was Karl Kautsky. His primary work, *The Class Struggle* (1895), was an elaboration of the SPD's Erfurt Program— which attempted to reconcile the radical and reformist wings of the party while responding to Marx's *Critique of the Gotha Program*. The fact that Kautsky had not been involved in the Eisenacher-Lassallean conflicts made him the logical choice to forge a degree of unity. But the fact that his views were heavily influenced by John Stuart Mill and Darwinian evolution and "He rejected the Hegelian dialectic with its teleological overtones" should alert the reader to the nondialectical basis of his thought.[34] With the recognition that the primary spokesman for "orthodox" German social democracy could be consciously anti-dialectical, we can appreciate the overwhelming importance of Engels' mechanistic (and evolutionary) interpretation of the Marxian synthesis. Recall Engels' critique of the Hegelian influences on Marx's thought, as well as his argument that "neither Kautsky nor Bernstein" were interested in the Hegelian dialectic. We have noted that Bernstein's rejection of the dialectical interaction between material conditions and revolutionary class consciousness led him to completely deny the proletarian revolution. Kautsky attempted to maintain the broad historical goal but, by disregarding the dialectic, he was left with the argument that the revolution would inevitably happen, even if the workers did not become aware of themselves as a revolutionary class and commit themselves to the transcendence of human alienation. Hence, the German workers could relax and enjoy whatever economic and social benefits they were provided by the German state, while waiting for capitalism to inevitably disintegrate—at which time they could assume their historical role and dominate society. And if capitalism and the bourgeois state were destined to fall apart, why take any risks to hasten the events?

The Class Struggle is divided into two parts; one treats broad theoretical issues, while the other focuses on day-to-day tactics. The early chapters leave no doubt that Marx's "laws" of capitalist development were officially retained. Increased concentration of economic power was taking place, as "the industrial development . . . steadily decreases the number of enterprises."[35] In addition, Kautsky argued that the size of the proletariat is "steadily on the increase."[36] Surplus value was recognized as the basis of the capitalist system of profit, though Kautsky's discussion of this point is matter-of-fact—completely lacking in the moral outrage that comes through Marx's writings on the subject. The "law" of crises was also defended, and referred to in terms of "the certainty of natural law."[37]

With the final "law" (that the collapse of capitalism is imminent, based upon its contradictions) Kautsky's "orthodoxy" is established:

> The capitalist system has run its course; its dissolution is now only a question of time. Irresistible economic forces lead with the certainty of doom to the shipwreck of capitalist production. The substitution of a new social order for the existing one is no longer simply desirable, it has become inevitable.[38]

Given the contradictions of capitalist production, its destruction and replacement are inevitable and the goal of the Social Democratic Party should be "the conquest of the government in the interest of the class which it represents."[39] The tactics to be used, however, need not involve bloodshed and violent revolution; instead, the social transformation can be brought about through the use of reformist means to achieve revolutionary ends. This position is clearly at odds with Bernstein, who argued that the existing system should be maintained as the basis for improvement.

While others tended to emphasize either reform (Bernstein) or revolution (Lenin), Kautsky attempted to maintain their unity. He argued that not only is it mistaken to dismiss the revolutionary goal and focus entirely on reforms, but it is also wrong to reject the revolutionary validity of reforms:

> reforms may be supported from the revolutionary standpoint because . . . they hasten the course of events and because, so far from doing away with the suicidal tendencies of the capitalist system, they rather strengthen them.[40]

The key phrase is "hasten the course of events," which suggests that Kautsky, unlike Bernstein, assumed that the radical transformation of capitalist society would take place, based on the natural course of its development.

With the inevitability of the self-destruction of capitalism accepted as a given of history, Kautsky argued that the parliamentary struggle for universal suffrage, freedom of speech, assembly and union activity was a revolutionary act. Notice that several of the goals of both the Lassalleans and the middle-class revolutionaries of 1848 were incorporated into "Orthodox Marxism." The idea that the working class should immediately rise up and overthrow the system was discounted as a "children's disease which threatens every young socialist movement."[41] Instead of pursuing such a childish goal, the socialist movement should attempt to expand its influence within the existing system, striving to increase its representation in the parliamentary bodies, and strengthen the position of these bodies in relation to the other branches of government. Kautsky, then, viewed participation in parliamentary activity as the primary tactic to be used in the proletariat's struggle, concluding that it was "the most powerful lever that can be utilized" to pursue working-class interests.[42]

While Kautsky attempted to maintain the connection between capitalist development and the proletarian revolution, his rejection of the Hegelian mind-matter unity as the foundation of Marx's thought led to major problems. The Hegelian and subsequent Marxian unity of mind and matter (revolutionary class consciousness and material conditions under capitalism) is precisely what made the revolution inevitable for Marx. If this critical bond is denied, then a gap is created between reality and ideas that is easily extended into distinctions between the reformist tactics and the revolutionary goal. Again, Engels' and Kautsky's disavowal of the importance of the Hegelian link emerges as a critical factor leading to the fragmentation of "orthodox" Marxism. Without this unity, Marx's mixture of tactics (reform) and strategy (revolution) crumbles.

This tendency to drift from Marxian precepts was exacerbated by the introduction of Bernstein's reformist arguments. Although Bernstein was influenced by the Fabians he was primarily a leader of the German SPD. He returned to Germany in 1901 and was elected to the Reichstag in 1902, 1912 and 1920. His views were particularly appealing to the rank and file members, as well as to the moderate socialists in the Reichstag. The clearest summary of his impact on German social democracy can be found in a letter he received from Ignaz Auer, longtime party secretary and influential moderate, in 1889:

> My dear Ede, one does not formally make a decision to do the things you suggest, one doesn't say such things, one simply does them.[43]

With Kautsky's theory combined with Bernstein's practice, the German SPD grew to be an influential force in the Reichstag. But the tension between the party's ideals and its daily reality left it poorly prepared when the opportunity to alter the course of German history presented itself during the period between the two World Wars.

The Elite's Reaction

When combined with the state-sponsored social welfare programs, the Anti-Socialist Laws accomplished Bismarck's goal of fragmenting the party without pushing the rank and file membership toward violent revolution. Compared to the British Socialists, the Germans were repressed; compared to the Russians, they were merely harrassed from 1878 through 1890. With the death of William I in 1888, the personal relationship between the Emperor and Bismarck—which had created and reinforced the constitutional structure of the Empire—dissolved. William II and Bismarck disagreed on numerous issues, including the Chancellor's plans to intensify the pressure on social democrats by outlawing socialist representation in the Reichstag and disenfranchising socialist voters. The personal conflicts between the new Emperor and the old Chancellor, combined with the anti-Prussian electoral results of 1890, led to Bismarck's dismissal. Guenther Roth summarizes the environment:

> There were, logically, three alternatives for the government in the 1890s: (1) The complete repression of the Social Democrats. . . . (2) Democratization. . . . (3) Continued isolation of the Social Democrats. Bismarck failed in his attempt at the first alternative before and after his dismissal. The second alternative was beyond the vision of William II and his officials. The Emperor and the government elected the easiest course; they continued to isolate the labor movement while not blocking its expansion among the working class.[44]

There is little doubt that increased represson would have strengthened the hand of the SPD radicals, while true reform would have elevated the status of the moderates. Option 3 perpetuated the status quo. The party continued to post electoral gains under William II but, given the constitutional structure of the Empire, these advances were not directly transferred into influence over public policy.

Bismarck and the new Emperor also clashed over the issue of imperialism. Bismarck's Prussian nationalism made him suspicious of imperialist expansion, while William II insisted on propelling Germany into the European race for colonies. As Arendt notes, pursuing this course served to further undermine forces seeking to limit the power of the strong central government. The thrust of highly militarized nationalistic expansion opened the door for World War I. The vote for war credits in the Reichstag on August 4, 1914 provided the SPD with the opportunity to make a stand against the existing power structure. Socialists and pacifists throughout the world denounced the War but, in Germany:

> The Social Democrats, in truth, had long been waiting to enter into alliance with the authoritarian Reich . . . and in August 1914 they returned eagerly to Lassalle's programme of alliance with Prussian militarism against capitalist liberalism, this time on an international stage.[45]

With the moderate socialists defending the interests of the Empire, the elite no longer had to guard itself from "revolutionary" social democracy. Disgusted with their moderate comrades' acquiescence, several radical socialists bolted from the party; most of them agreed to organize an Independent Socialist Party, while others prepared for violent revolution.

The Social Democrats were given an opportunity to assert their power during the winter of 1918–19. Anti-war sentiment had spread throughout Germany during the previous year, provoking mutinies, desertions and strikes. In August of 1918 the generals reported that the war was lost, due to the crumbling of the southeastern flank and the arrival of U.S. troops in the west. In September Prince Max was appointed Chancellor and two months later William II abdicated. Without a monarch, and with a non-Prussian Chancellor, the constitution of 1871 became meaningless. With Prussian power fragmented and the moderate socialists in control of the Reichstag, Germany might have been on the verge of fundamental change. But the radical socialists decided that the time was right for violent revolution and a series of revolts erupted from November to January throughout Germany. The dilemma of the moderate socialists was clear: support their former comrades or defend the state—they opted for the latter. The Prussian military brutally repressed the revolt and murdered its leaders.

Russia: The Radical Intelligentsia

The isolation and frustration of the Russian intelligentsia grew throughout the nineteenth century. With Herzen's views providing the foundation, revolutionary Populism became increasingly committed to the total destruction of the Czarist system. Prior to his exposure to Marx's writings, Lenin was involved in the Populist movement. His political activity began in 1887 in response to the execution of his older brother—a devoted Populist who led an attempt to assassinate Alexander III. Prior to the execution, Lenin scoffed at revolutionary activity and devoted his energy to achieving the highest honors in his graduating class. Virtually all scholars stress the impact of his brother's execution on the 17-year-old honors student. In addition, most emphasize the influence of Populist ideas—especially the revolutionary singlemindedness of Chernyshevsky, Nechaev and Tkachev.

The impact of Chernyshevsky's ideas on Lenin seems undeniable, if for no other reason than the fact that the title of Lenin's first major work, *What is to be Done?*, was adopted verbatim from Chernyshevsky's novel. The first *What is to be Done?* was written during Chernyshevsky's imprisonment for political agitation from 1862 to 1864. Hans Kohn refers to the novel as "the bible of the young generation."[46] And Theen draws the parallels with Lenin's thought:

> Like scores of other Russian revolutionaries in the second half of the nineteenth century, Lenin was inspired by Chernyshevsky's hero Rakhmetov, the revolutionary who denies himself the pleasures of life, sleeps on a bed of nails, and leads the ascetic existence, pursuing with singular determination and fanatic dedication his sole purpose in life: to prepare and steel himself for the coming revolution.[47]

Lenin had read the novel at the age of fourteen, but it took on new meaning following his brother's execution. He re-read the novel during the winter of 1887–1888, more than a year before his exposure to Marx.[48] And, in his own words:

> Chernyshevsky's novel, for example, fascinated and captivated my older brother. It also captivated me. It ploughed me over again completely. . . . It is a work which gives one a charge for a whole life.[49]

The acceptance of the necessity of violent revolution was further reinforced by Sergei Nechaev in 1868. Like Lenin, he was familiar with Marx as well as Populism, and Lenin was impressed with his writings.[50] In their "Catechism of the Revolutionary," Nechaev and Mikhail Bakunin propounded the need for totally-committed revolutionaries to destroy the Czarist system:

The revolutionary is a doomed man. He has no interests, no affairs, no feelings, no habits, no property, not even a name. Everything in him is wholly absorbed by a single, exclusive interest, a single thought, a single passion—the revolution.

The only revolution that can save the people is that revolution which will destroy totally the entire state apparatus and will eliminate all state traditions, orders, and social classes in Russia.[51]

Peter Tkachev's life seems to have been modeled on Chernyshevsky's "new man" and Nechaev's "revolutionary." First arrested for revolutionary activity at the age of 17, he was exiled to Siberia in 1868. He escaped, went to Geneva, and began publishing *Nabat,* a revolutionary journal that was smuggled into Russia. Theen notes that "Lenin was . . . interested in Tkachev and highly recommended the 'rich literature of this original writer' to his followers."[52] In the pages of *Nabat,* Lenin found guidelines which influenced his thought:

It was Tkachev, finally, who in the 1870s developed views on revolutionary organization, the nature of the forthcoming revolution in Russia, and, most important, a concept of the revolutionary state, which in a striking fashion anticipated Lenin's political program.[53]

Prior to his exposure to Marx's thought, Lenin was well-versed in the Russian revolutionary tradition.

By the 1860s the secret societies had grown and become increasingly politicized, including the constitutionalist group Great Russia (1861) and the first Land and Freedom Society (1862). By the 1870s numerous "cultural societies" had been formed to organize and agitate for political revolution. Scholars are in agreement concerning the diversity of these populist groups, with Masaryk concluding that:

It can by no means be said that these efforts were guided by a uniform spirit. Individual groups (Societies for Self-Culture and Practical Activity) consisted of adherents of Bakunin, Herzen, Lavrov, and Tkachev. The teachings of the narodniki, socialism and communism, liberalism and anarchism, were frequently disseminated by members of one and the same circle.[54]

The one thing they did have in common was their illegality:

From 1874 the government openly attempted to suppress the entire movement. Hundreds of young men and women were imprisoned. After a lengthy term of preliminary arrest, which would sometimes last for years, the accused were tried in batches ("the trial of the fifty," "the trial of the hundred and ninety-three," etc.).[55]

The second Land and Freedom organization was created in 1876. By 1879 it had split into the avowedly terrorist People's Will and the anti-terrorist group devoted to "Total Land Reapportionment." Initially, both groups maintained the goal of awakening the peasant's revolutionary potential through mass agitation. The People's Will, however, introduced the argument that terrorism should be added in order "to intimidate the tsarist government into granting constitutional rights without which no serious mass agitation could be conducted."[56] By the late summer of 1879 terrorism was the focal point of the entire organization, having become:

the very symbol of the individual combat between revolutionaries and authorities in a social and political situation where no room for further manoeuvre was left.[57]

The People's Will was involved in at least seven attempts on the Czar's life from October 1879 until the final successful one on March 1, 1881.

Plekhanov and Russian Marxism

Georgi Plekhanov was one of the leaders of Land and Freedom to speak out against terrorism, and he led the anti-terrorist faction until he was forced to flee from Russia in 1879. By 1883 he had adopted Marx's ideas and formed the group Emancipation of Labor, in the attempt to unite all of the Russian Marxists; but the entire leadership, including Lenin, was arrested in December 1895. Lenin spent fourteen months in prison and three years exiled in Siberia.

The First Congress of the Russian Social Democratic Labor Party met in Minsk on March 1, 1898, with the radical political leadership out of the country, in jail or exiled in Siberia. The police had been particularly effective in emasculating the Petersburg group:

> By the time the "First Congress" was finally held, in March 1898, there were only four members left in Saint Petersburg to elect a delegate.[58]

In addition, the vigilance of the police extended to Minsk:

> Eight of the nine delegates, and two of the three central committee members chosen by the congress, were picked up within a few days of its adjournment. The victory of the police and the rout of the new party seemed complete.[59]

An organizational committee was established to plan for a second congress in November 1902; its members were arrested shortly after they met.[60] The congress was convened on July 30, 1903 in Brussels, with the Czar's agents and the Belgian political police in attendance. Numerous delegates were arrested and, by August 5, the congress was moved to London.[61] It was in London that Lenin argued that, given the power of the Russian autocracy, it was necessary to create a conspiratorial group of professional revolutionaries, as delineated in his answer to the question *What is to be Done?*

The Russian Social Democrats were torn between the desire to follow Marx's view of history and his prescriptions for violent revolution. The "orthodox" faction argued that Russian conditions necessitated an alliance with the middle class to overthrow Czarist autocracy and stimulate the development of capitalism, and thus create the political and material conditions necessary for the growth of a strong socialist movement. In addition to this political compromise, they supported trade union activity as a tool for organizing the working class. Lenin argued for immediate violent revolution without any bourgeois allies. He succeeded in splitting the party into two separate groups, the Bolsheviks (who supported Lenin) and the Mensheviks (the more "orthodox" Marxists).

Lenin and the Bolsheviks

To appreciate Lenin's position, a discussion of the all-important concept of the "dictatorship of the proletariat" is necessary. Recall that Marx defined all political power as dictatorial. As noted in his *Critique of the Gotha Program,* the proletariat's dictatorship would be a transition period between the fall of capitalism and the establishment of socialism. From Marx's perspective, it would be a relatively brief and uneventful period concluding the historical scenario of the bourgeoisie destroying all pre-industrial classes, creating the proletariat and then being destroyed itself. At least the majority of society would already have been thrown down into the ranks of the dehumanized proletariat. Hence, for the first time in history, the dictatorship would be in the interests of the majority of society. But capitalism had barely begun to develop in Russia, which meant that only a very small segment of the population could be classified as industrial workers.

With this critical difference in mind, it should be obvious that Lenin's dictatorship of the proletariat would bear little resemblance to the concept envisioned by Marx.

Both Bernstein and Kautsky exerted a great deal of effort to reconcile their views with Marx's theoretical arguments. In Russia, however, Marx's thought tended to be viewed as a rallying cry for an already-radicalized segment of the population. In describing a "typical [Russian] Social-Democratic study circle of the period 1894–1901," Lenin summarizes the attraction to Marx's thought:

> We have noted that the entire student youth of the period was absorbed in Marxism. Of course, these students were not only, or even so much, interested in Marxism as a theory; they were interested in it as an answer to the question, "What is to be Done?," as a call to take the field against the enemy.[62]

Empirical laws concerning the decline of capitalism, then, were not of major concern to the young intellectuals who focused their attention on violent revolution. The aims of the socialists stood above question to Lenin, and the goal was the total destruction of the czarist system through violent revolution and the dictatorship of the proletariat.

The key to Lenin's goal of revolutionary change seems to lie in his recognition that socialism would not be the inevitable result of class struggle, especially in Russia with its low level of industrialization. In order to achieve the already-accepted end, a professional organization would be necessary to define the workers' goals and lead them in the proper direction. Amateurs could not be expected to bring about the revolution because the Czar's secret police was too sophisticated in its ability to thwart revolution.

Given these conditions a vanguard of professionals was necessary to lead the movement. Spontaneous action, while not necessarily bad, could be turned into effective revolutionary activity only through the party:

> The fact that the masses are spontaneously being drawn into the movement does not make the organization of this struggle less necessary. On the contrary, it makes it more necessary; for we socialists would be failing in our direct duty to the masses if we did not prevent the police from making a secret of every strike and every demonstration (and if we did not ourselves from time to time secretly prepare strikes and demonstrations).[63]

Lenin was quick to stress that the rationale for the conspiratorial party was the result of Russia's particular historical circumstances. The key to his position lies in the relative lack of economic development in Russia and the adaptation of Marxism to conditions far different from those originally pictured. Again, he repeatedly emphasized that his thoughts were meant to apply only to Russia, a far cry from the later Soviet attempts to generalize the validity of the Russian party:

> Everyone will probably agree that "the broad democratic principle" presupposes the two following conditions: First, full publicity, and secondly, election to all offices. . . . Try to fit this picture into the frame of our autocracy![64]

And:

> Only an incorrigible utopian would have a broad organization of workers, with elections, reports, universal suffrage, etc., under the autocracy.[65]

Broad organizations, elections and universal suffrage, of course, had been the outcome of the development of capitalism and bourgeois society in the west—and were viewed by Marx as necessary stepping stones toward the revolution. But for Lenin, the goal of political revolution was too urgent to wait for similar conditions to evolve in Russia; and besides, the party could lead the proletariat without them.

Lenin's position is the classic illustration of the alteration of Marx's thought to fit a context in which the development of capitalism, and its corresponding political institutions, had not even destroyed the traditional power structure—let alone created the material basis for the growth of proletarian class consciousness and the transcendence of human alienation:

> The national tasks of Russian Social-Democracy are such as have never confronted any other socialist party in the world . . . emancipating the whole people from the yoke of autocracy.[66]

It stands to reason that if the Bolsheviks were successful in this goal, equally monumental tasks would await them. They would have to destroy the traditional powers and initiate the process of economic development if scarcity were to be transcended. They would have to forcefully transform the peasantry into efficient industrial workers and resort to the dehumanization of the assembly line. In short, the revolutionary party was likely to become the Russian counterpart to the bourgeoisie in the west.

The Elite's Reaction

In 1894 Nicholas II, the last Czar of Russia, ascended to the throne. With total disregard for the growing discontent around him, he attempted to maintain the traditional Russian power structure:

> It is known to Me that recently in zemstvo assemblies have been heard, voices of people carried away by senseless dreams of participation by zemstvo representatives in the affairs of internal administration. Let everyone know that I, who am dedicating all My strength to the welfare of the people, will preserve the foundation of Absolutism as strongly and as undeviatingly as did My lamented late father.[67]

But growing segments of the population were organizing to bring about change in Russia, and they were not interested in the Czar's attempt to calm them by stressing his continuity with the past.

The political atmosphere in Russia grew increasingly tense in the first years of the twentieth century, while the Czar became consumed with imperialistic dreams of controlling northeast Asia. Japanese interests in Manchuria presented the major obstacle to such expansion so, in February of 1904, Russia and Japan went to war. The war proved to be disastrous. Battle after battle was lost and, in January of 1905, Russian society erupted in revolution. By October the workers in Petrograd had organized a general strike that spread throughout the urban areas. In December they made their move to overthrow the Czar but the army remained loyal and suppressed the insurrection. Nicholas II then offered to introduce major reforms, including a representative assembly (the Duma), thereby undermining the diverse coalition of revolutionaries that had nearly deposed him. The First Duma immediately challenged the Czar and was dismissed. The Second Duma followed suit and was also dismissed. The Third and Fourth Dumas were more accommodating but, by 1916, the obvious incompetency of the Czarist system during World War I created widespread opposition within the elected body.

Russia's defeats at the hands of the Japanese paled in comparison to its experience in World War I. By 1917 the military was near collapse, hunger was rampant throughout the country, and riots and mutinies were increasing. By March the cities were in chaos and the army refused to restore order. In Petrograd the workers council (the soviet) assumed control, while the Duma established a Provisional Government that was dominated by liberal, middle-class politicians. On March 15, Nicholas II abdicated in favor of his brother, Grand Duke Michael—but Michael refused and the czarist system dissolved.

Facing threats from the radical Petrograd workers on one side and conservative military officers on the other, the Provisional Government continued to pursue the war—suffering even more defeats. Deserting soldiers aligned themselves with the workers, while the peasants began organizing for meaningful land reform. Lenin returned from exile in April with a pragmatic appeal to the most disgruntled groups in Russia: peace, land, bread and all power to the soviets. While the Bolshevik organization had little to do with inciting the February revolution, the small group of revolutionaries effectively built support among the soldiers, peasants and industrial workers during the summer of 1917. Refusing to surrender or institute land reform, the Provisional Government became increasingly estranged from the people.

The Bolshevik coup in November spread rapidly from Petrograd to Moscow and throughout the urban areas, as local soviets seized power. The leaders of the Provisional Government were arrested or fled the country and, by December, the Church's land was confiscated for distribution to the peasants and private property was officially abolished. In March of 1918, Russia surrendered to Germany.

The dreams of generations of Russian revolutionaries seemed to have been fulfilled. The autocracy had crumbled, the Russian Orthodox Church was dismantled and the nobility was emasculated. But new challenges soon confronted the revolutionaries. Conservative generals were organizing a counterrevolution that, with the aid of Poland, Japan, Britain, France and the United States, escalated into a devastating civil war that lasted until 1920. On top of centuries of oppression, two destructive wars in ten years and two years of murderous civil war, the western powers imposed trade embargoes on the new regime. It is difficult to imagine an environment further removed from Marx's requisite of "abundance" as the material foundation for communism.

The 1920s: Preface to Madness

Weimar Germany

The Weimar Republic was created out of the ashes of World War I and became the kindling for World War II. While the circumstances associated with its creation did not guarantee its demise, they did not contribute anything to its longevity. This first real experiment with representative government in Germany coincided with severe punishments under the Treaty of Versailles. Under the Treaty, Germany was forced to accept full responsibility for the War. Backbreaking reparations payments were imposed by the victors while, at the same time, Germany's capacity to make them was impaired:

> Germany had to hand over to the allies most of its merchant marine, a quarter of its fishing fleet, and a good part of its railroad stock. For five years Germany had to build annually 200,000 tons of shipping for the victors. It had to make yearly deliveries of coal to France, Italy, and Belgium, and to pay the costs of the occupation of the Rhineland by the allied armies.[68]

In addition, it was stripped of its colonies and its future military capacity. While any society would resent such punitive action, the highly nationalistic Germans considered it to be intolerable.

Domestically, the progressive elements in German society suffered from the stigma of Versailles, a stigma that was encouraged by the conservative's argument that the moderate socialists and democrats had "stabbed Germany in the back." While the Weimar Constitution established a remarkably advanced system of representative government, the judiciary, military, presidency and educational system remained under the firm control of conservative nationalists. The spiraling inflation of the mid-1920s destroyed the hopes of the middle classes, while the depression crippled the working class. Under these circumstances, extreme solutions from the left and right flourished.

The Soviet Union

Joseph Stalin escaped from the confines of his rigid education in the Russian Orthodox Church to become a revolutionary activist at the age of 20. Like virtually all of the Bolshevik leaders, much of his life from 1903 to 1917 was spent in prison or Siberian exile. He was a trusted aide to Lenin, and was promoted to the position of General Secretary of the Communist Party in 1922. In short, he was Lenin's chief of staff. But Lenin began to doubt the wisdom of this promotion shortly after it was made and he started to make preparations to remove Stalin from this potentially powerful position in December of 1922. But in the same month the founder and leader of the Bolsheviks was partially paralyzed by a stroke. Another stroke severely disabled him three months later and in January of 1924 the pivotal figure of Bolshevism died.

The party leadership had already begun to factionalize over issues of tactics and strategies for the future. Trotsky and the radicals argued for the extension of the revolution into Europe in order to take advantage of the advanced levels of industrialization in the west. Bukharin and the conservatives stressed the need for the Soviet Union to turn inward and concentrate all of its resources on modernizing Russia. Stalin used his control over the bureaucracy to lend support to the conservative position and by 1928 Trotsky was exiled and his supporters were purged. By the early 1930s Stalin began to move against Bukharin and the remaining leaders of the Bolshevik revolution and, within a few years, he emerged as the dictator of the Communist Party of the Soviet Union—a party that exercised total control over the Russian people. Lenin was right—Stalin was dangerous, and Soviet "communism" diverged as far from the Marxian synthesis as any system possibly could.

1930–1945: The Vengeance of Economic Man

In 1929 international capitalism collapsed. The impact of the Great Depression on Germany was sufficiently pronounced to elevate the Nazi Party—viewed by many Germans as a lunatic fringe group in the 1920s—to power in 1933. The traditional conservatives viewed Hitler as a puppet who could be controlled and manipulated to support their opposition to the growing communist movement. The industrialists saw him as a means to enhance production. The middle classes saw a common man who could understand their problems. The workers saw him as a saviour who would guarantee them employment. And most Germans saw him as a twentieth-century Bismarck who would unite them in mass vengeance against those who had challenged their national pride. Desire and passion swept Germany into the arms of aggressive nationalism to restore economic productivity and control the world. Unlimited economic expansion, racism, the alliance of capital and the mob, political expediency and the unlimited power of the state were unleashed on the people of Europe, just as their governments had unleashed them on their colonized subjects.

The Third Reich moved with unprecedented rapidity. While eliminating its domestic critics, it tested the water in Spain during its Civil War. With pilots experienced in bombing civilian targets, the Luftwaffe was prepared to lead the attack on Poland; then into Czechoslovakia and back to France, where Nazi sympathizers accommodated fascism, terrorizing their own people through the Vichy regime; then back to Russia, while attempting to burn London to the ground. Japan joined in and conquered most of Asia.

By 1945 approximately 60 million people were dead—the vast majority civilians. The nature of warfare had been altered forever, as total war between societies, not just armies, reigned supreme. Millions were maimed. Many Europeans were homeless and thousands were scattered throughout the continent, attempting to make their way back to what had been home from Nazi concentration camps. Central Europe had been bombed into rubble and Allied troops were dividing Berlin—the bastion of Prussian militarism. People throughout the world had grown accustomed to subordinating their individual interests to the needs of their state, as the war effort took precedence over every aspect of life. Anti-colonial nationalism flourished throughout Asia. In short, a process that can be traced to the desire to expand the world economy through European imperialism in the nineteenth century—that contributed to World War I—which contributed to World War II—resulted in the bankruptcy and destruction of the empires themselves, along with most of the principles that European civilization purported to defend. In August of 1945 nuclear warfare, bringing with it the capacity to incinerate the planet, was accepted as an expedient way to defeat Japan and, according to United States Secretary of State Byrnes, "make Russia more manageable in Europe."[69] Nuclear warfare, with its threat of total annihilation, provided the link between World War II and the Cold War.

While Hitler was rallying Germany to economic recovery and aggressive nationalism, Stalin was using his dictatorial control of the party to force the Russian people into adopting the values of efficient economic man. Having purged the internationalists as well as the conservative leaders, Stalin promulgated the doctrine of "Socialism in One Country" and unleashed state terror against those Russians who did not subordinate their lives to the imperative of rapid economic modernization. The collectivization of agriculture was justified as an economic requisite for boosting agricultural efficiency; many small farmers opposed it and many were killed. Rapid industrialization necessitated the destruction of individuality and the regimentation of the entire industrial sector for the sake of productive efficiency. One generation of Russian people was coerced into adopting the values of economic man that several generations of western Europeans had gradually opted for or were forced to adopt. Many workers opposed this regimentation and many were killed.

Without the benefit of the protestant work ethic that grew out of the insecurity inherent in the doctrine of predestination, the Russian worker had to be convinced that he was insecure by the Soviet Commissar. The total subordination of one's life to his calling became total subordination to the state-owned factory, where social status and security could be acquired through productive labor. In the words of a veteran of Stalinist industrialization:

> Now let's assume that your personal records aren't so good. You have a pretty good idea it's so because you more or less know that your social origin and past work wouldn't be eyed favorably by the personnel authorities of the factory. You are perfectly aware of the fact that at any moment the management or the factory council may decide to add you to a list of workers assigned to some newly built factory.
> Thus you are facing the end of the world.
> So you take a 'production pledge'. . . . Suddenly you're a personality.

You work like a dog and you succeed in delivering the 40 percent over your norm. . . . And into your personal file goes the note 'shock worker in socialist work.' So they undertake an effort too big for their strength in the hope that this will permit them to get rid of the sense of guilt and sin which is always and everywhere with them. Even the medieval Orthodox Church didn't go so far in creating this guilt complex in the faithful.[70]

The shock of a world turned upside down—where human fulfillment is defined in Hegelian-Hitlerian terms as subordination to the state, and Marx's tirade against alienated labor is distorted to justify Stalinist repression—sets the stage for the emergence of existential man.

References

1. G. D.H. Cole and A. W. Filson, p. 373.
2. Henry Pelling, *A History of British Trade Unionism,* (New York: St. Martin's Press, 1963) p. 55.
3. Michael Mulhall, *The Dictionary of Statistics,* 4th ed., (Detroit: Gale Research, 1969) p. 813.
4. G. D. H. Cole and A. W. Filson, pp. 552–600. D. Douglas, vol. XII, part 2, pp. 632–633.
5. S. Pierson, p. 65.
6. Ibid., p. 69.
7. Ibid., p. 82.
8. Ibid., p. 107.
9. Henry Pelling, *The Origins of the Labor Party,* 2nd ed., (New York: Macmillan, 1965) p. 209.
10. Peter Clark, *Liberals and Social Democrats,* (New York: Cambridge Univ. Press, 1978) p. 32.
11. S. Pierson, p. 123.
12. George Bernard Shaw, ed., *The Fabian Essays in Socialism,* (London: Allen and Unwin, Ltd., 1948) p. 99. Originally published in 1889.
13. Peter Gay, *The Dilemma of Democratic Socialism,* (New York: Collier-Macmillan, 1962) p. 109. Also see G. Lichtheim, pp. 274–280. And H. Stuart Hughes, p. 71.
14. Eduard Bernstein, *Evolutionary Socialism,* trans. Edith C. Harvey (New York: Schocken Books, 1961) pp. 213–214.
15. Ibid., p. 81.
16. Ibid., p. 39.
17. Ibid., p. 83.
18. Ibid., p. 87.
19. Ibid., p. 142.
20. Ibid., pp. 143–144.
21. Ibid., p. 121.
22. Ibid., p. 125.
23. Ivor Bulmer-Thomas, *The Growth of the British Party System,* 2 vols., (London: John Baker Publishers, 1965) vol. I, p. 171.
24. Hannah Arendt, *The Origins of Totalitarianism,* (San Diego: Harcourt Brace Jovanovich, 1973) p. 152.
25. Cecil Rhodes quoted in Heinz Gollwitzer, *Europe in the Age of Imperialism,* (London: Thames and Hudson, Ltd., 1969) p. 136.
26. H. Arendt, p. 126.
27. Ibid., pp. 147–157.
28. Ibid., p. 155.
29. Guenther Roth, *The Social Democrats in Imperial Germany,* (Tatowa, N.J.: Bedminster Press, 1963) p. 47.
30. See Theodore Hamerow, *The Social Foundations of German Unification,* (Princeton, N.J.: Princeton Univ. Press, 1972) p. 359 and "The Eisenach Program," reprinted in Gary Steenson, *Not One Man! Not One Penny!,* (Pittsburgh, Penn: Univ. of Pittsburgh Press, 1981) p. 244.
31. Vernon Litdke, *The Outlawed Party,* (Princeton, N.J.: Princeton Univ. Press, 1966) pp. 117–118.
32. Carl E. Schorske, *German Social Democracy,* (Cambridge: Harvard Univ. Press, 1955) p. 3.
33. Ignaz Auer quoted in Litdke, p. 198.

34. John Kautsky, "Karl Kautsky," in David Stills, ed., *The International Encyclopedia of the Social Sciences,* 17 vols., (New York: Crowell Collier and Macmillan, 1968) vol. 8, p. 357.
35. Karl Kautsky, *The Class Struggle,* Trans. William E. Bohn, (New York: Norton, 1971) p. 63.
36. Ibid., p. 18.
37. Ibid., p. 71.
38. Ibid., p. 117.
39. Ibid., p. 189.
40. Ibid., p. 93.
41. Ibid., p. 198.
42. Ibid., p. 188.
43. Ignaz Auer quoted by Mary-Alice Waters, Introduction to Rosa Luxemburg, *Reform or Revolution,* (New York: Pathfinder Press, 1973) p. 7.
44. G. Roth, pp. 83–84.
45. A. J. P. Taylor, *The Course of German History,* (New York: Capricorn Books, 1962) p. 166.
46. Hans Kohn, ed., *The Mind of Modern Russia,* p. 139.
47. Rolf H. W. Theen, *Lenin,* (New York: Lippincott, 1973) p. 75.
48. Ibid., pp. 58–61.
49. Ibid., p. 60.
50. Ibid., p. 76.
51. Basil Dmytryshyn, ed., *Imperial Russia, A Source Book,* (New York: Holt, Rinehart and Winston, 1967) pp. 241–247.
52. R. Theen, p. 76.
53. Ibid.
54. Thomas G. Masaryk, *The Spirit of Russia,* 2nd ed. trans. Eden and Cedar Paul, 3 vols., (New York: Macmillan, 1955) vol. 1, p. 154.
55. Ibid.
56. Leopold Haimson, *The Russiann Marxists and the Origins of Bolshevism,* (Boston: Beacon Press, 1966) p. 37.
57. F. Venturi, p. 639.
58. Bertram D. Wolfe, *Three Who Made a Revolution,* (New York: Dial Press, 1964) p. 138.
59. Ibid., p. 139.
60. L. Haimson, p. 167.
61. Ibid., pp. 173–174.
62. V. I. Lenin, *What is to be Done?,* trans. Joe Fineberg and Victor Jerome, (New York: International Publishers, 1969) p. 180.
63. Ibid., p. 108.
64. Ibid., pp. 134–136.
65. Ibid., pp. 116–117.
66. Ibid., p. 26.
67. Nicholas II quoted in L. Haimson, pp. 50–51.
68. Felix Gilbert, *The End of the European Era,* (New York: W. W. Norton and Company, 1970) p. 170.
69. Gar Alperovitz, *Atomic Diplomacy: Hiroshima and Potsdam,* (New York: Vintage Books, 1967) p. 242.
70. Joseph Novak, *The Future is Ours, Comrade,* (New York: E. P. Dutton and Co., Inc., 1964) pp. 91–95.

Chapter 15
Existential Man

Philosophers have traditionally thought that meaning depends on essences and that questions about the meaning of life and the difference between good and evil could therefore be answered only in the context of a clear understanding of the essence of man. In the twentieth century a point of view called existentialism has challenged this traditional wisdom with insightful and provocative analyses of human existence, meaning, and value. Existentialism is best represented in the work of Martin Heidegger and Jean-Paul Sartre. It can be understood to culminate in a way of seeing beyond the fragmentation of Marx's vision to an understanding of human beings, society, and history which is true to Marx while it speaks directly to those who have lived through the absurdities and cruelties, the materialism and self-centeredness of our century. Although it is a twentieth-century position which has developed and become influential partly in response to the chaos and inhumanities of the two World Wars, the Holocaust, and ideologies such as Stalinism, existentialism has roots in the nineteenth century thinkers like Kierkegaard, Nietzsche, and Brentano, and it is with these that we begin our account.

Søren Kierkegaard

Søren Kierkegaard was born in Denmark in 1813. As a boy he was strongly affected by his father's stern and somber protestantism, which left Søren with a profound sense of guilt and sin. As a young man he managed for a time to throw off this influence, at least on the surface. He entered what he was later to call the "aesthetic stage" of his life—a stage in which he dedicated himself to the pursuit of pleasure, in which he flitted from the pleasures of society to those of art, music, and the theatre, and back again. Kierkegaard eventually came to see this and later periods in his own life as stages typical of all human beings, although not all people would move through all three stages. The lowest stage, the aesthetic, is one in which values and choices are not taken seriously, a period in which one takes the view that it doesn't really matter which choices one makes. Though it may be expressed as happy-go-lucky spontaneity, any sense of freedom it provides is illusory, and it is likely to lead to either cynicism or indifference.

While in the aesthetic stage the young Kierkegaard lived a frivolous social life, impressing acquaintances with his wit, but his happiness was only a mask. Living for the moment precluded any serious commitment or continuity. Life was directed neither by moral principle nor by logical consistency, but solely by social pressure and personal whim. The aesthetic stage may be either hedonistic or intellectual. The hedonist lives to be the "life of the party," and while this pursuit can be either amusing or tedious, it can never be serious. The intellectual finds excitement in hypothesizing and theorizing, but commits to nothing. Underneath Kierkegaard's aesthetic surface was a deep melancholy and despair:

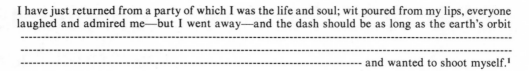

> I have just returned from a party of which I was the life and soul; wit poured from my lips, everyone laughed and admired me—but I went away—and the dash should be as long as the earth's orbit
> --
> --
> --- and wanted to shoot myself.[1]

Kierkegaard concluded that the aesthetic stage was a lie—an attempt to hide from himself and from the need to make serious choices:

> From childhood I was under the sway of a prodigious melancholy, the depth of which finds its only adequate measure in the equally prodigious dexterity I possessed of hiding it under an apparent gaity and *joie de vivre*.[2]

The second and higher stage Kierkegaard calls the "ethical stage." It is very different from the aesthetic. The ethical person is responsible, reliable, impartial, and impersonal. His life is guided by logic and moral principles. Promises are kept and lies avoided not for the love of any individual, but for the sake of duty. To live the ethical life is to believe in objective ethical principles which determine the purpose of life as well as the right and wrong in all specific situations. It is to believe that some philosophy or religion has the truth, and that reason or revelation will give us access to the universal principles we should all follow. The ethical life is therefore serious. Choices are dictated by an objective and universal code rather than by whim or social pressure.

Philosophers, theologians, and intellectuals of all kinds have traditionally extolled the ethical life as a way of getting in harmony with the essence of man and living the only truly good life. Immanuel Kant provides perhaps the best example of the thoroughly ethical life. Kierkegaard saw such a life as an advance over the aesthetic stage, but he also saw it as infected with the illusion that there are objective standards by which we can make and judge our choices. If there are such standards, then it is always possible that any choice one makes is in error. We are limited and fallible beings and can never be absolutely sure that we have correctly understood the standards or accurately assessed the circumstances in which we are applying them. By its own standards, then, the ethical stage is subject to uncertainty and despair. To accept its conviction that there are absolute truths which one must try to discover is to recognize that there is a possibility that one has not attained the truth, but is deceived. This is the point Jean-Paul Sartre was to make much later when he suggested that to know that one knows is always not quite to know, for it is to be aware that one might be mistaken. The only way to overcome this despair, Kierkegaard held, is to advance to the highest, or religious, stage.

The religious stage is one of passionate commitment to a belief for which there is no possible objective justification. This commitment Kierkegaard calls a "leap of faith." The religious stage is not to be confused with the so-called religions of the established churches. Kierkegaard insisted that those who do not live their faith with "passionate inwardness" and those who sleep contentedly because they have convinced themselves that their religious beliefs are objectively justifiable do not have true faith and are not truly religious. Accepting the claim that religion has objective sanctions makes calling oneself a Christian, for example, easy. It puts it on a par with other decisions one can make from a universal and detached point of view—such as that 25 is the square root of 625. But it does not change one's life, and it does not make one a true Christian. True Christianity is not easy, nor should it be. The leap of faith is difficult, but it is the only way to overcome despair and replace it with genuine meaningfulness.

Kierkegaard was fascinated by the story of Abraham, who one day was commanded by God to sacrifice his only son Isaac.[3] Imagine Abraham's despair. How could God ask this of him? Is it really God who is asking this? Surely it isn't God, but Satan instead? But if it is God, Abraham must obey; if Satan, he must not. And there is no proof either way. Abraham must decide, and there is no objective guide. His decision will be made in agony and despair. His suffering is a sign that although he is in touch with the uncertainty intrinsic to belief in objective truth, he has not yet made the leap of faith which will rescue him. Abraham's situation is, of course, a paradigm for the human condition that we all share. The important decisions, those that affect our existence, are those for which there are no universal and objective guides.

If there are no such guides, reason is, of course, powerless to discover them. Kierkegaard writes that "it is impossible to exist without passion."[4] Philosophers had often advocated a life in which reason completely conquers the passions as if it would be possible and desirable to make all of one's thinking logical thinking. But such an existence would not only be, as Aristotle had said, "too high for man," but it would not be a fully human existence at all:

> All logical thinking employs the language of abstraction, and is *sub specie aeterni*. To think existence logically is thus to ignore the difficulty, the difficulty, that is, of thinking the eternal as in process of becoming. But this difficulty is unavoidable, since the thinker himself is in the process of becoming. It is easier to indulge in abstract thought than it is to exist, unless we understand by this latter term what is loosely called existing. . . . But really to exist, so as to interpenetrate one's existence with consciousness, at one and the same time eternal and as if far removed from existence, and yet also present in existence and in the process of becoming: that is truly difficult . . .[5]

Not only is it difficult, but real existence—that is fully human existence—is anxious and despairing. Will, not reason, the faculty of choosing rather than the ability to recognize rational relations, is at the core of one's being. The Enlightenment's optimism and faith in reason are nowhere to be found in Kierkegaard's writings. Since truth is not accessible to reason, our only access to it is through will, through *choosing* to accept it. Revelation, not rational thought, is the way to salvation. Our freedom is revealed to us through the anxiety we experience whenever we have to make significant choices without any objective justification. The titles of many of his books—*Fear and Trembling, The Sickness unto Death, Either/Or, The Concept of Dread,* and *The Gospel of Suffering,* for example—testify to his sense of melancholy, anxiety, and dread.

If there is no objective justification for any choice—for any leap of faith—then how can Kierkegaard justify his Christianity? His answer seems to be that one's choice is justified subjectively by the passionate intensity with which it is made. But might opposing choices not be just as "true" because they are just as passionately intense? Aren't the Jew, the Hindu, the Muslim, and even the atheist just as likely to be "right" as is the Christian? It would seem so. But then what has happened to the meanings of "true" and "right?" They now refer, of course, to subjective criteria rather than to anything objective. Yet Kierkegaard is a Christian who holds that the Christian choice is the only adequate or satisfactory one. There is certainly an unresolved tension in Kierkegaard's thought between his insistence that only Christianity provides an adequate route to salvation and his recognition that the ultimate test of a choice is personal and subjective. What is most important to us is that part of Kierkegaard's message which has had the greatest impact, i.e., that man is not essentially rational, that those truths which are most significant in our lives are grounded subjectively, and that we, not any objective truth, are responsible for what we believe and do.

Friedrich Neitzsche

Friedrich Nietzsche was only fifteen when Charles Darwin's *Origin of Species* presented the theory of the evolution of living organisms, and Darwin's work strongly influenced Nietzsche, whose analysis of truth was to lead him to conclusions about religion and the nature of salvation drastically different from Kierkegaard's, although he would agree with Kierkegaard that we are not essentially rational and that truth is subjectively grounded. As a leading contemporary authority has pointed out, Nietzsche:

> was not a Darwinist, but only aroused from his dogmatic slumber by Darwin, much as Kant was a century earlier by Hume; and Nietzsche, too, sought to counter the positivistic challenge from across the channel (which seemed nihilistic to him) by developing a new picture of human dignity.[6]

Although he declared himself a Lamarckian because he believed in the inheritance of acquired characteristics rather than in Darwin's mechanistic theory of natural selection, Nietzsche nevertheless applied Darwin's idea of the struggle for survival to values, to knowledge itself, and to the human spirit, as well as to human biology. If life is a struggle for survival, what implications does this have for our understanding of ourselves as knowing and valuing beings? It means, Nietzsche concluded, that values, beliefs, and, indeed, knowledge itself are what they are because they fulfill needs—because they serve a fundamental motive to survive and prosper. Nietzsche called this fundamental motive the "Will to Power."

But, of course, there are many beliefs, many values, and many moralities. How do we choose between them? How do we know which are true and which false? Nietzsche would reject this last question, for it supposes that there is an objective truth which is independent of the particular choices and decision we believers, we valuers, make. Nietzsche's position is much more radical. For him there is no truth prior to a human choice to believe in a particular way—to interpret evidence this way rather than that, or even to select the evidence that will be considered. Indeed, the very idea of truth exists because it serves certain of our needs rather than because it names some objective reality:

> The intellect, as a means for the preservation of the individual, unfolds its chief powers in simulation; for this is the means by which the weaker, less robust individuals preserve themselves, since they are denied the chance of waging the struggle for existence with horns or the fangs of birds of prey.[7]

So it is our needs, which are manifestations of the will to power, that determine how we understand the world and what we consider to be valuable or true.

Needs—and therefore values—are often individual and subjective. They are certainly relative to, or dependent on, our characteristics as human organisms as well as on those factors which distinguish us from one another. The conclusion seems inevitable: there is no objective truth. The classical ideal, all subsequent theories of human nature, all religions, ideologies, and moralities, are true to the extent that they satisfy the will to power as it expresses itself in those who formulated them. And they are false in the sense that there is no objective truth that could validate them. What we call "truth" is a reflection of our needs and not of the nature of reality.

The notion that one's religion, one's values, or even one's science are objectively true is an illusion which prevents us from understanding ourselves. Nietzsche considers objective truth a kind of error. "Truths are illusions about which one has forgotten that this is what they are."[8]

"Physics, too, is only an interpretation and arrangement of the world (to suit ourselves, if I may say so!)—and *not* an explanation of it."[9]

So truth in any traditional sense is impossible. But truth is indispensible. Unless we have values, beliefs, and truths, life is meaningless and without purpose. Yet there are no objective truths. There are no revelations for which there are no counter-revelations, no theories without counter-theories, no uncontested interpretations. What is the solution? What should we believe? How can those of us who recognize this dilemma live? Nietzsche's answer is that we must recognize the subjectivity of all truth and value, and its dependence on our own creative powers. We must embrace and identify with those powers, and with the will to power. We must rejoice in our freedom. We all create truth; those who understand this most profound truth (for Nietzsche is, fundamentally, a defender of truth against positivism, skepticism, and nihilism) and accept their creativity without the crutch or excuse of an illusory "objective" truth are the most likely to dare to accomplish great things and to be what Nietzsche called *"Übermenschen"* (superior human beings; supermen).

Nietzsche understood that Christianity, unable to withstand the simultaneous attacks of philosophy and science, greed and technology, had lost its hold in Europe. Hume, Marx, and Darwin had each called religion into question. Many people no longer had faith in God. For them "God is dead," said Nietzsche. And without God all values and beliefs seem to disappear, so that there is nothing left except an eternity of meaninglessness. To be in this position and yet to cling to the traditional notion that truth has to be grounded in objective reality is to deny the possibility of any truth or meaning; it is to become nihilistic:

> Nihilism stands at the door: whence comes this uncanniest of all guests? Point of departure: it is an error to consider "social distress" or "physiological degeneration," or corruption of all things, as the cause of nihilism. Ours is the most honest and compassionate age. Distress, whether psychic, physical, or intellectual, need not at all produce nihilism (that is, the radical rejection of value, meaning, and desirability). Such distress always permits a variety of interpretations. Rather: it is in one particular interpretation, the Christian moral one, that nihilism is rooted.[10]

Of course, there were even more who clung steadfastly to their conception of traditional Christianity or to some moral, political, or even scientific ideology in a desperate attempt to avoid the despair which had led others to nihilism. Nietzsche saw this insistence on living a lie to be, like all beliefs and attitudes, an expression of the will to power. It is a response that is often necessary for those who are unable to accept the subjectivity of truth and their own consequent responsibility for determining what is valuable and what is true.

Nietzsche considered most people to be poor, weak, and above all, common. In their cases, psychic survival—happiness, if you will—is promoted by the lie that God exists and that He has decreed that it is better to be poor, weak, and humble than to be wealthy, powerful, and proud. Accepting this lie has transformed their poverty into an illusion of spiritual wealth, their weakness into the power to attain salvation, and their humility into the pride of possessing a superior truth. Christianity has inverted natural morality. Nietzsche would certainly accept Marx's observation that "religion is the opiate of the masses."

In contrast to the morality of the masses, which Nietzsche calls "slave morality," is the morality of *Übermenschen,* or "master morality." Master morality does not distinguish between good and evil as slave morality does, but between good and bad. Good and evil are religious, objectivistic, and anti-life notions, while good and bad are natural and life-affirming ideas. Master morality calls good that which contributes to success in this life and therefore prizes wealth, health, intelligence, creativity, and power. These are precisely the attributes that slave morality, for which subservience and obedience are the highest virtues, is most likely to be suspicious of and to reject as evil. Yet the slave is morally schizophrenic, for at the same time that his traditional morality tells him that wealth and power, for example, are evil, his natural intelligence tells him that they are good. So those who cling to slave morality are, if they have any native intelligence, at odds with themselves, confused and paralyzed. Small wonder that the masses have never amounted to much. How much better to renounce the lies of slave morality and, with clear vision, adopt the values of the masters, of nature, of the will to power, to dare to be whole and to exercise one's powers without apology. It is those who have had the courage, creativity, and means to assert themselves in the service of their visions who have led lives worth celebrating, and it is certainly no accident that "every enhancement of the type 'man' has so far been the work of an aristocratic society."[11]

Thus Nietzsche rejects Christianity and other slave moralities as well as nihilism. He challenges us to accept master morality even though it is no more objectively true than slave morality. Certainly he sees it to be nobler, more compatible with a higher type of man and a more accomplished level of civilization. He is distressed at the tendency, best exemplified by the nobility who joined the French revolution, of the European aristocracy to participate in their own corruption. Having attained wealth, power, and the opportunity to do great things, they were, in large numbers, adopting the democratic ideology of the herd and joining in the destruction not only of their own power but also of the possibility of a civilization they might be proud of. Greatness, Nietzsche insisted, is forever out of the reach of the democratic mediocrity he saw emerging in the Europe of the late nineteenth century:

> I describe what is coming, what can no longer come differently: *the advent of nihilism* . . . Our whole European culture is moving for some time now, with a tortured tension that is growing from decade to decade, as towards a catastrophe: relentlessly, violently, headlong, like a river that wants to reach the end, that no longer reflects, that is afraid to reflect.[12]

According to Neitzsche this central problem of his time and ours is that we inceasingly find that "everything lacks meaning." Our values seem arbitrary, our pleasures do not bring happiness, life appears to have no purpose. Nihilism is a curse. It can paralyze and defeat us, but only if we submit to it. Nietzsche's message is that to attain the sort of dignity that will make life a worthwhile project we must throw off the traditional moral, religious, and scientific notions of objective truth and replace them with a more reflective and profound notion of truth.

Both Kierkegaard and Nietzsche represent a crisis which began in the nineteenth century but continues, perhaps even more strongly, in the twentieth. It is a crisis of meaninglessness and despair. They both offer solutions: Kierkegaard the leap of faith and Nietzsche the joyous, empowering, adoption of master morality. In the middle of the twentieth century Jean-Paul Sartre encountered the same crisis but could accept neither Kierkegaard's nor Nietzsche's solution. Before entering the world of Sartrean existentialism, we must first look at phenomenology and the work of Edmund Husserl and Martin Heidegger. It was Husserl's phenomenology that provided one of the bases from which Sartre constructed his existential analysis of the human condition, and it was Heidegger who first applied Husserl's method to the description of human being-in-the-world in a way that was fully existential.

Phenomenology and the Origins of Existentialism

Phenomenology can be said to have begun with the work of the German psychologist and philosopher Franz Brentano (1838–1917). Brentano was responsible for formulating a new way of understanding the difference between mental and physical things and states. He saw that whatever is physical is self-contained in a way that mental things and states are not. Physical things can be understood and described without reference to other things in a way that whatever is mental cannot. It is the mark of the mental to refer to, or "intend", some other thing. Ideas are ideas *of* something or other, emotions are hopes *for,* fears *of,* loves *of,* or angers *at* something. There is no such thing as an idea which is not an idea of anything or a feeling which is not directed at anything. Consciousness, then, is very different from the objects that make up the world, for those objects exist in themselves, while consciousness is consciousness only when it intends something other than itself. As Jean-Paul Sartre was later to put it, an object is *en-soi,* or "in-itself," while consciousness is *pour-soi,* or "for-itself." Consciousness is not an object among other objects, but has a unique status. This doctrine has come to be called the doctrine of intentionality, and the exploration and elucidation of the status of consciousness which it implies was a primary concern of the phenomenologists and existentialists.

Edmund Husserl

Brentano's student, Edmund Husserl (1859–1938) is usually considered to be the founder of phenomenology. Trained as a mathematician, he earned his Ph.D. in 1881 and then discovered philosophy. He attended Brentano's lectures in Vienna from 1884 to 1886, and became obsessed with searching for unshakable foundations for human knowledge. During the nineteenth century, many philosophers had begun to realize that our knowledge of ourselves and the world is formed or structured by the concepts we use, by the subject-object structure of our language and thought, and by the assumptions, presuppositions, and prejudices we bring to experience. The realization that the world as it is known reflects the mind that does the knowing was the heritage of Kant and was basic to the subjectivism of Kierkegaard and the perspectivism of Nietzsche. It had become obvious that the natural sciences themselves were infected with an inevitable subjectivity. Husserl set out to find a method for the discovery of truth more objective and more exact than that of the natural sciences, which, despite their enormous success and prestige, seemed to Husserl to depend upon some very questionable assumptions. The notion that all adequate knowledge must be scientific rested on what Husserl called "the natural standpoint."[13] This point of view holds 1) that there is an objective world which is the totality of what is, 2) that to understand ourselves correctly is to understand ourselves as objects among other objects in that world, 3) that the methods of natural science are objectively determined by the nature of these objects, and 4) that whatever is subjective must be avoided. Clearly, the natural standpoint is incompatible with what Husserl had learned from Brentano about the uniqueness of consciousness. Husserl called the belief that this natural standpoint is the only adequate point of view "the myth of scientific objectivity." He accused the scientific establishment of promoting the notion that whatever exists or is important can be brought under the umbrella of objective science.

If science cannot give us pure and unquestionable knowledge, what can? How do we attain the truth? Husserl was convinced that the way to attain the truest vision of reality was to put aside, or "bracket," all of our prejudices and presuppositions and then observe and describe the phenomena which constitute the pure content of our experience. We should abandon all theorizing, for theories and their presuppositions color and alter our perceptions and our conception of the world. Husserl's phenomenology is descriptive, not theoretical. It is a method, not a set of conclusions. What Husserl called "bracketing," or "phenomenological reduction," is a method for apprehending the purest possible content of experience, thereby attaining an objectivity more fundamental than that of the sciences. It is a way of suspending, rather than altogether abandoning, our usual assumptions and points of view. To bracket an assumption is not to discard it permanently, for in most cases that would be impossible. Rather, it is to disengage it temporarily—to see around it.

But Husserl discovered one thing that could not be bracketed. That was consciousness itself. Consciousness is implicit in any experience at all, not as a content, but as a precondition without which there would be no experience and no phenomena, or objects of experience. The world consists of all possible objects of experience, but consciousness is not one of those objects and, consequently, is not *in* the world alongside them. It transcends the world. It is absolutely essential for the world, for to be an object is precisely to be an object *for* consciousness, without which there would be no objects and no world. Consciousness became Husserl's starting point.

To give an account of ourselves and our relation to the world is therefore fundamentally to give an account of ourselves as conscious beings, which is to give an account, or description, of consciousness. This became a central part of Husserl's project. Husserl also dedicated himself to the accurate apprehension and description of the essences revealed to him in experience—that is, to a description of the natures of things as apprehended in what he called the *Wesenschau,* or "intuition of essences." Only such a description could be the basis of a true science. But such a description must never lose sight of what most objective science ignores: the subjectivity that achieves science. True science must be reflective, or phenomenological; it must be grounded in a description of consciousness at the most fundamental level.

To describe consciousness at this level is to encounter what Husserl called the "transcendental ego," the absolute foundation of the world of experience. The transcendental ego is the absolute subject for which everything else is an object, and is distinct from the empirical ego which is an object of ordinary observation. The task of Husserl's phenomenology became the description of the transcendental ego and the way in which its activities constitute the world. Husserl later concerned himself with the problem of the intersubjectivity of transcendental egos, which is necessary if we are to live in a common world.

Husserl's doctrine of the transcendental ego was controversial. Many philosophers who had adopted his method regarded this aspect of his philosophy to be an unfortunate excursion away from the objectivity of descriptive phenomenology and into idealistic metaphysics. It was his phenomenological method rather than doctrines like that of the transcendental ego that became Husserl's most important legacy. His student, Martin Heidegger, made this method an integral part of existentialism.

Martin Heidegger

Martin Heidegger (1889–1976) saw the central task of philosophy to be answering the question "what is Being?" This question was first raised by the pre-Socratic Greek philosophers and, Heidegger insisted, had been systematically obscured by the tradition ever since Parmenides wrestled with it in the fifth century B.C. In fact, to ask "what is Being?" is misleading, since it seems to presuppose that Being is some object in the world, or some objective property belonging to all objects. Heidegger preferred to ask "what does it mean to Be?," or "what is the meaning of Being?"

Now this is a rather abstract question, and the only way Heidegger saw to approach it was to examine the Being that we know the best, i.e., human Being. *Being and Time,* his monumental study of human Being, or *Dasein,* as he called the Being of human beings, was originally intended to be the first of two volumes. The second volume, which was to uncover the secrets of Being itself, was never written. *Being and Time,* however, was so full of insights into the nature or meaning of being human that it has become one of the most influential books of twentieth-century philosophy. Heidegger's account is a phenomenological description of the basic structures of being human.

To be human is to be situated in the world, surrounded by others and by objects. It is to be in the world for no apparent reason, to have been thrust into the world without having asked to be born—to be "thrown into the world," as Heidegger puts it. And it is to be aware, as no other beings are, of one's own death. It is therefore to encounter one's own Being in recognizing the possibility of not being. Dasein "does not just occur among other entities. Rather, it is distinguished by the fact that, in its very Being, that Being is an issue for it."[14] To be human is therefore to suffer *Angst* (anxiety, dread) and, in an attempt to escape *Angst,* to flee from one's own Being toward the kind of beings or objects one finds in the world. To avoid being overwhelmed by the freedom and nothingness of our own Being, we attempt to see ourselves as things or as members of a crowd, and we express this view of ourselves in idle prattle about T.V., cars, football, or the weather. Serious conversation, on the other hand, bespeaks a willingness to accept the burdens of our humanity.

Heidegger found it necessary to distinguish between Being itself and beings (things). The function of objective science is to know and manipulate beings of various sorts, but the task of philosophy is much more fundamental. Philosophy is the search for Being. Scientific thought is calculative, while philosophy must be meditative and reflective. The thought of the geologist or engineer need not take itself into consideration, but that of the philosopher—indeed that of anyone who lives his humanity to the fullest—must be self-aware. It is *Angst* that reveals our Being to us and from which we are always fleeing. This flight from Being is flight from meditation and reflection, and from the true self-understanding that Heidegger calls "authenticity." It is flight toward the inauthentic and trivial concerns with the world of beings which occupy most of our attention and about which we are so good at calculating. Heidegger described our contemporary situation as "flight-from-thinking" and warned that:

> the approaching tide of technological revolution in the atomic age could so captivate, bewitch, dazzle, and beguile man that calculative thinking may some day come to be accepted and practiced *as the only* way of thinking. . . . Then man would have denied and thrown away his own special nature— that he is a meditative being.[15]

The "flight-from-thinking" Heidegger talks about is, of course, flight from meditative thinking and, because meditation is the uniquely human kind of thinking, it is also flight-from-ourselves, or flight-from-humanity.

Meditation differs from calculation because it is reflective, which is to say that it is conscious of the difference between the objects of thought and the subject of the thought, who is the thinker himself. Meditation is self-conscious and aware of the relation between the thinker and the things he thinks about in a way that calculation is not. It takes the self seriously and recognizes it as radically problematic in a sense in which the objects about which we calculate never are. To reflect on the questions "what is man?" or "who am I?" is a very different matter from attempting to formulate calculative or technological answers. To understand ourselves is not merely to know all there is to know about ourselves as objects. Certainly such disciplines as medicine and sociology provide important and legitimate kinds of objective knowledge about man. They are useful in helping us solve certain kinds of medical or social problems, once we have established the value of finding these solutions. But they are not part of the philosophical enterprise. They give us knowledge of our bodies and our institutions, but not of ourselves.

A fundamental distinction between *Dasein* and things in the world is that things are explained as the products of their pasts, while the actions of human beings are understood adequately only in relation to the future. To be human is to have purposes, projects, and values. It is to live toward the future rather than simply out of the past. It is to transcend the given, the present, and the merely factual. It is perhaps most fundamentally to be concerned, to care. It is to be free from determination solely by what is, and to be determined instead by what is not—by what Heidegger calls the Nothing. An adequate understanding of the meaning of Being involves, therefore, an encounter with nonbeing.

Traditional metaphysics (like Descartes'), as well as traditional natural science (such as Newtonian physics), has insisted on seeing reality, including human bodies and minds, as a collection of things present alongside each other, related only externally and accidentally. In order to understand the world it has been considered enough to know facts about objects in the world, and to understand any object—including the human mind—it has been thought that one must either reduce it to its constituent parts or trace its causal connections to other objects and facts. But to think in this traditional way is not only to accept what Husserl called "the myth of scientific objectivity," but it is also to ignore the distinctions Heidegger pointed out between human Being *(Dasein)* and beings which are objects for *Dasein,* and between things experienced merely "present-to-hand" (part of the background, the presence of which is a neutral fact) and things which are "ready-to-hand" in that they can be used as instruments in the pursuit of one's projects. It is this latter aspect of the world which transcends facts and is the locus of value. A hammer, for example, is merely present-to-hand when I have no project for which it is useful and am therefore indifferent to it, but as soon as I want to drive a nail or defend myself it stands out from the background and I see it as ready-to-hand, or valuable. The source of all value is, of course, human concern. Natural science has achieved enormous success and prestige in explaining and manipulating things present-to-hand but has been unable to understand consciousness, concern, or values. It has promoted a reductionistic and objectivistic view of human beings which is at odds with the most fundamental truths about human existence as revealed by phenomenological scrutiny or, for that matter, by any ordinary honest reflection. Poets and farmers and other ordinary folk have been more likely than professional scientists and philosophers to have escaped the myth of scientific objectivity and therefore to understand the truly human, value-laden, world. Science has been successful partly because it aids us in our flight from ourselves by seeming to deny the subjectivity which is the foundation of our being.

Jean-Paul Sartre

Jean-Paul Sartre was born in Paris in 1905. The following year his mother was widowed and took the young Sartre to live with her family. Sartre's grandfather was a professor of German. An unhappy child, Sartre turned to the books in his grandfather's library, where he was left pretty much to his own devices. From 1924 to 1928 he attended the prestigious École Normale Supérieure, and later went to Berlin where he studied the work of Husserl and Heidegger. Back in France, he taught at several *lycées* until called into the army at the outbreak of the Second World War. Captured by the Germans, he was paroled after some months and spent most of the war

236

years in Paris working with the resistance, writing, and teaching. He achieved literary success with such brilliant works as the novel *Nausea* (1938), the short story *The Wall* (1938), the plays *No Exit* (1944) and *Dirty Hands* (1948), and several essays. The first of his two most important philosophical works, *Being and Nothingness,* which appeared in 1943, was profoundly influenced by the work of Heidegger, but gave original explications of the basic tenets of existentialism which were so enormously influential that "Sartre" became almost synonymous with "existentialism." After the liberation of France Sartre helped found and edit *Les Temps Modernes* (Modern Times), a leftist journal of opinion and, although he saw it as the only legitimate voice of the French proletariat, he alienated the French Communist Party by establishing a political movement to reorganize all the parties of the left. In 1960 he published a second major philosophical work, the *Critique of Dialectical Reason,* in which he declared himself a Marxist and attempted a synthesis of Marxism and existentialism which managed to offend most orthodox Marxists. Sartre vehemently opposed the Soviet interventions in Hungary and Czechoslovakia, and the U.S. intervention in Vietnam.

Sartre had met Simone de Beauvoir when they were both students and they remained lifelong companions, although they maintained separate apartments and never married. In 1964 he was awarded the Nobel Prize for literature, but refused to accept it. He always seemed reluctant to identify with bourgeois institutions like marriage and the Nobel Prize. Sartre died in 1980, after a period of worsening blindness and declining health.

For Sartre, to be human is most importantly to be conscious, and *Being and Nothingness* is a phenomenological ontology of consciousness. Ontology is the study of the nature and meaning of being. Sartre's book is a description, using Husserl's phenomenological method, of what it means to be human. It is thus firmly in the tradition of Socrates, who insisted that the most important kind of knowledge is self-knowledge, as well as in the modern tradition which has held, since Descartes, that before we can know the world we must take stock of the mind which does the knowing. But Sartre's analysis of consciousness is very different from that of most earlier philosophers. It has been traditional to try to understand ourselves by asking "What kind of a *thing* is a human being? What kind of an *object* is consciousness? What is the *essence* of man? What is human *nature?*" These questions presuppose the myth of scientific objectivity and therefore that to be human is to be some particular kind of thing, an object with a certain essence. The phenomenological approach that Sartre adopted rejects such presuppositions and, therefore, the question about human nature. The problem is not to define human nature, but to describe human *existence.* Hence the term "existentialism."

Human existence is always concrete. Traditional philosophers grasped after abstractions, "essences," in terms of which they thought they could capture the most fundamental truths about human beings and the world. But the history of philosophy has been a history of different theories, each of which rested on assumptions which seemed obvious to its defenders, but which, precisely because they were assumptions, could not be proven. Human beings have been considered to be, for example, essentially rational beings, essentially creatures of God, essentially products of evolution, essentially pleasure seeking or psycho-sexual beings, essentially economic beings, and essentially responders to stimuli. These theories all reduce human beings to abstractions, but the fact that such theories exist and that I must decide how seriously to take them is not an abstraction; it is a fact or situation typical of those we encounter every day. The phenomenological method lends itself to a philosophy of existence, for it is a way of describing concrete, lived, experience.

What is most fundamental about any experience is what Brentano taught: experience entails consciousness, and consciousness is intentional. It is always consciousness of something. Consciousness has a subject-object structure. Not only are objects always objects for consciousness, so that the world depends in some way on the knower, but in order to be a subject one must be conscious of an object, so that the mind has a kind of dependence on the world. Intentionality does not imply any particular object, although to be conscious requires already having chosen to think of this object or that, in this way or that, with these assumptions or those. We must constantly choose, and we cannot escape choosing. What we cannot choose is not to choose, for even that would be a choice. Sartre's description of the human condition as one in which we are condemned to choose is not a psychological description, but an ontological one. The choices he describes are ontological choices—those that constitute the very *being* of consciousness—and the description is ontological because it describes what it means to *be* as a conscious being. Ontological choice is not necessarily something we make deliberately or are conscious *of*. It is not an object of consciousness; it is on the side of the subject.

Ontological choice is radically free. Any theory that tells me that all my choices are determined is itself the consequence of assumptions and ways of thinking that were freely chosen. The most fundamental fact about any of us is consciousness, which is identical with choice, with subjectivity, and with freedom. Consciousness is not a thing, but an activity, a directionality, a choice. It is negation, the ability to say "no" to what is the case. As such it is freedom from what is. What is the case can never completely determine any human act. "For an act is the projection of [the self] toward what is not, and what is can in no way determine by itself what is not."[16] We are the beings, Sartre points out, who introduce negation into the world. Objects are determined by what is the case, while conscious subjects are also aware of what is not the case. A camera, for example, will photograph a group without ever noticing that my friend is not there. For the camera there are no absences or lacks; there are no holes in being. What is, is, and that's the end of the matter. But for me, searching the group or the photograph, her absence is glaring. Likewise, the movement of a physical object I push is determined by objective factors such as its mass, the coefficient of friction between it and the surface it's resting on, and the force I exert. On the other hand, the movement of a human being I push is determined by something very different: by the idea, perhaps, that he has that I should not have pushed him, or by the idea he has of his own dignity. This is a determination by value rather than by fact, by the ideal rather than the actual. And it is freedom. It is freedom from the actual, and it is freedom in the sense of self-determination, since it is I who choose my values.

Consciousness is freedom. It is the source of all value, and therefore of all meaning. Meaning exists only for conscious beings. A world devoid of conscious beings would not even be a world, for "world" implies meaningful relationships like those between part and whole, mind and object, important and unimportant, and means and ends. To look in the world itself for the source of meaning and value is to search for objective answers to questions about the meaning and purpose of life. Sartre calls the notion that there are such answers "the spirit of seriousness." It is the same notion that Kierkegaard rejected when he surpassed the ethical stage, and it is certainly related to what Husserl called the myth of scientific objectivity. To accept this notion and then look honestly for the objective meaning of life is to set oneself up for disappointment. The world contains no ultimate meaning. In itself it is absurd, for there are no final answers and no reason that things are as they are. Science may offer answers, and so may religion—but to no avail. Scientific answers explain facts in terms of natural laws, and some natural laws in terms of other more fundamental laws, but must always fail to explain the most fundamental laws. Religious answers have the same flaw. Any appeal to an ultimate principle or ultimate being invites the question "Why that principle? Why this being?" A familiar form of the question is "What made God?" In the last analysis there is no reason for which one can give convincing reasons, since any reason can be questioned. Things are absurd. The world is revealed as one big meaningless accident. And this includes God, if He exists. So He can't really help either. This realization that there is no objective meaning contributes to what Heidegger called *Angst*. Kierkegaard had referred to the same thing when he titled two of his books *Fear and Trembling* and *The Sickness unto Death*. Literature of the absurd is dedicated to making the meaninglessness of the world apparent to the reader. Few of us reflect, for example, on the absurdity of the human body, but a thoughtful reader of Kafka's *Metamorphosis* will recognize Gregor Samsa's situation as he awakes to find himself transformed into a giant bug to be a metaphor for the human condition we all share. Certainly Gregor's condition made no sense, but neither does ours. The difference is that we are so accustomed to the usual that we don't notice its absurdity until a Kafka or a Sartre reveals it to us.

But all is not lost. If we cannot find meaning in the world itself, we cannot deny the existence of meaning either. Even the claim that the world is meaningless assigns a certain meaning to it. And it is replete with other meanings. The point, of course, is that those meanings do not have their origin in the world, but in consciousness. To understand the world one must therefore understand consciousness. "Subjectivity must be the starting point."[17]

To talk more precisely about the relation between consciousness and the world, Sartre devised some technical terminology. Consciousness, which as intentional is not complete in itself but always intends an object, Sartre called "being for-itself," or simply the "for-itself." The object of consciousness he called "being in-itself," or the "in-itself." The subject-object structure of consciousness is thus always this: the for-itself intends the in-itself. When he talks about consciousness, Sartre is not resurrecting Husserl's transcendental ego. He rejects Husserl's transcendental because Husserl seemed to have conceived it as an absolute subject which was really the most fundamental object—one on which the world depends but which doesn't depend on the world. Husserl thus seemed to fall into a metaphysical idealism that made the being of objects, as well as their meaning, dependent on the ego. Husserl's conception of the ego implied, moreover, that its essence was our true essence, and therefore that we were not free, in the way Sartre insisted we must be, to determine our own essences.

For Sartre, then, consciousness is nothingness. It is the absence of an essence. It is spontaneous, absolutely undetermined, and transparent. It is not a thing. It is pure intentionality, but intentionality is the fact that it is nothing in itself. There is a problem here that Sartre admitted but thought did more to throw light upon the human condition than to weaken his account. If the subject is always the knower and the known is always an object, how can anyone ever know himself? How can we ever know others? If my friend is really a subject, but to know him is to know him as an object, it would seem to follow that I can never know him as he really is. And indeed this does follow for Sartre. We see others, and others see us, as objects—as having essences which define and determine. My teachers saw me as a student; I saw them as teachers. But although I was a student, I was more than a student, and that essence was one I had chosen and was free to abandon. I both was a student, and was not really a student (since I was free to quit school and still be myself). Sartre describes the for-itself as "a being which is what it is not, and which is not what it is."[18] Objects, or beings in-themselves, on the other hand, are what they are. They are not problematic, as is consciousness. Sartre's comments about consciousness often seem paradoxical because we persist in thinking of consciousness as if it were an object, to be understood according to the law of non-contradiction.

But others always do see us as objects, and we know ourselves as objects. " 'Really to know oneself' is inevitably to take toward oneself the point of view of others, that is to say, a point of view which is necessarily false."[19] So self-knowledge is both possible and impossible. To know oneself most completely is to know one's own freedom. It is to know that whatever knowledge one has of oneself is misleading, because one is not an object that can be pinned down or grasped by an act of knowing. It is to know that whatever essence one has, one has chosen. It is to encounter one's responsibility for what one is at the same time that one realizes that one is not really, or necessarily, what one is.

Condemned to Be Free

Most of us flee from the responsibility for all that we have chosen to be and from our "dreadful freedom." We deny to ourself that we are free and responsible and take refuge in deterministic excuses. It is comforting to think of oneself as determined by one's situation or by an essence one considers inevitable, for the burden of making choices in the absence of any objective reason for one choice rather than another is a heavy one. Yet we are all condemned to our freedom and our responsibility; such is the human condition. To accept it and make one's choices in the full realization of one's freedom and responsibility is to be in good faith. To hide from one's condition by deceiving oneself, Sartre calls being in bad faith. Sartre insists that he is merely describing two structures of human being, or two ways of understanding oneself. He claims that bad faith is neither totally avoidable nor necessarily immoral, but instead is typically human. His implication, however, is clearly that one is more fully human to the extent one is in good faith, for then one is in touch with one's own subjectivity, freedom, and responsibility, and therefore with one's humanity.

Sartre's analysis of interpersonal relations was dominated by his description of "the Look"—the gaze which one person focuses like a spotlight on another and with which the other is invariably seen as an object rather than as a free subject. This description is a consequence of Sartre's making Brentano's doctrine of intentionality the foundation of his analysis of consciousness. It seems to imply that we are never truly conscious of each other, but are always limited to knowing an external appearance. But Sartre recognized experiences in which we are indeed in direct contact with the consciousness and freedom of others, though at a terrible price. These are experiences like those of shame or pride in which we see ourselves as objects for the Look of another. We live the freedom of the other, but surrender our own. Because of the fundamental subject-object structure of consciousness there seemed to Sartre no possible way for two or more individuals to attain a mutual and reciprocal togetherness. We are, in fact, doomed to be rivals or enemies, each of us struggling to preserve his own freedom by turning the other into an object lest the other turn him into one first. As Garcin says in the play *No Exit*, "Hell is other people."[20] This pessimistic description made each of us a free individual at the expense of a terrible isolation and alienation from others and ourselves. It was not until he was working out his existential version of Marxism that Sartre found a way to understand the possibility of truly reciprocal togetherness.

Society and the State

Sartre's existentialist account of being human as it is presented in *Being and Nothingness* is an account of the solitary human consciousness confronted with its own absolute freedom and responsibility. It is an insightful and exciting account from which much can be learned, but it is incomplete, for it lacks any meaningful social or political analysis of the human condition. Sartre had emphasized the importance of the context or situation within which we make our choices, and had argued that the limits which our situation puts on the choices available to us in no way diminishes the absolute character of our freedom to make those choices which we do have. He had rejected the quest for the sort of absolute and eternal truth that the tradition had sought. Now he sees that Marx was right to understand that we are historical through and through. Reason itself is always situational; reason invariably stems from, and is exercised within, a context that is cultural and historical. With his discovery of Karl Marx's social philosophy and historical dialectic, Sartre found a way to talk about the facticity of the concrete human being as well as about the historical nature of thought. It was only with the publication of *Search for a Method* and the *Critique of Dialectical Reason* (of which *Search for a Method* was, in the French edition, the first part) that Sartre announced that he had come to recognize that Marxism was the dominant philosophy of our time and that all other philosophies, including existentialism, must be understood in relation to Marxism. Sartre maintained that every philosopher expresses the thought of his age and is therefore to be understood historically. Those, like Marx, who best express the thought of one's age can only be supported and commented on. "Marxism . . . has scarcely begun to develop. . . . We cannot go beyond it because we have not gone beyond the circumstances which engendered it."[21] Since Marx expresses the consciousness of our age, to explicate and develop his thought is our surest route to self-knowledge, and it was this task that Sartre undertook in the *Critique*.

Sartre formulated an existential version of Marxism which he thought was true to the original Marxism of Karl Marx as well as to the most important doctrines of his own existentialism. This meant emphatically rejecting the many rigid and doctrinaire versions of Marxism that had emerged by the mid twentieth century, including the sterile mechanical formulas to which it had been reduced in the Soviet state. Stalinism, for example, presented caricatures of the class struggle and of the relations between the individual and the class and party. Engels had erred in proclaiming the dialectic most fundamentally a law of nature, rather than of history, and thus left no room for human freedom. Sartre also insisted that Engels' doctrine presupposed a desituated or divine point of view from outside of being from which eternal ahistorical truth can be known. But such knowledge is impossible, for all knowledge is situated, positional, and historical. For Sartre nature has no inherent meaning; whatever meaning it has for us, we give it. History, on the other hand, as the record of men's actions as well as the context within which they make choices, is meaningful. To understand history is to understand the actions of men, and to understand those actions is to understand the projects and values that make them meaningful. Thought is dialectical as well as historical because, arising in a given situation, it is able to surpass that situation by conceiving, and then acting to bring about, one it values more. And history is dialectical because out of the context it provides arise human actions which bring about a new context within which new human action will take place. The dialectical nature of history is a consequence of human freedom. When he wrote that "we were never more free than under the German Occupation,"[22] Sartre meant that the situation during the occupation confronted all Frenchmen with unavoidable choices between resistance and collaboration which would define them as patriots or collaborators. "The often frightful circumstances of our struggle enabled us finally to live, undisguised and unconcealed, that anxious, unbearable situation which is called the human predicament."[23] They were condemned by their situation to choose and therefore to surpass the situation in one way or another. They were therefore more intensely aware of their freedom and its implications than during normal and less demanding times.

Sartre had held in *Being and Nothingness* that all human action presupposes consciousness of a lack, or a nothingness, and in the *Critique* he points out that human history has hitherto been a history of human needs in the face of scarcity. History is the history of human projects which

241

are determined not only by what is the case, as any determinism must have it, but also by what is not the case. Scarcity is not an objective natural fact, but rather a condition which appears only in the light of human projects. Just as an obstacle is not an obstacle for me unless I have a project which demands that I overcome it, so the very idea of scarcity, like that of needs, is an idea that presupposes human values, human projects, and a human future which does not yet exist.

So Sartre rejected the mechanistic materialism of Stalin and Engels according to which history moves by an objective necessity, inevitably and inexorably, independent of the will of individuals. Such positivistic and finalistic versions hopelessly distorted true Marxism and had become instruments for preserving oppressive totalitarian regimes in a way that true Marxism never could.

Marx had recognized that men make history, although in the context of circumstances which they have not chosen. To understand history, therefore, is to understand it as the product of human creativity in the face of circumstance, as the result of free choices which might have been different, and not as a steady and inevitable movement in a fore-ordained direction. But without the existentialist ontology of consciousness that Sartre offers it, Marxism cannot account for the dialectic at the deepest level:

> Everything changes if one considers that society is presented to each man as a *perspective of the future* and that this future penetrates to the heart of each one as a real motivation for his behavior. That the Marxists allow themselves to be duped by mechanistic materialism is inexcusable.[24]

History is haunted by human freedom, human choices, and human values, all of which transcend the past and point to the future. It was the description of freedom, choice, and value to which he had given first expression in *Being and Nothingness* that Sartre offered Marxism in the *Critique*. To understand history as a series of moments, each a product of its past, or as the manifestation of some transcendent law which makes men mere puppets, is to misunderstand not only history, but ourselves as well. Marxists who embrace such a determinism while living, as we all do, their own freedom, he accused of bad faith.[25]

Sartre's earlier analysis of consciousness and freedom had seemed to make each person a threat to the freedom of others. Each of us was viewed as a solitary consciousness making lonely decisions in the light of a freedom which was grounded entirely in the self. There was no adequate social philosophy or way of understanding phenomena such as comradeship, political solidarity, or the enhancement of one's freedom when it is exercised in concert with the freedom of others. In the *Critique* Sartre addresses these issues. He describes the difference between a *series* of individuals, each with his own projects, each perceiving others as potential obstacles to the realization of his own projects, and the *group,* in which all the members share the same project and recognize in the others fellow subjects and allies with whom, together, their common goal can be realized. Sartre described this fusion of individual freedoms and activities into what he calls a *group praxis*—a collective purpose and action which is the expression and enhancement of the freedom of each member of the group. His favorite example of this fusion of individual freedoms is the storming of the Bastille—an event which inaugurated the French Revolution. The goals and frustrations of a great many individuals who had hitherto led seemingly separate and unconnected lives were fused in a group praxis which made possible an accomplishment beyond any which an individual could have achieved on his own. The freedom of each was truly affirmed and magnified in the process. Sartre held that one can achieve one's freedom in a way that makes a difference historically only through the recognition of the freedom of others, which is to say only by overcoming alienation and participating in the fused consciousness of a group with a common praxis.

For Sartre, then, the best life is the life in which one acknowledges one's freedom and one's responsibility for what one has made of oneself. One lives as much as possible in good faith, or what Heidegger called "authenticity." One refuses to hide behind deterministic excuses. One accepts that one's essence is determined by one's choices and realizes that since nothing is determined, everything is possible. One recognizes one's responsibility for what one does and for what one accepts. One lives for the future in the context of the past and present and, since the future is yet to be determined, one conceives and strives to determine it in terms of values which transcend any facts. Such values are chosen, as Heidegger says, in meditation. Yet Sartre goes beyond Heidegger to give an account of how the projects we adopt in contemplation or meditation can, in concert with the projects of others, be successfully realized. It is clear that the best possible life is no longer simply the authentic life as it can be considered in isolation. It is also the active and creative participation with others in the dialectic of situation, thought, and action.

Implications for Leisure

A central problem for contemporary man is the one Nietzsche foretold. Nihilism threatens us. Life often seems empty and not worth living. We have more and more spare time but less and less do we know what to do with it. Our possessions and our pleasures do not bring happiness or fulfillment. The good life eludes us.

There is no *a priori* essence in terms of which we are to understand the nature of man or of the good life. To live life to its fullest is to live creatively and to understand the freedom which underlies human existence. To understand and accept this freedom is to be authentic. To live meaningful lives we must understand who we are—that is, we must have reflected on our values and our projects. Those who have not achieved an authentic self-understanding are what Heidegger called *verfallen,* or lost in the crowd. They are in bad faith.

Authentic self-understanding recognizes the difference between being and having and is incompatible with consumerism, which is a rampant kind of alienation. To judge oneself and others in terms of material possessions, in terms of the kind of automobile one drives, the number of television sets one owns, or the brand of tennis shoe one wears, is to be alienated from the most fundamental truths about the meaning of being human. The catalogues we browse in and television programs like "The Price is Right" and channels like "The Cable Value Network" go so far as to make consumption a passive spectator "activity."

In order to be a significant part of a meaningful life, leisure must involve the active realization of our most fundamental projects. It must be authentic self-creation rather than amusement, for the function of amusement is to distract us from ourselves. Amusement is a form of what Heidegger called flight-from-thinking. It is what Sartre called bad faith. Its pursuit is an expression of nihilism. It is alienation and the antithesis of contemplation and, therefore, an abdication of one's humanity.

Major Philosophical Points

Sartre's early work was devoted to a phenomenological description of the existence of human beings as individuals. Building on the work of Husserl and Heidegger, he describes the roles of consciousness, choice, and commitment in establishing the meaningfulness of the world. He described two fundamentally different ways of being human, good faith and bad faith, and suggested that to be most fully human was to be in good faith, i.e., to be aware of one's subjectivity and freedom—and therefore of one's responsibility for the choices one makes and the person one becomes. Later, in search of an adequate social philosophy, he synthesized his ontology of consciousness and the humanistic social and political philosophy of Karl Marx.

- Consciousness is intentional and, as such, it is not an object.
- Consciousness has no necessary essence.
- To be human is to be conscious, which is to be free and to have no necessary essence.
- To be fully human is to accept one's freedom and the responsibility that it entails.
- Most of us flee from our freedom and responsibility, but we cannot choose not to choose or escape our responsibility for what we make of ourselves by our choices.
- To be conscious is to intend an object, so to be conscious of another is to be conscious of him as an object and not as the subject he really is.
- True reciprocity between human beings is therefore impossible when they focus their gazes on each other; it can happen only when they share a common project and activity (group praxis) and each experiences his own freedom and that of the other as mutually reinforcing.
- In such situations of reciprocity the humanity of each person is enhanced by his relations with others.
- To the extent that leisure is creative self-expression it must involve self-knowledge, or good faith. Our freedom and, therefore, our humanity, is enhanced by genuine reciprocity with others.
- Creative leisure is active and authentic self-creation rather than passive amusement.

References

1. Søren Kierkegaard, *The Journals of Kierkegaard,* trans. and ed. Alexander Dru (London: Collins, 1975) pp. 50–51.
2. Søren Kierkegaard, *The Point of View for My Work as an Author,* trans. Walter Lowrie, ed. Benjamin Nielson (New York: Harper & Row, 1962) p. 62.
3. Søren Kierkegaard, *Fear and Trembling and The Sickness unto Death,* trans. Walter Lowrie (Princeton: Princeton University Press, 1954) pp. 67–72.
4. Søren Kierkegaard, *Concluding Unscientific Postscript,* trans. D. F. Swenson (Princeton: Princeton University Press, 1941) p. 276.
5. Ibid., p. 273.
6. Walter Kaufmann, *Nietzsche: Philosopher, Psychologist, AntiChrist,* 4th ed. (Princeton: Princeton University Press, 1974) pp. xiii–xiv.
7. Friedrich Nietzsche, "On Truth and Lie" in *The Portable Nietzsche,* trans. and ed. Walter Kaufmann (New York: Viking, 1958) p. 43.
8. Ibid., p. 47.
9. Friedrich Nietzsche, *Beyond Good and Evil,* trans. Walter Kaufmann (New York: Vintage Books, 1966) p. 21.
10. Friedrich Nietzsche, *The Will to Power,* trans. Walter Kaufmann and R. J. Hollingdale, ed. Walter Kaufmann (New York: Vintage Books, 1968) p. 7.
11. *Beyond Good and Evil,* p. 201.
12. *The Will to Power,* p. 3.
13. cf. Edmund Husserl, *The Idea of Phenomenology,* trans. William P. Alston and George Nakhanikian (The Hague: Martinus Nijhoff, 1964) pp. 3–32.
14. Martin Heidegger, *Being and Time,* trans. John MacQuarrie and Edward Robinson (New York: Harper and Row, 1962) p. 32.
15. Martin Heidegger, *Discourse on Thinking,* trans. John M. Anderson and E. Hans Freund (New York: Harper & Row, 1966) p. 56.

16. *Being and Nothingness,* p. 235.
17. Jean-Paul Sartre, *Existentialism,* trans. Bernard Frechtman (New York: Philosophical Library, 1947) p. 15.
18. Jean-Paul Sartre, *Being and Nothingness,* trans. Hazel Barnes (New York: Philosophical Library, 1956) p. 58.
19. Jean-Paul Sartre, *The Transcendence of the Ego,* trans. F. Williams and R. Kirkpatrick (New York: Farrar, Straus & Giroux, 1957) p. 86.
20. Jean-Paul Sartre, *No Exit and Three Other Plays,* trans. Stuart Gilbert and Lionel Abel (New York: Vintage Books, 1955) p. 47.
21. Jean-Paul Sartre, *Search for a Method,* trans. Hazel Barnes (New York: Vintage Books, 1968) p. 30.
22. Jean-Paul Sartre, *Situations III,* translated and quoted in Robert Denoon Cumming, ed., *The Philosophy of Jean-Paul Sartre* (New York: Random House, 1965) p. 233.
23. Ibid.
24. *Search for a Method,* p. 96.
25. Ibid., p. 48.

Part V Conclusion

The optimism that Marx had resurrected from the Enlightenment was shattered by the first half of the twentieth century. Beginning with Engels, his closest associate, Marx's dynamic theory of history as a successful struggle for greater human fulfillment gave way to a myriad of interpretations. With its unity of material reality, the idea of freedom and the transcendence of human alienation broken, his system of thought lost its uniqueness.

In Britain, twentieth-century socialism grew out of nineteenth-century utilitarianism and, with the notion of efficient economic man intact, it became a movement that coexisted with and reinforced the definition of humans as economic animals. Concluding that human beings were incapable of making the quantum leap toward the total personal and social harmony propounded by Marx, the Fabians and Bernstein opted for a program of gradual reform of the political institutions and economic assumptions that had originally given rise to the concept of economic man. The goal of the "Greatest Happiness for the Greatest Number" was clearly expanded to include the working class, but the "Greatest Happiness" was defined as higher wages, shorter hours and social welfare. Gone was the glimmering hope of transcending economic man by integrating classical leisure, as essence-fulfillment, with industrial society. The Marxian call for conscious, cooperative human action to shape history and radically transform society was supplanted by efficient economic man's demands that the state modify the economic system in order to soften the impact of hard times while enhancing his standard of living and capacity to consume.

The link between the extension of the European empires and domestic social reform is well established. Of the numerous accounts of imperialism, Hannah Arendt's seems to highlight the most profound historical points: by the late nineteenth century, the economic systems of western Europe, which had developed under the banner of laissez-faire capitalism, had become increasingly dependent on imperialism. As a result, the eighteenth-century call for a limited state was replaced by the demand for a strong, vigorous political entity capable of expanding worldwide economic interests. In slightly more than a century, Adam Smith's insistence on a limited state gave way to widespread support for the state's role in actively promoting economic growth and protecting overseas investments. Hence, the once ostensibly incompatible interests of the working and middle classes were unexpectedly reconciled, resulting in their mutual acceptance of a powerful, active state to guarantee social welfare at home while extending imperial interests abroad.

While western Europe was busy altering its ideals to fit the reality of the international market, Germany was emerging as a major European power. By the time Germany became a united nation state the western European systems had already begun to divide the world into areas of economic influence. The addition of a frustrated Germany attempting to make up for lost time in the race to build an empire added to worldwide tensions. This drive for economic expansion merged with aggressive nationalism to divide Europe into well-armed hostile camps and, ignited by the spark from the Balkans, World War I erupted.

For two decades the size, influence, and program of the German Social Democratic Party made it appear to be the staunchest defender of the Marxian synthesis in Europe and, hence, an internationalist guard against aggressive nationalism. But below the surface, the party (which came into existence through the merger of the highly competitive Lassallean and Eisenacher factions in 1875) was extremely fragmented. Its leadership had separated from its rank and file members and its link with the trade unions had been broken during the outlaw period from 1878 to 1890. While the workers were gradually assimilated into the archetype of the modern welfare state, the bulk of the leadership continued to consider themselves "Orthodox Marxists"—a label that referred to Engels' mechanistic interpretation that denied Marx's dialectic. Bernstein returned from England in 1901, further dividing the organization and its leadership by openly promoting his clearly reformist position. Hence, by 1914, a highly fragmented leadership combined with the factionalized party structure to undermine whatever checks the SPD might have been able to impose on the Emperor and military.

The real test for the German socialists came on August 4, 1914 during the Reichstag vote for war credits. The socialist deputies assented to mobilizing Germany for war, thereby abdicating their internationalist role and betraying their revolutionary Marxism. During the winter of 1918–19 the fragmentation turned to fratricide when the moderate Majority Socialists (who, by then, controlled the government) allied themselves with the Prussian-dominated military to brutally repress the Sparticist Revolt that was led by their former comrades.

If the Germans were frustrated before the War, they were furious about the conditions imposed on them by the surrender. They were forced to bear all of the responsibility for the War, despite the indisputable fact that there were other contributory causes. Backbreaking reparations were forced on them, along with the loss of their colonies and military—a devastating blow to their material interests and nationalistic pride. It would seem that the victors were also motivated by economic factors and their own pride—weaknesses that Homer and the prophets cautioned against centuries ago. During the 1920s, the historically-fragmented Germans began to unite in response to a shared perception of the need to avenge all of the wrongs perpetrated against them: the Treaty of Versailles provided a focal point for national unity which even Bismarck could not have deliberately engineered.

The preconditions of Nazism may be traced to the original organization of the Prussian state, Hegelian attitudes toward authority, and the widespread economic hardship and hunger for vengeance created by Versailles. The depression provided the accelerator which moved Hitler's organization from the status of lunatic fringe group to controlling power. Whatever remnants of Enlightenment optimism had survived the First World War were shattered by the experience of World War II.

With Mussolini and Hitler leading the attack, several European societies supported the consciously irrational, violent assault on everything western civilization purported to represent. For every resistance fighter there was a collaborator, and the members of societies as diverse as Hungary, Yugoslavia and France found themselves ruled by pro-Nazi regimes established by their fellow countrymen. The War engulfed most of the world, killing an estimated 60 million people—over 40 million of whom were civilians. In addition, it sparked new fires of nationalism among the indigenous people controlled by the European colonial powers at precisely the time that these powers were battering each other into bankruptcy and cutting an immense swath of destruction. Indiscriminate carpet-bombing of Germany's urban areas had devastated the industrial capacity of central Europe. An estimated 20 million people had died in Russia and its industrial infrastructure was severely damaged. The stench of death still permeated the air around the Nazi extermination camps when the United States introduced the unparalleled destructive capacity of nuclear warfare into the annals of human history. With the exception of the U.S. (which had not been invaded and emerged from the war with its industrial facilities not only intact but flourishing—and its "manifest destiny" no longer confined to the western hemisphere), the western world was shattered. Many people who had become disenchanted with the shallow materialism and aggressive nationalism of economic man had looked to the Soviet Union during the 1920s with hope for a brighter future. But even this spark of hope was extinguished by the 1940s, as revelations of the atrocities committed by the Stalinist regime against its own people filtered to the west. Stalinist repression had thoroughly discredited whatever remnants of the Marxian synthesis survived the initial Bolshevik distortion. The revolutionary movement for human emancipation from Czarist autocracy had degenerated into a highly bureaucratized totalitarian regime that continued to pay homage to Marx—while forcing the Russian people to become efficient economic animals. Without an adequate religious or social impetus in Russian history to stimulate the voluntary adoption of the values associated with the modern work ethic, the Communist Party, under Stalin's dictatorship, emerged as a highly coercive power to compel the Russian people into industrial efficiency.

With still another dream shattered, only a blind ideologue could avoid being shaken. George Orwell's moderate leftist sympathies (he fought with the Republicans in the Spanish Civil War and was highly critical of British imperial arrogance in his novel *Burmese Days*) were destroyed during the 1940s, prompting him to write *Animal Farm* (1945) and *1984* (published in 1948). Arthur Koestler (who had also been in Spain during the Civil War) provided another influential and obviously disappointed reevaluation of the potential for positive social transformation through violent revolution following the degeneration of Stalinism in *Darkness at Noon* (1941) and *The Yogi and the Commissar* (1945).

The complete distortion of the Marxian synthesis under Stalinism pulled the plug on whatever traditional hope remained after two world wars, the great depression, the holocaust and the vaporization of tens of thousands of human beings in two split-second blasts over Hiroshima and Nagasaki. The hope for improving the human condition had sunk to an all-time low.

Against this background of a world gone mad and the bankruptcy of all positive conceptions of human nature which might offer hope for the future of mankind, the existentialists' analysis of the human situation began to offer insights and even to provide reason for optimism. Existentialism provided a way of understanding and relating to the absurdities of the world while still affirming that life has meaning. Its doctrine is that meaning has its source in the conscious subject, rather than in the world itself. No objective situation, in itself, is any more or less significant than any other. By the middle of the twentieth century Kafka, Sartre, and the literature of the absurd were no longer needed to bring home the meaninglessness of the world; Stalinism, the holocaust, and the bomb had done the job only too well.

Sartre had more to offer than a mere description of this meaninglessness. He pointed out that because meaning is always grounded in human choice and value, and history is the history of human actions and the choices that underlie them, human history is intelligible as the dialectical surpassing of facts toward the realization of value. It is, of course, in terms of those values that facts, meaningless in themselves, become significant. Sartre and his friend and fellow existentialist, Maurice Merleau-Ponty (1908–1961) saw how the existentialist understanding of the dialectic of fact and value, of situation and action, provided a way of rethinking and restoring the Marxian synthesis which had been destroyed by Engels, Stalin, and the other "orthodox Marxists." Recognizing the failures of the Soviet experience and sympathizing with Arthur Koestler's disillusionment with orthodox Marxism—what Koestler called "the philosophy of the Commissar"—Merleau-Ponty wrote that:

> We realize that after breathing the suffocating philosophy of the commissar so long, he [Koestler] is happy to leave it. What we understand less is that he blames Marxism for it and in so doing rejects Marxism itself.[1]

Marxism itself is, according to Merleau-Ponty, a philosophical position which provides the only possible truly humanistic way of understanding human beings in their political and historical situations. It is not a scientific theory which allows us to predict the future course of history:

The decline of proletarian humanism is not a crucial experience which annuls the whole of Marxism. It is still valid as a criticism of the existing world and of other humanisms. By virtue of this at least, it cannot be surpassed. Even if it is incapable of giving form to world history it remains strong enough to discredit the other solutions . . . Marxism is not just any hypothesis which can be replaced tomorrow by some other. It is the simple statement of those conditions without which there would be neither any humanism, in the sense of a reciprocal relation between men, or any rationality in history.[2]

Merleau-Ponty went on to insist that Marxism continually reminds us that "humanity is humanity in name only as long as the greater number of men have abdicated their sovereignty and some are masters and the others slaves," and that, therefore, "outside Marxism there is only the power of some and the resignation of others."[3] Sartre and Merleau-Ponty did not always agree, but for both of them existentialism permits a revitalization of the Marxian synthesis. The humanism which emerges conceives consciousness as the freedom which allows us to transcend our material situation. This conception of consciousness is basic to understanding the reciprocity between human beings who transcend alienation and act in concert with others to make history.

This humanistic vision born of Marxism and existentialism has serious implications for our conception of ourselves and, therefore, for our understanding of all human activities, including human leisure. In that to be human is precisely to be free, to have to choose, to have no necessary essence, and always to transcend one's situation, it is clear that to be most fully in touch with oneself is to recognize this freedom, to accept it, and to act on it. To be most fully human is to be active, creative, responsible, and contemplative. It is to be what Heidegger called "authentic."

The authentic contemplation which is essential to any truly significant leisure is in part a return to the classical ideal of the contemplative life, but there is an enormous difference between contemplation as conceived by Plato and Aristotle and authentic reflection as the existentialists understand it. For the ancients, contemplation put one in touch with eternal verities such as the natures of man, the universe, God, and the good life. These essences were thought to exist independent of our contemplation of them. The existentialist vision, on the other hand, is that it is the honesty or authenticity of the contemplation itself rather than any essences which are its objects that make contemplation essential to the good life.

Exactly what activities will constitute genuine leisure cannot be specified *a priori*, for such a specification would be incompatible with the creativity and freedom which are essential to any adequate expression of our humanity. It is clear, however, that if leisure is authentically contemplative it will necessarily be active rather than passive, creative and meaningful rather than idle and meaningless. Genuine leisure must be creative self-expression and not mere amusement.

References

1. Merleau-Ponty, Maurice, *The Primacy of Perception,* ed. and intro. James M. Edie (Evanston: Northwestern University Press, 1964) p. 219.
2. Ibid., p. 213.
3. Ibid., p. 215.

Conclusion

You can Talk about it—
Yea, talk about it,
But it really doesn't matter if it
doesn't do someone good.

Hoyt Axton

To analyze the interrelationship between historical change and ideas is to remove much of the mystery surrounding the distinctions between classical and modern concepts of leisure. The historical evidence suggests that, in many ways, we are still struggling to transcend the human weaknesses of desire and passion that initiated the ancient quest for the good life in western religion, science and philosophy. In stark contrast to the less-than-optimistic accounts of people and societies continually repeating the mistakes of the past, our intellectual heritage shines through as a testimony to human creativity and hope. Those who have decided to view human beings as what we appear to be have tended to deny the importance of creative leisure: if we are inherently evil, then our discretionary time is likely to be used to pursue evil. But if we are potentially something more than violent, egotistical, economic animals, then discretionary time becomes the most important time in our lives: time to pursue our potential.

As post-industrial realities continue to dominate our society, the issue of discretionary time will become more important. We are living in a period of profound transition that is as significant to the history of the species as the adoption of agriculture and industrialization. This transition has provided many of us (a relatively miniscule group compared to the rest of the world) with a previously-unimaginable blossoming of free time. We have what others could only dream about: increasing freedom from economic necessity. But what have we done with this dream that has become reality?

We jog to relieve tension. We numb our minds with alcohol and drugs. We escape into the fantasy world created by others for our entertainment through passive hours in front of a television. We seek amusement, diversion, denial and escape. Then, to show that our lives are not as empty as they feel, we go shopping with credit cards. By the time the bill arrives we have often forgotten what was purchased where, and why. Then, to pay the bill, we work more and jog to relieve the tension. We work very hard to be able to enjoy our free time, but tend to be nagged by guilt when we do.

We rely on clever bumper stickers (with slogans created by someone else) to make our statements to the world. While one generation announces that it is "spending our children's inheritance," another proclaims that "he who dies with the most toys wins." Others proclaim that they would rather be doing something else. Meanwhile, children who are not yet old enough to drive are making their statements through drug overdoses and suicide.

At the beginning of Part I we quoted Robert Heilbroner: You don't know if you can have any real impact on the future, but you act as if you can. Our decision to use this suggestion from an eminent twentieth-century thinker as a preface to "Leisure as Essence: The Athenian Ideal," summarizes our perspective on the current dilemma of leisure. Plato's world must have appeared to him to be as chaotic, disappointing, hypocritical and dangerous as ours is today. Thucydides' ob-

251

servation of the destruction of Athenian values as a consequence of imperialistic greed, aggressive nationalism and the plague haunts the twentieth century—as continually-expanding nuclear arsenals offer us a future of instant vaporization or a slow painful death while begging for a drink of water. While Socrates and Plato struggled to discover a creative response to their crises, most Athenians opted to:

> spend quickly and enjoy themselves, regarding their lives and riches alike as things of a day. Perserverance in what men called honour was popular with none, it was so uncertain whether they would be spared to attain the object; but it was settled that present enjoyment, and all that contributed to it, was both honourable and useful. Fear of gods or law of man there was none to restrain them. As for the first, they judged it to be just the same whether they worshipped them or not, as they saw all alike perishing; and for the last, no one expected to live to be brought to trial for his offences. . . .

Plato, Aristotle, the prophets, Aquinas, Marx and Sartre, without any assurance that they could "have any real impact on the future," chose to act as if they could.

Taking responsibility to create the future is a monumental choice that cannot be made and pursued if our leisure time is devalued by passive acceptance of what is. Recreation, diversion, escape and amusement—the cornerstones of modern leisure—subtly deny any capacity that we might have to take control of our own lives and consciously create a positive legacy for future generations.

We introduced this book with a series of quotes chosen to summarize the modern dilemma of leisure, and it is fitting that we close with a series of quotes for you to think about in your leisure time—if you have decided to become an active, creative force in your own life and the future of this planet.

As individuals express their life, so they are.

Karl Marx

Men who live in ages of equality have a great deal of curiosity and little leisure; their life is so practical, so confused, so excited, so active, that but little time remains to them for thought.

Alexis de Tocqueville

. . . the love of possession is a disease with them. . . . They claim this mother of ours, the earth, for their own and fence their neighbors away; they deface her with their buildings and refuse.

Tatanka Yotanka
(Sitting Bull)

The future rests, then, with the cultivation of those sides of our nature which are, in terms of immediate productivity and success, almost useless.

John Nef

To use leisure intelligently and profitably is a final test of a civilization.

Jay B. Nash

Bibliography

Ackrill, J. L. *Aristotle the Philosopher*. New York: Oxford University Press, 1981.

Albee, Ernest. *A History of English Utilitarianism*. New York: The Macmillan Company, 1957.

Allen, Reginald E., ed. *Greek Philosophy: Thales to Aristotle*. New York: The Free Press, 1966.

Alperovitz, Gar. *Atomic Diplomacy: Hiroshima and Potsdam*. New York: Vintage Books, 1967.

Anderson, Eugene N. *The Social and Political Conflict in Prussia*. New York: Octagon Books, 1968.

Anderson, Nels. *Work and Leisure*. New York: The Free Press of Glencoe, Inc., 1961.

Aquinas, Thomas. *Philosophical Texts*. Translated by Thomas Gilby. New York: Oxford University Press, 1956.

————. *The Philosophy of St. Thomas Aquinas*. Translated by Etienne Gilson. Cambridge: W. Heffer and Sons Ltd., 1924.

————. *Summa Theologica*. Translated by Fathers of the English Dominican Province. San Francisco: Benziger Bros., 1947.

Arendt, Hannah. *Between Past and Future: Eight Excercises in Political Thought*. New York: Penguin Books, 1977.

————. *The Human Condition*. Chicago: The University of Chicago Press, 1958.

————. *The Origins of Totalitarianism*. San Diego: Harcourt Brace Jovanovich, 1973.

Aron, Raymond. *Marxism and the Existentialists*. New York: Simon & Schuster, 1970.

Ashley, Maurice. *England in the Seventeenth Century*. 3rd ed. Baltimore, Md.: Penguin Books, 1961.

Augustine. *City of God*. Translated by M. Dods. New York: The Modern Library, 1950.

Avineri, Shlomo. *The Social and Political Thought of Karl Marx*. London: Cambridge University Press, 1968.

Bainton, Roland H. *The Age of the Reformation*. New York: Van Nostrand Reinhold Company, 1956.

————. *The Reformation of the Sixteenth Century*. Boston: The Beacon Press, 1952.

Balsdon, J. P. V. D. *Rome: The Story of an Empire*. New York: McGraw-Hill, 1970.

Barker, Sir Ernest. *Greek Political Theory: Plato and His Predecessors*. New York: Barnes & Noble, 1960. First published in 1918, London: Methuen & Co., Ltd.

————, ed. *The Politics of Aristotle*. Translated with an Introduction, Notes, and Appendixes by Ernest Barker. London: Oxford University Press, 1973.

————. *Principles of Social and Political Theory*. London: Oxford University Press, 1961.

Barraclough, Geoffrey. *The Origins of Modern Germany*. London: Basil-Blackwell, 1947.

Beck, Lewis White and Holmes, Robert L. *Philosophic Inquiry: An Introduction to Philosophy*. New Jersey: Prentice-Hall, Inc., 1968.

Becker, Carl L. *The Heavenly City of the Eighteenth-Century Philosophers*. New Haven, Conn.: Yale University Press, 1932.

Bentham, Jeremy. *The Principles of Morals and Legislation*. Introduction by Laurence J. Lafleur. Darien, Conn.: Hafner Publishing Co., 1970.

Berlin, Isaiah. *Karl Marx: His Life and Environment*. New York: Time Incorporated, 1963.

Bernstein, Eduard. *Evolutionary Socialism*. Introduction by Sidney Hook. Translated by Edith Harvey. New York: Schocken Books, 1961.

Billington, James H. *The Icon and the Axe*. New York: Vintage Books, 1970.

Black, Cyril E., ed. *The Transformation of Russian Society*. Cambridge: Harvard University Press, 1967.

Black, Eugene C., ed. *British Politics in the Nineteenth Century*. New York: Walker & Co., 1969.

Bottomore, T. B. and Rubel, Maxmilien, ed. *Karl Marx: Selected Writings in Sociology and Social Philosophy*. Translated by T. B. Bottomore. New York: McGraw-Hill, 1964. First Published by C. A. Watts and Co., 1956.

Brandes, George. *Ferdinand Lassalle*. New York: Bergman Publishers, 1968.

Braudel, Fernand. *Civilization and Capitalism 15th–18th Century. Vol. I.: The Structures of Everyday Life.* Translation from the French Revised by Siân Reynolds. New York: Harper & Row, 1981. First published in 1979, Paris: Librairie Armand Colin.

————. *Civilization and Capitalism 15th–18th Century. Vol. II.: The Wheels of Commerce.* Translation from the French by Siân Reynolds. New York: Harper & Row, 1982. First published in 1979. Paris: Librairie Armand Colin.

————. *Civilization and Capitalism 15th–18th Century. Vol. III.: The Perspective of the World.* Translation from the French by Siân Reynolds. New York: Harper & Row, 1984. First published in 1979, Paris: Librairie Armand Colin.

Brightbill, Charles K. *The Challenge of Leisure.* Englewood Cliffs, N.J.: Prentice-Hall, 1960.

Brightbill, Charles K., and Mobley, Tony A. *Educating for Leisure-Centered Living.* New York: John Wiley & Sons, 1977.

Bulmer-Thomas, Ivor. *The Growth of the British Party System.* 2 vols. London: John Baker Publishers, 1965.

Burke, Edmund. *Reflections on the Revolution in France.* Edited by Thomas H. D. Mahoney. Indianapolis: Bobbs-Merrill, 1965.

Burns, Delisle C. *Leisure in the Modern World.* Washington, D.C.: McGrath Publishing Company, 1932.

Callahan, John F. *Augustine and the Greek Philosophers.* Pennsylvania: Villanova University Press, 1967.

Caute, David. *Essential Writings of Karl Marx.* New York: Collier Books, 1970. Originally published by MacGibbon and Kee Limited, London, 1967.

Chappell, V. C., ed. *The Philosophy of David Hume.* New York: Modern Library, 1963.

Cipolla, Carlo M. *Before the Industrial Revolution: European Society and Economy, 1000–1700.* 2nd ed. New York: W. W. Norton & Co., Inc., 1980.

————. *Guns, Sails and Empires.* New York: Pantheon Books, 1965.

Clarke, Peter. *Liberals and Social Democrats.* New York: Cambridge University Press, 1978.

Cole, G. D. H. *British Working Class Politics.* London: Routledge & Kegan Paul, 1941.

Cole, G. D. H., and Filson, A. W. *British Working Class Movements, Select Documents.* New York: St. Martins Press, 1965.

Coulborn, Rushton, ed. *Feudalism in History.* Princeton, N.J.: Princeton University Press, 1956. reprint ed., Hamden, Conn.: Archon Books, 1965.

Dampier, Sir William Cecil. *A History of Science: And Its Relations with Philosophy and Religion.* 4th ed. New York: Cambridge University Press, 1971.

Dawson, Christopher. *The Making of Europe: An Introduction to the History of European Unity.* New York: The World Publishing Co., 1971.

de Grazia, Sebastian. *Of Time, Work and Leisure.* New York: Twentieth Century Fund, 1962.

de Ruggiero, Guido. *The History of European Liberalism.* Translated by R. G. Collingwood. Boston: Beacon Press, 1959.

Dmytryshyn, Basil. *A History of Russia.* Englewood Cliffs, N.J.: Prentice-Hall, 1977.

————. *Imperial Russia, a Source Book.* New York: Holt, Rinehart and Winston, 1967.

Douglas, David C., gen. ed. *English Historical Documents.* 12 vols. New York: Oxford University Press, 1977.

Dray, William H. *Philosophy of History.* Englewood Cliffs, N.J.: Prentice-Hall, 1964.

Dumazedier, Joffre. *Sociology of Leisure.* Translated by Marea A. McKenzie. New York: Elsevier Scientific Publishing Company, 1974.

Dunn, John. *The Political Thought of John Locke.* Cambridge: Cambridge University Press, 1969.

Durant, Will. *Caesar and Christ.* New York: Simon & Schuster, 1944.

————. *The Life of Greece.* New York: Simon & Schuster, 1939.

————. *The Reformation.* New York: Simon & Schuster, 1957.

Durant, Will and Ariel. *The Age of Voltaire.* New York: Simon & Schuster, 1965.

Ellwood, Jr., Robert S. *Many Peoples, Many Faiths: An Introduction to the Religious Life of Mankind.* Englewood Cliffs, N.J.: Prentice-Hall, 1976.

Feuer, Lewis S. *Marx and Engels: Basic Writings on Politics and Philosophy.* Garden City, N.Y.: Anchor Books, 1959.

Finley, M. I., ed. *The Greek Historians: The Essence of Herodotus, Thucydides, Xenophon, Polybius.* New York: The Viking Press, 1959.

Florinsky, Michael T. *Russia: A History and an Interpretation.* 2 vols. New York: Macmillan, 1953.

Freeman, Kathleen. *The Pre-Socratic Philosophers*. Oxford: Basil Blackwell, 1953.

Freud, Sigmund. *New Introductory Lectures on Psychoanalysis*. Translated by James Strachey. New York: W. W. Norton & Co., Inc., 1964.

Fried, Albert and Sanders, Ronald, eds. *Socialist Thought: A Documentary History*. Garden City, N.J.: Anchor Books, 1964.

Fromm, Erich. *Escape from Freedom*. New York: Avon Books, 1965.

———. *Marx's Concept of Man*. With a translation from Marx's Economic And Philosophical Manuscripts by T. B. Bottomore. New York: Frederick Ungar Publishing Co., 1963.

Fuller, B. A. G. *History of Greek Philosophy. Vol. 1: Thales to Democritus*. New York: Henry Holt and Company, 1923; reprint ed., New York: Greenwood Press, Publishers, 1968.

Garraty, John A. and Gay, Peter, ed. *The Columbia History of the World*. New York: Harper & Row, 1972.

Gay, Peter. *The Dilemma of Democratic Socialism*. New York: Columbia University Press, 1962.

Gibson, James. *Locke's Theory of Knowledge: And Its Historical Relations*. London: Cambridge University Press, 1917; reprint ed., Cambridge University Press, 1968.

Gilbert, Felix. *The End of the European Era: 1890 to the Present*. New York: W. W. Norton & Co., Inc., 1970.

Gilbert, Felix, ed. *The Historical Essays of Otto Hintze*. New York: Oxford University Press, 1975.

Girvetz, Harry K. *The Evolution of Liberalism*. Toronto: Collier-Macmillan, 1966.

Gollwitzer, Heinz. *Europe in the Age of Imperialism*. Translated by David Adam and Stanley Baron. Norwich, England: Harcourt, Brace and World, Inc., 1969.

Gray, David and Pelegrino, Donald, ed. *Reflections on the Park and Recreation Movement*. Dubuque, Iowa: William C. Brown, 1973.

Grossmann, Reinhardt. *Phenomenology and Existentialism*. Boston: Routledge & Kegan Paul, 1984.

Gurley, John G. *Challengers to Capitalism: Marx, Lenin, Stalin, and Mao*. 2nd ed. New York: W. W. Norton & Co., Inc., 1979.

Guthrie, W. K. C. *The Greek Philosophers: From Thales to Aristotle*. New York: Harper & Row, 1960.

Haimson, Leopold H. *The Russian Marxists and the Origins of Bolshevism*. Boston: Beacon Press, 1966.

Halévy, Elie. *The Growth of Philosophic Radicalism*. Translated by Mary Morris. Boston: Beacon Press, 1955.

Hamerow, Theodore S. *The Social Foundations of German Unification*. Princeton, N.J.: Princeton University Press, 1972.

Hamilton, Edith., and Cairns, Huntington., ed. *The Collected Dialogues of Plato*. New York: Pantheon Books, 1961; reprint ed., New York: Pantheon Books, 1964.

Hamilton, Peter. *Knowledge and Social Structure*. Boston: Routledge & Kegan Paul, 1974.

Hegel, G. W. F. *Reason in History*. Translated with an Introduction by Robert S. Hartman. New York: Bobbs-Merrill, 1953.

Heidegger, Martin. *Being and Time*. Translated by John MacQuarrie and Edward Robinson. New York: Harper & Row, 1962.

———. *Discourse on Thinking*. Translated by John M. Anderson and E. Hans Freund, with an Introduction by John M. Anderson. New York: Harper & Row, 1966.

———. *What Is Philosophy?* Translated by William Kluback and Jean T. Wilde. New York: Twayne Publishers, Inc., 1958.

———. *What Is a Thing?* Translated by W. B. Barton, Jr. and Vera Deutsch. Chicago: Henry Regnery Company, 1967.

Heilbroner, Robert L. *An Inquiry into the Human Prospect*. New York: W. W. Norton & Co., Inc., 1975.

———. *The Worldly Philosophers*. Rev. ed. New York: Simon & Schuster, 1961.

Hobbes, Thomas. *The Leviathan*. Edited by Michael Oakeshott. New York: Crowell-Collier Publishing Co., 1962.

Holborn, Hajo. *A History of Modern Germany*. 3 vols. New York: Alfred A. Knopf, 1969.

Holy Bible. King James Version.

Homer. *The Iliad of Homer*. Translated by Richard Lattimore. Chicago: Phoenix Books, 1961.

Horowitz, Irving Louis. *Philosophy, Science and the Sociology of Knowledge*. Springfield, Ill.: Thomas Books, 1961.

Hughes, H. Stuart. *Consciousness and Society*. New York: Vintage Books, 1961.

Hume, David. *An Inquiry Concerning Human Understanding and Concerning the Principles of Morals.* Edited by L. A. Selby-Biggs. Oxford: Clarendon Press, 1967.

————. *Political Essays.* Edited with an Introduction by Charles W. Hendel. Indianapolis: Bobbs-Merrill, 1953.

Husserl, Edmund. *The Idea of Phenomenology.* Translated by William P. Alston and George Nakhanikian with an Introduction by George Nakhanikian. The Hague: Martinus Nijhoff, 1964.

————. *Phenomenology and the Crisis in Philosophy.* Translation and Introduction by Quentin Lauer. New York: Harper & Row, 1965.

Hussey, Edward. *The Presocratics.* London: Gerald Duckworth and Company Limited, 1972.

Jennings, Sir Ivor. *Party Politics.* 2 vols. New York: Cambridge University Press, 1961.

Jones, W. T. *A History of Western Philosophy.* New York: Harcourt, Brace and World, 1952.

————. *A History of Western Philosophy.* 2nd rev. ed., 5 vols. New York: Harcourt Brace Jovanovich, 1975.

Kafka, Franz. *Metamorphosis.* Translated by A. L. Lloyd. New York: Vanguard Press, 1945.

Kant, Immanuel. *Fundamental Principles of the Metaphysics of Morals.* Translated by T. K. Abbott. Indianapolis: Bobbs-Merrill, 1949.

————. *Prolegomena to any Future Metaphysics.* Translated by James W. Ellington, Indianapolis: Hackett Publishing Co., 1977.

Kaufmann, Walter. *Nietzsche: Philosopher, Psychologist, Antichrist.* 4th ed. Princeton: Princeton University Press, 1974.

Kautsky, Karl. *The Class Struggle.* Introduction by Robert C. Tucker. Translated by Willian E. Bohn. New York: W. W. Norton & Co., Inc., 1971.

Kierkegaard, Søren. *Concluding Unscientific Postscript.* Translated by D. F. Swenson. Princeton: Princeton University Press, 1941.

————. *Fear and Trembling and the Sickness unto Death.* Translated by Walter Lowrie. Princeton: Princeton University Press, 1954.

————. *The Journals of Kierkegaard.* Translated and Edited by Alexander Dru. London: Collins, 1975.

————. *The Point of View for My Work as an Author.* Translated by Walter Lowrie. Edited by Benjamin Nielson. New York: Harper & Row, 1962.

Knoles, George H. and Snyder, Rixford K., ed. *Readings in Western Civilization.* Revised Edition. Chicago: J. B. Lippincott Co., 1954.

Kohn, Hans. *The Mind of Germany.* New York: Harper Torch Books, 1965.

————, ed. *The Mind of Modern Russia.* New York: Harper Torch Books, 1962.

Kraus, Richard. *Recreation and Leisure in Modern Society.* New York: Appleton-Century-Crofts, 1971.

Krieger, Leonard. *The German Idea of Freedom.* Chicago: University of Chicago Press, 1957.

Lavine, T. Z. *From Socrates to Sartre: the Philosophic Quest.* New York: Bantam Books, 1984.

Lenin, V. I. *What Is to Be Done?* Translated by Joe Fineberg and George Hanna. Edited by Victor J. Jerome. New York: International Publishers, 1969.

Lichtheim, George. *Marxism.* 2nd ed. New York: Praeger, 1965.

Lidtke, Vernon L. *The Outlawed Party.* Princeton, N.J.: Princeton University Press, 1966.

Locke, John. *Two Treatises of Government.* Introduction by Peter Laslett. New York: New American Library, 1965.

Luxemburg, Rosa. *Rosa Luxemburg Speaks.* New York: Pathfinder Press, 1970.

MacKendrick, Paul. *The Roman Mind at Work.* Princeton, N.J.: D. Van Nostrand Co., 1958.

MacKenzie, Norman, and MacKenzie, Jeanne. *The Fabians.* New York: Simon & Schuster, 1977.

Mackie, Thomas T., and Rose, Richard. *The International Almanac of Electoral History.* New York: Free Press, 1974.

Macpherson, C. B. *The Life and Times of Liberal Democracy.* Oxford, England: Oxford University Press, 1977.

————. *The Political Theory of Possessive Individualism: Hobbes to Locke.* London: Oxford University Press, 1962.

Mannheim, Karl. *Ideology and Utopia.* Translated by Louis Wirth and Edward Shils. New York: Harvest Books, 1936.

Marcuse, Herbert. *One-Dimensional Man.* Boston: Beacon Press, 1964.

————. *Reason and Revolution.* New York: Humanities Press, 1954; Reprint ed., New York: Humanities Press, Inc., 1968.

Maritain, Jacques. *St. Thomas Aquinas*. New York: Meridian Books, Inc., 1958.

Marx, Karl. *Capital: A Critique of Political Economy*. Edited by Frederick Engels. Translated from the Third German Edition by Samuel Moore and Edward Aveling. New York: Random House, 1906.

Masaryk, Thomas Garrigue. *The Spirit of Russia*. 2nd ed. Translated by Eden Paul and Cedar Paul. 3 vols. New York: Macmillan, 1955.

McKeon, Richard, ed. *The Basic Works of Aristotle*. New York: Random House, 1941; reprint ed., New York: Random House, 1968.

McLellan, David. *Marxism after Marx*. New York: Harper & Row, 1979.

McNeal, Robert H. *The Bolshevik Tradition*. Englewood Cliffs, N.J.: Prentice-Hall, 1963.

Meinecke, Friedrich. *The German Catastrophe*. Translated by Sidney B. Fay. Boston: Beacon Press, 1963.

Merleau-Ponty, Maurice. *Humanism and Terror*. Translated by John O'Neill. Boston: Beacon Press, 1969.

————. *The Primacy of Perception*. Edited by James M. Edie. Evanston, Ill.: Northwestern University Press, 1964.

Mill, John Stuart. *Autobiography*. Introduction by Currin V. Shields. New York: Bobbs-Merrill, 1957.

Miller, Norman and Robinson, Duane. *The Leisure Age*. Belmont, Cal.: Wadsworth Publishing Co., 1967.

Mitchell, B. R. *European Historical Statistics, 1750–1975*. 2nd rev., ed. New York: Facts on File, 1981.

Montesquieu. *Persian Letters*. Translated with an Introduction and Notes by C. J. Betts. Baltimore, Md.: Penguin Books, 1973.

Moore, Barrington, Jr. *Social Origins of Dictatorship and Democracy*. Boston: Beacon Press, 1967.

Mosse, George L. *The Crisis of German Ideology*. New York: Universal Library, 1964.

Mulhall, Michael. *The Dictionary of Statistics*. 4th ed. London: George Routledge & Sons, 1892; reprint ed., Detroit: Gale Research Co., 1969.

Myers, Milton L. *The Soul of Modern Economic Man: Ideas of Self-Interest; Thomas Hobbes to Adam Smith*. Chicago: The University of Chicago Press, 1983.

Neumeyer, Martin H., and Neumeyer, Esther S. *Leisure and Recreation*. New York: The Ronald Press Company, 1958.

Nietzsche, Friedrich. *Beyond Good and Evil*. Translated by Walter Kaufmann. New York: Vintage Books, 1966.

————. *The Portable Nietzsche*. Translated and Edited by Walter Kaufmann. New York: The Viking Press, 1958.

————. *The Will to Power*. Translated by Walter Kaufmann and R. J. Hollingdale. New York: Vintage Books, 1968.

Novak, Joseph. *The Future Is Ours, Comrade*. New York: E. P. Dutton and Co., Inc., 1964.

Oates, Whitney J., ed. *The Stoic and Epicurean Philosophers*. New York: The Modern Library, 1940.

Oberländer, Erwin, exec., ed. *Russia Enters the Twentieth Century*. New York: Schocken Books, 1971.

O'Brien, Elmer. *The Essential Plotinus*. New York: Mentor Book, 1964.

Ollman, Bertell. *Alienation; Marx's Conception of Man in Capitalist Society*. Cambridge: Cambridge University Press, 1971.

Orwell, George. *Coming Up for Air*. New York: Harcourt, Brace and World, 1939.

Pares, Sir Bernard. *Russia Between Reform and Revolution*. Edited by Francis B. Randall. New York: Schocken Books, 1962.

Parker, Francis H. *The Story of Western Philosophy*. Bloomington: Indiana University Press, 1967; reprint ed., Bloomington: Indiana University Press, 1972.

Parker, G. F. *A Short Account of Greek Philosophy: From Thales to Epicurus*. New York: Barnes and Noble, Inc., 1967.

Parker, Stanley. *The Future of Work and Leisure*. New York: Praeger Publishers, 1971.

Parrinder, Geoffrey, ed. *World Religions: From Ancient History to the Present*. New York: Facts on File, 1983. First published as "Religions of the World" in 1971, New York: The Hamlyn Publishing Group Limited.

Paulson, Friedrich. *Immanuel Kant: His Life and Times*. Translated from the Revised German Edition by J. E. Creighton and Albert Lefevre. New York: Frederick Ungar Publishing Co., 1963.

Payne, Robert. *Ancient Rome*. New York: American Heritage Press, 1970.

Pease, Edward R. *The History of the Fabian Society*. 3rd ed. London: Frank Cass & Co., 1963.

Pegis, Anton C. *Basic Writings of Thomas Aquinas*. New York: Random House, 1945.

Pelling, Henry. *A History of British Trade Unionism*. New York: St. Martin's Press, 1963.

————. *The Origins of the Labour Party*. 2nd ed. New York: Macmillan, 1965.

Petitot, L. H. *The Life and Spirit of Thomas Aquinas*. Translated by Cyprian Burke. Chicago: The Priory Press, 1966.

Pieper, Joseph. *Leisure: The Basis of Culture*. New York: Pantheon Books, 1952.

Pierson, Stanley. *Marxism and the Origins of British Socialism*. Ithaca, N.Y.: Cornell University Press, 1973.

Pinson, Koppel S. *Modern Germany*. 2nd ed. New York: Macmillan, 1966.

Plamenatz, John. *German Marxism and Russian Communism*. Westport, Conn.: Greenwood Press, 1975.

Plotinus. *The Philosophy of Plotinus*. Translated by Joseph Katz. New York: Appleton-Century-Crofts, Inc., 1950.

————. *Plotinus: The Enneads*. Translated by S. MacKenna. London: Faber and Faber Ltd., 1930.

Polanyi, Karl. *The Great Transformation: The Political and Economic Origins of Our Time*. With an Introduction by R. M. Macluer. Boston: Beacon Press, 1944.

Poster, Mark. *Existential Marxism in Postwar France*. Princeton, N.J.: Princeton University Press, 1975.

————. *Sartre's Marxism*. London: Pluto Press, 1979.

Riasanovsky, Nicholas, V. *A History of Russia*. 2nd ed. New York: Oxford University Press, 1969.

Rice, Eugene F. Jr. *The Foundations of Early Modern Europe 1460–1559*. New York: W. W. Norton & Co., Inc., 1970.

Robinson, C. E. *Hellas: A Short History of Ancient Greece*. Boston: Beacon Press, 1955.

Rosenberg, Arthur. *Imperial Germany*. Boston: Beacon Press, 1964.

Rosenberg, Hans. *Bureaucracy, Aristocracy and Autocracy*. Boston: Beacon Press, 1966.

Rostovtzeff, M. *Rome*. Translated by J. D. Duff. Paperback edition Editor, Eligs J. Bickerman. London: Oxford University Press, 1960.

Rostow, W. W., ed. *The Economics of Take-off into Sustained Growth*. New York: St. Martin's Press, 1963.

Rostow, W. W. *Politics and the Stages of Growth*. New York: Cambridge University Press, 1971.

————. *The Stages of Economic Growth*. 2nd ed. New York: Cambridge University Press, 1971.

————. *The World Economy*. Austin, Tex.: University of Texas Press, 1978.

Roth, Guenther. *The Social Democrats in Imperial Germany*. Totowa, N.J.: Bedminster Press, 1963.

Rousseau, Jean-Jacques. *The First and Second Discourses*. Edited by Roger D. Masters. Translated by Roger D. and Judith R. Masters. New York: St. Martin's Press, Inc., 1964.

————. *The Social Contract and Discourses*. Translated by G. D. H. Cole. New York: E. P. Dutton and Company, Inc., 1950.

Russell, Bertrand. *A History of Western Philosophy*. New York: Simon & Schuster, 1945.

Sabine, George H. *A History of Political Theory*. 3rd ed. New York: Holt, Rinehart and Winston, 1961.

Saint-Simon, Henri de. *Social Organization, the Science of Man and Other Writings*. Edited and translated by Felix Markham. New York: Harper and Row, 1964. First published in 1952, Oxford: Basil Blackwell.

Sartre, Jean-Paul. *Being and Nothingness*. Translated by Hazel Barnes. New York: Philosophical Library, 1956.

————. *Between Existentialism and Marxism*. Translated by John Mathews. New York: William Morrow, 1979.

————. *Critique of Dialectical Reason*. Translated by Alan Sheridan-Smith. Edited by Jonathan Reé. Atlantic Highlands, N.J.: Humanities Press, 1976.

————. *Existentialism*. Translated by Bernard Frechtman. New York: Philosophical Library, 1947.

————. *Nausea*. Translated by Lloyd Alexander. New York: New Directions, 1964.

————. *No Exit and Three Other Plays*. New York: Vintage Books, 1955.

————. *Search for a Method*. Translated by Hazel Barnes. New York: Vintage Books, 1963.

————. *The Transcendence of the Ego: An Existentialist Theory of Consciousness*. Translated and annotated with an Introduction by Forrest Williams and Robert Kirkpatrick. New York: Octagon Books, 1972.

Schmidt, Albert-Marie. *John Calvin: And the Calvinistic Tradition*. Translated by Ronald Wallace. New York: Harper and Brothers, 1960.

Schorske, Carl E. *German Social Democracy*. Cambridge: Harvard University Press, 1955.

Servan-Schreiber, J. J. *The American Challenge*. Translated by Ronald Steel. New York: Avon Books, 1968.

Shaw, George Bernard, ed. *The Fabian Essays in Socialism*. Gloucester, Mass: Smith, 1967.

Smith, Adam. *An Inquiry into the Nature and Causes of the Wealth of Nations*. Edited with an Introduction, Notes, Marginal Summary and an Enlarged Index by Edwin Cannan. With an Introduction by Max Lerner. New York: Random House, Inc., 1937.

Snyder, Louis L., ed. *Documents of German History*. New Brunswick, N.J.: Rutgers University Press, 1958.

Steenson, Gary P. *Not One Man! Not One Penny!*. Pittsburgh, Pa.: University of Pittsburgh Press, 1981.

Stern, Fritz. *The Politics of Cultural Despair*. Garden City, N.Y.: Anchor Books, 1965.

Stock, St. George. *Stoicism*. New York: Kennikat Press, 1969.

Strayer, Joseph R. *On the Medieval Origins of the Modern State*. Princeton, N.J.: Princeton University Press, 1970.

Stromberg, Roland N. *An Intellectual History of Modern Europe*. New York: Meredith Publishing Co., 1966.

Supple, Barry E., ed. *The Experience of Economic Growth*. New York: Random House, 1963.

Tawney, R. H. *The Acquisitive Society*. New York: Harvest Books, 1920.

———. *Religion and the Rise of Capitalism*. New York: Mentor Books, 1954.

Taylor, A. J. P. *The Course of German History*. New York: Capricorn Books, 1962.

Taylor, Alfred Edward. *Aristotle*. New York: Dover Publications, Inc., 1955.

———. *The Mind of Plato*. Ann Arbor: Ann Arbor Paperbacks, The University of Michigan Press, 1964.

Theen, Rolf H. W. *Lenin*. New York: Lippincott, 1973.

Thomas, William. *The Philosophic Radicals*. New York: Oxford University Press, 1979.

Thomson, David. *England in the Nineteenth Century*. Baltimore, Md.: Penguin Books, 1950.

Torrance, T. F. *Calvin's Doctrine of Man*. Grand Rapids, Iowa: Wm. B. Erdman's Publishing Company, 1957; reprint ed., Westport, Connecticut: Greenwood Press, Publishers, 1977.

Torrey, Norman L., ed. *Les Philosophes*. With an Introduction by Norman L. Torrey. New York: Perigee Books, 1980.

Trevelyan, George Macauley. *A Shortened History of England*. Baltimore, Md.: Penguin Books, 1959. First Published in 1942, New York: Longmans, Green & Co.

Troeltsch, Ernst. *The Social Teaching of the Christian Churches*. Vol. 1. Translated by Olive Wyon. Introduction by H. Richard Niebuhr. New York: Harper Torch Books, 1960. First published in 1931, London: George Allen & Unwin Ltd. and New York: Macmillan.

Tucker, Robert C., ed. *The Marx-Engels Reader*. 2nd ed. New York: W. W. Norton & Co., 1978.

Tucker, Robert. *Philosophy and Myth in Karl Marx*. 2nd ed. London: Cambridge University Press, 1972.

Ulam, Adam B. *Ideologies and Illusions*. Cambridge: Harvard University Press, 1976.

Venturi, Franco. *Roots of Revolution*. New York: Alfred A. Knopf, 1960.

Vernadsky, George, ed. *A Source Book for Russian History from Early Times to 1917*. 3 vols. New Haven, Conn.: Yale University Press, 1972.

Voltaire. *Philosophical Letters*. Translated, with an Introduction, by Ernest Dilworth. New York: Bobbs-Merrill, 1961.

Walker, Angus. *Marx: His Theory and Its Context*. New York: Longman, 1978.

Wallis, R. T. *Neoplatonism*. London: Duckworth, 1972.

Walzer, Michael. *Exodus and Revolution*. New York: Basic Books, 1985.

Warnock, Mary. *Existentialism*. Oxford: Oxford University Press, 1970.

Warnock, Robert and Anderson, George K., ed. *Centuries of Transition*, Book 2 of *The World in Literature*. Chicago: Scott, Foresman & Co., 1950.

Weber, Max. *The Protestant Ethic and the Spirit of Capitalism*. Translated by Talcott Parsons. With a Foreword by R. H. Tawney. New York: Charles Scribner's Sons, 1958.

Wilson, Edmund. *To the Finland Station: A Study in the Writing and Acting of History*. New York: Farrar, Straus And Giroux, 1972.

Wolfe, Bertram D. *Three Who Made a Revolution*. New York: Dial Press, 1964.

Zeller, Eduard. *Outlines of the History of Greek Philosophy*. Translated by L. R. Palmer. New York: The Humanities Press, Inc., 1931; reprint ed., New York: Meridian Books, The World Publishing Company, 1963.

CHRISTIAN·L

Index